Celebrated Weekends

The **Stars' Guide** to the Most Exciting
Destinations in the World

Mark Seal

Rutledge Hill Press®
Nashville, Tennessee

A Division of Thomas Nelson Publishers
www.thomasnelson.com

To four women whose faith, support, and confidence
made this book possible:
Laura Blocker, Jan Miller Rich, Evelyn Abroms Seal Kraus,
and the late, great Marcia May

A percentage of the royalties from this book will be donated to the Actors Studio.

Published by Rutledge Hill Press, a Division of Thomas Nelson, Inc., P.O. Box 141000, Nashville, Tennessee 37214.

Rutledge Hill Press books may be purchased in bulk for educational, business, fundraising, or sales promotional use.
For information, please e-mail SpecialMarkets@ThomasNelson.com.

Celebrity photos provided by Getty Images, unless indicated otherwise.

Library of Congress Cataloging-in-Publication Data

Seal, Mark, 1953–
  Celebrated weekends : the stars' guide to the most exciting destinations in the world / Mark Seal.
      p. cm.
  Includes index.
  ISBN-13: 978-1-4016-0243-7 (trade paper)
  ISBN-10: 1-4016-0243-6 (trade paper)
  1. Hotels—Directories. 2. Restaurants—Directories. 3. Celebrities—Travel. 4. Celebrities—United States. I. Title.

TX907.S387 2007
910.46—dc22   2007012734

Printed in the United States of America
07 08 09 10 11 — 5 4 3 2 1

Contents

Contents

Introduction

For years, I'd watched passengers rushing off of airplanes: business travelers striving for instant insider status, lovers hungry for overnight magic, families bent on immediate fun, everyone seeking the best-of-this or the don't-miss-that, but having no definitive place to turn. Sure, there were infinite guidebooks, all purporting to fling open the doors to a city. But in so many cases, the "best" turned out to be the pedestrian, the overhyped and overpriced, the over and the out.

I was among those masses of travelers, boomeranging back and forth on magazine assignments for *American Way*, the magazine of American Airlines, rushing off planes with an encyclopedic collection of guidebooks, only to frequently end up disillusioned and disappointed. Maybe it was one too many miserable meals or sleepless nights in substandard hotels that had been enthusiastically touted by some guidebook that gave rise to the idea that eventually became this book. I like to think that I tossed my napkin on the table in some mediocre restaurant, or bid adieu to a surly desk clerk on one too many red-eyed dawns, when the idea bubbled up whole: *the ultimate guide to the best and sometimes secret places in the major cities of the world*.

It wouldn't be another collection of opinions from some ink-stained journalist (like me) or some bureaucrat in the labyrinthine hallways of the publishing companies that produce travel guides, relying on reports from anonymous soldiers in the field. No, this would be a guide to each city by an authority: hometown heroes who have the run of their city, people whose fame flings open any door. It would be a guide to the planet by the stars, which, in today's world, means one thing: *celebrities*.

The perfect place to begin? Writing the guide city-by-city, star-by-star, in the pages of *American Way*, in the form of a travel column. I considered this a very important mission, not merely needed, but *required*—an invaluable tool. All travelers would have to do is reach into the seat pocket in front of them on the plane and learn the secrets of, say, John Cusack's Chicago or Jennifer Lopez's New York or Penélope Cruz's Madrid or Kevin Costner's Aspen. Enlightened, they could rush off the plane no longer a stranger, but an instant insider.

It was a whale of an idea, a surefire hit! All I had to do was sell it to my editor.

I was a hungry freelance writer—still am—who had a notebook full of story ideas—still do—and I've always loved the selling of a story as much as the tougher, disciplined work of writing one. My editor had already sent me on assignments that took me back and forth between my homebase of Dallas/Fort Worth and points around the world too many times to count. This time, I was pitching something better than ever before: a regular column that would appear in every issue of the magazine, which is published on the first and fifteenth of each month. For the reader, it would be a "service" column, a magic term in magazine journalism, meaning something that you don't merely read—but *use*. "Every two weeks I'll interview a celebrity about their hometown or a city that they know and love . . ." I began my pitch, as my editor dug into his lunch.

I used Jack Nicholson's Los Angeles as an example, and said I would interview Jack at his favorite restaurant, where he'd reveal his secrets. Not the typical Hollywood narrative of breakups and breakthroughs, but secrets far more valuable to the inveterate traveler. Jack would tell me his favorite places in the city he calls home.

"I'm ready to begin *immediately*," I said.

My editor liked the idea, but doubted that I could wrangle enough A-list—or even B-list—celebrities to agree to interviews to make it a regular column. We struck a compromise: I'd present a list of names for him to approve, and we'd see how many interviews I could get. The list was formidable: six top stars, topped off by the biggest of them all, Jack Nicholson.

They all said yes—except for Jack—and those airplane doors opened wide.

The first few interviews were done in one frenetic week of flying across the U.S. and Europe, listening as some of the world's most famous citizens discussed in detail the cities they love. I was in a hotel in Honolulu when the galleys of the first columns rolled off the fax. My editor called, excited, saying a contract would be forthcoming for a regular column, Celebrated Places, which eventually became Celebrated Weekend, twenty-four columns a year featuring twenty-four celebrities, each detailing their respective cities.

The column made its debut in the January 1990 issue with Jackie Collins's Hollywood—and we were off and running. Harrison Ford served me half a sub sandwich for our lunch on the deck of his Montana ranch house. Kiefer Sutherland showed up for his interview despite an excruciating kidney stone attack only an hour before, soldiering on to extol the glories of his hometown of Toronto. Gloria Estefan practically sang about the wonders of her Miami as she sat in her all-white recording studio offices near the beach. Jackie Chan waxed poetic about Hong Kong between acrobatic action scenes on a movie set. Dennis Quaid and I walked up and down a beach in Los Angeles as he got increasingly homesick for Austin, Texas, where he once lived. The list goes on, more than three hundred stars discussing wildly diverse places, but each sharing the singular passion that holds these columns together—*every soul has a home*. Famous or not, we're all from somewhere, and we carry that "somewhere" wherever we go.

Now, it's in the pages of this book.

Author's Note: Although some of these columns originally appeared several years ago, all the information in the listings has been verified and updated.

Key for Hotel and Restaurant Prices

$	Inexpensive
$$	Moderate
$$$	Expensive
$$$$–$$$$$	Very Expensive

U.S.
Destinations

Aspen

When I interviewed Kevin Costner, he had just directed and starred with Robert Duvall and Annette Bening in *Open Range*, the big-budget Western about a group of cowboys driving their cattle across the vast prairies, guided by a steadfast code of honor that puts them in a fight-to-the-finish with a corrupt sheriff and kingpin rancher. It's another last-gasp-of-the-West saga from Costner, who won multiple Oscars with *Dances with Wolves*, in which he also starred and directed. But for Costner, the West is no mere movie fantasy; it's a destination he's spent a lifetime searching for, scouring every corner of America for his vision of a perfect Western paradise.

He found it in the early nineties in what seemed like an unlikely place—five minutes outside of Aspen, Colorado. During the next dozen years, he bought parcels of what would eventually total the 165-acre ranch he calls home, a place he loves so much he wants to be buried there. "I've got the best view in the world," he said, calling from his ranch house, where he shares the grounds with elk, deer, and bear. "I've got the best bar in town. I've got the best breakfast place in town. I can fix a drink out here, and you won't ever want to leave."

Friday

PACKING There are some people who look pretty snappy downtown, but I'm looking down at myself right now and everything I have on has to go in the wash as soon as we're done talking here. I'm just in Levi's, a sweater, and boots. I've always got a little raincoat, too.

LODGING The **Hotel Jerome** and the **Little Nell** are great—I've frequented both of those places. I stayed at the Little Nell when we made *For the Love of the Game*. That hotel is the hub of activity. If you haven't met the person you wanted to, you're bound to during the course of your stay, because people just make their way through there. There's nothing quite like room service, right? But I really enjoy having lunch at the Little Nell. It's really fine dining and I guess next to **Cache Cache,** I find myself there.

DINNER The place we always go to have dinner with the kids is a restaurant called **Cache Cache.** Jodi Larner, the owner, is like a grande dame, and she has always taken care of me. The first day I walked in, Jodi had this great smile and said, "I was wondering when you were going to walk in here." And we've been friends ever since.

Saturday

PERCEPTION VS. REALITY I know there is a reputation out there, "Oh, the glitzy Aspen," but I don't think so. I think you can find glitz wherever you go. I think you can chase money

Cache Cache

and the party wherever you want. But if you find your collection of friends, you don't feel that effect, and if I did, I clearly wouldn't be here. I just had this thought: Our lives are in the balance, right? Every time I drive up here I think, *do I have one hundred more times to come up here in my life, or ten?* Because we don't know what fate really gives us. Let me say this: I feel more at home here than anyplace in the world. There are some places that have been real spiritual for me, like the Black Hills of South Dakota. I always have a special feeling there, but I have made my home here. I plan on being buried here.

ARCHITECTURE The greatest thing about downtown Aspen is that you can drop your kids off there. Not that I want to do that, but it's the one town I've been in that I felt like I could have left them by themselves when they were ten or twelve for a little bit. It feels safer than anyplace I've ever been; it's a very contained place. It's not like one street is very charming; there are four or five streets that have really held on to their architecture. It makes for fun walking, and you can see it on everybody's faces. They are just real happy to be here from wherever in the U.S. or the world they've come.

LUNCH Woody Creek Tavern [Woody Creek] has such a great rep. It's a burger joint near the river where people feel real comfortable. If you were to ask them, my guess is they feel like the Woody Creek Tavern has maintained itself and hasn't moved with any trend that Aspen has experienced. I've also eaten at

The place we always go to have dinner with the kids is a restaurant called Cache Cache.

Little Annie's, a real casual place downtown, a ton of times.

SHOPPING Well, I was sad when we lost the fishing shop next to the Little Nell. But my favorite store is the **Miner's Building,** which is sort of Aspen's general store. I go in there and get the stuff I need. I'm not at home more than an hour and I'm already digging or doing something. So I go down to Miner's, and I'm not really the handiest guy in the world, and I'm always trying to half explain what I'm trying to do, and the guys come out from behind the counter and there's always a good exchange. I let them come and fish with their kids up here. There is an exchange.

CULTURE I've been to the **Wheeler Opera House** a number of times to hear music, and the beat goes on. They had something in mind when it was being built in the 1880s, and here we are in the twenty-first century enjoying it. I actually enjoy the architecture, that style— the windows and moldings out in front of the shops. The extra-thick enamel paint where you feel like there are about fifty coats on. I like that.

GOLF I usually get in a game or two, even though golf's not really my sport. At the **Maroon Creek Club,** the people are great. I have been taken down to the **Roaring Fork Club** [Basalt] by guys who are members there. I enjoy the company and I'm always biting to get back there. But the first course we started playing was the public course, **Aspen Golf Club.** It doesn't really matter to me, because I'm looking for the company, not the challenge.

[I asked whether the balls go higher because of the altitude.] Yeah, but that means they also go to the right and left farther, too. With the gain, you get the pain.

DINNER Kenichi is a really good place for my family. My theme, my whistle, my song is pretty much the same. You know, if you're good to me, I'll usually be back. I love the bar there and having drinks. **Takah Sushi** also has great food. There's this back table, and that's where we generally sit. If Kenichi isn't open, I wouldn't think twice about going to Takah or **Matsuhisa** [the Aspen outpost of L.A. sushi chef Nobu Matsuhisa]. I like **Syzygy.** The bartender there is a guy that I hang with. Syzygy is a great restaurant, but also a great place to hear some jazz. I've had some great nights in there, no kidding. The big musical event is **Jazz Aspen Snowmass.** I really recommend that to anybody. It's three or four days where you're going to see some of the biggest acts in the world. You can do your outdoor thing all day, and about three o'clock you start getting yourself over there and you can hear world-class music.

DESSERT It's always good to have ice cream at **Paradise Bakery,** right in the center of town. You can see almost anything there at any given time. It's a very communal place.

NIGHTLIFE The **Caribou Club** is one of those places that you can really count on. People seem like they want to somehow bash it, but whenever I've been in there, I've seen everybody. I think that it has provided an incredible environment for out-of-towners and the people who go there. I guess the best way to describe the Caribou would be almost like a smoking club, although no one is smoking. It's really dark wood, like a library feeling. There's a big dining room.

LIVE MUSIC Little Blue is a local band, and they let my daughter sing one night. Lily is a very beautiful singer, but right away, my nerves started to play. Lily was reading the lyrics. She didn't even know the song. Here she was, fifteen years old, and singing in front of all these adults who had to stop all their talking and turn around to see this thing. She wasn't up to the mike, so nobody heard a word. I looked down at her sister, Annie, who was kind of mouthing the words, helping her, and I saw Lily going down in flames. My heart broke. When the song ended, the people clapped, even though they were clapping for nothing, because they couldn't hear her. I asked Lily if she was going to do another song and she said: "You bet your ass I am!" I saw something in her face and it reminded me of granite. Her second song was another one she didn't know, a Sheryl Crow song. She started to sing, and this time she blew the room away. What I saw in my daughter that night was her courage. So the people really had something to clap about. When they did, it marked the moment in her life—and in mine.

Sunday

RAFTING There's great rafting here. The **Roaring Fork River** spills into the Colorado. You get on somewhere in Basalt. Then there's one as you go over the Continental Divide that's really, really nice. The significance of the Continental Divide is that, without a doubt, you're closer to God, and at that point is where the rivers split. Everything to the east is running to the Mississippi and everything to the west is running to the Pacific. It's not so much for us to cross it now, because we can travel over it at fifty miles an hour. But at one time it was a life-and-death moment to get over the Continental Divide before the snows came or just figure out how you would actually cross a mountain range and still hold on to your possessions.

FISHING Sometimes I go down on the lower **Frying Pan River.** It's down valley toward Basalt. The fish are much, much bigger there than they are in the higher altitudes. I'll do a float trip, and one of the fishing guys has been really great, Kea Hause. We met him when we started coming up here. When somebody is good to you, there's no reason to change. He takes me down on the lower Frying Pan, but I bring him up on the property here sometimes.

BACKCOUNTRY I don't really feel the need to go anywhere else. But I enjoy being invited. We are always invited down to Don Johnson's. He has a fabulous place down there in Woody Creek, and he makes everybody feel welcome. But I come here and I really kind of nest. I'm probably not here more than an hour before I'm on the tractor, and away I go. In fact, I just about tipped it over today. Yeah, I was in a tough spot. I take ATVs into the backcountry, and we start at Lincoln Creek Road and head back into the upper lakes. My favorite season is summer and pushing into the fall. I'm not a snow person, although when I'm up here I appreciate it. I like it when the leaves come and go.

Kevin Costner's Aspen Essentials

LODGING

Hotel Jerome, $$$$, (970) 920-1000
330 East Main Street

The Little Nell, $$$$, (970) 920-4600
675 East Durant Avenue

DINING

Cache Cache, French, $$$, (970) 925-3835
205 South Mill Street

Kenichi, Pan Asian, $$$, (970) 920-2212
533 East Hopkins Avenue

Little Annie's Eating House, American, $$,
(970) 925-1098, 517 East Hyman Avenue

Matsuhisa, Japanese, $$$$, (970) 544-6628
303 East Main Street

Paradise Bakery & Café, bakery/ice cream, $,
(970) 925-7585, 320 South Galena Street

Syzygy, continental, $$$, (970) 925-3700
520 East Hyman Avenue, second floor

Takah Sushi, Japanese, $$$, (970) 925-8588
320 South Mill Street

Woody Creek Tavern, American/Mexican, $$,
(970) 923-4585, 2 Woody Creek Plaza

SHOPPING

Miner's Building, general store, (970) 925-5550
319 East Main Street

NIGHTLIFE/ENTERTAINMENT

Caribou Club, restaurant/nighclub, (970) 925-2929
411 East Hopkins Avenue

Isis Theater, movies, (970) 925-7591
406 East Hopkins Ave

Jazz Aspen Snowmass, concert series, (866) 527-8499

Wheeler Opera House, (970) 920-5770
320 East Hyman Avenue

GOLF

Aspen Golf Club, (970) 925-2145
39551 Highway 82

Maroon Creek Club, (970) 920-1533
10 Club Circle Road

Roaring Fork Club, (970) 927-9000
100 Arbaney Ranch Road, Basalt

FISHING/RAFTING

Frying Pan River, fishing,
runs from Aspen to beyond the town of Basalt

Roaring Fork River, rafting,
runs from west side of Independence Pass for seventy
miles, including Aspen and Snowmass

Lyle Lovett

Aspen/Vail

It makes sense that Lyle Lovett would love Colorado. Both singer and state are basically rough-hewn country folk, equally at home on the back roads and in the big city. Born and raised in Texas, Lovett first came to Colorado in the 1980s to ski with his father. Today, he and his Large Band regularly bombard the state, playing Denver and Boulder in the summer and the ski areas of Aspen and Vail in the winter. "What I enjoy about Colorado," said Lovett, "is that you can go there and imagine it back when, especially in the towns that were vital before skiing—Breckenridge and Aspen and Telluride. I look around and I see the streets teeming with people and activity and feel the life that once was there." Here's a weekend with the music and movie star in the ski towns of Colorado, starting in Vail and ending in Aspen.

Friday: Vail

LODGING The **Lodge at Vail** is the old standard. For something smaller, try the **Galatyn Lodge.** The **Park Hyatt** in Beaver Creek, the ski area just outside of Vail, is right below the ski mountain, so you can get the lift right at the hotel. Outside of town is the **Lodge at Cordillera,** which looks like a French château in the middle of the Rockies. It has a spa, four golf courses, and three restaurants.

DINNER Sweet Basil is international, and right in the center of Vail Village, which was created especially for skiers back in the sixties. The **Left Bank** is a French restaurant and one of the top places in town. You have to take a sleigh ride up to **Beano's Cabin** [Beaver Creek], which is a private club during the day, but open to the public at night. The old cabin was built by a Chicago lettuce farmer named Beano back in 1919.

NIGHTLIFE We most frequently play **Dobson's Hockey Rink** in Vail. They put a floor down and we play. It feels like you're playing in a hockey rink. It's a nice, small arena, but it's cold.

Saturday: Aspen

LODGING The **Snowflake Inn** is a very cool place. There seems to be a lot of families, and it's just down the street from the Wheeler Opera House and two blocks from the St. Regis. It's like a little apartment complex kind of deal. The **Aspen Meadows Resort** is a very cool place to stay. The **St. Regis** and the **Little Nell** are the ultimate in luxury. They're as nice as any hotel you can ever stay in anywhere. You run into all sorts of folks. It's what the Aspen people conjure up when they think of Aspen, but it's nice. I don't mind hanging out with those guys.

SKIING In Aspen I ski at **Buttermilk.** I've skied **Aspen Mountain,** but I ski a little bit nervous. At the top, I'm fine, but going down sometimes really good skiers ski Aspen Mountain and sometimes they go by you really fast. At Buttermilk, it's nice and relaxed. There are a lot of families and people who are out there just to have a good time. I have skied **Highlands,** and **Snowmass** is really great, but Buttermilk is so close to town.

DINNER Ajax Tavern has a wonderful hamburger. Great food! Right at the bottom of Aspen Mountain. **Matsuhisa** is really good sushi. When we're working out of L.A., we go to Matsuhisa there. Nobu Matsuhisa, the chef/owner, is a brilliant guy. **L'Hostaria** is great Italian. **Campo de Fiori** has murals and great food.

The Wheeler Opera House is just beautiful. It's so wonderful that Aspen saved the Wheeler.

CULTURE The **Wheeler Opera House** is just beautiful! It's so wonderful that Aspen saved the Wheeler. It is supported by city funds, or at least partially. It's just one of those wonderful nineteenth-century opera houses. It's the perfect size room—holds five hundred people but feels like you're playing to about fifty. We've played the **Music Tent** in the summer and we've played **Harris Hall,** which is beautiful, like the modern symphonic version of the Wheeler. It's a perfectly designed acoustic space.

NIGHTLIFE The **Caribou Club** is one of those places full of intrigue. It's underground; there are several different rooms—it's not like this big, open space. Of course, I've been to the bar at the **Jerome Hotel.** It's one of those great historical buildings. In Colorado, you have a chance to reflect on where our world has gone, because the old world is so well represented.

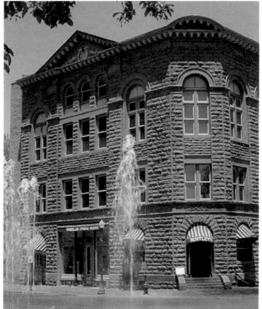
Wheeler Opera House

LODGING

Aspen Meadows Resort & Conference Center, $$, (800) 452-4240, 845 Meadows Road, Aspen

The Galatyn Lodge, $$$$, (970) 479-2418
365 Vail Valley Drive, Vail

The Little Nell, $$$$, (970) 920-4600
675 East Durant Avenue, Aspen

The Lodge & Spa at Cordillera, $$$, (970) 926-2200
2205 Cordillera Way, Edwards

The Lodge at Vail, $$$, (970) 476-5011
174 East Gore Creek Drive, Vail

Park Hyatt Beaver Creek Resort and Spa, $$$$,
(970) 949-1234, 50 West Thomas Place, Avon

Snowflake Inn, $$, (970) 925-3221
221 East Hyman Avenue, Aspen (reopening 2008)

The St. Regis, $$$$, (970) 920-3300
315 East Dean Street, Aspen

DINING

Ajax Tavern, Italian, $$$, (970) 920-9333
695 East Durant Avenue, Aspen

Beano's Cabin, American, $$$, (970) 949-9090
Beaver Creek Mountain

Campo de Fiori, Italian, $$$, (970) 920-7717
205 South Mill Street, Aspen

The Left Bank, French, $$$, (970) 476-3696
183 Gore Creek Drive, Vail

L'Hostaria, Italian, $$$, (970) 925-9022
620 East Hyman Avenue, Aspen

Matsuhisa, Japanese, $$$$, (970) 544-6628
303 East Main Street, Aspen

Sweet Basil, international, $$$, (970) 476-0125
193 East Gore Creek Drive, Vail

NIGHTLIFE/ENTERTAINMENT

Benedict Music Tent, concert venue, (970) 925-9042
2 Music School Road, Aspen

Caribou Club, restaurant/nightclub, (970) 925-2929
411 East Hopkins Avenue, Aspen

Dobson Arena, multi-purpose venue, (970) 479-2271
321 East Lionshead Circle, Vail

Harris Concert Hall, concert venue, (970) 925-9042
960 3rd Street, Aspen

Hotel Jerome, bar, (970) 920-1000, 330 East Main Street, Aspen

Wheeler Opera House, music venue, (970) 920-5770
320 East Hyman Avenue, Aspen

SKIING

Aspen Skiing Company, local mountains,
(800) 308-6935, www.aspensnowmass.com

One Great Night in Aspen

Hunter Thompson was one of the highlights of Aspen for me. I'm such a fan of his. I bought a car from him once, a gold 1976 El Dorado convertible. He had driven it to our show that night at the Wheeler and he said, "Where you guys going?" I said, "We're driving to Salt Lake City tonight." He said, "Well, that El Dorado would make a great pace car. You oughta buy it." I said, "How much?" He said, "Two thousand dollars." Buying a car from Hunter Thompson is quite an experience. We stopped on the way out of town at one in the morning, and he went over the car with me on the side of the road with a flashlight. We drove it away. It ran great. We returned it some time later that same night. I've never actually taken possession of it. I gave him the money and I get to drive the car around whenever I'm there. I love to drive it in the summer out on that road that goes out to Maroon Bells. So it was a great deal.

Austin

Matthew McConaughey's journey to Austin was an odyssey of self-discovery. In the summer of 1988, the Texas native was part of an exchange program in Australia, with plans to study pre-law at Southern Methodist University in Dallas. Then his father, former pro-footballer-turned-oil-field-supplier "Big Jim" McConaughey, called and said, "What about 'Hook 'Em, Horns'?" referring to the University of Texas in Austin. Matthew remembered, "My brother calls me a day later and says, 'Pop ain't gonna tell you this, but the reason he's saying Hook 'Em, Horns is because it's about $10,000 a year cheaper and the oil business is not in good shape right now. But let me tell you about Austin. You like running around in your bare feet, no shirt, hippying around town?' He started telling me about the outdoor life, the weather, the women—Austin has beautiful women—and he said, 'Man, it's more you than SMU!'"

Thus, Matthew McConaughey found his place in the world, both geographically and professionally. He switched from law to radio, television, and film, and landed his first acting role in 1993's *Dazed and Confused* after meeting a casting director in an Austin bar. Three years later, he starred in *A Time to Kill*, and McConaughey began a roll that hasn't slowed yet. Here's Matthew McConaughey, whom his friend and fellow Austinite Sandra Bullock once called "The Mayor of All Good Time," deep in the heart of Texas.

Friday

LODGING If you want to get a little more rural, there's the **Hotel San José.** It's on Congress Avenue, but it's like something you'd find on the side of a highway in the middle of nowhere. Sometimes I stay at my brother's in Dripping Springs. He's got eleven acres, and I sleep in his double-wide Winnebago.

DINNER Sullivan's, on Colorado Street, cooks a good steak, and they bring you out a big ol' half a head of iceberg lettuce with blue cheese dressing. I like sauces, so I get every sauce they've got. It's a finer dining restaurant, a cool, high-end spot downtown. A lot of times you get those places that everybody thinks are so cool and so hot, and you go in there, and it's all packaging. This place, the food's really good.

NIGHTLIFE I like the Saxon Pub on weeknights. It's a dark, smoky little joint, and there's always live music. It's a slightly older crowd, plus it's out there on South Lamar, not downtown. People talk about 6th Street, Austin's version of Bourbon Street. As we know with Bourbon Street, the best spots are really off the main street. On weekends, they block off the streets around 6th Street, and it's just a cattle call. You're always gonna hear some good music at the Continental Club. That's an eclectic music crowd. Plus, if you're staying at the Hotel San José, you can walk right across the street to the Continental Club.

Saturday

SIGHTS Obviously, you've got the state capitol. But for me, my landmark—and the best way to introduce anybody to Austin—is a University of Texas football game on Saturday. I don't know of a better college atmosphere. I've got a box there at Darrell K. Royal Memorial Stadium, so I go whenever I can get back for a game. Family and friends, there's usually about sixteen of us in the box. There are no boxes I've ever been in that are near as fine as what Texas has.

SWIMMING If you want to relax and get refreshed in the cold water, Barton Springs is a great spot. I used to take my school bags there

and do my homework. There's also Zilker Park, where I'd take the dog and throw the Frisbee. There are trails all up and down Lake Austin and the Colorado River. I like Hamilton Pool, too. It's a huge waterfall, a little oasis outside of town. It's got a small beach and a beautiful trail leading down to it. It's like a little lagoon.

LUNCH A great burger joint is Hut's on 5th. They do good burgers, and they have nice waitresses. There's a waitress there I met and dated for a couple of years. They didn't have music then, but now they have it some nights. And they put a pizza parlor in the back. They do twenty different kinds of burgers, but I always get the Number 8. It's got guacamole and cheese on it.

SPORTS My favorite Saturday begins with a 2:30 UT game. That gives you time to sleep in, have some breakfast, get the crew together. I like to get to the game a little early. You have lunch and everyone starts getting tuned up for the game, which will go until 5:30 or 6:00, and you usually get sundown about that time. Hang until the rest of the stadium clears out, then either catch cabs or walk to Scholz's, which is just a big, fun beer garden where they do the Longhorn postgame radio show. Obviously, if you win, that place is pretty fun. Then we go to Antone's. It's great if you really want to go shake it out and break a sweat on the dance floor. It's a legendary place in Austin.

DINNER Matt's El Rancho is pretty authentic Mexican food and a big family atmosphere. They're not afraid to spice it up and give you a little fire. If you want good Tex-Mex, Chuy's over on Barton Springs is a lively, kind of eclectic Austin spot. And their portions are huge. There's a string of good restaurants on Barton Springs, like Shady Grove. I love to eat outside if I can. What I like about Shady Grove is that the outside porch is sort of connected to the parking lot, which makes it seem like it's connected to a trailer park.

MUSIC Stubb's Bar-B-Q is a great place to get a group together to hear some music. I'm not going to say it's the best barbecue in town, but it's a good place to see live music.

MIDNIGHT SNACK The best pizza I've ever had is Domenick's on 6th Street. Oh, it's so good, and it stays open late. It's a hole in the wall with about four stools, a shaker of garlic, oregano, red pepper, and Parmesan. Gimme a slice of hamburger and pepperoni at 2 a.m.

Sunday

LUNCH I love Sonic—for a few reasons. One, I get the double jalapeño with cheese. They melt the cheese with the top bun; that's one of their secrets. The other thing I like is driving in. I get to control my climate, play my own music, and when I'm through eating, I don't have to wait for the bill. Get yourself a double jalapeño burger. That's my first meal of the day, man.

GOLF My mother lives at Del Webb's Sun City retirement community in Georgetown. I go out there and play some golf with her.

For me, my landmark—and the best way to introduce anybody to Austin—is a University of Texas football game on Saturday.

They've got two courses, and it's pretty nice. The back nine at Sun City is really good. Even if you get off the box big, you gotta swing some 7-irons. They didn't pinch up on the real estate, on the dirt, which a lot of these places do. The Hills Country Club has a Nicklaus course with a killer par 3 on 7, their signature hole. Barton Creek has a couple of good golf courses—a Fazio course, and they just built another one that's really fine.

CAMPING Take the Canyon Lake exit off I-35 when you're going south toward San Antonio to a campground called White Water. It's right there by the bridge in New Braunfels. I got introduced to it while I was there in college. With summer school, you'd take three hours of classes, just so you could stay in Austin. So you could go down there and skip class and go float the river. We pitch a tent at the riverside, and you get your tubes there, plus one extra tube for the cooler of beer. So you camp at night, party on the river, and then the next morning you get up and go catch about a four-hour float. River rats and that river, that's sort of a subculture all its own.

Austin Convention and Visitor's Bureau

Matthew McConaughey's Austin Essentials

LODGING
Hotel San José, $$, (512) 444-7322
1316 South Congress Avenue

DINING
Chuy's, Tex-Mex, $$, (512) 474-4452
1728 Barton Springs Road

Domenick's Pizzeria, pizza, $, 414 East 6th Street

Hut's Hamburgers, American, $, (512) 472-0693
807 West 6th Street

Matt's Famous El Rancho, Southwestern, $$,
(512) 462-9333, 2613 South Lamar Boulevard

Shady Grove, American, $, (512) 474-9991
1624 Barton Springs Road

Sonic Drive-In, fast food, $, multiple locations
throughout Austin

Sullivan's, steak house, $$$, (512) 495-6504
300 Colorado Street

SIGHTS
Barton Springs Pool, swimming, (512) 476-9044
2201 Barton Springs Drive

The Capitol Complex and Visitors Center,
(512) 305-8400, 112 East 11th Street

Hamilton Pool, recreation area, (512) 264-2740
30 miles southwest of Austin

University of Texas Longhorns, football tickets,
(800) 982-2386

White Water Campground, recreation area,
(830) 964-3800, 35 miles south of Austin, New Braunfels

Zilker Metropolitan Park, recreation area,
(512) 974-6700, 2100 Barton Springs Road

NIGHTLIFE
Antone's, live music, (512) 320-8424, 213 West 5th Street

The Continental Club, live music, (512) 441-2444
1315 South Congress Avenue

Saxon Pub, live music, (512) 448-2552
1320 South Lamar Street

Scholz Garten, bar, (512) 474-1958
1607 San Jacinto Boulevard

Stubb's Bar-B-Q, live music, (512) 480-8341
801 Red River Road

GOLF
Barton Creek Resort and Country Club, (512) 329-4000
8212 Barton Club Drive

Del Webb's Sun City, retirement community and golf
course, (512) 864-1243, 150 Dove Hollow Trail, Georgetown

The Hills Country Club, (512) 261-7200, 26 Club Estates
Parkway

One Interesting Night in Austin

Well, I can tell you one place I don't want to go in Austin—the city jail. I got arrested in Austin once for playing some music too loud. I was jamming two days after the Nebraska game. We had beat 'em, so it was a big celebratory weekend. It was 2:30 in the morning and I was buck-naked at home with the congas. Had the windows open and a new neighbor who'd just moved in back on the block behind me. It was a hot night. Just banging away to some music. Until two cops came in and arrested me. I was so adamant about being in the right, I went all the way to the station buck-naked. I got out of the car and they were like, "Mr. McConaughey, would you please put some pants on." And I was like, "No. This proves my innocence. This shows I was minding my own business." I was in jail for about ten hours. You don't want to be there, but I made it as fun as possible. I had some sing-alongs with some cell mates next to me and riddles going from cell to cell. I met some characters. Not that I wanted to stay and hang with them for a lifetime. What does that story tell me about Austin? You can do whatever you want. Just shut the windows so you don't wake your neighbor.

Austin

Dennis Quaid sat on a bench on the beach in Los Angeles, dreaming of home. Not Houston, where he was born and raised, but of Austin. Early Dennis Quaid and early Austin were meant for each other: the former wild-child-turned-star of scores of films like *The Right Stuff*, *The Big Easy*, and *Far from Heaven*, and the deep-in-the-heart-of-Texas home of country music, politics, and "anything goes." But now both entities have changed—the once laid-back Austin is the home of hi-tech powerhouses like Dell, and Dennis Quaid has ditched his celebratory ways for a more spiritual existence. On the beach, he struggled to remember the places that fed his fiery soul. "That was back in the days when . . . I don't remember much," he said, then smiled. "Actually, that's my trouble—I remember everything." Here's a weekend in Dennis Quaid's Austin.

Friday

LODGING The **Four Seasons** is . . . well, a Four Seasons is always a Four Seasons. It's a great hotel to begin with. You know what you're going to get. It's right on the Town Lake. It's a block or two from 6th Street near the bridge that all the bats live under. It's got a great ambience. It's nice, but not fancy-schmancy. The **Driskill Hotel** on 6th Street is gorgeous. They redid it about ten years ago. It's right in the middle of town.

BAT WATCHING At dusk, you can see all the bats come flying out from under the **Congress Avenue Bridge.** It's the biggest colony of bats in the country and they all come flying out from underneath the bridge like a cloud. They're Mexican bats, fruit bats, and they fly out at night to feed on insects. You can watch them from either side of the lake.

DINNER There are lots of Mexican restaurants, which is the traditional way to go. Texas, I think, has the best Mexican food around. There's something about the particular sauce that's involved. For me, Austin's always been the best Mexican food. The Mexican place I remember is **El Rancho.** It's excellent. Austin

Mexican food is supposed to be different from Dallas or Houston, but Austin and San Antonio kind of have the same sort of Mexican food. There's something about the way the enchiladas come out a little flatter, and there's a little bit more abundance of cheese on it, and they put the fresh onions on it, and the sauce is usually chili sauce.

ENTERTAINMENT Austin is one of the best places to hear live music in the country. On one night you might see Willie Nelson, then you go next door and it will be Wynton Marsalis. Go to 6th Street, where all of the music places are lined up one after another. It's all different kinds of music, all different kinds of people. Sixth Street is very vibrant. It's just a cacophony of sound and a great mix of people. **Antone's** is where we always used to go that was away from 6th Street. It's a great low-down dive club, man, where you could see just about anybody—very eclectic in style. I used to go there with [the musician] Jimmy Vaughn, back when the Thunderbirds were together. Jimmy's brother, Stevie, was an amazing virtuoso guitar player, but Jimmy could really play the hell out of one note, which is quite a talent. And Antone's featured all the old blues guys as well. You never knew who was going to show up. If you want an old-style Austin bar, check out the **Cedar Door.** I remember that place.

Saturday

BREAKFAST Breakfast would be one of those Mexican joints where you can get huevos rancheros. There's **Las Manitas.** I remember the decor is very Mexican, kind of pueblo almost. It's a really casual place and they have huevos rancheros and all that. **Cisco's** is another place downtown where LBJ used to eat breakfast. Again, great huevos rancheros.

SIGHTS You've got to know about the University of Texas and its tower. They light it up different; it's usually orange at night. I didn't go to UT, but when I was a kid, Austin was your first great destination. I grew up in Houston, so when I got my driver's license, Austin was the first place I went because it was a college town. I slept on somebody's dorm room floor. Basically, we had no money at all. We just walked the streets, especially Guadalupe, the main street at UT, which everybody calls "the Drag." It was during the early seventies, and there would be a lot of street musicians and parties.

The **state capitol** is in the middle of Austin, with its statue of a goddess holding a star at the top. It's taller than the Capitol in Washington and is one of the most beautiful capitol buildings in America. The capitol building sort of reminds you that Texas used to be a country unto itself, and in so many ways it still is.

NATURE You can always swim in **Barton Springs,** the big, old, spring-fed natural swimming pool where the water's always around sixty-something degrees. But one of the wonderful things about Austin is that it is right at the edge of the **Texas Hill Country,** and that's really the most beautiful part of Texas. The Hill Country is a very mystical, magical place. There's something about the way the light bounces around those hills. The oak trees are gnarled and beautiful, and the mesquite and the cedar smell fantastic. It's pretty natural, but you do have different towns there. There's Kerrville, Bandera—where I remember seeing Willie Nelson play at his Fourth of July picnic when I was about twelve years old and he still had short hair—and Johnson City. I grew up in flat Houston, so I longed for mountains and valleys.

LUNCH Threadgill's, the former gas station that's now a restaurant and was the club where Janice Joplin first played, is still there for chicken-fried steak.

SHOPPING At Texas Hatters you can get any kind of hat you want with an actual real RCA rodeo roll. A great place to buy boots is Capitol Saddlery, whose famous boot-maker, Charlie Dunn [now-deceased], made boots there for decades. I had some great boots

made there. Jerry Jeff Walker wrote a song about Charlie Dunn. You can still get great boots at Capitol Saddlery—and they can make you a saddle, too.

CULTURE The Humanities Research Center at the University of Texas has collections of many writers' works—literally millions of manuscripts and photographs. They have book readings and exhibits.

GOLF I like to play golf at Barton Creek Resort, which is outside of town at the edge of the Hill Country. There are three golf courses out there, including a Fazio course and a Ben Crenshaw course. I played the Crenshaw course, which has huge greens. Crenshaw is from Austin, of course, and the greens are big, I guess, because he's a putting fanatic. The Fazio Course, which

The state capitol is in the middle of Austin, with its statue of a goddess holding a star at the top. It's taller than the Capitol in Washington.

The State Preservation Board, Austin, Texas

is probably the most popular course there, is a work of art. They were adding a third course—called the Arnold Palmer Lakeside Course—when I was there.

DINNER There's a great place to eat barbecue that we used to go to—great ribs—off the I-35 freeway. There's also the County Line. Great ribs, man! We're talking spare ribs—that's what we're talking when I say ribs. Pork ribs. There's something about the sauce and the way they cook them, the wood that they use, good mesquite, you know. There are two County Lines, one on the lake and one in the hills. About ten miles out of town in the Hill Country there's a great barbecue place called the Salt Lick that's worth the drive.

ENTERTAINMENT The Scholz Garten is an old-fashioned beer garden with German and Mexican food. People sit outside. It's next to a bowling alley. You can hear them bowling and they have these lights that are all strung up. Stubb's Barbecue has great barbecue and great music. Stubbs was C. V. Stubblefield and he had a place in Lubbock and he moved it to Austin, and now they have bands that play there. It's on Red River Street, and there's a gospel brunch on Sundays. The Paramount Theater is the old theater right downtown. They recently redid it. It's a really old, kind of classic theater. They did it as a movie theater, but they also have music and Broadway shows.

Sunday

EXERCISE I played a concert when I had my band at Town Lake Metropolitan Park.

It was for thirty thousand people for Riverfest. The park runs along the lake, then along the Colorado River. Riverfest is held every year in April. Yeah, it must be April because it was my birthday when we played there. The park has jogging trails and walking trails all through it. I used to run along those. You're alongside the river the whole time. It's a fantastic place.

EXCURSION On a Sunday, you could take a jag down to San Antonio, which is a short drive. It's a nice drive through the edge of the Hill Country. You can get down to San Antonio and go to SeaWorld, or see the Alamo, or see the River Walk through town. It's a couple of hours away. There's a great snake farm halfway between Austin and San Antonio on one of the blue highways, which is the best way to travel through Texas, by the way. You really get a feeling for the country. You pass through the great little small towns in Texas where, if you really look, time hasn't changed all that much since the forties. They have a couple of thousand snakes—everything from pythons to rattlesnakes—each one in a different environment. This lady who ran the place had a cobra. I got a T-shirt; I've still got it.

EXCURSION If you're there in October, you can go to the Wurstfest in New Braunfels, which is Texas's version of the Oktoberfest. I went once. I had a great time, so they tell me. There's another one too, near Johnson City, in Fredericksburg. It's in the middle of the German area. Both are weeklong festivals where people drink beer, eat sausage, and have German bands. A lot of "oompah" stuff.

Dennis Quaid's Austin Essentials

LODGING

The Driskill, $$$, (512) 474-5911, 604 Brazos Street

The Four Seasons, $$$$, (512) 478-4500
98 San Jacinto Boulevard

DINING

Cisco's, Mexican/bakery, $, (512) 478-2420
1511 East 6th Avenue, downtown (open for breakfast and lunch)

County Line on the Hill, barbecue, $$, (512) 327-1742
6500 West Bee Cave Road

County Line on the Lake, barbecue, $$, (512) 346-3664
5204 Ranch Road 2222

Las Manitas, Mexican, $, (512) 472-9357
211 Congress Avenue

Matt's Famous El Rancho, Southwestern, $$,
(512) 462-9333, 2613 South Lamar Boulevard

The Salt Lick, barbecue, $$, (512) 858-4959
18001 FM 1826, Driftwood

SIGHTS

The Alamo, historic attraction, (210) 225-1391
300 Alamo Plaza, downtown, San Antonio

Barton Springs Pool, (512) 476-9044
2201 Barton Springs Drive

The Bats at the Congress Avenue Bridge,
(512) 416-5700, #3636, 100 Congress Avenue

The Capitol Complex and Visitors Center,
(512) 305-8400, 112 East 11th Street

Harry S. Ransom Humanities Research Center,
(512) 471-8944, 21st and Guadalupe, University of Texas

Hill Country Information Service, www.txinfo.com

New Braunfels Wurstfest, annual celebration, (830) 625-9167, 35 miles south of Austin, New Braunfels

San Antonio River Walk, entertainment district, (210) 227-4262, Commerce Street, downtown, San Antonio

SeaWorld Adventure Park, (800) 700-7786
10500 SeaWorld Drive, San Antonio

Town Lake Metropolitan Park,
along the Colorado River, running from Tom Miller Dam to the U.S. Highway 183 bridge

SHOPPING

Capitol Saddlery, custom leather, (512) 478-9309
1614 Lavaca Street

Texas Hatters, (512) 312-0036
15755 South IH-35, Buda

NIGHTLIFE

Antone's, live music, (512) 320-8424
213 West 5th Street

The Cedar Door, bar, (512) 473-3712
201 Brazos Street

The Paramount Theater, live music, live theater, film, (512) 472-5470, 713 Congress Avenue

Scholz Garten, bar, (512) 474-1958
1607 San Jacinto Boulevard

Stubb's Bar-B-Q, live music, (512) 480-8341
801 Red River Road

Threadgill's, restaurant/nightclub, (512) 451-5440
6416 North Lamar

GOLF

Barton Creek Resort and Country Club, (512) 329-4000
8212 Barton Club Drive

Edward Norton

Baltimore

In his breakthrough film, Edward Norton astonished audiences with his portrayal of a seemingly naive country boy battling dual personalities in 1996's *Primal Fear,* costarring Richard Gere. When the performance won Norton a Best Supporting Actor nomination at the Academy Awards and the Golden Globe Award for Best Supporting Actor, as well as comparisons to a young Dustin Hoffman and Robert De Niro, the big question was: Who is Edward Norton? Being unknown suited Norton just fine. "Every little thing that people know about you as a person impedes your ability to achieve that kind of terrific suspension of disbelief that happens when an audience goes with an actor and character he's playing," Norton said. Norton is happy, however, to tell all about one particular subject: his hometown of Baltimore, where his roots run deep.

The grandson of famed real estate developer James Rouse, who developed Baltimore's Harborplace complex as well as the Faneuil Hall Marketplace in Boston, Norton grew up in the Baltimore suburb of Columbia, the oldest son of an attorney father and a schoolteacher mom. At age five, he was captivated by a community theater play and he has wanted to be an actor ever since. After his breakout role in *Primal Fear,* he won starring roles in films like *The People vs. Larry Flynt, American History X* (for which he won a second Oscar nod), *Fight Club, Keeping the Faith,* in which he both directed and starred, and *The Illusionist.* But the big screen isn't the only place to catch Norton's fireworks. Here's a Fourth of July weekend with him in his hometown of Baltimore, the city where "The Star-Spangled Banner" was born.

Friday

LODGING It's fun to stay at the **Admiral Fell Inn** or the **Inn at Henderson's Wharf,** both small, traditional waterfront inns. They're in Fells Point, which is full of old taverns and bars and seafood restaurants. It's a really great place to walk around—kind of dynamic, with old cobblestone streets. If you want to stay someplace more modern, the new **Marriott** right on the harbor is pretty fantastic, especially if you can get rooms high up on the waterside. They have tremendous views of the harbor, the Inner Harbor, Fort McHenry, and all of downtown Baltimore. For the uninitiated, however, I would definitely recommend the Admiral Fell Inn or the Inn at Henderson's Wharf, because they're much more the flavor of old Baltimore.

DINNER My uncle used to work at **Martick's** [midtown], a very interesting, eclectic little French restaurant.

NIGHTLIFE Pick up a paper and see what's playing at **Center Stage** [downtown], one of the really great regional theaters. When I was growing up, it was run by a guy who later went on to run the Yale drama school. It's a tremendous theater. I grew up seeing everything from Shakespeare to really contemporary, avant-garde stuff there.

Saturday

HOW TO LOOK LIKE A LOCAL You'll see a lot of what I call "Southern preppy." You'll see the madras shirts and the docksiders and penny loafers. It definitely has sort of a Southern inflection, with a particularly Baltimore spin. There's lots of funky-colored madras jackets and even people with shorts and sports jackets. Baltimore's pretty laid-back, pretty casual, and it's hot in the summer. So people don't stand on ceremony. Going to the ballgame or going out and about, people will be dressed for the heat.

MUST-DO One of my highest "musts" is the **American Visionary Art Museum.** I've tried so many times to explain this museum to

One of my highest "musts" is the American Visionary Art Museum.

people, and at the end of the day, I end up just taking them there. I've never taken anyone there who hasn't walked away saying it was their favorite, most inspiring museum. The best I can say is that it's a museum on visionary artists who are working outside the academy in a way—everything from people in mental institutions to people who did their work through sort of a divine inspiration, without training. It's one of the most remarkable collections you'll ever see. I worked on a film—*Death to Smoochy*—with Robin Williams, and he collects some of the same artists they display.

SIGHTS Any weekend in Baltimore should include strolling around the **Inner Harbor** or even better, strolling around in a U and then taking a water taxi or one of the paddleboats you can rent in and around the harbor. Baltimore has a very dynamic harbor environment. The city is situated sort of in the northwest corner of the Chesapeake Bay, and when you first enter off the bay, it's kind of a big, wide mouth of a harbor.

Photo by Alain Jaramillo

As you come inland it narrows, into almost a serpent's tongue. I remember as a kid, there was literally a garbage dump and junkyard on the harbor. In the late seventies, they started the redevelopment plan of the Inner Harbor. They built the big marketplace called **Harborplace.** They built the **National Aquarium** [Inner Harbor] in Baltimore, an enormous edifice whose design has been emulated a lot of places. It's a terrific place for kids. There's also the **Maryland Science Center** [Inner Harbor], and those projects sort of radiated outward to the redevelopment of downtown Baltimore. It's been a twenty- or twenty-five-year project of the rebirth of downtown Baltimore.

SHOPPING The old defunct power plant has been renovated into an enormous multiuse facility, the **Harborplace** [Inner Harbor]. There's an **ESPN Zone** and a big **Barnes & Noble.** The Harborplace is great in the summer. There are always music and cultural festivals. It's teeming with people, and in the center of it all are two pavilions that have a lot of eclectic little stores and open raw bars and markets. It's a great, festive atmosphere. Across the street is the **Gallery,** which has great shopping and high-end stores.

LUNCH If you've never been to Maryland, I definitely recommend having the "crab experience." I've had arguments all of my life with people from the Gulf coast of Louisiana about who's got the better crabs. I would say you will arguably never have a better seafood experience than in Baltimore and the Chesapeake Bay. The way the crabs are prepared is completely unique to Maryland. **L.P. Steamer's** [Locust Point] is

probably the best place. It's on the other side of the harbor on the Fort McHenry side. They'll spread newspaper on the table and give you a mallet, and then they'll bring out the crabs with the spicy Old Bay seasoning on them. If you don't know how to eat hard-shell crabs, they'll come out and show you how to work your way through one.

FIREWORKS Baltimore is a great place to be on the Fourth of July. There are always fireworks in the harbor, which will be plastered with boats, and people will be on every roof. I really think that the tradition of rockets and explosions and everything on the Fourth of July comes from Francis Scott Key writing "The Star-Spangled Banner" after the Battle of 1814 at Fort McHenry. Not far from there is the Francis Scott Key Bridge over one of the extensions of the harbor.

CULTURE I can hear [avant-garde Baltimore director] John Waters yelling in my ear, saying, "You're telling them all of the straight places. Tell them some of the eclectic!" In the old days, I might have said you could walk along old Baltimore Street, the old adult theater, porn district. But they've pretty much cleaned that up. There's the **Edgar Allan Poe grave site** [Westminster Burial Grounds]. He died in Baltimore. It never ceases to amaze me that our football team was actually named after an Edgar Allan Poe poem, "The Raven." You can walk to Poe's grave. If you have a literary bent and you want to put a rose on his grave, you can.

DINNER Atlantic was one of the nicer restaurants. One of the things Baltimore is obviously famous for is seafood from the Chesapeake Bay. [Editor's note: Unfortunately the Atlantic closed down, and the **Full Moon Barbeque,** which is owned by Baltimore Raven Ray Lewis, took its place in the old American Can Company factory. Although the Atlantic no longer exists, Baltimore abounds with tremendous seafood establishments. **Pisces** (Inner Harbor) was voted Best Seafood Restaurant in Baltimore by Zagat Survey.]

NOSTALGIA If you're a movie fan, don't miss seeing a show at the **Senator Theatre** [North Baltimore], one of the last remaining art deco movie palaces left in the Maryland/ Virginia area. I would rate it up there with the Ziegfeld in New York and Mann's Chinese Theatre in L.A. as one of my favorite, favorite places to see a movie. It's a twenty-minute cab ride from downtown. Whenever I have a

movie, I take it back to Baltimore and do a benefit première at the Senator. It is a nine-hundred-seat theater with a gigantic screen and a phenomenal sound system. It's still family owned. We're hoping that it's about to be given historic landmark preservation status. Some of the films I've done haven't been appropriate to invite the hometown crowd out to for a benefit, but I guess I've done four or five big benefits there.

NIGHTLIFE We almost always go out to Fells Point. You never do it by heading toward one place. You just stroll along and head into any likely bar. That's the fun of it. You can walk around and just sort of barhop. You'll see the new and the old. There's a place called **Bertha's,** which is really funny. Sometimes they have live jazz combos there. There's a good bar, and you can obviously get good mussels there.

One Great Day in Baltimore

I saw Cal Ripken Jr.'s rookie game in 1982 with my whole family. Then my brother and I were at both of the games at Camden Yards when he tied and broke Lou Gehrig's record for the consecutive game streak—2130 and 2131. He got a twenty-eight-minute standing ovation, one of the longest applause moments I've ever been involved in. The next day, everybody's hands were all bruised and sore. It was one of those transcendent moments. He had been a part of Baltimore life for such a long time and is so representative of the simple working-class work ethic. His father was a coach and manager for the Orioles. Cal has stayed with the Orioles throughout his career and broke the record that most people said would never, ever be broken. It's about getting up every day and going to work, even if you're feeling lousy. The quiet nobility of that particular feat is an appealing one. I work in Hollywood, where you script these things to come out better than they do in life. But you couldn't have scripted this better, because in the game he hit a home run in his first at-bat after breaking the record to give the go-ahead run. And then the last two outs of the ballgame were both hard-hit balls to him at shortstop. You just sat there holding your head because you couldn't believe that the forces in the universe were letting things fall so perfectly on that evening. It was one of those transcendent moments in a lifetime of sports watching.

SPORTS My number one thing to do would be to get tickets to an Orioles game at **Oriole Park at Camden Yards** [downtown]. I grew up in a family of rabid Orioles fans. We probably went to thirty or forty games a summer from the time I was eight years old on, and we had season tickets all my life. My mother was one of the only women I ever knew who actually did the Orioles spring training fantasy camp. When they announced they were going to move to a stadium downtown, a lot of my family members were horrified because they were sure it would be one of these terrible new modern stadiums. Miracle of miracles, they happened to get this wonderful, brilliant group of architects, who went around studying all of the great old parks in America before designing Camden Yards. It is such a gorgeous, almost miracle of a stadium that it could be argued that the whole trend in modern baseball stadiums toward smaller, more beautiful parks has been specifically modeled after the success of Camden Yards. Sitting anywhere in the stadium out through center field, you have a view of downtown Baltimore. I remember the first time my grandfather went into the park, he practically cried because it reminded him so much of going to the ballparks of his youth. It has an almost hallowed feel to it.

Edward Norton's Baltimore Essentials

LODGING

The Admiral Fell Inn, $$$, (410) 522-7377
888 South Broadway, Fells Point

Baltimore Marriott Waterfront Hotel, $$$,
(410) 385-3000, 700 Aliceanna Street, Inner Harbor

Inn at Henderson's Wharf, $$$, (410) 522-7777
1000 Fell Street, Fells Point

DINING

Bertha's, seafood, $$$, (410) 327-5795
734 South Broadway, Fells Point

Full Moon Barbecue, barbecue, $$, (410) 327-5200
2400 Boston Street, Canton

L.P. Steamers, seafood, $$, (410) 576-9294
1100 East Fort Avenue, Locust Point

Martick's, French, $$$, (410) 752-5155
214 West Mulberry Street, midtown

Pisces, seafood, $$$, (410) 605-2835
300 Light Street, Hyatt Regency Hotel, Inner Harbor

SIGHTS

American Visionary Art Museum, (410) 244-1900
800 Key Highway, Inner Harbor

Edgar Allan Poe Grave Site, (410) 706-7228
519 West Fayette Street, Westminster Burial Grounds and Catacombs

Maryland Science Center, (410) 685-5225
601 Light Street, Inner Harbor

National Aquarium, (410) 576-3800
501 East Pratt Street, Inner Harbor

Oriole Park at Camden Yards, baseball, (888) 848-BIRD
333 West Camden Street, downtown

SHOPPING

Barnes & Noble, bookstore, (410) 385-1709
601 East Pratt Street, Inner Harbor

ESPN Zone, sports memorabilia and dining,
(410) 685-3776, 601 East Pratt Street, Inner Harbor

Harborplace and the Gallery, shopping center,
(800) Harbor-1, 200 East Pratt Street, Inner Harbor

NIGHTLIFE

Center Stage, live theater, (410) 332-0033
700 North Calvert Street, downtown

The Senator Theatre, movies, (410) 435-8338
5904 York Road, North Baltimore

Boston

"One of the things I appreciate more and more about Boston is that out of all the cities in the United States it has its own history," said leading man Ben Affleck. When he was eight, the city of Paul Revere and the American Revolution gave Affleck two gifts. One, he landed his first acting job on the marine biology PBS series *The Voyage of the Mimi.* The same year, on a basketball court, he met a new kid in the neighborhood: Matt Damon. The two became best friends, participating in their school's drama program and working in Boston-area films.

After college, Affleck moved to L.A. to become an actor. Work was sporadic, and he returned to Boston to work with his friend on a screenplay that Damon had started at Harvard about two Boston youths and their quest to become somebody. The result was *Good Will Hunting,* which won Affleck and Damon Best Screenplay Oscars in 1997. But before you check him out on the screen, check out this weekend with Ben in Boston, the city that gave him a foundation on which he's built his career.

Friday

LODGING The Four Seasons [Back Bay] is nice, as is the **Ritz-Carlton** [Public Garden]. But when I go home, if I don't stay at the house I grew up in with my mother, I stay at the **Charles** in Cambridge. It's an excellent place to stay because you don't have that sense that you could be staying in any hotel from Seattle to Miami. It's got a unique feel to it and an excellent restaurant, **Rialto.** In fact, I've gone to Rialto without even staying at the hotel, which says something. I'm a pretty simple guy, with what some of your readers might consider pretty pedestrian tastes. I can't recall food with my palate, but I know every time I've gone there it's been good. And the decor is lovely and the service is excellent.

DINNER/NIGHTLIFE My father used to work at a bar called the **Cantab,** which was kind of a working people's bar in Central Square in Cambridge. Now it's become a more college, alternative place. I might go to **B-Side** in Cambridge. Good food, nice atmosphere, sort of like your diner atmosphere except nicer, upscale, with a little bit of deco. It's a young crowd, but not oppressive in the overly "college" sense. We used to go to a bar called Drumlin's, which has now become a bar called the **People's Republik** [Cambridge]. So you can see how the flavor has changed—that's one of the flip sides of gentrification. But there's still a lot of really wonderful places to go.

Saturday

BREAKFAST When I go home, the first thing I do is get some coffee at **Dunkin' Donuts** in Central Square. There is something absolutely magical about Dunkin' Donuts' coffee that you can't get on the West Coast. The coffee there is clearly the greatest coffee on earth. I wish they were in more places. **Brookline Lunch** in Cambridge is a tiny little place, an old-fashioned mom-and-pop greasy spoon that has great breakfasts.

SIGHTS The **Back Bay** area is another gorgeous place to go. In *Good Will Hunting*, we selected places to film that were kind of, we thought, our landmarks. We shot on the Red Line as it went over the bridge, where you see the whole city on the subway. You can go on the swan boats in the **Boston Public Garden.** It's the place that every public school kid goes to on a field trip at least once in his life. It's an experience, these little swan boats that unite all the public school kids of Boston. It's where the Robin Williams character and Matt's character sit down and he gives him a lecture about life.

You'd really be doing yourself a disservice if you didn't go to Fenway Park. It's sort of a holy place in Boston.

There's something beautiful and serene and yet distinct and Boston-specific about it.

LUNCH I like places that seem to have some authenticity and sense of place. You can get a great slice of pizza at **Pinocchio's** in Harvard Square. It's just a tiny walk-in place that's been around forever. They've got great deep-dish and thin-crust pizza. If you're looking for a cheeseburger and fries, the absolute best place to go is **Leo's** [Cambridge]. The double-cheeseburger plate there is one of the most sinfully exquisite treats you'll ever know in your life. There's a place called **Grendel's Den** [Cambridge], whose name was taken from the Beowulf character in English literature, and you get a nice cross section of your academics and your college people. They've got good wings. It's got a medieval tavern kind of vibe. **Charlie's Kitchen** [Cambridge] is a nice divey kind of diner/bar.

SPORTS You'd really be doing yourself a disservice if you didn't go to **Fenway Park.** It's sort of a holy place in Boston. At least it was to me growing up. It's our local "Saint of Lost Causes." It's a beautiful old ballpark. If you go

Julie Cordeiro, Boston Red Sox

in spring, summer, even in the autumn, the air hangs low and heavy, and the whole city seems to slow down and hold its breath to wait and see if the Red Sox can maybe pull one out this year. The ballpark is basically just as it was back in 1918. Babe Ruth played there before Harry Frazee [Red Sox owner] sold him to the New York Yankees.

SHOPPING A good reason to go to Fenway Park is for baseballs and souvenirs. **Newbury Street** has your upscale shopping and stores and fancier stuff. There's an amazing shop in Cambridge called **Nomad.** The owner is a woman who buys art in places like Africa and Afghanistan. It's all handcrafted stuff and really beautiful. There's no other place that I know of quite like it. It's one of the little secrets of Boston.

DINNER For New Year's on the millennium, we had a party at **Sonsie** on Newbury Street. That's your generally upscale restaurant where the food and atmosphere are good and you might, every now and again, run into one of the Red Sox eating there. The **Elephant Walk** [Cambridge], a French/ Cambodian restaurant, is excellent. It's sort of quiet, tucked away, and private. The food is exquisite. They have a great spring roll and wonderful pad thai. They use really fresh ingredients and are very attentive.

THEATER The **American Repertory Company** is in Cambridge, and they have a little theater where they do really terrific work. They put on some astonishing productions there. It's where I have seen some of the best theater in my lifetime. If you want to drive forty minutes, the **Trinity Repertory Company** in Providence also does excellent work.

NIGHTLIFE There's a great place for live music called the **Middle East** in Central Square. The music's always good and the food is superb. It's a little bit raucous. It's in what used to be the non-university side of Cambridge, which is where I grew up. It's now kind of encroached upon by MIT. On the same side of the street is **Hi-Fi Pizza,** a place you can get pizza at two in the morning—if you want to stand in line behind a bunch of drunk kids with purple hair. But the pizza's worth the wait.

Sunday

SOLITUDE **Mount Auburn Cemetery** is a beautiful old cemetery that's very well kept. It sounds like a morbid place to go, but it's actually exquisitely beautiful, particularly in the fall as the leaves change. They don't mind if people come for a walk. There's an old tower in the middle that you can climb up and look out. It's a lovely place to spend an afternoon if you're looking for quiet and some time to think and reflect.

STROLL In summer on Sundays, they close Memorial Drive on the Cambridge side of the Charles River. There are people out there selling stuff and people riding bikes and rollerblading and walking. It's like a little street fair. From the Cambridge side, you can see all of Boston. You can see the capitol dome, which was plated in gold because originally Boston thought of itself as the hub of the universe and believed that their model of government was going to be "a city on a hill" and a beacon for all other nations. That's why there's an area called Beacon Hill, even though it only has an altitude of twenty feet.

Ben Affleck's Boston Essentials

LODGING

The Charles Hotel, $$$$, (617) 964-1200
1 Bennett Street, Cambridge

The Four Seasons, $$$$, (617) 338-4400
200 Boylston Street, Back Bay

The Ritz-Carlton, $$$$, (617) 536-5700
15 Arlington Street, near Public Garden

DINING

Brookline Lunch, diner, $, 9 Brookline Street, Cambridge

B-Side Lounge, new American, $$, (617) 354-0766
92 Hampshire Street, Cambridge

Charlie's Kitchen, American, $, (617) 492-9646
10 Eliot Street, Cambridge

Dunkin' Donuts, $, (617) 354-8944
616 Massachusetts Avenue, Cambridge

The Elephant Walk, French/Cambodian, $$$,
(617) 492-6900, 2067 Massachusetts Avenue, Cambridge

Grendel's Den, eclectic, $, (617) 491-1160
89 Winthrop Street, Cambridge

Hi-Fi Pizza & Subs, $, (617) 492-4600
496 Massachusetts Avenue, Cambridge

Leo's, burgers, $, (617) 354-9192, 35 JFK Street, Cambridge

The Middle East, Middle Eastern, live music, $$,
(617) 864-3278, 472 Massachusetts Avenue, Cambridge

Pinocchio's, pizza, $, (617) 876-4897
74 Winthrop Street, Cambridge

Rialto, Mediterranean, $$$$, (617) 661-5050
1 Bennett Street, Charles Hotel

Sonsie, international, $$$, (617) 351-2500
327 Newbury Street, Back Bay

SIGHTS

Boston Public Garden, park with swan boats,
(617) 927-7444, bounded by Charles, Arlington, Boylston,
and Beacon Streets

Fenway Park, Red Sox tickets, (617) 482-4769
4 Yawkey Way, Kenmore Square

Mount Auburn Cemetery, (617) 547-7105
580 Mount Auburn Street, Cambridge

SHOPPING

Fenway Park Souvenir Shop, Red Sox paraphernalia,
(617) 421-8686, 4 Yawkey Way, Kenmore Square

Newbury Street, upscale shops

Nomad, global art, (617) 497-6677
1741 Massachusetts Avenue, Cambridge

NIGHTLIFE/ENTERTAINMENT

American Repertory Company, theater, (617) 547-8300
64 Brattle Street, Cambridge

Cantab, bar, (617) 354-2685
738 Massachusetts Avenue, Cambridge

People's Republik, bar, (617) 491-6969
878 Massachusetts Avenue, Cambridge

Trinity Repertory Company, theater, (401) 351-4242
201 Washington Street, Providence, Rhode Island

One Great Walk in Boston

Boston is contained and you can get almost anywhere on foot. When I was a little kid, my dad and I used to walk in the afternoons in the summer. We could walk from where we lived, down over the river, across the Boston University Bridge, and over to Fenway Park. You could still buy bleacher seats for a couple of bucks. We'd go sit in the bleachers and watch the Sox. That walk I used to take with my dad still means a lot to me. I go back and take those little walks again, walk over to Fenway Park, walk down through the North End, the Italian neighborhood, all the way down over to South Boston and down through the Back Bay. You can do all that in a day. I think about my dad and where I grew up and the way I grew up. It's nice. We can still go home again.

Mark Wahlberg

Boston

Mark Wahlberg went from being the youngest of nine kids to street tough to rapper Marky Mark to mainstream movie star in record time. One minute he was half-naked above Times Square on Calvin Klein billboards, the next he was starring in films like *Boogie Nights*, *Three Kings*, and *The Perfect Storm*. But through every epoch, he's remained firmly rooted in home. "Acting came naturally for me because of my ability to survive on the street in Boston," said Wahlberg. "I was always trying to convince somebody of something. It usually wasn't the truth. That's what acting is. As long as you believe it, then you feel like you can convince someone else. I learned how to survive. I was a troubled teen. Sometimes, I used to be jealous that I didn't get to go to a school where I could have played sports and gotten a better education. But I learned the really important things, the real life experience. That's what got me to where I am today. I credit that to growing up on the streets."

Wahlberg wore a V-necked T-shirt and backward baseball cap at our meeting in the Alfred Hitchcock Building at Universal Studios, where he was doing some last-minute work on his film *The Italian Job*. More recently, he produced his first television series, the HBO hit *Entourage*. But Wahlberg remains, at heart, a kid from the streets of Boston where, he said, every trip back home is a reality check. "They make a point to make me feel like I am no better than anybody else," he said. "It's nice, because you can get spoiled after a while. Back home, I remind myself of where I came from and where I hope to go back to."

Friday

LODGING I can stay at my mom's again because my days of going out and having fun are pretty much over, but **Fifteen Beacon** is an amazing hotel. It's right downtown in Beacon Hill. It's got a great restaurant with great steaks and a fantastic wine list. The hotel rooms are huge; they have some suites that have a living room and dining room. It's a really nice hotel. Then there's a **Marriott,** near Braintree, that's really close to my mom's house. Growing up in Dorchester, we thought Braintree was like Beverly Hills, because it's all one-family houses. Some people have yards and some people have pools. It's about forty-five minutes outside of the city. It's just like a small town.

DINNER Every time I go back to Boston, I want to eat seafood. But my mom eats it so often, she usually wants to go to the **Capital Grille** [Back Bay], a steak house. In Boston, I like **Jimmy's Harborside** [waterfront; closed for renovation until Spring 2008], a seafood place, and **Anthony's Pier Four** [waterfront] is famous. I also like the **Atlantic Fish Company** [Back Bay] on Boylston Street. It's great for me because not a lot of people recognize me. But the people who work there know me, so I can kind of squeeze in and get a table without having a reservation, which is nearly impossible. So there are a few upsides to being famous.

NIGHTLIFE There is some great nightlife in Boston. **Aria** [theater district] is a great club. It's the music, the crowd, and they have different rooms. Boston is such a great party town, because it's one of the biggest school towns in the country. If the Celtics win, you see a lot of players out at places like Aria. If they lose, of course, they are nowhere to be seen, because Boston sports fans aren't that forgiving.

Saturday

BREAKFAST I usually end up flying to New York and then driving to Boston, and the first thing I do is go to this little place called **Nick's,** eat some breakfast, then go home to my mother. Nick's is in Weymouth and it's amazing. It's open seven days a week—a very, very small place. It's the best breakfast I have ever had. Afterward, I visit my mom and try to sleep until my niece and nephew start jumping on me.

SHOPPING **Faneuil Hall** [downtown] is the big outdoor marketplace where they have all these really cool shops. It's a popular place for tourists. I used to work at [the now closed] Bailey's Ice Cream in Faneuil Hall. I got fired after three months. I remember eating so much ice cream and feeling sick to my stomach, so I just went in the back and lay down. Probably three or four hours later, the assistant manager came back and fired me. Fantastic ice cream, but too much of anything isn't good for you.

SPORTS You can't go to Boston without going to a Red Sox game in the summer. **Fenway** is an amazing ballpark. To me, Boston has a lot of historical sites and a lot of history, but Fenway Park is where Bill Buckner missed that ground ball. You know, it's got this curse. Yet to me it's one of the most exciting places to watch a game. It's a small field, but with the Green Monster [the left field wall], it's still a tough field to play.

LOCAL HISTORY I visit the town of **Plymouth** often. I tend to go down there to the gym, but I'll go down to Plymouth Rock. I don't know if it's the original rock—I mean, people say that. It's just at the edge of the water, where they say the Pilgrims landed.

LUNCH Plymouth has one of my ten favorite restaurants in the world, a place called the **Colonial.** It's a little mom-and-pop place that has the best fish, the best of everything. It's always packed, and you have to wait for a table. I get baked haddock or grilled haddock or broiled haddock with mashed potatoes. It takes me probably forty minutes to drive from my mother's house to Plymouth, and when I'm home I probably go three or four times a week. In Boston, I'd go to the **Palm** [Copley Place] or **Legal Sea Foods** [waterfront], where you can always get a decent piece of fish. You can't get haddock anywhere but New England—or I have never seen a piece of haddock on a menu anywhere else. I'll have it any way—fried, baked, broiled. But the best haddock is at Colonial, and then I'd say Atlantic Fish Company second.

MORE SHOPPING My friend owns a store on Newbury Street called **House of Culture** [South End]. He used to be a stylist for me when I was in the music business. He goes to London and New York and Paris, and he gets all the stuff that you can't get around here. He has very casual stuff and athletic wear, but also suits. Newbury Street is the SoHo of Boston. That's where all the upscale shops are. **Northside Family Sportswear** [Boston Common] is where we used to go as kids and look in the window at all the stuff that we couldn't have, the Nikes and the sweat suits, and everything that was new and cool that we couldn't afford. So I'll go in there and buy stuff that I don't need just because I couldn't as a kid. But now I'm not doing that as much anymore.

SIGHTS There are some great parks like the **Boston Common.** You can go to the **Boston Public Garden** and they have swan boats and just beautiful lush greens where you can play football and Frisbee like in Central Park. The **Children's Museum** is great. It's right there in downtown Boston, actually near where the

The New England Aquarium is incredible! I used to love going there as a kid.

Boston Tea Party took place. And the **New England Aquarium** is incredible! I used to love going there as a kid.

DINNER I have an early dinner at my mother's house because I like to eat, and she eats early. So she'll make one of my favorites because I'm not home that much and she likes to spoil me. Then I'll end up going for dinner again at 10 or 10:30 at the **Atlantic Fish Company** or the **Capital Grille.** If I have pasta early, then maybe I'll have steak at night and get a beautiful bottle of wine. I'd get something nice, something expensive—Chateau Latour. The last time I went, me and Father Flavin, my parish priest, had a bottle of '82. We grew up together. He's a little bit older than me, but he was the one that got me on the straight and narrow, and he was always there for me. My brother, Paul, is the executive chef of **Bridgeman's** in Hull. It's right on the water on Nantasket Beach. It's got a great wine list.

NIGHTLIFE I'd probably go to **Venu** [theater district]. A friend of mine is a DJ there, a kid that I grew up with. I ask them not to [announce that I'm there]. You know, "We've got a movie star in the house who claims he's from Boston, but he's not from Boston anymore. He's from

New England Aquarium

Hollywood." They like to bust my chops. Or they'll play my old song "Good Vibrations," or one of the songs that I sang in my early days. It goes with the territory. People are tough on you, but it's just tough love.

TATTOOS The first one I got I did myself with India ink. It was on my leg here. [He pulled up his pant leg.] I got it covered up with this stupid cartoon character because it was the only thing I could cover it up with—Sylvester the Cat. But I had a shamrock with a club. Of course, I had to hide that from my mother until I was eighteen; I got it when I was thirteen. This one [the rosary beads around his neck] I got when I was twenty-two. I always wore rosary beads, and they were always getting broken and I was losing them. So I said, *you know what? I want to get it done.* I had to drink a lot of beer before I got in the chair at **Tattoo Fever** [Pelham], because it's extremely painful right here, especially over your collarbone and down the center of the chest. I was supposed to get one tattoo and I ended up getting three. I got Bob Marley and then I got my parents' initials. Then I found out five months later that the same guy, my friend Mike, gave my mother a tattoo. My mother has a little teeny tattoo on the small of her back. She got it done at sixty years old. I am like, "What are you doing? It's a little late to start trying to be a rebel." But she wanted to get it done, and Mike was like, "Please, don't tell Mark that I did it." He was scared that I was going to be really upset. But she's a grown woman.

Sunday

WORSHIP Go to church. I grew up going to St. Williams, but now I go to **St. Edwards** in Brockton, because that's where Father Flavin is. It's a gorgeous, gorgeous service. There are a lot of wonderful, God-loving people there, and the energy—you feel it. Father Flavin is amazing. He's loved by everybody.

GOLF There are lots of great courses in Braintree, all along the South Shore. The **Presidents Golf Course** in North Quincy is nice. **Braintree Golf Course** is nice. There are some nice public courses out there. The Sheraton in Danvers has a great golf course [**Ferncroft**]. I stayed there part of the time I was doing *The Perfect Storm*.

EXCURSION If you're a fan of the movie *The Perfect Storm* and you want to see where these people live, go twenty-five minutes from Boston to Gloucester and to the **Crow's Nest.** You want to go there for some chowder or a sandwich and to have a drink, play a little pool, smell the fish off the fishermen in there. But you also want to go to **Halibut Point,** an amazing little seafood restaurant, where you're going to get the best fish chowder, the best sandwiches. There is some serious history in Gloucester. It's amazing to go to the City Hall, where you'll see the lists of Gloucester—all the names, the memorials for the fishermen. I mean, there are probably ten thousand names on that wall of all the fishermen who have died at sea since the 1890s.

Mark Wahlberg's Boston Essentials

LODGING

Boston Quincy Marriott, $$, (617) 472-1000
1000 Marriott Drive, Quincy

Fifteen Beacon, $$$$, (617) 670-1500
15 Beacon Street, Beacon Hill

DINING

Anthony's Pier Four, seafood, $$$, (617) 482-6262
140 Northern Boulevard, waterfront

Atlantic Fish Co., seafood, $$$, (617) 267-4000
761 Boylston Street, Back Bay

Bridgeman's, American, $$$, (781) 925-6336
145 Nantasket, Hull

The Capital Grille, steak house, $$$$, (617) 262-8900
359 Newbury Street, Back Bay

Colonial Restaurant, seafood, $$, (508) 746-0838
39 Main Street, Plymouth

The Crow's Nest, bar and grill, $, (978) 281-2965
334 Main Street, Gloucester

Halibut Point Restaurant, seafood, $$, (978) 281-1900
289 Main Street, Gloucester

Jimmy's Harborside Restaurant, seafood, $$$,
(617) 423-1000, 242 Northern Avenue, waterfront
(closed for renovation until Spring 2008)

Legal Sea Foods, seafood, $$, (617) 227-3115
255 State Street, waterfront

Nick's Restaurant, diner, $, (781) 337-3270
33 Washington Street, Weymouth

The Palm, steaks and seafood, $$$$, (617) 867-9292
200 Dartmouth Street, Copley Place

SIGHTS

Boston Public Garden, park and swan boats, bounded by
Charles, Arlington, Boylston, and Beacon Streets

The Children's Museum Boston, (617) 426-8855
300 Congress Street, downtown

Fenway Park, Red Sox tickets, (617) 482-4769
4 Yawkey Way, downtown

The New England Aquarium, (617) 973-5200
1 Central Wharf, waterfront

Plymouth Rock, (800) 872-1620
Plymouth Information Center, 130 Water Street, Plymouth

SHOPPING

Faneuil Hall Marketplace, shopping/dining complex,
(617) 523-1300, 4 South Market Building, 5th floor, downtown

House of Culture, (617) 236-1090
585 Columbus Avenue, South End

Northside Family Sportswear, (617) 265-1010
601 Washington Street, Boston Common

Tattoo Fever, (603) 635-3129
63 Route 38, Pelham, New Hampshire

NIGHTLIFE

Aria, nightclub, (617) 338-7080, 246 Tremont Street,
theater district

Venu, bar, (617) 338-8061, 100 Warrenton Street, theater
district

GOLF

Braintree Municipal Golf Course, (781) 843-9780
101 Jefferson Street, Braintree

Ferncroft Country Club, golf (978) 739-4032
50 Ferncroft Road, in the Sheraton Danvers, Danvers

Presidents Golf Course, (617) 328-3444
357 Squantum Road, Quincy

One Seasick Day in Boston

I went on a whale watch when I was doing *The Perfect Storm*. No, George [Clooney] didn't go. It was all fine and dandy until I started getting sick. We went out in a "Boston Whaler," these big trucks that are also flotation devices. So you go out right into the water, which is scary at first. Then, once you start getting out there, those floats aren't very stable, so you get a little seasick. I was with long-liners and sword fishermen. I got sick. We were at the Crow's Nest, which is the bar in the movie, and we were having a bunch of beers and some fish chowder, then went out there, and I just couldn't handle it. Well, they cracked up and told everybody that I was a wimp, and they didn't put it that nicely. They called me a movie star, a Hollywood chump, and all that stuff. That's the last thing I ever want to be, a fisherman, but I really admire those guys—they do some serious work. You know, we never think about it when we're eating a piece of fish, but I think about it every time I sit down at a table. I think about some guy had to actually go out there and risk his life.

Carmel/Monterey

I t was someplace I'd always dreamed about going to," said John Travolta of that slice of perfect California coastline encompassing the picturesque seaside villages of Carmel and Monterey. A native of Englewood, New Jersey, who initially gained fame in the TV series *Welcome Back, Kotter*, he first visited in late 1976. It was just before the release of *Saturday Night Fever*, in which Travolta, as Tony Manero, would launch both the disco boom and his own superstardom, winning a Best Actor Oscar nomination. He stayed at the Highlands Inn above the ocean in Carmel. "I had seen ads with the cypress trees overlooking the ocean," he remembered, but pictures paled when compared with the real thing. Seventeen years later, in 1993, he was still so hopelessly in love with the area he rented a house and moved outside Carmel for a year, just before the release of *Pulp Fiction*, in which his role as a philosophical hit man won him his second Oscar nomination. Since then, he's barely had time for a getaway, but at the time of our interview, he was fitting in at least three Carmel/Monterey visits a year.

Through starring roles in *Get Shorty, A Civil Action,* and *Primary Colors,* Travolta has made the second half of his career as impressive as the first, when he sizzled on-screen in *Grease, Urban Cowboy, Carrie,* and *Blow Out.* Between films, if you look skyward, you might spot Travolta, a qualified pilot, flying up from Los Angeles at the helm of one of his many airplanes, including a Boeing 707, with his wife, actress Kelly Preston, and their two children as his passengers. Here's where you'll find him when he touches down.

Friday

HOTEL I like either the **Lodge at Pebble Beach** or the **Inn at Spanish Bay.** And if either of those were booked, then I would go to the **Highlands Inn.** The Lodge is a classic. It's an upscale golf resort at its best. It's rustic elegance. The Inn at Spanish Bay is along similar lines, but because it's newer and the architecture is different you have more of a California comfortable, pristine kind of elegance. It's not as old world, but more "comfortable-new." The Highlands Inn is classic Carmel-hill-overlooking-the-ocean kind of living. Cypress trees. Each room with its own fireplace. On the hill overlooking the ocean, which is different from on a golf course overlooking the ocean. The ocean is always tumultuous and beautiful from all of these hotels. It's exciting and dramatic.

DINNER The restaurants at both the Lodge at Pebble Beach and the Inn at Spanish Bay are excellent. If you start at the Lodge, you've got **Club XIX** and you've got **Stillwater's,** which is more of a casual grill overlooking the eighteenth green and amazingly fresh fish. And if you just want sandwich fare, you've got the **Tap Room.** So those three restaurants at the Lodge are outstanding. And then the restaurant at the Inn at Spanish Bay is **Roy's,** the first continental U.S. branch of the famous Roy's in Hawaii. The food is a mix of things but closest to French-Chinese. You can't miss with the cuisine at any of these places.

Saturday

BREAKFAST Normally, I go to **Club XIX** because I wake up late and I have a brunch there. You're sitting there overlooking the eighteenth green beside the sea. It's an amazing place to start your day.

SIGHTS I think there's something in Carmel/ Monterey for everybody. The overall feeling of Carmel reminds you of Ireland a little bit.

Carmel Village is basically a Main Street with about ten offshoots of that Main Street, which is just wonderful shopping, wonderful restaurants. The **Carmel Mission** is interesting, the second of twenty-one missions founded by Father Junipero Serra in the 1700s. Then, when you've explored Carmel, move into Monterey, the former whaling town that became a sardine capital that became the setting for John Steinbeck's novel *Cannery Row,* named for Monterey's sardine canning factory. It's an amazing old town where you get the sense of the turn-of-the-century, of the gold diggers and the fishermen and the fisherman's wharf. You get more of a Steinbeckian feel to the whole thing—and if you're a Steinbeck fan you can visit the **National Steinbeck Center,** the museum of the author's life, twenty minutes away in Salinas. There, again, the walks on the ocean are great in Monterey, and the bay with its seals and otters is always interesting to see. For the kids, there's the **Dennis the Menace Playground,** created by cartoonist and local resident Hank Ketcham—it has tons of apparatuses to climb on and go through. And trains and paddle boats. It's a very expansive concept for kids to play in; it's outdoors and it's been there since the fifties.

SEA LIFE The **Monterey Bay Aquarium** is the best aquarium I have ever seen. There are literally hundreds of species of fish and sea plants. It's got a three-story wall of glass that's about thirty feet high, about seventy-five to one hundred feet wide, where you've got everything from sharks to manta rays to every sea life you can imagine. It is breathtaking. They even have an upper level where you can observe. And it's in the dark so the water's illuminated and you can see the fish. And then it continues on to be this extraordinary museum of fish: an Outer Bay exhibit, featuring schools of species from the ocean, and the Mysteries of the Deep exhibit, a huge assemblage of deep-sea creatures. It's an amazing aquarium.

Golf Golfers flock to **Pebble Beach,** an oasis of golf where Bing Crosby hosted his famous annual tournament and where Elizabeth Taylor filmed *National Velvet* in the forties, set in the extraordinary Del Monte pine forest with the most amazing cypress trees and blacktail deer. You get there via the famous **17-Mile Drive** at Pebble, which is an outrageous residential road, winding through twenty-six points of interest— from the Seal and Bird Rocks to the Cypress Point Lookout. 17-Mile Drive has a little bit of every place that you love. It's set alongside the most stunning coastline and has five of the world's greatest golf courses, including the **Pebble Beach Golf Links,** which most people say is their favorite golf course in the

world, and **Spyglass Hill,** one of the world's toughest courses. I play golf intermittently and I enjoy it. But to be honest I don't go to Monterey/Carmel for the golf, even though that's what most people go for. I go for the atmosphere and the ambience and the food.

LUNCH There's a mall, the **Barnyard** area, in Carmel that looks like a farmhouse, on Highway 1. Their Japanese place, the **Robata Grill,** is always packed. In Monterey, the **Sardine Factory** is fun. That's more of a wild west, kind of a Gay Nineties feeling to it.

SHOPPING The shopping in Carmel is fabulous. Whether you go at Christmastime or the middle of the summer, the shopping— whether it's clothes, gift buying, or whatever— is really great. There are hundreds of shops in the town, which is officially called Carmel-by-the-Sea. There are so many antique places and clothing places. I go to this aviation store, **Wings of America,** that's quite fun. They have nostalgic aviator-type things—memorabilia from airlines, vintage aircraft, things like that.

EXERCISE I like the main beach in Carmel at the end of the main drag. It's quite white and hilly, with the sea-green ocean. With the combination of the crashing waves, it's glorious. At sunset, you can't beat it. If you drive farther south, you can visit the **Carmel River State Beach,** which is a bird sanctuary and a great

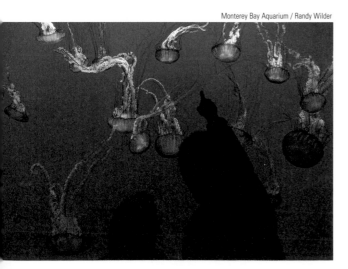
Monterey Bay Aquarium / Randy Wilder

The Monterey Bay Aquarium is the best aquarium I have ever seen. There are literally hundreds of species of fish and sea plants.

place to walk along the water. The spas are great at both the Inn at Spanish Bay and the Lodge at Pebble Beach. You get every kind of service imaginable, from hands and feet to facials to massage to steam. At the spa near the Lodge, you can relax in the big Jacuzzi overlooking the ocean.

DINNER There's an Italian restaurant in Carmel that I go to called **Piatti.** It's modern, Italian cuisine—gourmet Italian. The atmosphere is contemporary, fireplace with glass where you overlook a town park. It's comfortable. There's paper on the tables where kids can draw with crayons—or adults. It's a gimmick that they use while you're waiting for your glass of wine or whatever. The **Flying Fish Grill** is a French-Japanese restaurant in downtown Carmel. It's small, very quaint, with semiprivate dining, with redwood booths built by the chef, and the food is so delicious. There's a sea bass dish that they make, which is amazing. Everything they serve is very special and very flavorful. I've also been to **Casanova** [Carmel], a romantic Mediterranean restaurant housed in a building once owned by Charlie Chaplin's chef.

Sunday

BRUNCH Sunday is the day to stroll through downtown Carmel and shop. Clint Eastwood used to own the **Hog's Breath Inn.** Years ago, I'd go there. But it's more of a bar, hamburger fare, more of a tourist stop.

EXCURSION I hang out at Big Sur, which is, of course, ninety miles of the most stunning coastline on earth, above the ocean on Highway 1 between Carmel and San Simeon. Heading to the famous Big Sur resorts, you'll pass the **Point Lobos State Reserve,** where you'll see seals, otters, seabirds, and quite possibly, migrating California gray whales, then cross the Bixby Bridge, one of the highest concrete bridges in the world. The **Post Ranch Inn** is set above the ocean. The rooms are comprised of tree houses and ocean houses, some literally hanging over the sea. The **Ventana Inn and Spa** is on the other side of the road on more than two hundred acres of the national park called the **Ventana Wilderness,** and the Ventana Inn is dotted with Jacuzzi tubs. You can hike the resort's acreage or the adjoining mountains, which are filled with hiking trails and trail camps. Both are excellent places to stay, excellent places to dine. If you like the more rustic in-the-mountains feel, overlooking the ocean, you've got the best of it in Big Sur.

CULTURE If you're in Big Sur, you can drive farther south to the village of San Simeon, home to the **Hearst Castle,** one of the most famous private homes in the world, made famous in the movie *Citizen Kane.* I've been to San Simeon several times—and it's history. Being a film actor, you can just imagine being up there during Hearst's time at his Casa Grande, the one-hundred-room castle filled with the art and antiques he purchased around the world. Standing there today, you can imagine Clark Gable and Carol Lombard, David Niven, Norma Shearer, and Charles Lindbergh arriving from L.A. by Hearst's private railway car and being entertained by Hearst and his mistress and the whole bit. We had a private tour, but public tours are conducted several times throughout the day and night. Set it up early.

John Travolta's Carmel/Monterey Essentials

LODGING

The Highlands Inn, $$$, (831) 620-1234
120 Highland Drive, Carmel

The Inn at Spanish Bay, $$$$, (831) 647-7500
2700 17-Mile Drive, Pebble Beach

The Lodge at Pebble Beach, $$$$, (831) 647-7500
1700 17-Mile Drive, Pebble Beach

Post Ranch Inn, $$$$, (800) 667-2200, Highway 1, Big Sur

Ventana Inn and Spa, $$$$, (831) 667-2331
Highway 1, Big Sur

DINING

Casanova, Mediterranean, $$$, (831) 625-0501
5th Street, Carmel

Club XIX, contemporary, $$$$, (831) 625-8519
1700 17-Mile Drive, Pebble Beach

Flying Fish Grill, seafood, $$$, (831) 625-1962
Mission Street, Carmel

Hog's Breath Inn, burgers/steaks, $$, (831) 625-1044
San Carlos Street, Carmel

Piatti, Italian, $$$, (831) 625-1766, 6th Avenue, Carmel

Robata Grill, Japanese, $$$, (831) 624-2643
3658 The Barnyard, Carmel

Roy's, Hawaiian fusion, $$$, (831) 647-7423
2700 17-Mile Drive, Pebble Beach

Sardine Factory, seafood, $$$$, (831) 373-3775
701 Wave Street, Monterey

Stillwater Bar and Grill, contemporary, $$$$,
(831) 625-8524, 1700 17-Mile Drive, Pebble Beach

The Tap Room, American, $$$, (831) 625-8535
1700 17-Mile Drive, Pebble Beach

SIGHTS

Cannery Row, (831) 649-6690
Wave Street, Monterey

Carmel River State Beach, (831) 649-2836
Carmelo Street, one mile south of Carmel

Dennis the Menace Park, children's playground,
(831) 646-3860, Camino El Estero, Monterey

Fisherman's Wharf, 99 Pacific Street, Monterey

Hearst Castle, (800) 444-4445
750 Hearst Castle Road, San Simeon

Mission San Carlos Borromeo de Carmelo,
(831) 624-1271, 3080 Rio Road, Carmel

Monterey Bay Aquarium, (831) 648-4888
886 Cannery Row, Monterey

National Steinbeck Center, (831) 796-3833
1 Main Street, Salinas

Point Lobos State Reserve, (831) 624-4909
Highway 1, three miles south of Carmel

Ventana Wilderness and 17-Mile Drive,
(888) 221-1010 (Monterey Convention and Visitor's Bureau)

SHOPPING

The Barnyard, mall, (831) 624-8886, Carmel

Wings of America, aviation specialty store,
(831) 626-9464, Carmel

GOLF

Links at Spanish Bay, golf, (831) 647-7495
2700 17-Mile Drive, Pebble Beach

Pebble Beach Golf Links, (831) 622-8723
1700 17-Mile Drive, Pebble Beach

Spyglass Hill Golf Course, (831) 625-8563
68 West Pebble Beach, Pebble Beach

Chicago

T he guy on the bike is famous, but zipping up and down the skyscraper streets, along the famous lakeshore, and through the heady arts, restaurant, and nightclub districts of Chicago, he's no longer best identified as one of the most venerable actors of his generation. Returning to the city where he grew up, John Cusack reverts to the role he loves most. He

becomes just another Chicagoan, another guy on a bike in awe of the city sprawling beneath his pumping feet. "Chicago is the best-kept secret in America, in a weird way," he said. "It's an international city, and you have all the great architecture and all the stuff that any major international city would have. But it still has a great, down-home, down-to-earth, almost no-nonsense sensibility. They don't suffer fools well."

Cusack's favorite way to see Chicago is not from some sports car or limousine, but from the seat of a bike. And even though America's third largest city stretches across 229 square miles, Cusack insisted that the heart of the city is easily navigated. "It's a great city for biking around," he said, rattling off streets, sights, secret places. So with the wind in his hair and his grip on the handlebars of his bike, Cusack takes us on a tour of his hometown, the City of Big Shoulders, the Windy City, Frank Sinatra's kind of town. "So we're going to talk about Chicago," I said, and I could hear him brighten. "Hit me!" said Cusack—and he was off and riding.

Friday

CHOICES FOR AN AFTERNOON BIKE RIDE I'll ride up and down the waterfront, go by **Navy Pier,** then all the way down the public park toward Montrose. You can go all the way up and down Lake Shore Drive. There are parks all over there. Then you can go through the city and all of its different neighborhoods—Wrigleyville and near Halsted—everywhere. You can go up toward the south side, toward **Millennium Park,** to the **Shedd Aquarium** and **Soldier Field,** through Chinatown, and all the way back through the city to the Loop, and then through downtown.

DINNER/BASEBALL I could say, "Hey, I'll meet you over at **Smith & Wollensky** [River North]," and we would bike over there, have some food, and then make a mad dash to **Wrigley Field** [Old Town]. It totally connects me to Chicago and my childhood. My father took me there. We would sit behind third base—not in the box seats, but the grandstand. Then, when I got old enough, I would take the El—the elevated train—from Evanston, change to the Purple Line, and then we would go to Wrigley Field.

I remember just as we'd pull into the park, the whole train would be rocking with excitement. You could see the scoreboard, the flags waving, and I would usually have about three or four bucks. It would take 50 cents to get down there, then it was $1.50 to sit in the bleachers, so that would take about $2.00, which would give me about a buck and a half for food and a ride home. Usually, I would spend the whole thing and we would have to hop the train on the way back.

AFTER-GAME COCKTAILS Sports bars are a little trickier to go into if you are famous. Famous and alcohol can be not so good, but I like to go into them. There are great ones all around Wrigley Field. You can go into any of those and have a great time.

Saturday

ARCHITECTURAL BIKE TOUR I know the city inside and out. I don't think there's an area I haven't been to. There is a tour where you

I'll ride up and down the waterfront, go by Navy Pier, then all the way down the public park toward Montrose.

Navy Pier

can go up and down the river and see the architecture. It's just out of control. [He's talking about a boat tour called **Chicago from the Lake,** which hits the highlights of Chicago architecture. But Cusack prefers the bike to the boat.] You go past the **Wrigley Building** [downtown]. The **John Hancock** [the Loop] is great because you can see the whole city from all the way around.

LUNCH You can take your bike through Bucktown, which is terrific. Just a cool area with lots of great coffee shops and clubs and restaurants. We shot all over there for *High Fidelity*. It's where **Double Door** [a live-music venue] is. There are great record stores in Bucktown. Tiny little record stores like the one in *High Fidelity*. You can also find great funky art and stuff like that.

DINNER You can go out in Chicago and the day or the night happens to you. You run into people and they say: "Let's go over here, and let's do this . . ." **Gibson's Bar and Steakhouse** [Gold Coast] is the old standby. It's hard to get a better steak than at Gibson's in Chicago. It's like Old Faithful. It has a real Chicago feeling. There are great little Italian restaurants on Wells. **Edwardo's** [Gold Coast] is a great pizza place. They've got them all over. I get the stuffed spinach. **Topo Gigio's Ristorante** is a good Italian restaurant on Wells—traditional. There are so many places. **Charlie Trotter's** [Lincoln Park] is a terrific place. There is also **Spiaggia** [a two-level, upscale Northern Italian restaurant on the Gold Coast], in the One Magnificent Mile building. It's a fantastic restaurant overlooking the city, right across from the Drake

Hotel. I've gone there quite a bit. It's really superior.

NIGHTLIFE **Stanley's** [Lincoln Park] is a terrific bar. Stanley's is like mayhem, basically. Donnie Kruse is one of the owners, and he's kind of the mayor of Chicago. A lot of ballplayers go over there. It's like a sports bar and they have live-band karaoke on Sunday nights. It's a really loose, fun crowd. They have a little restaurant in back and serve great food. You can go down toward Halsted and see all the blues clubs and jazz clubs. I like to go to the **Green Mill.** We shot that in *High Fidelity*. It's this great old jazz club; it's in a really old building that is just fantastic. They say Al Capone drank there. You feel like you can see how the whole place must have been bustling in the twenties or something. Then the neighborhood decayed, and now it is coming back up. It's been around for so long, you can feel the history. The acoustics aren't great, but the room feels so great. It has a big long old bar, and it's a great place to hang out.

BLUES [Cusack noted that the clubs are lined up along Rush Street and beyond—all within biking distance of one another.] **Kingston Mines** is a tiny little blues place, the best place to hear the blues. You can hear the best blues in the world in these cramped little places. They have small, tiny little stages and the best blues players in the world. We used to go hear Sugar Blue play all the time. We would go out to dinner, then go over to Checkerboard Lounge [now closed] and hear Sugar Blue playing with his band from around 11 p.m. on. You can go barhopping all night.

Sunday

SPIRIT The people of Chicago survive all those tough winters and then everybody sort of explodes and goes crazy when the spring and summer come because they are so happy about it. You have the dead of summer and the dead of winter. There is not a better place to be.

I watched all six championships for the Bulls. You could always go to any bar on any given night in the winter and the whole city would stop for Michael Jordan. Everyone would hold their breath to see what he would do. The whole city went nuts for all six championships. I would also go to the old Soldier Field on Sundays and see the Bears. I was there for every playoff game when they went to the Super Bowl, when the Bears had that magical season in 1985. I was there for the last game, when they beat the Giants. The colder it got, the happier the fans got. Then, as soon as they knew they were going to the Super Bowl, it started to snow. The whole city was in this state of bliss.

I was also there the year before when the Cubs were two innings away from going to the World Series. I've been to every playoff game the Cubs have played, too, which haven't been that many. Hey, man, it's like enduring the winters. We will endure and persevere until the spring comes.

John Cusack's Chicago Essentials

DINING
Charlie Trotter's, nouvelle American, $$$$, (773) 248-6228
816 West Armitage Avenue, Lincoln Park

Edwardo's Natural Pizza, $–$$, (312) 337-4490
1212 North Dearborn Street, Gold Coast

Gibson's Bar and Steakhouse, $$$$, (312) 266-8999
1028 North Rush Street, Gold Coast

Smith & Wollensky, steak, $$$$, (312) 670-9900
318 North State Street, River North

Spiaggia, Regional Italian, $$$, (312) 280-2750
980 North Michigan Avenue, Gold Coast

Topo Gigio Ristorante, Italian, $$$, (312) 266-9355
1516 North Wells Street, Old Town

SIGHTS
Chicago from the Lake, boat tour, (312) 527-2002
North Pier Docks, downtown

John G. Shedd Aquarium, (312) 939-2438
1200 South Lake Shore Drive, Museum Campus

John Hancock Center, (312) 751-3681
875 North Michigan Avenue, the Loop

Millennium Park, (312) 742-1168
borders Michigan Avenue, between Randolph Street and Monroe Street, the Loop

Navy Pier, (312) 595-5300, 600 Grand Avenue,
Lake Michigan near Streeterville

Soldier Field, football, (312) 235-7000
425 East McFetridge Drive, downtown

The Wrigley Building, (312) 923-8080
400 North Michigan Avenue, downtown

Wrigley Field, baseball, (773) 404-CUBS
1060 West Addison Street, Wrigleyville, Old Town

NIGHTLIFE
Double Door, live music, (773) 489-3160
1572 North Milwaukee Ave., Wicker Park

The Green Mill, jazz club, (773) 878-5552
4802 North Broadway Street, uptown

Kingston Mines, blues club, (312) 477-4647
2548 North Halstead Street, Lincoln Park

Stanley's Kitchen & Tap, bar, (312) 642-0007
1970 North Lincoln Avenue, Lincoln Park

Chicago

On his birthday, Joe Mantegna sat in his Los Angeles–area living room fielding congratulatory calls from family members in Chicago, each call ending with the salutation, "See you soon!" Chicago calls Mantegna constantly, whether through friends and relatives on the phone or in his memory. It's not only the city where he was born and raised, it's also the town whose characters—specifically a shadowy brand of "businessmen"—inspired him in film roles like *Godfather III*, *Bugsy*, and *The Last Don*. The hardworking actor grew up in Chicago theater, starring in local theater, and later moved on to Broadway, acting in many plays written by his friend and fellow Chicagoan David Mamet. *Glengarry Glen Ross* won Mantegna a prestigious Tony Award. It was in Los Angeles, however, that he became elastic, working on a diverse collection of films. He also began coauthoring plays and producing movies. But in between, he finds time to return to his favorite role: Chicagoan. Here's a weekend in the windy city that Joe Mantegna will always call home.

Friday

LODGING The **Drake** [Gold Coast] is a great hotel. David Mamet used to stay there. We were doing one of his plays, *The Disappearance of the Jews*, at the Goodman Theater. It's about two men in a hotel room, so we rehearsed the play in his suite at the Drake Hotel. We got so used to using his two chairs that we actually borrowed them from the hotel and used them on stage at the Goodman Theater. We were rehearsing in his room one night after he had stayed up late the night before, writing. So he left us to rehearse in his suite—he went off around the corner and I assumed he had left. We rehearsed for a couple of hours and when it was time to leave, we said, "Well, geez, Dave never came back. I guess we'll just lock up." Something was laying out, maybe an umbrella, and I figured, *I'll put this away in the closet before we leave.* And I open up the closet and David's sleeping in the closet—just tucked in the closet sleeping. He didn't want to bother us in the rehearsal, yet he was so tired and couldn't use the bedroom because we were rehearsing there, so he just went in the closet and went to sleep. For the last two hours, he had been asleep. I didn't even wake him up.

DINNER I would probably go to the Rosebud in Little Italy on Taylor Street. I love their *pappardelle*—it's one of my favorite dishes there. Tuscany is another great Italian restaurant. Both are on Taylor Street, the original Little Italy of Chicago. This is where my parents grew up. When my grandparents came over from Sicily by way of New York they wound up in that neighborhood. There's a whole revitalization of that area. There's a pizza restaurant called Pompei that's been there forever. There are a lot of other good ones, but Rosebud and Tuscany are two that I particularly like.

ENTERTAINMENT After dinner, it's Jilly's [Gold Coast]. They play Frank Sinatra songs all the time. It's named after Jilly Rizzo, who was Frank Sinatra's best friend and bodyguard. I don't know where Jilly was originally from, but his son is involved with this place. It's a great club because it's always jammed. You'll see Rat Pack wannabes, a crowd that spans from their twenties up to guys like more my age in their forties and fifties, who can actually relate to that period from memory. I would go to Jilly's and have a martini. My wife likes that.

Saturday

BREAKFAST My idea of breakfast is going to Mr. Beef [River North] around 11 a.m. for a beef sandwich. That would definitely get me started! It's something that you can't just get anywhere. Italian beef sandwiches are to Chicago what Philly cheese steaks are to Philadelphia, and what po' boys are to New Orleans—a sandwich that defines the city. It's a sandwich of sliced beef and seasoned juices, and you can get it with sausages, sweet peppers, or hot peppers. Whenever I'm on *Jay Leno,* we always joke about it because Jay, I guess, is taken with the name Mr. Beef. He'll go in there and do a little bit whenever he's in town in Chicago. This is like a unique kind of sandwich. I would go there anytime, to tell you the truth, but it's not really for dinner.

PERSPECTIVE To me, Chicago is every adolescent and childhood memory I have. It represents all my memories of being a boy and a young man and also all of my family, because 99 percent of my family still lives there, as does my wife's. First of all, I'm really struck by how flat the Midwest is. You grow up there and you assume every place is like that, and then you leave and you realize other places have hills and mountains. Carl Sandburg put it very well. He said it was the "city with big shoulders." Here's this little tiny jewel of a city, but it's sitting in the middle of the Great Plains of the United States, with some of the most horrific weather that you probably have on the planet at various times. I mean, as much as people talk about the famous Chicago winds and Chicago winters, the summers would probably kill more people there in terms of the heat and humidity. I mean, it's not for the faint of heart. Chicago is a tough town, but its people, in a way, are soft.

VIEWS Everybody talks about going to the top of the Sears Tower, which is great because it's so high, but actually I think it's a lot of fun to go up to the top of the **Hancock Building.** It's a smaller building, but it's a little more in the heart, in the "Loop" of Chicago. The view from up there is interesting. The best view of Chicago is looking back from the promontory of the **Adler Planetarium.** If you drive up toward the planetarium, you drive up to the end of this little promontory—because the planetarium is on this little finger of land that sticks out from Grand Park near downtown—and the view looking back is probably one of the great skyline views on the planet. It's been on the cover of a lot of record albums.

DIRECTIONS The thing about Chicago is there is no east. Once you've got that figured out, it's one of the easiest cities in the world to get around. It's laid out on the grid system, so all you have to do is think, *Remember, the lake is east.* So all you have to really worry about is north, south, and west. There are a few blocks that are numbered east, but not much because eventually you're in the lake. Zero-zero is the corner of State and Madison—that's the big intersection in Chicago. So if somebody gives you an address that says, "I'm 3200 West, 400 North," you know that it's thirty-two blocks west of State Street and four blocks north of Madison. Everything goes off that zero-zero intersection. In Chicago, it all makes some logical sense so it's very easy to find your way around. Also, remember that Chicago is defined by the parks. Where you grew up, your neighborhood was defined by what park you were living near. I grew up near Garfield Park, which is one of the great flower conservatories in the country, a huge old park. There's Douglas Park,

Albany Park, and Lincoln Park, which was designed by the same guy who designed Central Park in New York. Lincoln Park is in the heart of the city of Chicago. It's where the Lincoln Park Zoo is located.

ARCHITECTURE Chicago is so well known for its architecture. That's why the skyline is so beautiful—they've paid such attention to the architecture in that city. It's a tradition. You have more Frank Lloyd Wright houses in the Chicago area than anywhere else on the planet. Go up near the University of Chicago and there are all kinds of famous Frank Wright houses and Mies Van der Rohe—it's an architect stream. The old library, which was built around the turn of the century, is right downtown on Michigan Avenue. It's just gorgeous. As a kid I used to go there when it was the library and I took it for granted. Now, it's a cultural center and they have on display memorabilia from Chicago. The **State of Illinois Building** is another one of these architecturally unbelievable things in Chicago, this huge building—all glass—that looks like a glass Christmas tree ornament that someone just plopped in the middle of the city. You walk in and it's totally hollow inside and the offices are all built in the circle of this globe. It's so unique.

CULTURE There's the natural history **Field Museum,** which is immortalized in the movie *Ferris Bueller's Day Off,* with the skeleton of a dinosaur in the lobby, and the **Shedd Aquarium** [Museum Campus]. They've done a lot of renovation there. The **Museum of Science and Industry** is still one of the great museums on the south side where they have the only submarine that was captured and attacked in World

War II—this huge German submarine that's sitting right outside the museum. You can walk through it. As a kid, it was always an adventure to go down to the Museum of Science and Industry.

And, of course, the Art Institute of Chicago [downtown]. I went to acting school at the Goodman School of Drama, which doesn't exist anymore. Back then it was located in the same building as the Art Institute. So I would very often cut through the art museum to get into the theater school, which was located in the basement in the back of the art museum. There's some great art there, like *American Gothic,* the famous picture of the couple with the pitchfork. There's some great stuff by Toulouse Lautrec, Picasso's finest, *Night Hawks*—the famous painting of the people sitting at the diner—by Edward Hopper. There's also the Picasso statue, the big bird that they always talk about. Picasso donated this small sculpture to the city of Chicago and in typical Chicago fashion, they said, "Let's make a big one!" They made this huge sculpture that's in front of the Federal Building. The Chagall Wall is right downtown in front of the First Illinois Building. It's this huge wall that Chagall painted.

LUNCH Well, since I had a Mr. Beef's for breakfast, that kind of cuts into my choices for lunch. Pizza is great in Chicago. The famous place is Uno's. Now they are all over. They're noted for their deep-dish Sicilian pan pizza, which everybody thinks is the definitive Chicago pizza. Actually, to me, Chicago pizza is more the thin, very crispy crust kind with a lot of cheese and a lot of sauce. I used to get it at a place called the Home Run Inn [Pitrowski Park], a real neighborhood joint, which has become famous in the sense that they started

marketing and freezing their stuff and selling it nationwide. A very famous barbecue place is Russell's [Elmwood Park], which has been there forever. They bottle their own sauce. It's one of those places that where, when I was a kid, we would get in the car and my dad would drive us up to Russell's. Anybody from that era in Chicago would know about it. It's still there and it hasn't changed much from the thirties.

SHOPPING Shore Galleries [Lincolnwood] is an auction house and gun store. The reason they got into the gun business was because they were estate auctioneers in the forties. They were making so much money off some of these private collections of very fine firearms, and they realized this was a profitable thing, so they branched off into a gun store. It's such a weird place! In the window they have stuff like Erte statues and Wedgewood bowls, and then they'll have a Beretta shotgun. You'll go in and find camouflage jackets and hunting supplies and then next to it you'll see fine art work. It's unique.

BASEBALL Wrigley Field is a must even if you don't like baseball. If you're a baseball fan, it's like going to Mecca. Wrigley and Fenway in Boston are really "it" in terms of great, great historical baseball parks. So if you're in Chicago during baseball season, I would say it would be a must to get tickets, which you can. You don't have to go around the city selling your soul to get a ticket. You get a ticket in the bleachers and go in and see a Cubs game. That is a real interesting thing to do.

WALK I like to walk down Michigan Avenue just because it's Michigan Avenue. It's just a great street, even though Sinatra sings, "Chicago . . . on State Street, that great street." State Street *is* a great street. State Street has a lot of memories because that's the street you walk down when you go into Marshall Fields. Wabash is also a great street. It was always different from any other street; it was always a little dark because it was covered by these elevated train tracks. It always had a certain look to it that was unique and so any time of year, winter or summer, it always had that similar kind of look. And then there's underground Wacker Drive. Part of it was immortalized by *Saturday Night Live* when they talked about Billy Goat Tavern—remember "chee–burger, chee–burger"—and all that? That's located in underground Wacker. They called it Emerald City because they had this one section of it that was all lit by green lights, so when you entered in the car, all of a sudden everything turns green and has this eerie glow to it. From what I've been told, that was the actual street level of Chicago prior to the Chicago fire. That level is the remnant of what Chicago was and they basically built the rest of the city of Chicago after the fire above that level.

CIGARS On Saturday afternoon, I'd go hang out at Jack Schwartz's Importers, a cigar store. It's this great little cigar store that's right in the financial district of Chicago. It's where all the stockbrokers and the guys who work at the Board of Trade and the Mercantile Exchange all buy cigars and hang out. It's been a cigar store since 1921.

DINNER Saturday, I might go to one of the great steak houses like Morton's. Or Gibson's, a great steak place with a great bar. Gene and Georgetti's [River North] is another and the Chicago Chop House [River North]. These are great traditional places filled with serious eaters—a clientele of steak lovers. This is not the California vegetarian sprout set. These people are wearing leather shoes and wool suits and the men might even be wearing hats. The Berghoff [the Loop] is a German restaurant that's been there forever. It always had male waiters and a lot of them were immigrants from Germany, old guys who would wear something almost like tuxedoes, but it isn't a fancy place. It started in 1898 as an outdoor beer garden. Now, it's a great, great restaurant. Get either the beer or their root beer and get their schnitzel and their creamed spinach, which they're famous for.

ENTERTAINMENT There are two worlds of Chicago theater—the big-time downtown houses and the small theater companies. My first professional play, *Hair,* was done at the Schubert, now known as the LaSalle Bank Theater [the Loop], which is a big old twenty-three-hundred-seat house that's still there—big,

Chicago Chop House

The Chicago Chop House is a great traditional place filled with serious eaters—a clientele of steak lovers. This is not the California vegetarian sprout set.

beautiful, old. But then, in the seventies, there was this whole kind of resurgence of smaller theaters for small theater companies. Obviously, Chicago's Steppenwolf Theater [Old Town] is world-famous now. They won a Tony Award and they got something from the president proclaiming them as one of the great regional theaters of the country. We knew them when they were just these young kids—John Malkovich, Gary Sinese, Joan Allen—just kind of starting out. Then, there's the Second City [Old Town], where John Belushi, Dan Aykroyd and Gilda Radner came from. The whole heart of *Saturday Night Live* was basically an extension of what Second City's been doing. It's all still rolling—still very popular.

Sunday

DRIVE Well, Sunday would be a nice day to actually take a drive north up on Lake Shore Drive, which becomes Sheridan Road, up to the Bahai Temple, which is listed on the National Register of Historic Places and is the first house of worship erected in the U.S. for the Bahai faith. It's this huge temple right on Lake Shore Drive, which is a really pretty drive. You drive up through some of the nicer communities of Chicago—Winnetka and these other places that are very affluent, old established sections of the Chicago area. Then, you get to this temple that looks like the Taj Mahal.

EXERCISE I like to ride my bike a lot along the Lake Shore Drive bike path, along the lakefront. I would usually pick it up around North Avenue because that's about where I lived, but you can pick it up anywhere. The bike path runs right along the lake there, starting probably on Oak Street at Michigan Avenue, which is called the Gold Coast. Growing up in Chicago, that's where you always think you would like to live. I was in a movie called *Things Change,* with Don Ameche, part of which was shot on Oak Street Beach—the

One Great Day in Chicago

When I was a kid, we moved to Cicero, Illinois, where Al Capone was from, and it's right on the border of Chicago. During election years, when the heat was on for him to get out of Chicago, he just moved right over the border into Cicero. When I was a teenager, my first car, which I still own, was a black 1947 Buick. We used to hang out at this coffeehouse right in Cicero, and everybody said that it was owned by mob guys—real mob guys. We were in there one day and I remember a bunch of us were just hanging out and this one guy came in who everybody knew was the mob guy from the neighborhood. He was impeccably dressed. It was like two in the afternoon on a Thursday. Most guys his age would be at their jobs, but here he was, in this coffeeshop, walking up to our table.

He said, "Who owns that black Buick out front?" And my heart went into my throat and I started thinking, *Oh, my God, did I park in his space? Did I scratch his car?* My friend next to me said, "Oh, that's Joe's car. " I'm thinking, *He's turning me in!* So the guy goes, "That's your car?" and I say, "Yes." He goes, "Yeah, I like that car. How much would you take for that car? I would like to buy it from you." I had to think fast. I said, "Oh, that's my dad's favorite car! I can't sell it, but if I ever see another one, I'll let you know!" He was fine with that. Little did I know that maybe twenty years later I would draw on experiences like that as research for the kind of roles that I would play in movies like *Godfather III.*

premier kind of beach area because you're surrounded by the most expensive real estate in the city. The setting is majestic. It looks kind of like that part of Monaco where they do the Grand Prix racing along the water. You'll pass all of this as you're jogging or biking along Lake Shore Drive. You can take the bike path from Oak Street and then you move up north and come through around the Lincoln Park area, and you can cut off into the park where the zoo and the conservatory are. Then you come up on Belmont Harbor and you can see the boats dock there. Then you go a little farther and there's Wrigley Field.

Joe Mantegna's Chicago Essentials

LODGING
The Drake Hotel, $$$$, (312) 787-2200
140 East Walton Place, Gold Coast

DINING
The Berghoff, German, $$, (312) 427-3170
17 West Adams Street, the Loop

Chicago Chop House, steak house, $$$, (312) 787-7100
60 West Ontario Street, River North

Gene and Georgetti's, steak house/Italian, $$$,
(312) 527-3718, 500 North Franklin Street, River North

Gibson's, bar/steak house, $$$$, (312) 266-8999
1028 North Rush Street, Gold Coast

The Home Run Inn, Italian, $$, (773) 247-9696
4254 West 31st Street, Pitrowski Park

Morton's, steak house, $$$$, (312) 266-4820
1050 North State Street, Gold Coast

Mr. Beef, Italian sandwiches, $, (312) 337-8500
666 North Orleans Street, River North

Pompei, pizza, $, (312) 421-5179
multiple locations throughout Chicago

Rosebud on Taylor, Italian, $$, (312) 942-1117
1500 West Taylor Street, Little Italy

Russell's Barbecue, American, $, (708) 453-7065
1621 North Thatcher Avenue, Elmwood Park

Tuscany, Italian, $$, (312) 829-1990
1014 West Taylor Street, Little Italy

Uno Chicago Grill, pizza, $$, (312) 321-1000
multiple locations throughout Chicago

SHOPPING
Jack Schwartz Importers, tobacco, (312) 782-7898
141 West Jackson Boulevard, financial district

Shore Galleries, firearms/auction house, (847) 676-2900
3318 West Devon Avenue, Lincolnwood

SIGHTS
Adler Planetarium & Astronomy Museum, (312) 322-0300, 1300 South Lake Shore Drive, Museum Campus

Art Institute of Chicago, (312) 443-3600
111 South Michigan Avenue, downtown

Bahai Temple, house of worship, (847) 853-2300
100 Linden Avenue, Wilmette

Chagall Wall, mural, 1 First National Plaza, the Loop

Field Museum, natural history, (312) 922-9410
1400 South Lake Shore Drive, Museum Campus

John G. Shedd Aquarium, (312) 939-2426
1200 South Lake Shore Drive, Museum Campus

John Hancock Center, (312) 751-3680
875 North Michigan Avenue, the Loop

The Museum of Science and Industry, (773) 684-1414
5700 South Lake Shore Drive, south side

Sears Tower, (312) 875-0066
233 South Wacker Drive, downtown

State of Illinois Building, (312) 793-3500
160 North La Salle Street, downtown

Wrigley Field, baseball, (773) 404-CUBS
1060 West Addison Street, Wrigleyville, Old Town

NIGHTLIFE/THEATER
Jilly's, piano bar, (312) 664-1001
1007 North Rush Street, Gold Coast

LaSalle Bank Theater, (312) 977-1710
18 W. Monroe St., the Loop

The Second City, live theater, (312) 337-3992
1616 North Wells Street, Old Town

Steppenwolf Theater Company, live theater,
(312) 335-1650, 1650 North Halsted Street, Old Town

Halle Berry

Cleveland

Halle Berry is a product of Cleveland, Ohio, the city that gave the world the first traffic light, first streetcar, Chef Boyardee, Stouffer Frozen Food, and Dorothy Dandridge, the first black actress to be nominated for an Academy Award. Halle Berry, born in the same Cleveland City Hospital as Dorothy, starred in HBO's *The Dorothy Dandridge Story*. Berry purchased the rights to the biography penned by Dandridge's former manager Earl Mills, then spent five years working to get the film version made. Named for Cleveland's late, great Halle's department store, Berry is accustomed to winning. She was a high school cheerleader, honor society member, newspaper editor, class president, and—in a hotly contested victory over a blonde, blue-eyed competitor—prom queen. She went on to win practically every beauty pageant on the planet, from Miss Teen Ohio to Miss World, before trying her hand at broadcast journalism, modeling, and finally, acting. She returned to her Cleveland roots as Dorothy Dandridge, with whom Halle's been obsessed since high school, when she caught Dandridge's award-winning performance in 1954's *Carmen Jones* on late-night Cleveland TV. Then, she made history in *Monster's Ball*, becoming the first African-American actress to win an Academy Award for Best Actress. Here's a weekend with Halle in the city she and Dorothy Dandridge once called home.

Friday

LODGING The rooms at the **Marriott Downtown** are nice and it has a state-of-the-art health club. It's the tallest building in Cleveland, located in the heart of downtown and accessible to many of my favorite places. It's only a ten-minute walk from the **Rock and Roll Hall of Fame;** the famous entertainment, dining, and shopping district called the **Flats; Jacobs Field,** where the Cleveland Indians play; and **Tower City,** the largest shopping mall in downtown Cleveland. You're literally in the middle of everything.

DINNER The Lancer [Hough District] is on Carnegie Avenue and it's the best fresh fish and broiled scampi you'll find anywhere. On Thursday nights, there's smooth live jazz and R&B. Sergio's in University Circle, right in the heart of the city's cultural center, has inside/outside dining and great Brazilian specialties, lots of fresh seafood. Sergio's has the feel of a Brazilian seaside resort. There's Brazilian jazz on the patio on Wednesday, Thursday, and Saturday nights.

ENTERTAINMENT The Karamu House [Fairfax] is one of the places that still exists from Dorothy Dandridge's era. The word *karamu* is Swahili for "a place of joyful gathering," and that's exactly what the Karamu is—the oldest theater in the country featuring plays by black playwrights. Many writers and actors got their start at the Karamu; Dorothy Dandridge attended classes there. The Cleveland Play House [Fairfax] is one of the oldest and largest theaters in the U.S. It's comprised of four different theaters. Paul Newman and many other stars got their start in the Play House's acting classes. A musical evening under the stars at Cain Park in Cleveland Heights is nice—you can either sit in the amphitheater or out on the lawn. Some of the best acts in music perform at Cain Park. The Flats, named for the flat banks of the Cuyahoga River, where there's a constant stream of river traffic, has been transformed into Cleveland's entertainment district. It's exciting because you can sit there, beneath the bridges and in the shadow of downtown,

and watch not only the shipping action on the river, but also the nightlife on both the east and west bank. Lake Erie is a world unto itself—the huge, famous lake just north of downtown, stretching from Cleveland to Detroit to Canada.

Saturday

BREAKFAST Yours Truly on Shaker Square is a small diner with great food—a well-known neighborhood hangout both for early morning and late at night. During the day, they specialize in hamburgers and broiled chicken, but my favorite is breakfast—everything with eggs, as well as pancakes. It's right in the middle of Shaker Square, and it opens every morning at 7 a.m.

SIGHTS The Rock and Roll Hall of Fame [downtown] has become a landmark, a $100 million testament to rock-and-roll. You can watch films that show how rock-and-roll was born, then see everything from Jim Morrison's Cub Scout uniform to the stage outfits of the Supremes, Elvis, and Chuck Berry.

CULTURE Severance Hall [University Circle], home of the world-famous Cleveland Orchestra, is one of the greatest buildings in the city, built in 1929 and named for John Severance, a local businessman who donated the money for the hall as a memorial for his late wife. The Botanic Gardens [University Circle] is a beautiful place to walk on a warm day, almost ten acres of every type of plant and tree and shrub. The African American Museum [Hough District] has incredible exhibits tracing African-American history from the kings and queens of Africa to the slave trade to the accomplishments of contemporary African-Americans, including Cleveland's great inventor, Garrett Morgan, who invented the stoplight, which, of course, is on display. The **Cleveland Museum of Art** [University Circle] has been around since the early part of the twentieth century and is filled with wonderful art.

LUNCH **Heck's Café** is in the historic Ohio City area. It's in an old house with a fabulous spiral staircase in the rear of the restaurant. Heck's is great for lunch. They serve all sorts of salads and sandwiches, and the best and biggest hamburgers in town. **Nighttown** is a turn-of-the-century Irish pub in the inner-ring suburb of Cleveland Heights. They have great soups, salads, seafood, and burgers and their specialty, the Dublin Lawyer—lobster sautéed in a cayenne butter.

Steve Hall @ Hedrich Blessing

SHOPPING I love the Rock and Roll Hall of Fame souvenirs: everything from T-shirts and leather jackets to authentic rock posters to limited edition Fender guitars. You can also go to the Ohio City/Tremont area, on the west bank of the river, where Cleveland began. It's a very bohemian experience with the antique shopping district called **Antiques on Lorain Avenue** and the **West Side Market,** the famous open-air market built in 1912 and still selling every type of meat, produce, cheese, baked goods, and more.

VIEW I love to watch the sun set at **Edgewater Park,** a one-hundred-acre park on the shore of Lake Erie, right near downtown. There's a long beach running along the famous lake, where the kids love to swim, but I like it best at sunset.

DINNER I go to **Giovanni's** in Beachwood, Ohio, for fine Italian dining. It's twenty miles from downtown Cleveland, a great Northern Italian/continental restaurant that's won just about every award. The decor is elegant and the food is fabulous—fresh seafood flown in from Boston, homemade pasta, and excellent veal. **Johnny's Bar** [West Side] is the place for power dining. It's in a hundred-year-old grocers' building, beautifully renovated, with a long mahogany bar and cozy booths for four. The food is Northern Italian, and their specialty is veal. **Classics** [Hough District], the four-star

Severance Hall, home of the world-famous Cleveland Orchestra, is one of the greatest buildings in the city, built in 1929 and named for John Severance, a local businessman.

restaurant in the Intercontinental Conference Center, is excellent. Club Isabella [University Circle] is another good Italian restaurant close to Little Italy. There's live jazz every night. It's pretty casual—you can eat either inside or outside on the patio.

ENTERTAINMENT Attend a theatrical, opera, or ballet performance at Playhouse Square. This was Cleveland's great theater district of twelve working playhouses in the 1920s. Not only were these theaters magnificent architectural landmarks, they hosted some of the greatest names in Vaudeville. Now, four of the theaters have been beautifully renovated and are linked together.

Sunday

BREAKFAST Attend church services at the historic, sixty-eight-year-old Olivet Institutional Baptist Church [Fairfax] with Reverend Otis Moss Jr., pastor. He's an inspiring speaker and he has a long history of fighting injustice internationally. He worked in the civil rights movement alongside Jesse Jackson and Martin Luther King Jr., who made the church his Midwest headquarters. Olivet features several choirs, all with great musicians, ranging from a 350-voice mass choir to smaller choirs. After church, stop by an all-star brunch at the Ritz-Carlton, downtown.

EXCURSION Drive an hour or so to the Amish country, where they have the best to offer in wine and cheese—they make an amazing variety of cheeses and let you watch them work. There are Amish farmhouses that you can tour, lots of interesting Amish restaurants, and great shopping. It's another world from another time.

One Great Night in Cleveland

I lived in the inner city until I was maybe in the third grade. Then we moved out to Oakwood Village. It was a very rural community. We didn't even have paved streets. They were more like tarred streets and I remember riding my bike, coming home with tar all over my feet, and I couldn't come in the house. My mom was a single parent, trying to make ends meet.

I can remember going into Cleveland with my fifth-grade teacher. She became my mentor—Yvonne Sims. I remember going to the Karamu Playhouse Theater to see *The Wiz,* and that impacted me. In a child's mind, the theater was very intimate and small, but at the same time it was very dark and, in a way, kind of spooky. Having all of the people there and having the lights be down—there was something a little scary about it at first. And then when the curtain came up and the show came on it just came to life. It was magical. I felt so good watching all of the other people's reaction and thinking, *Wow! How great is it that those people on the stage can impact every single person in the audience.* As I look back on it now, I think that was probably what inspired me, because it touched me so much.

Cleveland | Halle Berry

Halle Berry's Cleveland Essentials

LODGING
Cleveland Marriott Downtown at Key Center, $$$,
(216) 696-9200, 127 Public Square, downtown

DINING
Classics Restaurant, continental, $$$$, (216) 707-4157
9801 Carnegie Avenue, Intercontinental Conference Center,
University Circle

Club Isabella, Italian, $$$, (216) 229-1177
2025 University Hospital Drive, University Circle

Giovanni's Ristorante, Italian, $$$$, (216) 831-8625
25550 Chagrin Boulevard, Beachwood

Heck's Café, American, $$, (216) 861-5464
2927 Bridge Avenue, Ohio City

Johnny's Bar, European, $$$$, (216) 281-0055
3164 Fulton Road, West Side

Lancer's, steak house, $$$, (216) 881-0080
7707 Carnegie Avenue, Hough District

Nighttown, Irish pub, $$$, (216) 795-0550
12383 Cedar Road, Cleveland Heights

Sergio's, Brazilian, $$$, (216) 231-1234
1903 Ford Drive, University Circle

Yours Truly, American, $, (216) 751-8646
13228 Shaker Square, Shaker Square

SIGHTS
African American Museum, (216) 791-1700
1765 Crawford Road, Hough District

Amish Country, Holmes County

Cleveland Botanical Gardens, (216) 721-1600
11030 East Boulevard, University Circle

Cleveland Museum of Art, (216) 421-7340
11150 East Boulevard, University Circle

Edgewater Park, (216) 881-8141
6500 Cleveland Memorial Shoreway, downtown west

The Flats, dining/shopping district, North Cleveland

Jacobs Field, Cleveland Indians ballpark, (216) 420 4200
2401 Ontario Street, downtown

Lake Erie, Borders the northern side of Cleveland

Olivet Institutional Baptist Church, (216) 721-3585
8712 Quincy Avenue, Fairfax

Rock and Roll Hall of Fame and Museum,
(216) 781-7625, 1 Key Plaza, downtown

SHOPPING
Antiques on Lorain Avenue, antique shopping district
Lorain Avenue, Ohio City

Tower City, shopping center, (216) 771-0033
230 West Huron Road, downtown

West Side Market, open-air food market, (216) 664-3387
1979 West 25th Street, Ohio City

NIGHTLIFE/THEATER
Cain Park, live music, outdoor amphitheater,
(216) 371-3000, 1823 Lee Road, Cleveland Heights

Cleveland Orchestra at Severance Hall, live music,
(216) 231-7300, 11001 Euclid Avenue, University Circle

Cleveland Playhouse, live theater, (216) 795-7000
8500 Euclid Avenue, Fairfax

The Flats, entertainment district
Old River Road, Cuyahoga Riverfront

Karamu House, live theater, (216) 795-7077
2355 East 89th Street, Fairfax

Playhouse Square Center, live theater, (216) 771-4444
1501 Euclid Avenue, theater district

Dallas

Most people know film and TV actress Angie Harmon as the beautiful, tough assistant district attorney Abbie Carmichael on NBC's Emmy Award–winning drama *Law and Order*. But the role was merely one episode in the career of a woman who's been a star since she was born in one of America's most image-conscious cities: Dallas, Texas. Both of her parents were top models; their union produced a baby with the camera and the catwalk in her genes. "Dad was the Mary Kay man and the Sanger Harris man and the Kouros man—remember that cologne?" she said. "I mean, he was *it*." On the day Angie was born, Dallas's top modeling agent stood outside the delivery room door. She was there as a family friend, but the baby born that day would model almost as soon as she could yawn.

When Angie was fifteen, she beat out sixty-three thousand entrants to win *Seventeen* magazine's cover model contest, for which she won a new car before she was even old enough to drive. After graduating from high school—where she excelled on both the track and drill team—she moved to New York to model, then began traveling between New York and Los Angeles to study acting. On one cross-country flight, luck placed her next to David Hasselhoff, who was in the midst of a nationwide search to cast the role of Ryan McBride in the TV series *Baywatch Nights*. Harmon got the part and the rest, as they say, is history. But her heart has never strayed too far from Texas. Here's a weekend with the actress at rest in Big D.

Friday

LODGING The **Hotel Crescent Court** [downtown]—that's the one I love. I mean, the lobby is gorgeous. You feel like you're at the Peninsula in L.A. or something. It's so classy and it's so beautifully decorated. It's just got that real homey and rich feeling to it. I don't mean "rich" in a money sense. Just overstuffed cushions and things like that. The Crescent is a shopping and office complex designed by Phillip Johnson. The rooms either overlook the courtyard into where the **Stanley Korshak** clothing store is and all those other stores, or you can overlook the office building opposite. The thing I love most about the rooms are those little sitting tables, where you've got mirrors and lights all the way down, left and right. From some rooms, you can open the doors and watch a Texas sunset, which is my absolute favorite. I've been all over the world and nobody has sunsets like Texas.

DINNER Javier's [Highland Park] serves upscale Mexican food. But on the other hand, if you just want to go in and grab a margarita with friends or just hang out, it's a great place for that, too. I love the food—I think it's great. Javier, the owner, has his Ferrari out front, although I thought it belonged to a frequent customer. Javier's sautéed beef sirloin tips come in that fantastic sauce. Then, they've got those two hot sauces—one red and one green—that come before the meal. You fill up on chips because you can't help it. Oh, you're making me so hungry. Javier's is when we get a ton of people, because all my high school friends are still in Dallas. We always get that really big huge table and just sit and visit and have so much fun. It's like a family event.

Saturday

BREAKFAST This weekend we ended up going to the **Blue Goose** on Greenville Avenue. It's the place to go if you want a Tex-Mex breakfast, kind of a Mexican brunch. Their hot sauce will just knock you out of this world, it's so good. Yet another restaurant where you fill up on the chips and hot sauce—and this is at ten in the morning! Get their huevos rancheros.

SIGHTS I grew up there and I get lost all the time because Dallas is always changing. At DFW Airport, things are always moving around. I came out of Terminal B and that's new, so I took the south exit and I was, "Oh, no, I can't figure out where we are. Let me call Dad!" He said, "Texas Stadium is coming up on your left and Reunion Tower is coming up on your right." You always have to point out the Reunion Tower—the ball with the revolving restaurant that's part of the Hyatt Regency hotel. When the World Cup was going on, the ball was a soccer ball, when New Year's Eve was going on, it was the world. Whenever I come home, I always drive around by myself where Interstate 35 curves around to Woodall-Rogers Freeway and you're right in front of downtown. When downtown is lit up, it is so pretty. I practically crash my car because I'm too busy looking around. From that curve, you can see the big green building [Bank of America Plaza] outlined in green neon-type lights at night. There's the big "X" building designed by I.M. Pei. And then you see West End—well, the downtown entertainment district where all the tourists go. They don't know about Deep Ellum, and you want to go, "Yeah, West End is cool, but come look at this," and take them to all the shops over in Deep Ellum. As you can tell, I love to shop.

SHOPPING Highland Park Village is where I got every Christmas present and birthday present for everyone I know. They have the **Ralph Lauren** shop. They've got **Celebrity Bakery,** where we got all our Christmas cookies and our gingerbread house and every single pie you can imagine—pumpkin, pecan, cherry, apple, everything. Highland Park Village has every type of store. I love going to **NorthPark.** I would go there every day if I could. I was in there during the day on New Year's Eve, dragging my sweetie around trying to find a top for that night because I had left my stuff in New York. Of course, I went to **Neiman Marcus** [NorthPark], and I ended up buying a pair of Manolo Blanik shoes and a pair of Prada loafers and this, that, and the other—things that I had absolutely no use for until spring, which really didn't have to be bought on New Year's Eve. The Mackenzie Child collection upstairs at Neiman Marcus is the best. NorthPark also has **J. Crew** and **Victoria's Secret**—every woman needs that.

LUNCH Bubba's [University Park] is right across from Southern Methodist University. Bubba's, of course, has the best fried chicken on the planet. Then they've got these great rolls that they make right there and they are huge—just sin-

Neiman Marcus

ful. If you put butter on them, they are fantastic, and if you put honey on them, they're dessert. The fried chicken is so amazing—and mashed potatoes and green beans and black-eyed peas and okra. The **Burger House** [multiple locations] is across the street from SMU. Man, if I would have gone to SMU, I would have weighed four hundred pounds. They have some secret ingredient in their hamburgers, and I think it's in the seasoning. The Burger House is a place that you drive by and you just have to keep driving, because you know if you go in there, you're getting their French fries, which are so good. The best barbecue in Dallas is **Sammy's** [Uptown]. This place is packed during lunch—everything from business executives to families coming in. You just don't miss this place if you want barbecue. Their sauce is to die for.

MORE SHOPPING You can get lost in the **Galleria** [North Dallas]. I get in there and I don't come out for two days. I mean, you're just like, *Oh, this person wants this, and this person wants that,* and you can't get out of there because it's so huge and so much fun. And then, of course, you stand there watching people ice-skate in the indoor skating rink with the little kids in their skates and they can barely stand up. Oh, they are so cute.

CULTURE The **Dallas Aquarium** [West End] is one of the most relaxing places. When you walk in, you go through a shark aquarium. They are swimming over you and around you, and they are so gorgeous and beautiful. It's one of the nicest aquariums I've ever seen. It's got these

---

Of course, I went to Neiman Marcus, and I ended up buying a pair of Manolo Blanik shoes and a pair of Prada loafers and this, that, and the other.

great places where kids can sit and get close to the windows and close to the fish and look around. Then, there's the **Dallas Museum of Art** [Arts District], where I took my father and my uncle to see the Monet collection. I could not get them out of the museum.

AFTERNOON BREAK Mi Cocina [multiple locations], please. I love it! We go there in the afternoons. If we're going to go and have Mambo Taxis, we go to Mi Cocina. Anyone who has lived in Dallas and been to Mi Cocina knows what a Mambo Taxi is. It's half margarita, half sangria, but they put this special ingredient in it. You can only have three because if you have more than that, you're on the floor—at least I am. You get to the middle of your first one and you're, "Oh, I'm fine," and then at the end of your first one, you're, "You know what, I might need to hang on a second." You just grab hold of the nearest person. I love the tortilla soup at Mi Cocina.

NEIGHBORHOODS There are three areas for me to hang out in Dallas. First, **Highland Park** where I grew up. Highland Park is known as "the bubble." It's a really, really wonderful place to have a family and raise your kids and put your kids through school, because it's a community. Everybody knows everybody and everybody kind of watches out for everybody. There are two police stations. There's Highland Park police and University Park police, and it's just a real secure, safe area. It's hard when you grow up there to not want to go back. Then we'll hang out on **Greenville Avenue,** where there are just a bunch of different restaurants and different stores. It's kind of the artsy area. It's where all the artists live, and the musicians.

Then there's **Deep Ellum** downtown where they're starting to put up loft apartments and things like that, which was unheard of in Dallas less than five years ago.

STATE FAIR Oh, I love Fair Park! Please. Texas-OU weekend, the big game between the universities of Texas and Oklahoma, while the State Fair of Texas is going on, is one of the best times in Dallas. Because most of my family went to Texas, and then my father went to Oklahoma State University. So of course, he's naturally going to root for Oklahoma. We have so many people who are all friends of ours and family, and we all go to the game. During halftime, everybody meets out in front of the stadium, and you have corny dogs and funnel cake and nachos and those big huge turkey legs, and then you go get on all the rides at the fair. I can do every single ride they've got—well, the only one that I wig out on is the swings. You know, it's like first rides for five-year-olds? I wig. I completely just freeze. My friends sit there and think it's the funniest thing on the planet. I'm just, "Don't touch me!"

DINNER The **Green Room** has the best food. It's in Deep Ellum, the downtown bar and club area, so a lot of people think it's kind of this funky club that doesn't serve food. But it's got to be one of the top five restaurants in Dallas. We went for New Year's Eve, and it was so amazing. I had beef tenderloin and it just melted in your mouth. We had these wonderful salads and oysters. There was a duck confit, there was a risotto. It was so good, and everyone was just passing plates around because you didn't want to miss anything. The Green Room is funky and fun. It's got a bunch of musician paraphernalia, like one of the Nirvana album covers signed by all of them. They keep rotating everything with all of the new musicians who come in.

Sunday

LUNCH I love **Uncle Julio's** [multiple locations]. I'm such a fan of their hot sauce. I guess you can tell I enjoy Mexican food, because I can't have it here in New York. Uncle Julio's hot sauce is so good because—this is going to sound so gross—they have actual beef drippings in it. It gives it this flavor that will just knock your socks off, it is so delicious. You'll ask them if they can put a little thing of hot sauce together for you to take home. Of course, Uncle Julio's also has fantastic tamales. Part of it is that hot sauce. The sauce is so good I had to know what was in it and they said, "The secret is beef drippings."

SIGHTS Everybody from Texas knows the joke about **Texas Stadium** [Irving]. "You know why there's the hole in the ceiling? So God can watch his favorite team play." But it's just so much fun there. The **Corral** is so much fun. It's a big huge tent—actually, I think there are two of them now—outside of Texas Stadium on game days. Everyone meets there at halftime. The hard part is getting back into the game because it's like a private box with 150 of your friends instead of just 5. What's fantastic about it is it's not some kind of VIP restricted thing—anybody can get in. I don't think people in Dallas understand that the Corral is only in

One Great Day in Dallas

We went to the farm and as we were pulling in, we saw this big huge thing and we thought one of the rocks had rolled over from the pasture. Then we realized it was one of our cows and she had gotten caught in the barbed wire and slipped on her side and couldn't get up. It was the first cow in distress I'd ever seen. Here's this other creature that needs your help. Of course, it weighs seven hundred pounds more than you do. It was just me and Caroline, my stepmom, and we couldn't figure out how to hook the tractor up to her without hurting her. A cow can only be down for ten or twenty minutes before they give up; they die within another ten minutes. Her horn was caught in the ground and her feet were up above her body, and she was wrapped all in barbed wire. So my stepmom grabbed hold of her head and got her horn out of the mud and started pulling her. I was pulling her by her front feet. You've got to watch her because if she starts to think she can get up, she'll try it on her own and kick you and gouge you with her horns, not meaning to.

She was breathing real hard and making those helpless noises. I've got tears streaming down my face. Her eyes were rolling back in her head and we're giving this cow a pep talk. Finally, we got her turned around, but she couldn't get up because of the barbed wire. I reached in to get some of the barbed wire off of her and got a six-inch cut all the way down the inside of my arm. Then, we started rocking her so she would get the idea and she tossed her head back and got me right in the hip with her horn—I mean, launched me about four feet! But now she's up and it's this huge triumphant moment and she stands there for a second. It's all three girls: Caroline, myself, and this cow. She took a couple of shaky steps and then walked off and she was fine. Everyone thinks of Texas as great, wide-open spaces, and they're right. It's still there.

Dallas. Other little tents outside of stadiums in other parts of the country do not have seventeen televisions all stacked up on top of each other making one big picture and margarita machines down the walls. I mean, they don't have that.

EXCURSION We have land in New Summerfield, which is two and a half hours away from Dallas. It's really amazing because it's where Davy Crockett grew up. You think you've gone to another state, because a lot of people think of Texas as being really flat and that's so not true. It's so wonderful and peaceful. The towns are **Rusk** and **New Summerfield.** They're little, about five hundred people. It's all about the country cooking and getting stuff from the garden and bringing that in. I completely just raid their freezer. They've got peas that are frozen fresh out of the garden, and pepper sauce—this sauce that you can put on anything. I would put it on pumpkin pie if I could. We go there to get away. You can actually see the stars when you look up at night.

Angie Harmon's Dallas Essentials

LODGING
Hotel Crescent Court, (214) 871-3200
400 Crescent Court, downtown

DINING
Blue Goose Cantina, Mexican, $$, (214) 823-8339
2905 Greenville Avenue, Lower Greenville,

Bubba's Cooks Country, American, $$, (214) 373-6527
6617 Hillcrest Avenue, University Park

Burger House, American, $, (214) 361-0370
multiple locations throughout Dallas

Celebrity Bakery, café/bakery, (214) 528-6612
65 Highland Park Village, Highland Park

The Green Room, American, $$$, (214) 748-7666
2715 Elm Street, Deep Ellum

Javier's, Mexican, $$$, (214) 521-4211
4912 Cole Avenue, Highland Park

Mi Cocina, Mexican, $$, (214) 521-6426
multiple locations throughout Dallas

Sammy's, barbecue, $, (214) 880-9064
2126 Leonard Street, Uptown

Uncle Julio's, Mexican, $$, (214) 520-6620
multiple locations throughout Dallas

SIGHTS
Dallas World Aquarium, (214) 720-2224
1801 North Griffin Street, West End

Dallas Museum of Art, (214) 922-1200
1717 North Harwood Street, Arts District

Greenville Avenue, shopping, dining, and entertainment district

Highland Park Village, historic upscale shopping and dining

New Summerfield, rural community, (903) 726-3651
128 miles southeast of Dallas

Rusk, rural community, (903) 683-4242
141 miles southeast of Dallas

Texas Stadium, (972) 785-4000, 2401 East Airport Freeway, Irving

SHOPPING
The Galleria, mall, (972) 702-7100
13350 Dallas Parkway, North Dallas

J. Crew, clothing, (214) 987-9700
520 NorthPark Center, NorthPark

Neiman Marcus, department store, (214) 363-8311
400 NorthPark Center, NorthPark

Ralph Lauren Polo, clothing, (214) 522-5270
58 Highland Park Village, Highland Park

Stanley Korshak, clothing, (214) 871-3600
500 Crescent Court, downtown

Victoria's Secret, lingerie, (214) 987-1368
522 NorthPark Center, NorthPark

NIGHTLIFE
Deep Ellum, entertainment district, (214) 748-4332
three blocks east of downtown

Denver

Actor Don Cheadle stole the screen and won several awards as Mouse, Denzel Washington's gun-toting sidekick in *Devil in a Blue Dress*. He had already appeared in numerous films and television productions, but the role launched Cheadle as a star. His star rose even higher in *Boogie Nights*, a movie about the porn industry, and kept rising: he starred in *Hotel Rwanda*, for which he was nominated for a 2005 Best Actor Oscar, and joined the ensemble cast of the 2005 Best Picture Oscar winner *Crash*. Cheadle was raised in Denver, where he received numerous scholarship offers for his abilities as a jazz musician. But his future was set at Holm Elementary School, where his first stage role was playing Templeton the Rat in *Charlotte's Web*. "I remember walking around with my script, studying my lines and trying to think of motivation and character breakdowns for Templeton the Rat," he said. Here's a weekend in the mountains with Denver's own, Don Cheadle.

Friday

LODGING The **Brown Palace** is flat-out Denver's most famous hotel and deservedly so—it has a lot of history. Everybody stayed there. I guess all the presidents stayed there, except for Carter and Clinton. A lot of stars have stayed there. There's a funny story about Flo Ziegfeld, who wanted to stay there, but they wouldn't let him bring his dog in, so he stormed out.

DINNER When you eat at the **Buckhorn Exchange,** you feel like you're being watched, because of all the animal heads. There have to be more than five hundred of them [deer, elk, antelope, cattle, buffalo, boar, reindeer, caribou, birds, rabbits] and they didn't look happy. [The restaurant specializes in beef, buffalo, and elk steak.] There's also a spot that I remember my friend's mother took us to, and they served Rocky Mountain oysters. Do you know what Rocky Mountain oysters are? Well, my friend's mother waited until we were halfway through with the meal to tell us what they were—another meal that I didn't finish. The **Fort** [Morrison] is another restaurant that has Rocky Mountain oysters [also buffalo, elk, quail, ostrich, and beef].

Saturday

SIGHTS For me, the main sights were the theater places: **Helen Bonfils Theatre** and the **Denver Center of Performing Arts.** It's home to the Denver Center Theater Company, the Colorado Symphony Orchestra, and the Colorado Ballet, and the Opera of Colorado. A very pretty space, actually. I saw Sara Vaughn there. My parents took me because they were huge Sara Vaughn fans, and I remember thinking that she was the best singer and most dynamic performer that I had ever seen in my life—she inspired me. Denver also is home to the **Colorado State Capitol.** In school, we had an introduction to politics, where we got to go to the Capitol and act like we were writing bills and

David Zalubowski

proposals and trying to draft amendments and stuff like that Finally, you can't miss **Larimer Square.** They redeveloped all that. They did kind of a city walk thing downtown. It's a lot of shops and restaurants and bars in an old part of downtown. The train used to run around there; now it's upscale trendy shops, fern bars, and clubs.

CULTURE I went to the **Museum of Natural History** a lot when I was younger. It's kind of cool, because the museum is right there in **City Park,** next to the **Denver Zoo.** So you can make a whole day of it. My favorite section of the museum is the rocks and the minerals and the stones. They have them under different lights; they reflect the cracks and do all this cool stuff. They have big dinosaurs, too, and a cool Native American section and an Egyptian section. I took dates to the museum and then to the zoo next door. You could sit under a tree in the park and have a little impromptu picnic. City Park is a big park. I went to school at East High School, which is right across the street from City Park, so everything was kind of centralized. Finally, the **Black American Heritage Center** [downtown] is the museum of the African-American cowboys and soldiers. There were many black American cowboys, because they were accepted more readily into the Native American society.

LUNCH Casa Bonita is a Mexican restaurant where they have divers diving into the water like you're in Acapulco. There's a lot of greenery around and big pools and tanks with fish in them and everything—very tropical. It's a cool

The Brown Palace is flat-out Denver's most famous hotel and deservedly so—it has a lot of history.

place for kids; they have fake gunfights, a lot of eye candy for kids. The best thing was the sopapillas—pockets of bread that were hollow and you poke them and pour honey in them. They bring them to your table and they're warm.

SHOPPING Denver is a big mall town. The **Cherry Creek Shopping Center** is famous. I lived near the Cherry Creek Reservoir, not the mall, but we'd go to the mall at Christmas. It's a big mall with a lot of stores. [Bookstore lovers shouldn't miss the **Tattered Cover,** one of the largest bookstores in the world.]

VIEW The Denver skyline is beautiful. If you're looking from the east and you're on the other side of downtown, you can see the skyline and behind the skyline you see the mountains. Where I lived in southeast Denver, you could see an almost 180-degree view of the mountains.

NIGHTLIFE One of the best clubs is the **El Chapultepec.** I never played there, but that's a really great jazz club in Denver that pretty much everybody goes to. It's a very intimate jazz setting, where all the greats have played. It's a long bar and about ten booths and a little performance area up front. The **Wynkoop Brewing Company** also has live music; it's a brew pub. In Colorado, you get a lot of these local beers. They have a lot of microbreweries, like the Wynkoop Brewery—that's a real nice one.

Sunday

BRUNCH GoodFriends is like a bar, but they also have good food, really good low-fat food. It's a place where you could have a nice meal.
EXCURSION The **Garden of the Gods** is this really beautiful park in Colorado Springs. It's about thirteen hundred acres with all these different rock formations, red stones, sandstones. You can hike around them and walk around them and climb up on those rocks. It's a really spiritual place. All of these formations are naturally carved by the water and the winds. In the center of the park is the Hidden Inn. I just remember driving through and feeling really kind of mystical and spiritual. It was the winter camping ground of the Ute Indian tribe until a century ago. They have the balancing rock up there, this big natural arch stone configuration. It's really beautiful. The **Royal Gorge** in Cañon City has the world's highest suspension bridge. It's an hour's drive from the Garden of the Gods. You could walk over it if you were that brave. I don't remember being brave enough to walk over it.

LUNCH If you like pizza, try **Beau Jo's** on Colorado Boulevard. You can make up your own pizzas at Beau Jo's and they'll make it. They have a huge pizza called the Challenge. If two people can eat that whole pizza in one sitting in an hour, they'll give it to you free and you get fifty dollars and two T-shirts. It's monstrously huge, a twelve-to-fourteen pound pizza. No, I never tried. The pizza costs sixty dollars and if you don't finish, you pay. So no, I never went for that.

AFTERNOON THRILLS Elitch Gardens Amusement Park is famous. Elitch's had that old rickety wooden roller coaster that was really kind of terrifying and fun. You would sit in the last car and swing off a track. It was called the Wildcat, and it was scary, real scary. The coolest part about Elitch's is this three-hundred-foot-high observation tower, where you go up and see a lot of Colorado. Elitch's has been rebuilt—now it's a huge Six Flags, about sixty acres.

NATURAL MUSIC The **Red Rocks Amphitheater** [Morrison] is great—I saw Miles Davis there. It's a natural amphitheater; they took advantage of the topography and built in seats in a valley to make a theater. The seats are between two jutting sets of red rocks, so the sound comes out and reverberates against the rocks. A lot of artists say that's their favorite place to play. And because you're in the mountains of Colorado and because you don't have all that light pollution, you can see the stars. [The Red Rocks State Park is open daily.]

Don Cheadle's Denver Essentials

LODGING
Brown Palace Hotel, $$$, (303) 297-3111, 321 17th Street

DINING
Beau Jo's Pizza, $$, (303) 758-1519
2710 South Colorado Boulevard

The Buckhorn Exchange, American, $$$$,
(303) 534-9505, 1000 Osage Street

Casa Bonita, Mexican, $$, (303) 232-5115
6715 West Colfax Avenue, Lakewood

The Fort, American, $$$$, (303) 697-4771
19192 Highway 8, Morrison

GoodFriends, American, $$, (303) 399-1751
3100 East Colfax Avenue

SIGHTS
Black American West Museum and Heritage Center, museum, (303) 292-2566, 3091 California Street, downtown

Colorado State Capitol, (303) 866-2604, 200 East Colfax

Denver Center for the Performing Arts and Helen Bonfils Theatre Complex, (303) 893-4100, 1101 13th Street

Denver Zoo, (303) 376-4800, 2300 Steele Street, City Park

Garden of the Gods Park, (719) 634-6666
1805 North 30th Street, Colorado Springs

Museum of Natural History, (303) 322-7009
2001 Colorado Boulevard, City Park

Red Rocks Amphitheater, (303) 295-4444
18300 West Alameda Parkway, Morrison

Royal Gorge Bridge and Park, (719) 275-7507
4218 Fremont County Road, Cañon City

Six Flags Elitch Gardens, amusement park,
(303) 595-4386, 2000 Elitch Circle

SHOPPING
Cherry Creek Shopping Center, mall, (303) 388-3900
3000 East 1st Avenue, Cherry Creek

Larimer Square, shopping mall
Between 14th and 15th Streets, downtown

The Tattered Cover Bookstore, (303) 436-1070
1628 16th Street

NIGHTLIFE
El Chapultepec, jazz club and live music, (303) 295-9126
1962 Market Street

Wynkoop Brewing Company, brew pub and live music,
(303) 297-2700, 1634 18th Street

Life in the Wild

I lived in southeast Denver, the suburbs. Our house was on a cul de sac near the Cherry Creek Reservoir. My friends and I used to walk from my house to Cherry Creek and we'd see so much wildlife we couldn't believe it. We'd come around the trees and see deer standing there. We'd see a herd of deer, owls—just everything! We weren't up in the mountains, we were on Hampden Boulevard, one of the big streets that runs all the way through Denver. Denver is a city that hasn't gotten rid of all its critters.

Houston

Beyoncé Knowles is a dual superstar as an actress and as a performing artist, both in her current solo career and, before that, with Destiny's Child, the chart-topping group she led to international stardom. But she is still what she's always been: a Houstonian. It was

there in 1990, that her father enlisted eight-year-old Beyoncé and three other young girls to form an R&B group. After gaining a huge local following, the group won a record contract for the first Destiny's Child album. After making her feature film debut opposite Mike Myers as a seductress named Foxxy Cleopatra in the Austin Powers sequel *Goldmember,* she became a movie star. With film offers pouring in and her music career exploding, Beyoncé's gone global. But at heart she's never far from home. Here's a weekend with Beyoncé Knowles in Houston, the city where it all began.

Friday

LODGING The **St. Regis** [uptown] in the Galleria area is really nice; the sheets are really soft and the beds are so comfortable. The **Westins** [uptown] in the Galleria are also nice. There are two of them now. The **Galleria** [uptown] is right downstairs, and that's the best place for me in Houston. The Galleria has everything for everybody: it has all of the top designers, an ice-skating rink, and a food court with all kinds of restaurants.

DINNER The **Cheesecake Factory** [uptown] has the best menu. I stopped eating red meat, but just recently I had the steak there again after not eating it for three years, because you just can't resist it. And the cheesecake—they have all kinds. I usually go to **Pappasito's** [multiple locations] for Mexican food. The fajitas are really good; they have the best seasoning. The environment is really cool, too. **Lopez** [downtown southwest] also has some of the best Mexican food in Houston, with fast service.

NIGHTLIFE When somebody asks, "Where should I go?" I usually recommend the **Roxy** [uptown]. I know a lot of people have their after-parties there and a lot of celebrities go there. We've performed a couple of times at the **Alley Theater** [downtown]. They did a Motown show, and it was really great.

Saturday

BREAKFAST This Is It [Fourth Ward] is a soul food restaurant downtown. They have the best breakfasts, lunches, and dinners. Any kind of soul food you want. For breakfast, it's grits and eggs and just any kind of regular breakfast food. They cook it so good it tastes like your grandmother made it.

Greater Houston Convention and Visitor's Bureau

SIGHTS Right near the Galleria there's the **Water Wall,** this beautiful waterfall at the Williams Tower, the tallest skyscraper in Houston. It's a nice place to go on a date. The breeze is nice, because Houston is usually warm and you can feel the water blowing against your face. It's just a peaceful, beautiful place to go. I had one of my first dates at the Water Wall. And we did a photo shoot there. The Water Wall reminds me of summer. It reminds me of my childhood; it reminds me of growing up. When I didn't have anything else to do, I'd just go to the Galleria and watch the people. When I see the Galleria and the Water Wall, I know I'm home. When I see big hair and big jewelry, I know I'm home.

SHOPPING Bebe [uptown] has a lot of great clothes that aren't as expensive as other name-brand clothes. They have great sizes for every-body—my mother can shop there, my little sister can shop there, and I can shop there. Destiny's Child has a good relationship with the **Versace, Gucci,** and **MAC** [all uptown] stores in Houston.

EXERCISE We ran in **Memorial Park** [downtown west] every morning before we got our record deal. We would sing while we jogged to try to be in shape. I think it's a four-mile trail. We would run, and we would hate it because it was so hot and we'd be running and jogging and singing and trying not to stop, but four miles is a long time to run. It makes it easier because

The Galleria has everything for everybody: all of the top designers, an ice-skating rink, and a food court with all kinds of restaurants.

there are so many different things you can look at while you're running.

LUNCH The best thing in Houston that you can't get anywhere else is **Frenchy's** [University District] fried chicken. Frenchy's has the best chicken. The seasoning is unlike any other; it's very spicy. It tastes like home-cooked. I love their French fries, too. They have all kinds of great desserts—the pound cake is excellent. It's not anything really fancy, but it feels really down-home. **Goode Company** [Kirby District] has really great barbecue. It looks like a cabin; it's very Western. They have turkey sausage, which a lot of places don't have. I get the turkey-sausage sandwich, and they have the best jalapeño cheese bread and the best baked potatoes.

BEAUTY My mother owns a hair salon called **Headliners** [West University Place]. I grew up performing there every week for the people in the salon, trying to make tips. We would sing and dance in the salon. It's still there, only now Headliners is one of the top salons in Houston. But it's still like home to me when I'm there, because I grew up there.

DINNER I love **Pappadeaux** [multiple locations], which has the best seafood I've ever had. Whenever we have people come to town, we take them to Pappadeaux. A lot of our deals with record labels and with group members have been made at Pappadeaux. The Pappas family has lots of restaurants in Houston. Everything that has *Pappa* in front of it is delicious: **Pappasito's, Pappas Bar-B-Q** [downtown], **Pappas Bros. Steakhouse** [uptown].

Sunday

BREAKFAST I love **Shipley's Do-Nuts.** You'll find them all over Texas.

EXCURSION Kemah is forty-five minutes from Houston. It's like a boardwalk, similar to the San Antonio River Walk, with little shops and restaurants. Down in **Galveston,** they have nice beach houses you can rent out in Pirate's Cove. I like to ride the ferry. They have a little boat that travels to **Moody Gardens** [Galveston] and back. Moody Gardens has a beautiful rain forest, an IMAX theater, a nice pool, and a man-made beach. On Galveston Beach, I like to rent the bikes and ride on the seawall, then get dinner at **Landry's Seafood** [multiple locations].

One Great Day in Houston

We did the last performance ever at the Astrodome a couple of months ago. It was during the rodeo and every seat was full. It was such a historical place. So many events have happened there, so for us to end it was really great. It was definitely one of the most exciting performances we've ever had. There's nothing better than performing in your hometown. And to hear all of those people and to know that the Astrodome was such a huge landmark, such a historical place for Houston, and that we were the last people to perform there was an honor for us.

Beyoncé Knowles's Houston Essentials

LODGING

The St. Regis, $$$, (713) 840-7600
1919 Briar Oaks Lane, uptown

The Westin Galleria, $$$, (713) 960-8100
5060 West Alabama, uptown

The Westin Oaks, $$$, (713) 960-8100
5011 Westheimer Road, uptown

DINING

The Cheesecake Factory, American, $$, (713) 840-0600
5015 Westheimer Road, uptown

Goode Company Barbeque, barbecue, $$,
(713) 522-2530, 5109 Kirby Drive, Kirby District

Frenchy's Creole Chicken, soul food, $, (713) 748-2233
3919 Scott Street, University District

Landry's Seafood House, seafood, $$, (409) 744-1010
multiple locations throughout Houston and Galveston

Lopez Mexican Restaurant, Mexican, $, (281) 495-2436
11606 South Wilcrest Drive, downtown southwest

Pappadeaux Seafood Kitchen, seafood, $$,
(713) 665-3155, multiple locations throughout Houston

Pappas Bar-B-Q, barbecue, $$, (713) 659-1245
1217 Pierce Street, downtown

Pappas Bros. Steakhouse, steakhouse, $$$$,
(713) 780-7352, 5839 Westheimer Road, uptown

Pappasito's Cantina, Mexican, $$, (713) 520-5066
multiple locations throughout Houston

Shipley's Do-Nuts, bakery, $, (713) 869-8622
multiple locations throughout Houston

This Is It, soul food, $, (713) 659-1608
207 Gray Street, Fourth Ward

SIGHTS

Kemah, boardwalk, (281) 334-9880, 20 miles south of
Houston

Memorial Park, good running park, (713) 845-1000
6501 Memorial Drive, downtown west

Moody Gardens, aquarium, IMAX theater, and more,
(800) 582-4673, 1 Hope Boulevard, Galveston

Williams Tower Water Wall, (713) 850-8841
2800 Post Oak Boulevard, uptown

SHOPPING

Bebe, women's clothing, (713) 622-2113
5015 Westheimer Road, the Galleria, uptown

The Galleria, shopping mall, (713) 622-0663
5085 Westheimer Road, uptown

Gianni Versace, designer clothing, (713) 623-8220
5015 Westheimer Road, the Galleria, uptown

Gucci, designer clothing, (713) 961-0778
5085 Westheimer Road, the Galleria, uptown

Headliners Hair Salon, beauty salon, (713) 528-1001
2442 Bissonnet Street, West University Place

MAC, cosmetics, (713) 629-5566
5015 Westheimer Road, the Galleria, uptown

NIGHTLIFE

The Alley Theater, performing arts theater, (713) 228-8421
615 Texas Street, downtown

The Roxy, bar/nightclub, (713) 850-7699
5351 West Alabama Street, uptown

Jackson Hole

E verybody grows up with a vision in their head of paradise," Harrison Ford told me, sitting on an outdoor deck overlooking his ranch outside of Jackson Hole, Wyoming. His vision was of a world of "streams and woods and wildlife." Ford, one of the biggest box-office stars of all time—the hero of the *Star Wars* and *Indiana Jones* movies and scores of other films—had always envisioned his paradise, but had been unable to find it until he and his then-wife, screenwriter Melissa Mathison, drove from Idaho into Wyoming via the Teton Pass. Parking their rental car atop an 8,249-foot precipice, they stared across Jackson Hole, a broad valley framed by the majestic Grand Teton Mountains. The view matched the vision Ford had carried in his mind. "We were standing there and looking and looking and looking," he said with a grin, pantomiming them nudging each other, pointing and whispering: "That's it!" They checked into the Wort Hotel and began exploring, but didn't risk visiting a real estate office "until we got the stupid grins off our faces, which took about three days." Now, Ford owns this eight-hundred-acre Jackson ranch, sharing his property with moose, elk, deer, beaver, badger, coyote, and bear. From here he pilots his planes, rides his horses and motorcycles, and, during my visit, juggled his dual career as both rancher and actor from his office near the barn. Here's the world he dreamed of, a weekend in the Western paradise that Harrison Ford calls home.

Friday

ORIENTATION The official name of the town here is Jackson, but we all call it Jackson Hole. The "hole" itself is the place between the mountains, which is a high mountain valley. It was the bailiwick of Davy Jackson, who was a fur trapper, one of the first semipermanent settlers. Modern-day Jackson is in Teton County, which is the most populous county in one of the least populous states. It had been, until recently, a ranching community. But as the ranching business has become less and less profitable, our economy depends on tourism and we have many second homes. When we came here, the town only had one streetlight. Now, we're a resort destination, a ski resort, and a summer destination for fishing and whitewater rafting and a number of other things. Yellowstone is ninety miles north and the Teton Wilderness is ten miles from here. You can be back in wilderness by going ten miles in any direction, except up the valley floor. If you set off into the mountains, you'll quickly be beyond normal civilization.

LODGING There are any number of good places to stay here depending on what kind of experience you want—whether you want a bed and breakfast, or the more anonymous feeling of a hotel. The **Amangami** is a fine hotel. I've stayed at Aman Resorts—the parent company of the Amangami—in various parts of the world, that are terrific hotels. The **Wort** is still a good hotel. It's got brand-new rooms. It burned to the ground about fifteen years ago and was reconstructed, so everything is pretty much brand new, in the same place and same style. My aircrew sometimes stays at the **Grand Victorian Lodge,** but they're always looking for someplace cheap. It's run by some real personable people and it's a bed and breakfast. There are lots of places that have cabins and there are the lodges in the park. The **Jenny Lake Lodge** [Moran] has cabins, but they also have a main building. There's also the **Jackson Lake Lodge** [North Moran], which is like a camp for rich adults.

DINNER The **Snake River Grill** is probably our most ambitious restaurant at the moment. It's right in town and it's a well-run professional restaurant, which is tough to do when you're depending on seasonal help and people who would really rather be fishing or hiking or something else. But they've gotten theirs on a real professional footing and they do a good job. It's a seasonal menu—a menu you might expect to find in New York or Los Angeles.

ENTERTAINMENT The **Silver Dollar Bar** is in the Wort Hotel. The **Million Dollar Cowboy Bar** is around the corner, not in the hotel. I've been in them three or four times each, and it's usually when I'm taking somebody who wants to see the town at night. The Million Dollar Bar has saddles as bar stools, and the Silver Dollar Bar has silver dollars embedded in the bar. That's the difference. But there are other places. There's the **Stagecoach Bar** in Wilson, which is more of a local place. Sunday night they have a live band—a local live band and people dance a bit. It's just a little funkier.

Saturday

SIGHTS **Grand Teton National Park** is all up and down the sides of the Teton Mountains, so it includes everything that comprises the Teton Mountains: meadows, glaciers, mountain peaks, forests, and streams. It's quite beautiful, quite rough. The **National Elk Refuge** is that big open space you see to the left of the road as you're coming into town. It was created by the national government to feed elk because the town had been built right in their traditional migration path. You see elk there in the fall and early spring; there are about ten thousand of them. You take folks out there in horse-drawn hay wagons and you can pretty much ride amongst the herds. In early spring, the Boy Scouts and the U.S. Fish and Wildlife Service have an auction in the town square. They sell elk antlers to those people who think they have some particular medicinal power. They are supposed to actually be an aphrodisiac. That's what they are generally sold for in the Orient.

FISHING I'm not an expert fisherman, but when I float the Snake River, I put in up toward Moose, or up toward the park, and float down. You go in a drift boat, with a guide that keeps you out of the snags and eddies and you just continually fish right off the bank. That's "floating the Snake." I look for what the guide tells me to look for. I know a couple of places, but basically look for a place where fish will lie, where they're in an eddy of water, or there is some hydraulic situation that will allow them to watch the food floating past. That can be in the shade of a cut bank, it can be in a riffle, where the water is being forced into a discrete direction over some rocks or gyrates the water. This makes it easier for the fish to breathe and also carries food to them. Cutthroat trout is the native variety here.

© Vlad Turchenko/fotolia.com

Grand Teton National Park is all up and down the sides of the Teton Mountains, so it includes everything that comprises the Teton Mountains: meadows, glaciers, mountain peaks, forests, and streams. It's quite beautiful, quite rough.

LUNCH Nora's Fish Creek Inn is a local place in Wilson. They get their share of tourists, but it's mostly local—a breakfast, lunch, and dinner place, very informal. You're likely to see your neighbors there. Wilson has much more of a local feeling than Jackson. But I have people pick me up a sandwich from the New York City Sub Shop. It's about a ten-by-ten little storefront where they make subs. Otto Brothers was a microbrewery in Victor, now renamed Grand Teton Brewing Company, and they make darn good beer. It's more working class.

CULTURE The Jackson Hole Museum is a little historical museum that will give you a real good idea of the history of this place. They've got photographs and artifacts and journals and newspapers. That's the real repository of the history of this place. They have some Moleswood, who was the famous Western furniture maker. The Natural Museum of Wildlife Art [began as long-time local Bill Kerr's collection]. It happens to be across from the National Elk Refuge, but it's no way a quasi-government thing—it's a private collection. I did take a walk through it, but I don't judge somebody else's art. One man's art is another man's fishing rod.

HELICOPTERING I'd hike to the glacial lakes that are at the foot of the Tetons back in the old days. There's Matilda and there's String Lake, Jenny Lake, Phelps Lake. There are some very easy hikes up into the mountains and there are some real tough ones. The helicopter is a wonderful way to see the mountains as well. You get to stop in the odd mountaintop or Alpine meadow, the green meadows that are all over the place. That's not in the park, by the way, because you're not supposed to land the helicopter in the park. There's a local pilot named Ken Johnson who flies heli-skiing in the winter and who flies for a company called Hawkins and Powers. Mostly he does search and rescue work. He's a fine, fine pilot.

THE PERFECT RIDE I have motorcycles. I like to go out south of town through Snake River Pass along the Snake River up toward Salt Lake, and there's a stretch of road there that goes through Tin Cup Pass on the way up to Desoto Springs. It's one of the best motorcycle roads I've ever been on, a smooth two-lane asphalt road that swoops and curves and it's just sort of the perfect motorcycle road, not too much traffic, not too many police. You're already sixty miles away from here. The pass is over Snake River Canyon. It connects a town called Hoback to a town called Alpine.

WESTERN LIFE There are some ranches that run dude operations. Dude ranches are part of the history of this place and have been since the twenties or thirties. People used to come up here to have a Western experience. Today, dude ranches are mostly the littler operations where people stay in cabins and they ride every day. They sit around and sing campfire songs, wear bandanas and spurs.

RAFTING I think one of the great things to do here is a float trip on the Snake River. You put in up at the park or up at Moose and just float the river. You see a lot of wildlife and you get a beautiful view of the Tetons. The outfitter I would recommend is Mad River. You'll be floating with ten to sixteen people on a raft. There are white-water trips and then there are scenic trips. The white-water trips are conducted down in the Snake River Canyon, where there's more of an elevation drop, and the river runs a little faster.

DINNER Moose is a little town pretty much comprised of people who work in the park—a lot of federal housing for rangers. It's a nice, quiet little town. Other than a few little shops, there's really not anything there except for **Dornan's,** which is two restaurants and a bar and a grocery store. Dornan's has the best wine, the best selection. Bob Dornan is a guy who really cares about wine, so it's nice that in a town like this you get a great bottle of wine.

ENTERTAINMENT Well, there's a movie theater we call "the sticky theater," because your feet stick to the floor, there's so much Coke being spilled there. That's the old one downtown; it's called the **Teton Theatre.** We have a great summer music festival, the **Teton Music Festival,** which really brings world-class players from all the great symphonies here through the summer.

Sunday

EXCURSION We fly up to **Chico Hot Springs** every once in a while. There's no airport there. They close off the road and you land on it, and there's a hot spring. It's a big Olympic-size swimming hole filled with hot water that comes from a natural spring. It's a semi-funky type of pool. Actually, a good restaurant and a place you can stay overnight is **Chico Hot Springs Resort.** That's all there is there. It's near Pray, Montana [four and a half hours from Jackson], just north of the north entrance of Yellowstone Park.

One Great Day in Jackson Hole

The Dalai Lama stayed here for three or four days. We were having a meal out here in the garage, a buffet for the people who work for us and some of the people that were in his party. He came out to see what we were up to. I said, "Is there anything special you would like to see while you're here?" He said, "Moose." So I called the chief naturalist at Teton National Park and I said, "Do you have a moose jam working right now?" A moose jam is a place where traffic has accumulated to a dangerous extent because there's a moose just off the road. So he gave me the location of three different moose jams. So this whole caravan of about four or five cars moves out, and I'm going to show His Holiness some moose. We turned left on the Moose-Wilson Road, and there is a big sign with an arrow that points this way and says "Moose." I didn't know how to explain this to him. Certainly he has the mental capacity to understand it, but I just never got around to explaining that the sign was to the town. So the sign said "Moose," and sure enough, a half a mile down the road, there's the moose. It was off the road and a bunch of cars had pulled over, everybody stopping to look and gawk. There were about three or four or five monks by the time we all got out of the cars. I don't know if he expected to see the moose because of the sign or what, but he was delighted. He stood there for half an hour watching a moose and her calf.

THE TETONS *Tetons* is French for "tits." The French fur trappers named them. These mountains are magical. There are no foothills—they rise steeply up from the high mountain valley floor, which is like 6,500 feet, and the tops of the mountains are about 15,000, probably. But it's dramatic because of this lack of foreground hills, which makes you feel far away from the mountains. You're right there. Here's the thing about this place for me: No matter where I am, where I've been, what I've been doing, I land at this airport, and I am struck over and over and over again by the magical beauty of it, the display of nature. It gives you a sense of correct scale. Along the road toward Wilson, despite its being marred by high-tension power lines, there's a view of the Tetons that always makes me laugh; it always makes me smile. And that's the way this place is for me. I always decompress here.

Harrison Ford's Jackson Hole Essentials

LODGING
The Amangani, $$$$, (307) 734-7333
1535 North East Butte Road

The Grand Victorian Lodge, $$, (307) 739-2294
85 Perry Street

Jackson Lake Lodge, $$$, (307) 543-3100
US Highway 89, North Moran

The Jenny Lake Lodge, $$$$, (307) 733-4647
North Jenny Creek Junction, Moran

The Wort Hotel, $$, (307) 733-2190
50 North Glenwood Street

DINING
Dornan's Chuckwagon / Pizza Pasta Company,
American/Italian, $$, (307) 733-2415
10 Moose Street, Moose

Grand Teton Brewing Company, brewery, $$,
(208) 787-9000, 430 Old Jackson Highway, Victor, Idaho

New York City Sub Shop, sandwiches, $, (307) 733-4414
20 Jack Pine

Nora's Fish Creek Inn, American, $$, (307) 733-8288
5600 West Highway 22, Wilson

The Snake River Grill, American, $$$, (307) 733-0557
on the town square

SIGHTS
Chico Hot Springs Resort, (406) 333-4933
Pray, Montana

Grand Teton Music Festival, live music, (307) 733-3050
4015 West Lake Creek Drive, Wilson

Grand Teton National Park, (307) 739-3300
Route 26 north from Jackson

The Jackson Hole Museum, (307) 733-2414
105 North Glenwood Street

The National Elk Refuge, (307) 733-9212
Broadway east from Jackson town square for one mile

The Natural Museum of Wildlife Art, (307) 733-5771
2820 Rungius Road

NIGHTLIFE
The Million Dollar Cowboy Bar, (307) 733-2207
25 North Cache Drive

The Silver Dollar Bar, (307) 733-2190
50 North Glenwood Street, Wort Hotel

The Stagecoach Bar, (307) 733-4407
5755 West Highway 22, Wilson

The Teton Theatre, movies, (307) 733-4939
295 West Pearl Street

FISHING/HELICOPTER/RAFTING
Hawkins and Powers Aviation, (307) 733-1633
8350 Spring Gulch Road

Mad River Rafting Company, (307) 733-6203
Highway 89 and U.S. Highway 19

Wyoming Game and Fish Department, (307) 733-2321
420 North Cache Drive

Las Vegas

A ndre Agassi is a Vegas boy, born and raised. But he's not from the bright lights, roll 'em side of town. He's from the Vegas of neighborhoods, churches, and schools, the Vegas that the tennis vet says taught him that anything is possible. The son of a mother who worked at an unemployment office and a dad who helped run the *Jubilee* show, Agassi got his

first taste of pro tennis as a ball boy for tournaments at Caesars Palace and began his rise to what has become more than two decades in the upper rankings of his sport. Although he once blazed across the court in long hair and day-glo clothing, Agassi is now as down-to-earth as the next guy, living in Vegas with his wife, retired tennis pro Steffi Graf, and their two children. Although he still travels much of the year, Agassi has left a legacy to his hometown: the Andre Agassi Charitable Foundation, which has raised more than $60 million (and counting) for children's charities, and the Andre Agassi College Preparatory Academy, which educates hundreds of students. Here's a weekend in the city where Andre Agassi learned to win.

Friday

ORIENTATION Vegas has been the fastest-growing city in America for more than thirty years. It's a city of great vision. It's a city where the community believes that if you actually believe in something enough, you can create it and make it happen. It gets a tough rap because it's perceived as an adult Disneyland. But the community of people who live here is strong. It is a community that bonds together and looks out for each other. It's an incredibly inspirational city.

DINNER Vegas has come so far in their cuisine and dining options. I love **Nobhill** at the MGM Grand. It's a phenomenal restaurant. For steak, I love **Delmonico** at the Venetian. Go for the filet, charred medium. With the family, go up into Summerlin to a place called **Sedona.** I'm a partner in it, and it feels like home to go to the place that you helped create.

CASINO I'm second generation here, and the people I'm involved with are third generation Vegas. The **Nugget** [downtown] is a lot of fun because it's such old Vegas. You're talking about a place that has been there for a lot of years and has a great feel. It's hard to get nicer than the **Bellagio** [Center Strip]. But that said, every hotel offers its thing. **Caesars Palace** [Center Strip] now has Celine Dion camped there. You've got **Mandalay Bay** [Center Strip], which has an incredible bar and lounge at the top of the hotel called the **Foundation.** There's a deck overlooking the whole city. The **Hard Rock Hotel** has the **Joint,** with incredible music acts that come through. This city is about targeting what it is you are looking for, because you're going to find it. It's not about one place having it all and you never leave; there's just too much to experience.

Saturday

WALK Downtown is a place where you can park your car and walk around and experience that old feeling of just stepping two feet off the street into a casino that basically has no doors. And the lights are incredible. There are more lights downtown than you will see in New York at Christmas.

SHOPPING Yeah, we have all the great shops: the **Aladdin shops** [Center Strip] and the **Forum Shops at Caesars,** which are incredible. Go with the family. You go from having dinner to taking your kids to FAO Schwarz to looking around at different high-end retailers. You can't imagine how many thousands of pairs of jeans there are to choose from until you go

to the Forum Shops. It's a lot of fun. But I don't know if you should trust me with shopping.

LUNCH Out where we live, there's this place called Desert Shores, where there are these little lakes. There is a real cute French eatery called **Marché Bacchus** there on the lake where you can sit outside. You would never know you were in Vegas. Jaden, our two-year-old, entertains himself by feeding the ducks while we're eating.

GOLF **Shadow Creek** [North Vegas] is pretty amazing. It's the course Steve Wynn built through the Mirage Resorts. He put about $43 million into it and made it look like you were on some holes in Hawaii and some in Colorado. You just can't believe the terrain and the way he built this course. The thing that blows you away is that it's in the middle of the desert. There has been such a big boom in courses here. There's **Bali Hai,** a great course right on the Strip. But I am a creature of habit, and usually play at the courses closest to where I live, **Shadow Creek** and **Red Rock** [Summerlin].

SPA There is a great one at the **Bellagio,** and **Canyon Ranch** has a spa at the Venetian.

DINNER My wife and I are pretty similar. We think a great evening out together is to get some good sushi, so we go to **Nobu** [Hard Rock Hotel]. We enjoy sitting at the sushi bar because it's only the two of us. We take our time and pick through a lot of different flavors and tastes. **Seablue** at the MGM is amazing. It's a fish restaurant. There's also an old French restaurant downtown called **Andre's.** It's in an old house and has been around for decades. We used to go there when I was young and I still go back. It's really clean and nice.

SHOWS You've gotta see **O** [Bellagio]. It's incredible. *O* is a Cirque du Soleil show, but it's done in water. You find it so amazing that you are sitting in the middle of a showroom with a stage basically made out of water. The showroom is in a casino, and the casino is in the middle of the desert. It just blows you away that you're watching this. Another show I love is **Danny Gans** [Mirage]. He does impersonations of hundreds of legendary performers and singers. The show is really nostalgic; it almost brings to life characters that you always used to think about so fondly—the Frank Sinatras, the James Deans, and scenes from movies.

NIGHTLIFE Vegas gets more music acts coming through than any other city in the world. We have concerts nonstop. So the options for music are endless. The **MGM Grand Garden** is a concert hall here. They use it for a lot of things. **Mandalay Bay Events Center** had the *Three Tenors*; it's a big, 14,000- to 15,000-square-foot indoor hall. The **Joint** at the Hard Rock always has musical acts there. But I'm a family guy. I don't quite go out and hit it like I used to.

Sunday

SUNDAY BRUNCH Twenty-five dollars would be an expensive meal at most of the casinos. There are some nice restaurants now; we have so many five-star restaurants, it's crazy. But as far as being able to fill your stomach as cheaply as possible, there's probably no city in the world that offers more. I have heard speakers at colleges talk about when the kids travel in and out to compete, whether it's a tennis team or what have you, that Vegas is the only place in

You've gotta see O. *It's incredible.* O *is a Cirque du Soleil show, but it's done in water.*

"O" by Cirque du Soleil. Photo by Tomasz Rossa. Costumes by Dominique Lemieux. © Cirque du Soleil Inc.

the country that they can eat on the per diem. You can go to $3.99 buffets, where their only goal is to get you in the door.

EXCURSION There's a lot to be offered in the outskirts—the **Red Rock Canyon,** going hiking and biking. If you're on the Strip, you're probably about thirty-five minutes away from Red Rock. You just take Charleston as far west as you can possibly go. There are trails with waterfalls and beautiful red rocks, and great hiking.

WINNING Caesars used to have the Alan King Tennis Tournament, and I was a ball boy there. The top thirty-two in the world played there. I played tennis hard almost as soon as I could walk. I was competing at seven years old, playing tournament after tournament. But being a ball boy really got me in tune to what the players might or might not be thinking or feeling, and being up close, watching the concentration and seeing the sweat, hearing the movement and the grunting. Caesars would give $50,000 to the winner. They would pay you in silver dollars that they brought out in a wheelbarrow. Obviously, that was for show and you would get a check. I remember watching the greats win, and they would bring the wheelbarrow out. It was sort of symbolic: this is a dream world, a dream life. But it only happens if you have the backbone and strength to dream it. Las Vegas made me feel like I can dream.

Talking about Las Vegas with Andre Agassi

What do you remember about growing up in Vegas?

When I was a boy, my dad used to work from four in the afternoon until two in the morning, and my mom worked from eight in the morning until four in the afternoon. So we were with my dad all day and my mom all night. A lot of times when I was with my mom, whether we were going to go get dinner or go shopping, we needed some money from Dad, who was working. So we would pull into the old MGM Grand Hotel, and at eight years old, I would go running through the casino to the Jubilee showroom, where they had all the naked dancing ladies, the follies chorus-line-type stuff. I knew all the captains and maître d's and used to just wait for my dad to come through his little turn there in the office. He would give us some money and I'd go running back out, go to the grocery store, and go home. As a little boy, it felt strangely normal.

Could you ever live in a normal town?

The thing is, excluding the slot machines at grocery stores, there's nothing about living here that would seem any more or less odd than living anywhere else. We have an industry here: the gaming and tourism industry. We have a few casinos that have popped up in different areas of town, but we also have more churches per capita than most of the cities in America. That's not wedding chapels—that's real churches. We have twenty-seven high schools here. It's a very narrow perspective to think that a person who was born and raised here had an abnormal upbringing. It's like thinking if you live in New Orleans, that you've gotta get drunk every night.

Andre Agassi's Las Vegas Essentials

LODGING
Bellagio, $$$$, (702) 693-7111
3600 Las Vegas Boulevard South, Center Strip

Caesars Palace, $$, (702) 731-7110
3570 Las Vegas Boulevard South, Center Strip

Golden Nugget Las Vegas, $, (702) 385-7111
129 East Fremont Street, downtown

The Hard Rock Hotel & Casino, $$$, (702) 693-5000
4455 Paradise Road, eastside

Mandalay Bay Resort & Casino, $$, (877) 632-7800
3950 Las Vegas Boulevard South, Center Strip

DINING
Andre's Restaurant, French, $$$$, (702) 385-5016
401 South 6th Street, downtown

Delmonico Steakhouse, American, $$$$, (702) 414-3737
3355 Las Vegas Boulevard, Venetian Hotel

Marché Bacchus, French, $$$, (702) 804-8008
2620 Regatta Drive, Desert Shores

Nobhill, continental, $$$, (702) 891-3110
3799 Las Vegas Boulevard South, MGM Grand

Nobu, Japanese, $$$$, (702) 693-5090
4455 Paradise Road, Hard Rock Hotel

Seablue, seafood, $$$$, (702) 891-3486
3799 Las Vegas Boulevard South, MGM Grand

Sedona, American/fusion, $$, (702) 320-4700
9580 West Flamingo Road, Summerlin

SIGHTS
Red Rock Canyon, hiking and biking,
15 miles west of downtown Las Vegas

SHOPPING
The Forum Shops at Caesars, (702) 893-4800
3500 Las Vegas Boulevard South, Center Strip

The Shops in Desert Passage at the Aladdin, (888)
800-8284, 3667 Las Vegas Boulevard South, Center Strip

NIGHTLIFE
Danny Gans, (702) 792-7600
3400 Las Vegas Boulevard South, Mirage Hotel

The House of Blues Foundation Room, bar and lounge,
(702) 632-7631, 3950 Las Vegas Boulevard South,
Mandalay Bay

The Joint, live music, (702) 693-5000
4455 Paradise Road, Hard Rock Hotel

Mandalay Bay Events Center, (702) 632-7580
3950 Las Vegas Boulevard South, Center Strip

MGM Grand Garden Arena, concert hall, (702) 891-1111
3799 Las Vegas Boulevard South, Center Strip

Cirque du Soleil's *O*, (702) 796-9999
3600 Las Vegas Boulevard South, Bellagio Hotel

GOLF
The Arroyo at Red Rock Country Club, (866) 934-4653
2250C Red Springs Drive

Bali Hai Golf Club, (702) 450-8000
5160 Las Vegas Boulevard South, Center Strip

Shadow Creek (open only to Mirage Hotel guests),
(888) 778-3387, 5400 Losee Road, North Las Vegas

Jamie Lee Curtis

Los Angeles

Jamie Lee Curtis was born and raised in the City of Angels and is proud of it. As the daughter of Janet Leigh and Tony Curtis, Curtis lives up to her Hollywood-royalty bloodline. The award-winning actress has starred in both TV and films, including her own sitcom *Anything but Love* in the early nineties and movies from *Trading Places* to *True Lies* for more than twenty-five years. Several years ago, Curtis, the mother of two and wife of actor/writer/director Christopher Guest, launched an auspicious second career as an author of what's become a sizable number of children's books. Here's a story she's spent a lifetime learning: the tale of her hometown of Los Angeles, where she shines as brightly as her star on the Walk of Fame.

Friday

LODGING I'm always drawn to the ocean and the clean air and the fresh element the ocean brings. So I'm drawn to **Shutters,** which is right on the beach in Santa Monica. Very simple and yet beautifully elegant. If you need access to the whole city of Los Angeles, the **Beverly Hills Hotel** would be your best bet. I love the old-time glamour. They've completely refurbished it, and it's a beautiful place. I have friends who love the **Mondrian** [Hollywood], designed by Philippe Starck.

DINNER The **Getty Center** [Los Angeles] is my favorite outing. Make a reservation for dinner up at the Getty restaurant—have dinner and see the art at night. The setting is so appropriate for L.A. It's perched up on a hill and you can see it from everywhere in the city. It's a magnificent addition to our city. It's open late on Friday and Saturday. Otherwise, I would go to dinner at **Il Ristorante di Giorgio Baldi,** in Santa Monica near the ocean. It feels like you're eating at Giorgio's home. Giorgio cooks. I would do clam soup, grilled langoustines, or this fish called spigola. The food is truly unparalleled in the city.

Saturday

BREAKFAST **Le Pain Quotidien** is newish on Santa Monica Boulevard. It's a Belgian patisserie and bakery. They do fresh bread and granola and yogurt, which is my kind of breakfast. Very light. Good coffee. I might also go to the **Broadway Deli** down on the Third Street Promenade. It's pancakes and scrambled eggs, a hearty hash browns kind of breakfast.

SIGHTS There used to be a newscaster in California whose name was Jerry Dunphy, and how he opened the news every day was: "From the desert to the sea to all of Southern California, a good evening." Every single night of my childhood I heard him say, "From the desert to the sea . . . " That's my L.A. This morning I was thinking, *What are the main sights?* And I thought, *From the desert to the sea.* You can go from the desert to the sea and every-thing in between. I would recommend Santa Monica Beach and the great old pier. Santa Monica totally redeveloped the whole Third Street Promenade. And then there's the redevel-opment of Hollywood, the **Kodak Theater, Sunset Boulevard,** and the **Hollywood Walk of Fame,** where my star is right between Frederick's of Hollywood and a Halloween cos-tume store, which I thought was appropriate.

CULTURE The **L.A. Public Library** down-town is incredible; it's huge and magnificent. Beside the **Natural History Museum** [down-town], where you get to see all the dinosaurs, there are the fabulous **La Brea Tar Pits.** I remember going to La Brea as a child on school trips. There's something about seeing and smelling these ancient tar pits. They bubble up

The Getty Center is my favorite outing. The setting is so appropriate for L.A. It's perched up on a hill and you can see it from everywhere in the city.

right in the middle of this city. If you're a car buff—and if you're in L.A., you have to be a car buff—I'd go to the **Petersen Automotive Museum** [downtown].

LUNCH Ballona Fishmarket, in Marina Del Rey, has perfect California Pacific fish. I love **Ivy at the Shore** [Santa Monica], too, because it's right on the ocean and you get that lovely California cuisine, and you can walk to the pier and go shopping and to the movies and to the art galleries right there. They make these humongous salads—the portions are huge.

SHOPPING Clothing-wise, I love **Savannah** on Montana. They carry lovely designers, includ-ing Jil Sander. If there's ever a California shopping

© William Carroll / fotolia.com

experience, it's **Fred Segal** [Santa Monica]. It's been around since I was a teenager. It is a very eclectic, trendy clothing store with makeup, accessories, everything you could ever need. There are people who come to L.A. just to go to Fred Segal. I like one-of-a-kind artist-made ceramics and objets d'art, and there are two stores in West Hollywood, **Freehand** and **New Stone Age.** If you're looking for a gift for somebody, or you want to bring back something that you aren't going to find other places, you'll find it in those two stores.

DINNER Campanile is in the redeveloped area of La Brea/Highland. The building is an old movie studio. Campanile is California eclectic, but what stands out is the flavor of the food.

NIGHTLIFE The one thing that gets me out is a concert, and there are myriad places. You can go to an outdoor venue like the **Greek Theatre** [Griffith Park], which is this beautiful amphitheater, as is the **Hollywood Bowl** [Hollywood]. Then there are interior venues like the **Wiltern Theatre** [downtown]. I went to see Elvis Costello at the **Kodak Theater** [Hollywood], which is where they hold the Oscars. And there's a nice new Wolfgang Puck restaurant upstairs called **Vert.** The **House of Blues** [West Hollywood] is a safe bet. And then there's the **Troubadour** and the **Roxy** on Sunset Boulevard with teenage bands where my daughter attends concerts.

Sunday

OUTDOORS You can take a long walk or a rollerblade or a bike ride on the boardwalk all the way from Malibu down to Manhattan Beach and spend the day down by the ocean. Up in Malibu, at **Point Dume,** are these beautiful tide pools. You see sea lions—it's incredible.

LUNCH Sunday is at the **Polo Lounge** at the Beverly Hills Hotel. The food is what I call hotel food, which I love—like Cobb salad, a light fish and vegetable—something simple. The Polo Lounge is pink and green; there's this very dark bar area, and your eyes have to adjust. Then you walk outside and it's an incredibly bright patio. The great thing about the Beverly Hills Hotel is that you never have to leave. What's that line from "Hotel California"? "You can check out but you can never leave." The one great thing about this city and the climate is that you end up at a little place and you just don't want to leave. You want to stay there and relax.

Jamie Lee Curtis's Los Angeles Essentials

LODGING

The Beverly Hills Hotel and Bungalows, $$$$, (310) 276-2251, 9641 Sunset Boulevard, Beverly Hills

Mondrian, $$$, (323) 650-8999
8440 West Sunset Boulevard, Hollywood

Shutters on the Beach, $$$$, (310) 458-0030
1 Pico Boulevard, Santa Monica

DINING

Ballona Seafood Grill and Sushi Bar, seafood, $$, (310) 822-8979, 13455 Maxella Avenue, Marina Del Ray

Broadway Deli, California deli, $–$$, (310) 451-0616
1457 3rd Street Promenade, Santa Monica

Campanile, California cuisine, $$$, (323) 938-1447
624 South La Brea Avenue, La Brea/Highland

Il Ristorante di Giorgio Baldi, Italian, $$$,
(310) 573-1660, 114 West Channel Road, Santa Monica

Ivy at the Shore, American, $$$, (310) 393-3113
1535 Ocean Avenue, Santa Monica

Le Pain Quotidien, Belgian bakery, $–$$, (310) 859-1100,
www.painquotidien.com, multiple locations throughout L.A.

The Polo Lounge, California-Asian, $$$, (310) 887-2777
9641 Sunset Boulevard, at the Beverly Hills Hotel

The Restaurant at the Getty, California cuisine, $$$,
(310) 440-7300, 1200 Getty Center Drive, Los Angeles

Vert A Brasserie by Wolfgang Puck, French eclectic,
$$$, (323) 491-1300, 6801 Hollywood Boulevard #411,
Hollywood

SIGHTS

Central Library, (213) 228-7000
630 West 5th Street, downtown

Disneyland Resort, (714) 520-5060, Anaheim

Getty Center, (310) 440-7300
1200 Getty Center Drive, Los Angeles

Hollywood Walk of Fame, (323) 469-8311
Hollywood Boulevard and Vine Street, Hollywood

La Brea Tar Pits, (323) 934-7243
5801 Wilshire Boulevard, Los Angeles

Natural History Museum of Los Angeles, (213) 763-
3466, 900 Exposition Boulevard, downtown

The Petersen Automotive Museum, (323) 930-2277
6060 Wilshire Boulevard, Los Angeles

Point Dume State Preserve, (818) 880-0350
Westward Beach Road, Malibu

SHOPPING

Fred Segal, clothing and accessories
(323) 651-4129, 8100 Melrose Avenue, West Hollywood
(310) 394-4787, 500 Broadway, Santa Monica

Freehand, art and gifts, (323) 655-2607
8413 West 3rd Street, West Hollywood

New Stone Age, art and gifts, (323) 658-5969
8407 West 3rd Street, West Hollywood

Savannah, designer clothing, (310) 458-2095
706 Montana Avenue, Santa Monica

NIGHTLIFE/THEATER

The Greek Theatre, outdoor amphitheater, (323) 665-5857
2700 North Vermont Avenue, Los Angeles

Hollywood Bowl, outdoor amphitheater, (323) 850-2050
2301 North Highland Avenue, Hollywood

The House of Blues, live music, (323) 848-5100
8430 West Sunset Boulevard, West Hollywood

Kodak Theater, concerts, live theater, Academy Awards,
(323) 308-6300, 6801 Hollywood Boulevard, Hollywood

The Roxy Theatre, music venue, (310) 278-9457
9009 West Sunset Boulevard, West Hollywood

Troubadour Theater Company, live theater, (310)
979-7196, performance locations vary

The Wiltern, concert venue, (213) 388-1400
3790 Wilshire Boulevard, downtown

One Great Day in L.A.

I still remember going to Disneyland when I was a little girl. They call it the Magic Kingdom for a reason. We would get up early and stay at the Disneyland Hotel. You got a ticket book and the rides were separated into letters. The A tickets were for kiddie rides, and then you would progress to the B tickets for the aerial tramway—until you got to the E ticket, which was for the Matterhorn and the adventure rides. Every time I go I still get a Minnie Mouse hat with *Jamie* on it. I remember being transported to a different place, a fantasyland. What I've learned about living in Los Angeles is that you can do and be anything. L.A. is one big E ticket. You need a car, but you can take that little booklet and go all around our city and find everything you would ever want to do. It's truly a magic kingdom.

Willie Nelson

Maui

Willie Nelson was psychoanalyzing his pull to paradise. "Of all of the places in the world, why do I spend five or six hours flying over there?" he asked. "Well, when you get there, you know why immediately." It doesn't take a Sigmund Freud to reveal why the Red Headed Stranger—who, in his legendary music career, has recorded more than one hundred albums, and appeared in numerous films—has ricocheted back and forth for twenty years to the Hawaiian island of Maui. One reason: even Willie Nelson needs some rest! "To me, it's the 'hospital zone,' where I go to heal up from the rest of the world," he said. He rests up in his own home near the North Maui village of Spreckelsville, where he gazes out on a beach scene so pristine it inspired his 1990 song, "Island in the Sea." Here's a weekend on Willie Nelson's island.

Friday

LODGING Well, it depends on what you want to do. As a golfer, I'd stay somewhere around Makena, which is where **Makena Beach** and the **Makena Resort** golf courses are—two great courses. The **Maui Prince Hotel** is there, right across the street from the Makena golf courses. All those hotels over on that south side of the island are nice hotels [the **Grand Wailea Resort and Spa**, the **Four Seasons**, and many others]. It just depends on what part of the island you want to be on. That's the Wailea side. It's got great beaches. You can't go wrong over there. I mention the Maui Prince because it just happens to be where I stayed the last time I was over there, because my house was rented. [At the time of our interview, you could rent Willie Nelson's house if you could find the realtor who rented it; Nelson wouldn't advertise the name.] It's a beautiful, old-style Hawaiian house on the beach. [I asked him how many people it sleeps.] Oh, I don't know— there are five bedrooms. It just depends on how friendly you are.

SIGHTS Maui has two sides. The calmer side, the south side—Wailea and Makena—and then over on my side, the north side [around Spreckelsville and Paia], where the water and the waves are a lot higher. Our side is pretty windy and the waves get pretty good-sized, but it's great for the wind surfers. I would think the other side of the island, the Wailea side, would be better for swimming and better for the tourists. Because that's where all the hotels are, and that's where the nice beaches are. If you're going to camp out or get out on the beach or go snorkeling or something, I would go over around Wailea and Kihei and Makena, that area down there. But all of Maui is just one big huge garden of flowers and more flowers and trees. Everywhere you look, there's a picture. It's a small island. You can drive around it easily in a few hours. Some of the roads are better than the others. But in comparison to Texas, Maui is a very small piece of property.

DINNER For fish, I would go to **Mama's Fish House** [Paia]. That's one of the better spots to eat over on the north side of the island. We go there a lot. Mama's is one of those one-of-a-kind places, you know, where they've got great food and a great atmosphere. The view is wonderful, and of course their specialty is seafood, whatever the catch of the day is. But they have everything there.

Saturday

LODGING **Hotel Hana** on Hana Ranch is a great place to stay. Many years ago, me and [ex-wife] Connie and the girls stayed over there and had great food. Kris [Kristofferson] and I used to rent horses at the **Hana Ranch** with our kids

Last time I was there, I played thirty-six holes of golf at Makena. It's like having your own course when you play late in the afternoons.

and we would ride around. They have about three thousand acres over there at the Hana Ranch [a working cattle ranch]. That's a lot of fun. It's a nice drive over; you could spend the night and drive back the next day.

BREAKFAST There's a place in Paia called **Charley's.** I hang out over there a lot. It's just a little bar with a nice restaurant. Yeah, it's a good place to go for breakfast. At night, Charley's is a great bar. Anything you want.

SIGHTS My house is in Spreckelsville, a great little village. It's between the airport and Hana. You go out on the Hana Highway, and you only go a few miles before you come to my place. It's just before you get to a little town called Paia. Spreckelsville has a little nine-hole golf course, right on the water. It's the greatest windsurfing place in the world right there on that **Ho'okipa Beach.** That's where everybody from all over the world comes to windsurf because of the trade winds. On farther down

Makena Resort

the Hana Highway for a few miles, you get to the place where they have the competitions. When the weather and the winds are right, you can watch the windsurfers.

EXCURSIONS Take the Hana Highway. It's crooked; it's got more curves in it, I think, per square mile than any other highway [about six hundred curves and fifty bridges]. It comes out of Kahului, and you go from there through Spreckelsville and Paia, and then on toward Hana. You had better give yourself a good couple of hours to make the drive, even though it's only fifty or so miles. It's very green on that side of the island. The black-sand beaches in Hana are beautiful. But then as you go around the other side of Hana, you get up in the desert side; the climate changes immediately.

Kris Kristofferson has a house in Hana. One time, I went over to see Kris and the road fell in behind me. They had a big rain and the road caved in, and we had to wait a day or two to get back, until they could clean off the road. Sometimes they have big slides over there, and that road is not all that safe.

Once you pass Hana and go over on the other side, then you're going over toward the Seven Sacred Pools and that area [twenty-two pools]. I'm not sure what the stories are about it, but it's beautiful. Beyond that is Charles Lindbergh's Grave [Kipahulu].

LUNCH There's a great place to eat in Lahaina called Longhi's. Well, it's not exactly anything you could define in culinary terms. It's just Bob Longhi's idea of what good food is. He didn't used to have any menu there. It's just good food, good steaks, and specialties.

GOLF The Makena area is one of my favorites. There are so many great golf courses. I like them all. They are all just gorgeous. I like them for different reasons. The Makena Resort has two courses there. Last time I was there, I played thirty-six holes of golf at Makena; I played the north course and the south course. There's nobody there, and it's real private. It's like having your own course when you play late in the afternoons. Now, in the day-time, it gets pretty crowded.

NIGHTLIFE Lahaina is the hot spot. It's the nightlife—the activity. A lot of the young people go to Lahaina because they have some nice bars and good restaurants. They have some live music. I love Lahaina. Whatever you want to do, if you're golfing or fishing or just looking, it's a good spot. The whole town is a very historical village. It's an old whaling village, and the banyan tree there is worth the drive itself. It's huge and beautiful [the second largest banyan tree in the world].

Sunday

SIGHTS One of the top things to do is to go up to the top of Haleakala and watch the sun come up out of the volcano. The first time I did it was over twenty-something years ago, and you had better take a coat with you because you will freeze. Watching the sun come up on Haleakala is incredible. You can't describe it. You just have to see it.

EXCURSIONS You should go up to the Iao Needle [a rock formation in the world's wettest area] up there at Wailuku, on the top of the mountain where the rain forests are. Oh Lord, you should go there. They get four hundred inches of rain annually; it's just incredible. It's like you're going into the tropics immediately. There are businesses up there; people live up there. But it's an entirely different climate.

I've taken a helicopter over Maui. I guess it depends on who's flying the helicopter, but we had a great ride. They took us up and down the mountains, and all over the island. We had earphones on and had some hi-fi music going, and it was a pretty neat trip. I've done it a couple of times.

LUNCH An old friend of mine, Shep Gordon, owns Maui Taco. It's good Mexican food, great tacos.

SPORTS Well, I like to jog where there's not much traffic. Of course, over [the main streets of Maui] you've got back-to-back rental cars, so it's not a lot of fun to jog just anywhere, and it's not that safe. The roads are narrow and you're putting your life on the line. There are a lot of bicyclers, too. I used to run in the cane fields, but now they discourage runners there. Now, at my place in Spreckelsville, there's a great beach, and some roads next to the Ho'okipa Beach that I run on. It's quiet and there's no traffic. A lot of the days, I'm the only guy there. It's two, three, or four miles of just great beach.

If I had two days, then I would probably go over to Kapalua on the northwest side and play [golf] over there. On that end of the island, there are a whole lot of people. Some friends of mine live on that side of the island, so when we play, we go over there and play the courses that they like [Kapalua Bay, Plantation, and Village courses], and then we'll come back over and play Makena, or play Pukalani [up-country on the way to the summit of the Haleakala volcano]. The weather is great and you can play almost year-round over there. It's so beautiful. But you'd better keep your eye on the ball.

NIGHTLIFE You have to catch the bands coming through Maui. There's a Maui Arts and Cultural Center over there in Kahului. That's a good spot. At the cultural center, you

One Great Day in Maui

My idea of a great day is playing thirty-six holes of golf and then a show. [Here's how one such day ended.] You haven't been to Charley's? In the front, it's a restaurant and in the back it's a bar and a pool hall. A lot of locals come there at night and hang out, and sometimes they have little bands in there. I've played there maybe five or six times. The last time Leon Russell and I played Maui, we went on a night off. We had played the island [the Cultural Center in Kahului the night before] and we had a night off, so the next day we went over to Charley's and just set up and played for the locals. We had a little jam session. It was a Monday night, and there was nothing happening anywhere, really. Well, it's a pretty small island, and word got out pretty good, so we had a full house. They had the windows and the doors open. People from all over. They had their tailgate parties going. There were as many people outside as there were inside.

can get three or four thousand people over there. There's an indoor venue and an outdoor. It's very good, because it's new and the sound is good. There's especially a nice twelve-hundred-seat concert hall in there that we play. The sound is excellent. Over in Lahaina, they sometimes have little jazz bands that play around.

Willie Nelson's Maui Essentials

LODGING

Four Seasons Resort Maui at Wailea, $$$$,
(808) 874-8000, 3900 Wailea Alanui, Wailea

Grand Wailea Resort Hotel and Spa, $$$$,
(800) 888-6100, 3850 Alanui Drive, Wailea

Hotel Hana Maui, $$$$, (808) 248-8211
5031 Hana Highway, Hana

Maui Prince Hotel, $$$$, (808) 874-1111
5400 Makena Alanui, Makena

DINING

Charley's, American, $$, (808) 579-9453
142 Hana Highway, Paia

Longhi's, Italian, $$$, (808) 667-2286
888 Front Street, Lahaina

Mama's Fish House, seafood, $$$, (808) 579-8488
799 Poho Place, Paia

Maui Tacos,
Mexican fast food, $, (808) 661-8883
multiple locations throughout Maui

SIGHTS

Charles Lindbergh's Grave
Hana Highway, Kipahulu

Haleakala National Park, volcano, (808) 572-4400

Hana Highway, a winding road running between Kahului and Hana, Route 360

Hana Ranch, working cattle ranch/horseback riding, (808) 248-8211, 5031 Hana Highway, Hana

Ho'okipa Beach, windsurfing, Highway 36

Iao Needle, rock formation, (808) 984-8109
Iao Valley State Park, Wailuku

Makena Beach, Highway 31

The Maui Arts & Cultural Center, (808) 242-7469
1 Cameron Way, Kahului

Seven Sacred Pools
Hana Highway at the Seven Pools marker

GOLF

Kapalua Bay, Village, and Plantation Courses,
(877) 527-2582, 800 Kapalua Drive, Lahaina

Makena Resort, North and South Courses,
(808) 879-3344, 5415 Makena Alanui, Makena

Pukalani Country Club, (808) 572-1314
360 Pukalani Street, Pukalani

Miami

Jessica Alba is already envisioning retirement: a drink in one hand, a book in the other, her famous figure in a lounge chair on South Beach near Miami, the city she's come to love like a second home. "I'll definitely retire there," she said, adding that she had already been scouting real estate, specifically a condo either in the residential section of the W Hotel or in a high-rise called 900 Biscayne Bay.

For Alba, retirement seems very far away. But she tends to do things quickly. In two short years, she went from headlining her own TV series, *Dark Angel* (created by no less than James Cameron, who helmed the blockbuster *Titanic*), to reducing Bruce Willis to ruin as a smoldering femme fatale in the film *Sin City*. She's still on the go: Alba starred as superhero Susan Storm, the Invisible Woman in *Fantastic Four*, the film version of the longest running comic book series in history.

It's always been this way for the Mexican-French-English-Danish daughter of an Air Force officer who moved his family from California to Mississippi to Texas and back to California again. Alba dreamed of becoming an actress at age five. Months after attending her first acting class, she landed a part on a TV series at thirteen. It was filmed partly in Miami, where she lived while shooting the pilot and the first few episodes with her mother, brother, and tutor in tow. Her star was a well-muscled hunk named Flipper. *Flipper* wrapped, but Alba's love affair with Miami didn't. These days, she gets back as often as she can. And have no doubt—she'll eventually move there. But in the meantime, here's where you'll find Alba until she hits retirement.

Friday

ORIENTATION Miami doesn't feel like the States. It feels like you're in Latin America. It's real sexy. The people primarily speak Spanish and I just like the vibe. I like that it isn't American and conservative. I love that going to the beach, everyone is sexy and beautiful. Older men and women, younger men and women, all shapes and sizes—that's primarily why I like it. And the Cuban food is second to none.

LODGING I stay at the Shore Club [Miami Beach] mostly. And eat at their restaurant Nobu constantly, the Japanese-Peruvian one. The Shore Club is an older hotel that they revamped. Very simple. The floors are all sandstone and the beds are all white, and everything's pretty simple. I like that in Miami, because it's so hot. It's nice to not have a lot of clutter.

LUNCH/DINNER When I land, I go straight to San Loco Tacos [South Beach]. It's next to a gas station and across the street from this dive bar, and it's amazing. There are stools and you can sit up at the sort of bar area and watch them cook. It's a tiny little kitchen. There are two or three people, and they make everything right in front of you. It's authentic and it's yummy. You have a cold beer and a couple of tacos. I like the fish tacos and the chicken tacos. The restaurant makes really good chips and they have good burritos. They're moist and taste like my grandmother's. I was presenting at the Latin Grammys and I ditched the big party that everyone was in town for, so I could go to San Loco Tacos, grab tacos, and hang out at the beach.

Saturday

BEACH I wake up and grab a chair at the beach. There are three hotels: the Sagamore [Miami Beach], the Ritz-Carlton [Coconut Grove], and the Shore Club. And the best chairs are the ones facing the water, because you get to look at the ocean while you're lying down. They all have the little chairs that are set up for

you and you can order food. I stayed at the Sagamore for my *Fantastic Four* premiere. After I get super hot, I just go swim, and then more sunscreen and reading and sleeping. There's no other place in the States where the water is that warm and the sand is white and clean. In Miami, women with curves are celebrated and they just walk around differently. They're real proud of their bodies and I love that. You can tell the people who are from Miami—just their bods. They're usually really tan and they have light hair and don't wear a lot of makeup. They wear real sexy outfits, and no matter what size, what age, it's all accepted.

WORKOUT I like the gym at the Shore Club. I usually try to work out there because, you know, being at the beach or in a bathing suit all the time . . . They have a good spa there, too. I always try, as often as possible, to get a massage. The pool at the Delano [Miami Beach] is a good pool to hang out at. It's an infinity pool, so it doesn't have any edges. If you're staying in one of the rooms, you get to have your own bungalow and then have access to the pool area. And there's a huge chess set on the lawn. I went to a great party at the Delano. Rufus Wainwright played and we were eating outside under the stars.

LUNCH I really like the Blue Door restaurant at the Delano. I always go there because they have caviar. And you can eat outside. You're eating at the top of steps and you can look down to the pool, which leads to the beach. And then inside, there are a couple of pool tables and it's a bit loungey. If you want a romantic, quiet dinner, you can sit outside, but if you want to be part of the hustle and bustle, you can sit inside.

I'm usually the outside girl, though. I like to be on my own with my friends. I don't really care about being seen so much. I go to the Blue Door because I like the caviar.

CULTURE I always go by the Versace mansion, just because it's fabulous. His was such a senseless death, so there's always a little bit of paying respect to a genius. I mean, Gianni Versace was incredible—what he did for clothes and for women, and the glamour that he added to couture. It was very wearable couture, and he was an icon. The mansion is unreal. It covers an entire block in Miami Beach and it's right on the strip. I haven't been inside because I keep missing the tours. It feels like someone literally swapped it out of Italy and plopped it in Miami Beach. It's surrounded by so much art deco, it sticks out. It's this little gem and it's really, really lush and green. It feels historical.

SHOPPING I mostly go to Barneys Co-op in South Beach, which is all Barneys stuff from their stores in L.A. and New York. When I want to have big-time shopping, there's Bal Harbour Shops [Bal Harbour], a twenty-minute drive from South Beach. All the big stores are there. And then there's Scoop, which is inside the Shore Club. Scoop is a mixture of really cute things. When I'm going out and didn't bring a dress, or if I have an event and I didn't buy jewelry, I go to Scoop. There's Me & Ro Jewelry, as well, a sort of spiritual-based store in the Shore Club. It's just a great place to go to if you forget stuff.

Ocean Drive, whether you're on the beach or on the sidewalk, is a great place to walk in the day.

LOCAL LORE What makes Miami so great isn't hanging out with celebrities. What makes it great is the vibe of the city. You feel like you're in Latin America. It feels more liberal. I like that when I would go into the Rite Aid in Miami, everyone spoke Spanish to me. No one would speak English at all. It wasn't a mom-and-pop bodega—it was a Rite Aid! And I don't speak Spanish at all, so I just sort of piece-mealed my own version of Spanish to get out of the store. They don't care that you don't speak Spanish, but they're going to speak Spanish to you regardless. People are real proud to be who they are, and I like it. I like that when you go to a place like Rite Aid or Walgreens they're going to speak in Spanish to you just because they can.

WALK What happens on the beach, other than the paparazzi stalking me? And they always do. In Miami, they're the worst. You're there, and all of a sudden there are twenty guys surrounding you on the beach. It's horrible. It makes you not want to go to the beach and just

Andy Hwang

stay by the pool instead. The paparazzi just walk right up and take pictures of you while you're lying there minding your own business. Ocean Drive, whether you're on the beach or on the sidewalk, is a great place to walk in the day. Every hotel on the strip is really cool and unique. It's like being in a museum. But day or night, it's great. The paparazzi don't seem to hang out there. It's like all they want to do is take pictures of people in their bathing suits. I walk on Ocean Drive until the street ends.

DINNER AT TEN You don't even have dinner in Miami until 9:30 or 10. Nobu is pretty much like it is anywhere, in New York or L.A. There's also this Cuban place where they have music—it's called Versailles Restaurant. It's just good Cuban food. Cuban, Latin, and Mexican food—they're different, but they're the same. It feels like your mom was in the kitchen cooking it up. At Versailles, I usually eat plantains and black beans and chicken.

DRINKS AT MIDNIGHT I love mojitos. Skybar [Shore Club] has good mojitos. They're made with a lot of mint and fresh sugarcane and sugar. It's outdoor and indoor, and it's real comfortable. Nikki Beach [South Beach] is a great place to grab a margarita, hang out, and people-watch. People are hilarious in Miami. I usually drink either a martini or a Grey Goose and soda. When I'm lazy, I just stay at the Shore Club. But I usually go to the Mansion [Miami Beach]. It's a really big, fun club that has many different levels. There are different rooms and different music in the different rooms. Mynt Lounge [Miami Beach] is smaller and it usually plays sort of funk music, and that's a little

bit more of a hangout place after you go to the Mansion. You'll go to Mynt on your way home.

SNACK Jerry's Famous Deli [Miami Beach] is open all night long. I definitely have gotten some takeout from there at four or five in the morning. People stay up late in Miami. It feels like it's the middle of the day, not like it's four in the morning. It feels more like it's noon. People are bright-eyed and bushy-tailed. They're just wearing a little bit more makeup, guys and girls. What do I usually get when I go to Jerry's? I usually get a salad. I make my boyfriend get a dessert, though, so I can have some of his.

Sunday

EXCURSION We went to SeaWorld [in Orlando, to shoot some of *Flipper*]. It's pretty, like Disneyland. I never really cared about theme parks, so it was quite fitting that we went through the back entrance. My brother would run around and try to go to all the rides, but I didn't care—even when I was a kid. I just wanted to get in the water with the animals. I got to swim with a killer whale, which was pretty cool. I was totally with the dolphins the whole time. They're incredibly intelligent, way more intelligent than anybody would imagine. Their bodies are solid muscle. They're really, really, really strong. And they're really loyal. And they're just sweet. I usually would hug them too hard. Because you just have a hard time hugging them softly. That's when I thought, *You know, when I'm older, this is a great place to retire.*

FISHING I've gone fishing in the Keys, but we got stuck because the hurricane came. All of a sudden these black clouds rolled in, and in Miami it rains a couple of times a day. So you don't realize in five minutes it's going from being the sunniest, hottest place to full-on hurricane storm. So we were out fishing—my brother, my mother, my tutor, and her husband—and honestly, in five minutes, there were black clouds and it just started pouring sideways rain. It took us about twenty minutes to get out to where we were, and it took us an hour and a half to get back.

FLASH FORWARD FORTY YEARS In the United States, of any place to retire, I definitely would pick Miami. I won't be blue-haired; I'll be fabulous. Yeah. I'll be more like, let me think, who's really great? Raquel Welch. I'll be lying out on the beach, living.

Jessica Alba's Miami Essentials

LODGING
Delano, $$$$, (305) 672-2000
1685 Collins Avenue, Miami Beach

The Ritz-Carlton—South Beach, $$$$, (786) 276-4000
1 Lincoln Road, South Beach

The Sagamore, $$$$, (305) 535-8088
1671 Collins Avenue, Miami Beach

The Shore Club, $$$$, (305) 695-3100
1901 Collins Avenue, Miami Beach

DINING
The Blue Door, Brazilian/French, $$$$, (305) 674-6400
1685 Collins Avenue, Delano

Jerry's Famous Deli, $, (305) 534-3244
1450 Collins Avenue, Miami Beach

Nobu, Japanese-Peruvian, $$$$, (305) 695-3232
1901 Collins Avenue, Shore Club

San Loco Tacos, takeout, $, (305) 538-3009
235 14th Street, South Beach

Versailles Restaurant, Cuban, $$, (305) 444-0240
3501 SW 5th Street, downtown

SIGHTS
Ocean Drive
Between 1st and 15th Streets along South Beach

Casa Casuarina (formerly the **Versace mansion**)
1116 Ocean Drive, Miami Beach

SeaWorld, (800) 327-2424
7007 SeaWorld Drive, Orlando

SHOPPING
Bal Harbour Shops, mall, (305) 866-0311
9700 Collins Avenue, Bal Harbour

Barneys Co-op, clothing, (305) 421-2010
832 Collins Avenue, South Beach

Me & Ro Jewelry, (305) 672-3566
1901 Collins Avenue, Shore Club

Scoop, clothing, (305) 532-5929
1901 Collins Avenue, Shore Club

NIGHTLIFE
The Mansion, club, (305) 532-1525
1235 Washington Avenue, Miami Beach

Mynt Lounge, (786) 276-6132
1921 Collins Avenue, Miami Beach

Nikki Beach, bar, (305) 538-1111
1 Ocean Drive, South Beach

Skybar Miami Beach, bar and lounge, (305) 695-3100
1901 Collins Avenue, Shore Club

Gloria Estefan

Miami

Few people are as synonymous with their cities as Gloria Estefan is with Miami. An international superstar, the first Hispanic woman to be named BMI songwriter of the year, a member of the Songwriters Hall of Fame, and an American Music Award Lifetime Achievement recipient, Estefan was born in Havana, Cuba. But she's lived in Miami since she was a baby, growing up near a Dairy Queen with its own banyan tree, strolling South Beach long before it was a modeling Mecca, and simultaneously working three jobs during college: teaching guitar classes, performing with her band on weekends, and translating French for the customs inspectors at Miami International Airport. She met her future husband and partner, Emilio Estefan, at a wedding in 1975, where he was performing with his band, the Miami Latin Boys. He coaxed her into singing two songs with the group, which eventually became the Miami Sound Machine, featuring a talented, energetic, and charismatic Gloria Estefan front and center. The couple have been married more than thirty years, are the parents of two children, and run Miami's Crescent Moon Studios. Here's a hot weekend in the cool city that inspires Gloria Estefan's life and music.

Friday

LODGING The Fountainbleu [Miami Beach] is nice because the pool area is so incredible. I've filmed videos at the Fountainbleu, and when we used to play in Miami we played hundreds of times there. We knew that place inside out. I've visited the Loews Miami Beach a couple of times. I can't plug all of my places, but the Cardozo [Miami Beach] is our hotel. It's a small hotel, forty-four rooms. It's where they filmed Sinatra's movie *A Hole in the Head* in the fifties, with the song about the rubber tree plant. The Cardozo is for people who like small, family hotels. Delano [Miami Beach] is a great hotel. People go there to hang out. It's got a beautiful pool that plays music underwater—a very nice atmosphere. And they have some funky things to do on weekends.

DINNER Of course, I've got to tell you about Larios on the Beach [South Beach]. The original Casa Larios [Miami Beach] is still right across from the Mall of the Americas. But I wanted to have it closer to my house. So we asked the owners if they wanted to go into business with us. If you want Cuban food, you're not going to get better. It's like grandmother's cooking. Roast chicken is great. And *vaca frita*, fried cow as I call it, grilled flank steak with onions—crispy on the outside and tender on the inside. There's live music Wednesday to Saturday and old Cuban newspapers on the walls, interwoven with Larios family pictures with pictures of me as a baby. It's really fun and there's usually a long wait. The mojito is the drink. It's a nuclear lemonade, Hemingway's favorite drink. It goes down very easy and it goes to your head quickly.

ENTERTAINMENT There are a lot of clubs on Lincoln Road in South Beach, clubs for all tastes. In South Beach there's a live band at Mango's. It's always packed—Dominican music, Brazilian music, a very Brazilian atmosphere.

Saturday

BREAKFAST News Café was the first thing that was happening on South Beach. It's grown from a very small place to huge, bustling, and probably the center of that strip. It's always packed, the only twenty-four hour restaurant on South Beach. I go to the News Café for

I've got to tell you about Larios on the Beach. If you want Cuban food, you're not going to get better. It's like grandmother's cooking.

breakfast or a late-night meal. They've got great tomatoes there. I don't know where they buy them, but the salads are really good. They serve all kinds of food. I'll never forget the tomatoes.

SIGHTS The city of Miami includes Little Havana, Hialeah, Sweetwater, Miami, Miami Beach, and other little enclaves. Each is its own little city within a bigger city. But if I had to pick one place where the city's spirit is for me, it would be on Ocean Drive in the South Beach area. I have been going to that beach since I was five years old. I have pictures of me topless when I was five, standing on the little stone fence that's still there. As I grew up, I always used to wonder how long it would take people to realize what an incredible place it is and turn it into what it deserved to be. And I think that's happening. There's a lot of atmosphere and it's more unique than any place I've ever been to. Just the life that is there every night of the week. It's a wonderful place to go for a walk. There are little jazz clubs, restaurants, and a little playground right on the beach, Lummus Park, where my son and I used to ride the swings. There are little public parks along the beach that are nice and quiet.

Larios on the Beach

CRUISE During the day, I'd take you out on the boat. We'd sail past the skyline. We'd cruise up the Miami River so you could see downtown. We could park the boat in a mall called Bayside Marketplace, right on the bay where there are shops, like the Seaport in New York. We opened Bongos Cuban Café, which is a restaurant and at night a club, in Bayside. It's adjacent to American Airlines Arena, which we inaugurated on a New Year's Eve. They're still getting confetti falling from the roof.

STROLL If you want to capture the other flavor of Miami, there's Little Havana. It's like stepping back into Old Havana, with influences from Latin American countries. You can get espressos from windows on the street. They have Maximo Gomez Park, where the old guys play dominoes. The main street is 8th Street, Calle Ocho; take a walk through there. Drink a Cuban coffee at one of those little stands. Try the meat and guava pastries, which is so typically Cuban. That whole street is like being in a different country.

LUNCH The Big Pink, at the beginning of the beach, is a cool place, in an art deco building with an open kitchen and a bar. Seats right outside on the sidewalk, in a quieter part of the beach. Great turkey burgers, shakes, soups, pasta.

SHOPPING We go to Lincoln Road Mall, an open-air mall on South Beach. It used to be offbeat but now it has the Gap, William Sonoma, Pottery Barn, and an eighteen-screen movie theater. The theater is art deco, very different from every theater you have ever seen. We have an art deco Publix supermarket on Miami Beach that is an amazing sight. It's become a landmark already. I love the 9th Chakra on Lincoln Road. We buy incense from there in cases—all the kinds you could imagine. Very esoteric with metaphysical books. Bal Harbour Shops to the north has all the great stores. Details [Miami Beach] is a wonderful furniture and home shop.

DINNER We go to Café Abbracci [Coral Gables] a lot for dinner. It's Italian—excellent

One Great Night in Miami

Of course, my best days were the births of my two children and when we renewed our vows on our twentieth anniversary. But there was this boat called the Miss Florida. It's not really a boat; it looks like a boat. It's this building they rent for parties. I remember July 4, 1976, we were playing at a party there. Emilio and I had been working together for about a year, and he asked me to go and get some air with him on the third deck. There were fireworks. And he told me it was his birthday. He was always flirting with me, but we weren't dating yet; he was just my boss. He insisted that it was his birthday and that I should give him a birthday kiss—on the cheek. He had been after me for a while. I thought he was a big flirt. I didn't want to mix business and pleasure, but I believed him that it was his birthday, even though later I found out it wasn't true. I said, "All right, all right, I'll give you a birthday kiss!" And he put his cheek there, and right when I went to kiss him he turned his face and smacked me right on the lips. And we started dating after that. So that ship on that causeway holds very romantic memories for me.

food, very cozy, intimate feeling. The Forge [North Beach] is a steak house, a little more upscale. Lincoln Road has Yuca, a nouvelle Cuban restaurant.

Sunday

BRUNCH Monty's Stone Crab is a place in Coconut Grove where you can drive in with your boat and park. It's an outdoor restaurant with different kinds of bands every night of the week. It's a great feeling. I feel like I'm in the islands.

EXCURSION I love to go down to the Moorings in Islamorada in the Keys. It's a tiny little hotel, with little cabanas right on the beach—very private and very woody with beautiful trees. That's an hour outside of Miami. There's a nice restaurant on the beach. But we buy stuff and just cook it there or wander across the street and have some nice fish on the sand.

Gloria Estefan's Miami Essentials

LODGING

Cardozo, $$$, (305) 535-6500
1300 Ocean Drive, Miami Beach

Delano, $$$$, (305) 672-2000
1685 Collins Avenue, Miami Beach

The Fountainbleu Resort, $$$$, (305) 538-2000
4441 Collins Avenue, Miami Beach

DINING

Big Pink, American, $$, (305) 532-4700
157 Collins Avenue, Miami Beach

Bongos Cuban Café, Cuban, $$, (786) 777-2100
601 Biscayne Boulevard, Bayside

Café Abbracci, European, $$$, (305) 441-0700
318 Aragon Avenue, Coral Gables

Casa Larios, Cuban, (305) 266-5494
7705 West Flagler Street

The Forge, steak house, $$$$, (305) 538-8533
432 West 41st Street, North Beach

Larios on the Beach, Cuban, $$$, (305) 532-9577
820 Ocean Drive, South Beach

Monty's Stone Crab, seafood, $$$, (305) 856-3992
2250 South Bayshore Drive, Coconut Grove

News Café, American, $, (305) 538-6397
800 Ocean Avenue, South Beach

Yuca, Cuban, $$$, (305) 532-9822
501 Lincoln Road, Miami Beach

SIGHTS

Little Havana
Southwest 8th Street between I95 and Southwest 32nd Avenue

Lummus Park
Ocean Drive between 10th and 14th Streets

Maximo Gomez Park, 801 Southwest 15th Avenue

Ocean Drive
Between 1st and 15th Streets along South Beach

SHOPPING

The 9th Chakra, metaphysical shop, (305) 538-0671
811 Lincoln Road, Miami Beach

Bal Harbour Shops, mall, (305) 866-0311
9700 Collins Avenue, Bal Harbour

Bayside Marketplace, mall, (305) 577-3344
401 Biscayne Boulevard, Bayside

Details at Home, home furnishings, (305) 531-1325
1711 Alton Road, Miami Beach

Lincoln Road Mall, (305) 531-3442
Lincoln Road, South Beach

Publix, grocery, (305) 535-4268
1920 West Avenue, Miami Beach

NIGHTLIFE

Mango's, live music, (305) 673-4422
900 Ocean Drive, South Beach

Faith Hill

Nashville

For Faith Hill, Nashville is not only a home, it's the realization of a dream. The country music crossover star, whose worldwide album sales have surpassed the thirty-two million mark, dreamed of Nashville while growing up in Star, Mississippi. She performed publicly for the first time at age seven, but it wasn't until after a few months in junior college, when she packed her bags and moved to Music City, USA, that her career began to click. While working as a receptionist at a music production company, a songwriter heard her singing in the office one day and encouraged her to cut a demo and start sitting in on sessions at the famous Bluebird Cafe. Hill and her husband, fellow country superstar Tim McGraw, reign as Nashville royalty, taking Nashville's music to the world. Here's a weekend in the city of Faith Hill's dreams: Nashville, Tennessee.

Friday

LODGING I would stay at one of the hotels downtown or near Vanderbilt University. It puts you in the middle of all the action. My favorites are the **Hilton Suites,** downtown, across the street from the Country Music Hall of Fame and a block away from the Ryman Auditorium. There's also the new **Marriott** at Vanderbilt University. It's across from Centennial Park and next door to some great restaurants.

DINNER Other than my own kitchen at home, I'd probably go to **Fleming's** [Music Row] or **Ruth's Chris** [West End] for a steak. Ruth's Chris is a national chain that was started in New Orleans, but the Nashville location is right in the middle of everything in the Loews Vanderbilt Hotel. Fleming's is also national, but the one in Nashville is great—the dining room all around a big open kitchen, where you can watch them cooking. The atmosphere in both of these restaurants is dark and cozy, and they have the best au gratin potatoes.

NIGHTLIFE There are a lot of great spots, it just depends what you're looking for. If there's a big act in town, you'll usually find them at the **Gaylord Entertainment Center** [downtown]. If you're looking for something more intimate, try the **Bluebird Cafe,** which is a little club in a strip center out in a neighborhood called Green Hills. It's famous, a place where songwriters play their original songs.

Sometimes three or four songwriters will sit around and play, and sometimes famous people drop in. If you want some place even smaller than that, go to **Tootsie's Orchid Lounge** downtown. It's famous, too. Everybody hung out there—Willie Nelson, Kris Kristofferson—you name it. It's a living shrine to country music.

Saturday

BREAKFAST Hands down, it's the **Waffle House.** It's a must! Grilled pork chops, toast, and grits is the menu for me. You can sit in a booth or on a stool at the counter, listen to country music on the jukebox, and watch all of Nashville come in for breakfast on just about any morning—or late at night.

SIGHTS There are a lot of great landmarks in Nashville; not just in country music but history in general. First and foremost, there's the **Ryman Auditorium** [downtown], the "mother church of country music." Everybody—Hank Williams, Patsy Cline, Bill Monroe, you name it—performed on its stage. In the seventies, the **Grand Ole Opry** moved to the new **Opry House** [Opryland Hotel], where they broadcast live every Friday and Saturday night. President Andrew Jackson's home, the **Hermitage,** is just outside of Nashville. More Civil War battles were fought around Nashville than any place outside of Virginia. You can visit the sites, like

the **Stones River National Battlefield** and see how the South lived at **Belle Meade Plantation.**

OUTDOORS There are a lot of great parks, like **Warner Parks.** There are acres and acres of walking and hiking trails, baseball fields, open areas for picnics, horseback riding, etc. There's also **Cheekwood** [Belle Meade], which is an art museum and botanical garden. It has great garden exhibits and activities for kids of all ages.

LUNCH Monell's [downtown] is a fantastic restaurant in an old house—a real family restaurant. The tables are very large, seating from ten to sixteen. When the food is brought out, you pass it around the table. It reminds you of dinner at Grandma's house. They have great fried chicken.

CULTURE If I could only do one thing in Nashville, I'd go to the gigantic **Country Music**

The Country Music Hall of Fame and Museum; Architects: Tuck-Hinton; Photographer: Tim Hursley

If I could only do one thing in Nashville, I'd go to the gigantic Country Music Hall of Fame, which has every type of exhibit imaginable to honor the incredible history of country music.

Hall of Fame [downtown], which has every type of exhibit imaginable to honor the incredible history of country music. Then I'd go to the new **Frist Center for the Visual Arts,** which is downtown. It has an area featuring local artisans and also plays host to many exhibits, featuring Picasso, Georgia O'Keeffe, and others.

SHOPPING There are some great antique stores in Franklin, a perfect little town twenty minutes outside of Nashville with nineteenth-century buildings, Victorian cottages, and a downtown area listed on the National Register of Historic Places. For clothes, there's **Jamie's,** which is near Belle Meade Plantation and is a favorite boutique of Nashville's ladies, or one of the malls. What can you buy in Nashville that you can't buy anywhere else? Goo Goo Clusters, the famous candy made of peanuts, caramel, marshmallow, and milk chocolate that was invented here. It got its name when somebody told the inventor: the candy is so good you'll ask for it from birth.

DINNER I love **P. F. Chang's China Bistro** [West End], a big, loud, always busy restaurant, for Asian food. I like the **Palm** [downtown] for steaks.

NIGHTLIFE It depends what's going on in town. Tim and I would catch a movie or see a concert at the Gaylord Entertainment Center or the Ryman or check out the entertainment at one of Nashville's clubs like **12th and Porter** downtown—a restaurant and club where some of Nashville's best musicians perform.

Sunday

BREAKFAST I would go to the **Loveless Cafe** [west of Nashville] for breakfast. You can either have breakfast in the main restaurant or the buffet in one of the converted rooms. The biscuits, homemade preserves, country ham, and red-eye gravy are world-famous, and Martha Stewart once said it was the best breakfast she'd ever had. The café dates back to the 1950s and looks pretty much the same as it did back then.

EXCURSION After breakfast at the Loveless, hop onto the **Natchez Trace** for a day of wandering. The Trace runs 444 miles, from

One Great Night in Nashville

I was discovered at the Bluebird Cafe. I wore a black dress and a hat. I was singing background vocals for a songwriter here in Nashville named Gary Burr. We performed two shows that night and Martha Sharp, a vice president at Warner Brothers Records, Nashville, saw the first show and approached me afterwards and asked if I wanted to be a solo artist. I said yes, of course, and she wanted to hear a tape. I think I gave her a tape with some demos I had sung for Gary. She called me a couple weeks later and offered me a development deal with Warner Brothers. We set out to find the right team of producers, songwriters, manager, etc. Once they were in place, the development deal became a valid record deal with money to record an album. And the rest, as they say, is history.

Nashville, Tennessee, to Natchez, Mississippi. It's the trail once used by Indians, fur traders, and adventurers like Daniel Boone. You can pack a picnic lunch and explore some of the towns located off of the Trace. The speed limit is only fifty, so it makes for a leisurely drive.

Faith Hill's Nashville Essentials

LODGING
Hilton Suites Nashville, $$$, (615) 620-1000
121 4th Avenue South, downtown

Nashville Marriott at Vanderbilt University, $$,
(615) 321-1300, 255 West End Avenue, West End

DINING
Fleming's Prime Steakhouse & Wine Bar, steak house, $$$, (615) 342-0131, 2525 West End Avenue, West End

Loveless Cafe, American, $, (615) 646-9700
8400 Highway 100, west of Nashville

Monell's Dining and Catering, Southern, $$$,
(615) 248-4747, 1235 6th Avenue North, downtown

The Palm, steak house, $$$$, (615) 742-7256
140 5th Avenue South, downtown

P. F. Chang's China Bistro, Chinese, $$, (615) 329-8901
2525 West End Ave, West End

Ruth's Chris, steak house, $$$$, (615) 320-0163
2100 West End Avenue, Loews Vanderbilt Plaza Hotel, West End

Waffle House, American, $, (615) 262-9139
multiple locations throughout Nashville

SIGHTS
Belle Meade Plantation, (615) 356-0501
5025 Harding Road, Belle Meade

Cheekwood Botanical Garden and Museum,
garden/museum, (615) 356-8000
200 Forrest Park Drive, Belle Meade

The Country Music Hall of Fame, (615) 416-2001
222 5th Avenue South, downtown

Frist Center for the Visual Arts, (615) 244-3340
919 Broadway, downtown

The Hermitage, Andrew Jackson's home / museum,
(888) 888-9414, 4580 Rachel's Lane, twelve miles east of Nashville

Natchez Trace, scenic highway, www.nps.gov/natr

Percy Warner Park & Edwin Warner Park
50 Vaughn Road

SHOPPING
Franklin Antique Mall, antiques, (615) 790-8593
251 2nd Avenue South, Franklin

Jamie's, designer clothing, (615) 292-4188
4317 Harding Pike, Belle Meade

NIGHTLIFE/ENTERTAINMENT
12th and Porter, restaurant/nightclub, (615) 254-7250
114 12th Avenue North, downtown

The Bluebird Cafe, songwriter's showcase,
(615) 383-1461, 4104 Hillsboro Pike, Green Hills

Gaylord Entertainment Center, concert and sports
venue, (615) 770-2000, 501 Broadway, downtown

The Grand Ole Opry, (615) 871-6779
2802 Opryland Drive, Opryland Hotel

Ryman Auditorium, concert venue, (615) 458-8700
116 5th Avenue, downtown

Tootsie's Orchid Lounge, live music, (615) 726-0463
422 Broadway, downtown

Nashville

Billy Bob Thornton may hail from small-town Arkansas and live large in Los Angeles, but a big part of his soul resides in Nashville, Tennessee. Here, Thornton recorded his own albums while hanging out with Nashville stars Marty Stuart, Rodney Crowell, and Randy Scruggs. "I kick my heels up in Nashville," he said. "It's my 'fun' town." Country singer is another dream realized for Thornton, whom Robert Duvall dubbed "the Hillbilly Orson Welles."

Once hospitalized for severe malnutrition from weeks of subsisting on nothing but potatoes and supporting parts in low-budget fare like *Chopper Chicks in Zombie Town*, his life was filled with the pathos of a country music song. But then, after a bad day on a 1987 made-for-TV movie set, he began ranting and making faces at himself in the mirror like some hillbilly from hell, jutting out his upper lip like the patients he'd seen while working in nursing homes in the seventies.

The rant gave birth to Karl Childers, the mentally challenged killer with the heart of gold whom Thornton channeled in his breakthrough film, *Slingblade*. The movie won him a Best Screenplay Oscar and a Best Actor Oscar nomination, and made good on his psychic mother's prediction that he was born for greatness, maybe even to cross paths with her idol Burt Reynolds. Coronated by *Slingblade*, he starred in a variety of films, then turned director, helming an all-star cast including Matt Damon in novelist Cormac McCarthy's Western classic *All the Pretty Horses*. In between appearances, here's where I found Billy Bob Thornton kicking back in Nashville, Tennessee.

Friday

LODGING The first time I ever went to Nashville when I could actually stay in a hotel, I asked [late actor] Jim Varney, rest his soul, "Where should I stay?" He told me about the **Loews Vanderbilt Plaza** [West End]. They've got some really nice suites and you can have everybody over. They're used to a bunch of crazy artist types and entertainers. It's just right across the street from Vanderbilt University. One of the reasons I like the hotel is it's more modern. I get creeped out by antique furniture, especially any of that old Elizabethan times or Victorian kind of stuff. I can't be around it, I can't eat around it. I get the whole crew over there—we watch movies and videos and play music.

DINNER I go to the **Sunset Grill** [Hillsboro Village] every night. It's a place that I've closed down a few times that's a lot of fun and the people are real nice there. I'm allergic to dairy and wheat, and a lot of times in your standard Southern restaurant, everything is dairy and wheat, so it's kind of tough. The Sunset Grill has a bunch of stuff I can have. I always get some kind of salad with nuts and apples, and then I'll get fish or steak. There's a **Ruth's Chris** at the Loews Vanderbilt. You can't beat that. It's in-between a nice restaurant and just a regular joint. Any time you fry a steak in butter, you can't lose, right? I have to get mine dry now, but, boy, I used to eat it fried in butter. I would just go ahead and suffer the migraine. The hotel also has a cigar bar that's cool. I'm not the biggest cigar smoker in the world, but I don't mind it every now and then.

ENTERTAINMENT I don't really go to bars, but every now and then I'll hit one. I would go either to the one at the hotel—they usually have somebody in there playing the piano and it's pretty laid back—or the one at the Sunset Grill. I'm kind of a creature of habit, but Second Avenue has got a bunch of restaurants and clubs on it. When I used to go to bars, I didn't remember the names of them.

Saturday

BREAKFAST For some reason, going to the **Waffle House** in Nashville is different from going to it anywhere else. It's just kind of got a Nashville vibe. You can go to any of them. It's like they're the same thing—a lot of interesting characters and the people that work there are always interesting. I recently went to the **Loveless Cafe** [west of Nashville] with Marty Stuart. I've never had breakfast at the Loveless Cafe. I only had dinner there. It seems that almost any restaurant you go to, even breakfast joints, make good country ham. You can get good ham everywhere. The Loveless Cafe has great country ham and red-eye gravy. Red-eye gravy is gravy—it's just ham gravy. It's real thin. That's that kind of see-through gravy.

CULTURE WSM-AM [650] is the very famous country radio station. It plays top stuff and it's been around forever. You have to turn that on just because of its legend. The first thing you will probably see in Nashville is a sign for Music

For some reason, going to the Waffle House in Nashville is different from going to it anywhere else. It's just kind of got a Nashville vibe.

Row—everybody should see Music Row. Just drive up and down the streets on Music Row—Music Square West and East. It's rows and rows of all the publishing companies, studios, offices of all the famous music people. It's interesting to see an area that's "all music." The **Country Music Hall of Fame** is downtown. My friend Marty Stuart has a lot to do with all that and has a big private collection as well. He's donated some of his Hank Williams collection to the museum. Elvis's Cadillac is there and Minnie Pearl's hat. Oh yeah—you've got to have Minnie Pearl's hat.

THE SHRINE Visit the **Ryman Auditorium,** of course. [Located downtown, it's the former home of the Grand Ole Opry.] Certain places just have ghosts around, you know? Just to stand there and look at the Ryman is amazing, but then to actually go in there—I was taken in there by Jim Varney one time. He knew somebody that got us in there at an off time. And it was just—you get chills. I've got to tell you, it's spooky. It's such a wonderful piece of history, first of all, and you can tell there are spirits around that place. Honestly, I can stand outside and just feel it.

GETTING OUTFITTED Manuel is the guy who does all the snappy Western jackets with rhinestones. If you don't have a real good hairdo, you need a hip jacket. I've got several Manuel jackets myself. If you're looking for the really fancy stuff in terms of Western wear, Manuel is the guy. He's a dark guy with white hair, real distinguished looking and a character. His shop, **Manuel Exclusive Clothier** [downtown], is in a red brick building that used to be a bordello. I've got black short jackets with rhinestones and white piping. I've got a red jacket, I've got a royal blue Manuel jacket, loaded down with rhinestones, that Mel Tillis gave me. I wore it in the movie called *Waking Up in Reno*. I would buy something from Manuel, even if it's something little. He's probably got some bolos or something. Anything you buy from Manuel is going to be cool.

LUNCH People who visit Nashville always go to **Rotier's** [West End]. They have hamburgers and meat 'n' three—meat and three vegetables—that's your Blue Plate Special. **Jack's Barbecue** [downtown] is a place that the recording studio orders from. Golly, it's good. They've got beef, pork—of course, you get slaw with it and beans. I just ate a pile of their beef and pork when I was in Nashville last. It looked like a mountain.

SHOPPING The **Ernest Tubb Record Shop** is down on lower Broadway. It's got some instruments. It's another one of those places that you ought to see. Broadway is kind of the old-time street where a lot of stuff was. I remember sitting there one day and there was a guy who was obviously a songwriter, and he kept writing and tearing up paper, and he kept running his hand through his hair. It was like a scene out of a movie. Everybody should go to the Ernest Tubb Record Shop. Every now and then, I think they'll have an event there, too. They'll have somebody in the store signing stuff. **Lawrence Records** [downtown] is close to Manuel's place. They only sell used records, and it's full of vinyl records. It's got rows and rows of stuff. I bought two Connie Smith records and they had some Beatles 45s. They've got old posters; they sell memorabilia, too.

DRINKS Tootsie's Orchid Lounge [downtown] is a famous place. Back in the old days, that's where all the entertainers hung out after the shows. These days, I don't know if it's as much a real hangout as it is more for people that just want to see it. They say Roger Miller wrote "Dang Me" at the bar. I'm pretty sure that was the place where Hank Williams stood looking at the Grand Ole Opry the first time he played there [the back door connects to Ryman Auditorium's side entrance]. He stood there and walked around and went in, he was nervous—about to go out of his mind. It's another one of those places that's got a lot of history. Marty just sent me a box of stuff from there, like a T-shirt and all these different things. These days it must be more touristy than it was.

DINNER White Castle has those little bitty hamburgers. There's one not too far from the Loews Hotel. Since I can't eat wheat, I go to White Castle and just take those little squares of hamburger out of them and eat them with pickles. Without the bread I could probably eat a dozen. **Shoney's,** which used to be a Big Boy, became popular for hamburgers, but these days they've got salad bars. It used to have the kid with the sweptback hair holding the hamburger up on the plate out front. There used to be a big deal about people stealing the Big Boy from those restaurants. Shoney's has excellent hamburgers. In Nashville, Shoney's is near a McDonald's with a radio station.

ENTERTAINMENT I like to go out and listen to these guys play bluegrass music on the outside of town. Just find out where people are having a "singing." People are friendly enough that if you ever run into somebody outside of town, you can ask, "Hey, is there any bluegrass going on anywhere?" I would try to find anywhere there was going to be a group of musicians playing. You know, just an impromptu music session, because in Nashville, they're great. If you've got the chance to get in on a little shindig with people, it's a great town for it. It just rubs off on everybody.

Sunday

BREAKFAST I would go to the **Cracker Barrel** for breakfast. Cracker Barrels are all around in the South, but they started in

One Great Day in Nashville

One time in Nashville, I had breakfast with Johnny Cash and June Carter at their house. It was the first time in my life that I froze up around a famous person. I could barely talk to him. Now, June and I could talk real easy because she's a talker and a real energetic woman, so you just kind of naturally fall into it, but Cash was an imposing kind of legend. I couldn't even talk; I just sat there. They made breakfast like when I was a kid. I mean everything—biscuits and gravy and country ham and eggs. Of course, I can't eat most of that, but when Cash told me to, I did it. He said, "Get you some. Don't be shy." I didn't forget about my allergies, but I also didn't want to say no to him. I ended up with a migraine, but it was worth it. They were real gracious. They have a house full of all kinds of interesting stuff. Johnny had to go to the studio to do some recording after a while and then June took us through. It was a magical time.

Lebanon, near Nashville. It's a chain of restaurants that are made to look old-fashioned. They've got wagon wheels on the walls and the whole deal. They have country food, and shops where you can buy jars of molasses, pictures of Loretta Lynn, Loretta Lynn coasters, Conway Twitty oven mitts—that kind of thing. The food is good at a Cracker Barrel; It's the standard stuff: biscuits, gravy, bacon. Breakfast is real good there, and then at night, chicken-fried steak.

SIGHTS Of course, there's the **Hermitage** [twelve miles east of Nashville], the Home of Andrew Jackson. Andrew Jackson was supposed to have been a character. Jim Varney used to tell me stories of Andrew Jackson because Varney was a history buff. It's kind of funny to see the Hermitage and know that it was Andrew Jackson's home. Varney lived out in a place called White House, which is outside of town. It was the stopover, he told me, for Andrew Jackson when he came into town. I used to stay at Varney's house every now and then. This was a hillbilly with money. He's probably the only person in history who had a Delorian up on blocks in his front yard.

Billy Bob Thornton's Nashville Essentials

LODGING
Loews Vanderbilt Plaza Hotel, $$$, (615) 320-1700
2100 West End Avenue, West End

DINING
The Cracker Barrel, American, $, (615) 331-6733
multiple locations throughout Nashville

Jack's Barbecue, barbecue, $, (615) 254-5715
416 Broadway, downtown

Loveless Cafe, American, $, (615) 646-9700
8400 Highway 100, west of Nashville

Rotier's, American grill, $, (615) 327-9892
2413 Elliston Place, West End

Ruth's Chris, steak house, $$$$, (615) 320-0163
2100 West End Avenue, Loews Vanderbilt Plaza Hotel, West End

Shoney's, American, $, (615) 885-0568
2645 McGavock Pike

Sunset Grill, international, $$$, (615) 386-3663
2001 Belcourt Avenue, Hillsboro Village

Waffle House, American, $, 615-262-9139
multiple locations throughout Nashville

White Castle, fast food, $, 615-321-2291
multiple locations throughout Nashville

SIGHTS
The Country Music Hall of Fame, (615) 416-2001
222 Fifth Avenue South, downtown

The Hermitage, Andrew Jackson's home/museum, (615) 889-2941, 4580 Rachel's Lane, twelve miles east of Nashville

Ryman Auditorium, concert venue and former home of Grand Ole Opry, (615) 458-8700, 116 5th Avenue, downtown

SHOPPING
Ernest Tubb Record Shop, music, (615) 255-7503
417 Broadway, downtown

Lawrence Record Shop, music, (615) 256-9240
409 Broadway, downtown

Manuel Exclusive Clothier, clothing, (615) 321-5444
1922 Broadway, downtown

NIGHTLIFE
Tootsie's Orchid Lounge, live music, (615) 726-0463
422 Broadway, downtown

New Orleans

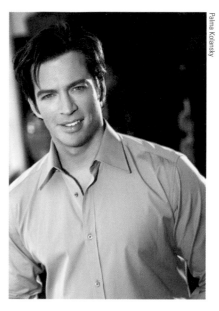

Palma Kolansky

Hey, Harry Jr.! We're going to have Harry Jr. come up and play a tune with us!" These words play endlessly in Harry Connick Jr.'s memory. For the young New Orleans musical prodigy, the words were a siren's call from the bandstand of the Maison Bourbon, a French Quarter club where Connick's parents took him from age five to fourteen to listen to—and eventually play with—the greats. The son of two lawyers who also owned a record store—his late mother was a judge and his father served as district attorney—Connick was sitting at a piano by age three, performing professionally at six, and recording at ten. At nineteen, he released his first major-label album. Two years later, in 1989, he contributed to the soundtrack of *When Harry Met Sally*, a hit comedy starring Meg Ryan and Billy Crystal.

Connick was proclaimed the "new Frank Sinatra." When he decided to try acting, Connick became a movie star almost overnight. Now, when Connick's not touring, he's filming. His veins are forever filled, however, with the gumbo of his hometown. "The whole point of going to New Orleans is to realize that you sleep when you're dead," he instructed. "If you're going to visit for a week or a weekend, forget your diets, forget getting your beauty sleep, because it's not going to happen."

When Huricane Katrina devastated New Orleans in the summer of 2005, Harry immediately flew home to help. He assisted in rescue efforts; headed a coalition to aid, house, and return displaced musicians to the city; and increased financial aid and public awareness. Because to Harry Connick Jr. and the world at large, New Orleans can never die. In fact, as of publication time, the places listed here are still alive and kicking.

Friday

GETTING ACCLIMATED You should know a couple of local expressions, like "Where you at?" That's something that we say. It means, "How are you doing?" Call everybody *baby* or *darlin'*. That works. Where you at, baby? Where you at, darlin'? You say that to anybody down here and they'll think you're a local. As far as what to wear, if you go anytime between April and October, you better not bring much to wear because it is hot.

LODGING The **Fairmont** [Central Business District] is the hotel that probably brings back the most memories, because I went there a lot as a kid. My mother died, but she was a politician, and my dad is a politician, and they used to have fund-raisers there. The **Omni Royal Orleans Hotel** is also great. That's an old-school French Quarter hotel right on St. Louis Street, within walking distance of most everything. It has elegance about it. The **Hotel Inter-Continental** [Central Business District] is where we stay when we go home for Mardi Gras. It's a full-service, big hotel. Then, there's the **Columns,** one of those hotels where you have to walk down the hall to use the bathroom. It's an old house on St. Charles Avenue. That's a cool place, if you're into that sort of thing.

Eddie Seal

DINNER Mandina's is a real local joint. It's my first stop. It's where locals go to eat, and they have the best food. Cajun isn't really New Orleans; it's more straight-up Creole food. Mandina's has crab fingers in this butter sauce and some of the best po' boys in town. They also have grilled pork chops and string beans, and stuff you can get anywhere. It just tastes better there.

NIGHTLIFE Of course, there's **Tipitina's** [Uptown], which is famous for rock-and-roll, New Orleans–funk kind of music. A lot of legendary New Orleans musicians have played there, like Professor Longhair. When you go in, there's a bronze bust of him right in the entryway, which is sort of neat because it's like his house. It's the kind of place where you wear jeans and a T-shirt and go drink beer and listen to the music. **Vaughn's** is another Uptown club, a small house—so small that people end up standing outside. Right outside of the French Quarter, there's **Snug Harbor,** a straight-ahead jazz club where I started playing when I was in my early teens. Snug Harbor makes great hamburgers, but they also have great music.

Saturday

SIGHTS The locals' and the tourists' places are almost one and the same, like **Jackson Square** and the Pontalba Apartments with St. Louis Cathedral right there in the middle. It's a real touristy spot, but it's just a phenomenal

Then you walk right across the street to Café du Monde and have coffee and beignets. That's a touristy things to do, but I do that every time I go home.

place to be. The history there is amazing. Then you walk right across the street to **Café Du Monde** [French Quarter] and have coffee and beignets. Those are touristy things to do, but I do that every time I go home. People think the French Quarter is sort of a Disney World kind of environment, and I guess the façade of it is, in a sense, because it's almost impossible to believe it's got more to it than that. But if you take a bird's-eye view of it all, you'll realize that it's a living, working community. The **French Quarter,** as touristy as it is, is very much a place where I love to spend most of my time.

LUNCH You really should have boiled crawfish, because that's a staple of the whole culture down there. Go to the Bucktown area. There are a lot of shrimpers, and, man, if you want some boiled seafood, this is it. It's messy, it's bright, it has sort of a family feel to it. You can get boiled crawfish, boiled shrimp, boiled crabs, all that stuff. Eating crawfish takes a little practice, but here's how: Break off the tail and crack that little armor that he has over his tail. Peel that off, squeeze the tail, and pull out the meat. The real lovers will suck the fat out of the head, which may turn some people off, but once you try it, it's really good. Yeah, I suck the heads; it just tastes good. It's also a habit thing; it's a rhythm you get into.

TREAT The **Williams-Plum Street Snowball Stand** is just a little teeny, teeny place. Everybody else calls them snow cones, but we grew up calling them snowballs. You know those little cardboard containers you get Chinese food in? They put the snowballs in that. You can get them in all kinds of flavors. I'm giving away a lot of stuff I shouldn't be giving away, because people will realize that I'm the white trash that I've been trying to avoid saying I am. But my favorite is chocolate with condensed milk. It's just terrible to eat, but man, is it good! I get the biggest one they have, and it is huge.

ART I'm a big George Rodrigue fan. You know, the artist who paints the Blue Dog? George is a Cajun painter who actually is quite a draftsman. You can see clearly in his earlier work how he is a talented technician as well. He spends 100 percent of his time painting this dog. There's a huge story behind it, about how she's trying to find her way back to him. In every single painting, the Blue Dog is trying to find her way back to George. No matter what the circumstances are, or what celebrities are in the painting, or what background it is, the Blue Dog is always there. He's a good example of a Louisiana artist who has become famous all over the world. He has his **Rodrigue Gallery** [French Quarter] right there in New Orleans.

COCKTAILS I used to take the streetcar to school every day. If you get on at, say, the corner of St. Charles and Canal Street, and ride it all the way down St. Charles, you could get off at the **Columns Hotel** and go in and have a drink. Or you could have a Pimm's Cup at the **Napoleon House** [French Quarter; open daytime only at time of publication]. Now that's old school—that really feels like New Orleans. You almost feel like you have to be wearing some white saddle oxfords and a seersucker suit and a linen shirt. It's one of the oldest bars in New Orleans—it's falling down. There's also a really old bar called **Lafitte's Blacksmith Shop.** Talk about falling down! Every time I pass it, I can't believe it's still standing.

DINNER Not a lot of people know about **Irene's,** which is an Italian restaurant in the French Quarter. It's really romantic. They have amazing food—I think it's Southern Italian, but it's really delicious. It's very casual, real laid back, candlelit, and there are tons of pictures on the walls. It's not a typical New Orleans kind of place.

NIGHTLIFE Maison Bourbon [French Quarter] is a real traditional club. That's where I spent most of my time. That place—that sign

out front, those doors, the slate floors, the pictures of the musicians above the bandstand—is my home in my heart.

Sunday

BRUNCH If I could only do one thing, I'd go to **Brennan's** [French Quarter] for Sunday brunch. When I walk in there, it feels like the calm before the storm. It feels like, *This is the last moment I'm going to have before I feel like I'm going to physically explode from eating so much food.* It's a nice feeling of anticipation. Every time I go, I get the same thing. I get the turtle soup with sherry. Then, I get the eggs Hussarde, which is almost like eggs Benedict, except it has a white wine sauce, too. It's unbelievable. Then I get Bananas Foster. The whole brunch takes

One Memorable Night in New Orleans

There are a lot of great musicians from New Orleans. When I was probably fifteen, I was studying with Ellis Marsalis, and Ellis would play at Snug Harbor all the time. Back then, he would play there a couple of times a week and a lot of his students would play there, too. One day he said, "I need you to sub for me with James Black." James Black was one of the greatest, if not the greatest, jazz drummers to ever come out of New Orleans. I was excited because I had never played with him. The first song I called was "Magnolia Triangle," which James wrote. It's in an odd meter, 5/4 time, which isn't necessarily that hard to play, it's just not the most common time. I remember the bass player looking at me like I was crazy because James was such a manipulator of rhythm that if you played one of these odd-time meters with him, there was a good chance that he would throw you off and you would get lost in the song. And that's exactly what happened.

He threw us off, we didn't know where we were, and I think he became frustrated with our inability to keep up with him, and he left after that song. He just walked to the bar, got a beer, and left the gig! We ended up playing the rest of the night as a duo without a drummer. That story just tells you that the music is hard-core down there. People are very serious about the arts. They are really serious about music, and the musicians are serious about what they do. When I was coming up, I felt an immense amount of pressure to keep this high level of music going.

you three hours to eat, and you want to just sleep the rest of the day. But it's the best food.

Harry Connick Jr.'s New Orleans Essentials

LODGING
The Columns Hotel, $$, (504) 899-9308
3811 Saint Charles Avenue, Uptown

The Fairmont New Orleans, $$$,
123 Baronne Street, Central Business District

Hotel Inter-Continental New Orleans, $$$,
(504) 525-5566, 444 Saint Charles Avenue, Central
Business District

Omni Royal Orleans Hotel, $$$$, (504) 529-5333
621 Saint Louis Street, French Quarter

DINING
Brennan's, French/Creole, $$$$, (504) 525-9711
417 Royal Street, French Quarter

Café Du Monde, coffee/beignets, $, (504) 525-4544
800 Decatur Street, French Quarter

Irene's Cuisine, Italian, $$$, (504) 529-8811
539 Saint Phillip Street, French Quarter

Mandina's Restaurant and Bar, Creole/Italian, $$
3800 Canal Street, midcity, New Orleans

Napoleon House, restaurant and bar, (504) 524-9752
500 Charles Street, French Quarter (Open daytime only at
time of publication)

Williams-Plum Street Snowball Stand, snow cones
(open seasonally), $, (504) 866-7996, 1300 Burdette Street

SIGHTS
French Quarter, historic district

Jackson Square, town square, center of the French Quarter

Rodrigue Studio, art gallery, (504) 581-4244
721 Royal Street, French Quarter

NIGHTLIFE
Lafitte's Blacksmith Shop, bar, 941 Bourton Street,
French Quarter

Maison Bourbon, jazz club, (504) 522-8818
641 Bourbon Street, French Quarter

Snug Harbor Jazz Bistro, restaurant/nightclub, (504)
949-0696, 626 Frenchmen Street, French Quarter

Tipitina's, nightclub, (504) 895-8477
501 Napoleon Avenue, Uptown

Vaughn's Lounge, nightclub, (504) 947-5562
4229 Dauphine Street, Uptown

Greenwich Village

I was lucky to grow up in the center of the world," said Matthew Broderick of his hometown, Greenwich Village, that quarter of bohemia in lower Manhattan. As he sat in a Village restaurant, the boyish Broderick attracted no stares, much less paparazzi or autograph hounds. People were used to seeing him there. It's the neighborhood he's lived in all his life and where he presently resides with his wife, actress Sarah Jessica Parker and their son, James. He has never ventured far for long, even when starring in films such as *Addicted to Love* with Meg Ryan or *The Cable Guy* with Jim Carrey, or earlier films such as *Glory* and *Ferris Bueller's Day Off*. He made his theater debut at age seventeen opposite his father, the late James Broderick, and has been appearing regularly on Broadway in smash hits like *The Producers* and *The Odd Couple* ever since. When we met in 1998, he had just starred in *Godzilla*, in which the giant lizard raids—where else?—Manhattan. "Thank God, he stays out of the Village!" said Matthew with a laugh. Here's a weekend in "the village" that it took to raise Matthew Broderick.

Friday

LODGING People like the **Washington Square Hotel.** When I was a kid, it was a welfare hotel that kept catching on fire; then somebody bought it and painted it and spruced it up. It's on MacDougal and Waverly, right in the heart of the Village. The **SoHo Grand Hotel** is a little nicer. SoHo is right next to the Village, a block's walk.

DINNER I might go to the **Minetta Tavern,** which is on MacDougal Street and Minetta Lane. It's very old; it was a speakeasy way back.

It has beautiful caricatures and silhouettes all over the walls—don't forget to look at those. It's an old-fashioned Italian restaurant with white tablecloths. If you want to see what the Village was like in the thirties and forties, this is a great place. On Thompson Street I know a great place for paella. It's called **Rincon de España.** It's real small with red booths and a banquette with chairs and tables. It's not very expensive. There's a guy with a guitar and he'll sing anything you ask him to, then he'll try to make you sing with him. They have delicious paella and the best mussels I've ever tasted.

NIGHTLIFE After dinner, you can have coffee at any one of the coffee shops on MacDougal Street—**Cafe Dante** and **Figaro.** NYU is in that area. There are students sitting there, studying and drinking coffee. There are a lot of famous old clubs on Bleecker Street. Then, there's the **Village Vanguard,** where Bob Dylan played.

Saturday

SIGHTS The Village is basically from Houston Street to the south. Below Houston they call SoHo. So it's up to maybe 14th Street. Above that you're probably in Chelsea. If you take 5th all the way down, it terminates right at **Washington Square Park.** It's nice to walk around that park. You can look on the north side of Waverly Street at the old townhouses, which, if you squint and close your ears, are much like the ones in the book *Washington Square* by Henry James. Then there's the fountain in the middle of the square where it's nice to sit around in the summer. There are a lot of young people on skateboards and with Frisbees—it's full of Village atmosphere.

St. Mark's Place is also very well known. It's much more eclectic than the other parts of the Village. A lot of stuff is sold on the street here and in stores. Some people sell their appliances from their houses. Teenagers sell sweaters laid out on the cement. My favorite part of the Village, though, is the West Village. If you start on Christopher Street and walk north or go down West 4th or on Bleecker Street and just sort of weave your way around, you'll pass a lot of bak-

eries and cafés. Mostly, you pass nice houses and interesting-looking people. I like Bleecker and West 4th, when you get over toward 11th Street or Perry; I grew up there. It's full of brownstones and little shops and antique stores.

LUNCH On Bleecker Street there's **John's Pizza** if you really want great pizza.

SHOPPING There's a small bookstore called **Three Lives.** It's on 10th and Waverly. It's the kind of bookstore where the people who work there have read what's there and they will tell you what the book is about or could recommend something. It's a very hands-on bookstore. The **Biography Bookshop** is fun because all they sell are biographies; it's on 11th and Bleecker. There's a store that sells nothing but LPs. It's

Michal Daniel

The Joseph Papp Public Theater is right at Astor Place. They have very innovative theater, a lot of Shakespeare.

called the **House of Oldies,** which is on Carmine Street. In SoHo, there's **Agnes B.** and a nice jewelry store called **Reinstein/Ross.**

CULTURE The **Joseph Papp Public Theater** is right at Astor Place. They have very innovative theater, a lot of Shakespeare. Sometimes the plays start here and go to Broadway, like *Rent* and *Bring in the Noise, Bring in the Funk.*

DINNER Il Mulino is an old-fashioned Italian place. The waiters are real theatrical. They wear tuxedos and really know what they're doing. It's on West 3rd Street. You sit down and they give you hunks of Parmesan and salami and eggplant—it's sensational food. There's another place called **Po.** It's Italian. It's delicious and simply fantastic. But it's a teeny little restaurant, hard to get in.

NIGHTLIFE Raoul's in SoHo is on Prince Street and Sullivan Thompson. It's the sort of place to see models and fashionable-looking people and feel very hip if you can get in. It looks like a very old Village restaurant, except it's totally not, as far as atmosphere goes. It has tin ceilings and dark wood. It's very dark with a huge, beautiful, long bar and a spiral staircase. On some nights, there's a woman up there who does palm readings and tarot card readings. It's a place where people go to smoke and drink martinis and look good.

Sunday

EXERCISE If you go as far west as you can in the Village, you'll be at the Hudson River, and there's a path along the river there that's nice for skating or biking and running. You can go from there all the way to the forties. There are millions of gyms in the Village. There's also the **Russian Bathhouse** and other Polish-Russian bathhouses in the East Village. It's something you can't do anywhere else. A lot of actors go to them. You steam, then jump into cold water and then back into the hot again. It's not a place

One Great Day in the Village

When I was five or six, my whole school walked to **Jefferson Market Library** to get our library cards. We were rounded up with our mittens and everything and held hands and walked out of school and down 11th Street, between 7th and 6th [Avenue of the Americas], which is a nice, two-lane street. We turned right and walked past the A&P and Ray's Pizza and P.S. 41—all so scared that someone from the public school might beat up one of us from the private school. The library looks like a castle—it has big towers and it's dark and very imposing. It always had a particularly ominous quality for me because it used to have a jail next to it called the Women's House of Detention, where we would see people screaming up to women in the windows.

I was very frightened when we got inside the library. I remember it being made very clear to me that these books were loaned and that you had to bring them back or you'd end up in the Women's House of Detention. I remember filling out my library card. Under "occupation" I wrote "actor." I didn't really know what that meant, but my father was an actor. Nobody laughed when they saw I had written "actor." In the Village, that was pretty normal.

to work out, but to relax and absorb tremendous New York atmosphere.

LUNCH I love **Union Square Cafe.** I'm cheating a little bit because it may not technically be in the Village, but it's very close on 16th Street near Union Square. That's maybe my favorite restaurant in the city. It's just simple decor, very clean looking, and fairly large, with great food and an extremely nice staff. The tuna burger is great.

SHOPPING There is a great food market that has been around forever. A little uptown is **Jefferson Market,** which is where those of us who live in the Village would shop. The butcher there is fantastic. There are a lot of old Irish guys who I've known since I was this big. If I come in, to this day they say, "Hi, Matthew, how are you?" They also deliver.

Matthew Broderick's Greenwich Village Essentials

LODGING
SoHo Grand Hotel, $$$, (212) 965–3000 310 West Broadway, SoHo

Washington Square Hotel, $$, (212) 777-9515 103 Waverly Place

DINING
Cafe Dante, Italian coffeehouse, $$, (212) 982-5275, 79 MacDougal Street

Il Mulino, Italian, $$$, (212) 673-3783, 86 West 3rd Street

John's Pizzeria, pizza, $, (212) 243-1680 278 Bleecker Street

Le Figaro Café, coffeehouse, $, (212) 677-1100 184 Bleecker Street

Minetta Tavern, Italian, $$, (212) 475-3850 113 MacDougal Street

Po, Italian, $$, (212) 645-2189, 31 Cornelia Street

Rincon de España (now called Cuba), Spanish, $$, (212) 260-4950, 226 Thompson Street

Union Square Cafe, American, $$$, (212) 243-4020 21 East 16th Street, Union Square

SIGHTS
Joseph Papp Public Theater, (212) 539-8500 425 Lafayette Street

New York Public Library, Jefferson Market Regional Branch, (212) 243-4334, 425 Avenue of the Americas

St. Mark's Place, Avenue A to 3rd Avenue

Washington Square Park, south end of 5th Avenue between MacDougal Street and University Place

SHOPPING
Agnes B., clothing, (212) 925-4649 103 Greene Street, SoHo

Biography Bookshop, bookstore, (212) 807-8655 400 Bleecker Street, West Village

House of Oldies, record store, (212) 243-0500 35 Carmine Street

Jefferson Market, gourmet grocery, (212) 533-3377 450 Avenue of the Americas, West Village

Reinstein/Ross, jewelry, (212) 226-4513 122 Prince Street, SoHo

Three Lives & Company Ltd., bookstore, (212) 741-2069 154 West 10th Street, West Village

NIGHTLIFE
Raoul's, French, (212) 966-3518, 180 Prince Street, SoHo

The Village Vanguard, jazz club, (212) 255-4037 178 7th Avenue South

SPAS/EXERCISE
Hudson River running path, west of Greenwich Village

Russian & Turkish Baths, (212) 473-8806 268 10th Avenue, East Village

New York City

Growing up in the Bronx, Jennifer Lopez learned how to dream big. And while she is an undeniable star today, she hasn't forgotten where she came from. Her first album, *On the 6*, was inspired by the number 6 train that took her from her family's Castle Hill neighborhood to Manhattan for dance lessons. The daughter of a kindergarten teacher and a computer specialist, Lopez literally rode the 6 train to stardom, as her lessons began paying off. She

first landed a spot as one of the Fly Girls, the dance troupe that led into commercial breaks on the TV series *In Living Color*.

Lopez then danced her way into television and films. First, she landed a role in the short-lived series *South Central*, before moving on to movies with *Mi Familia*. But it was the coveted lead in 1997's *Selena*, the story of the slain Hispanic singer, that made Lopez a star. She was named one of *People's* Most Beautiful People, then appeared with Jack Nicholson in *Blood & Wine*, Sean Penn in *U Turn*, and George Clooney in *Out of Sight*. In her film *The Wedding Planner*, Lopez became the first person to have both the nation's number one movie and number one album (her second, *J.Lo*) simultaneously. But a piece of her soul is still riding the 6 train into Manhattan. Here's where you'll find Jennifer Lopez in her hip hometown.

Friday

THE SOUND OF NEW YORK One of the reasons I love going back to New York is the Spanish radio stations. They play the best salsa music! As soon as I get there, I'll turn on the radio in the car, tuning back and forth between 97.9 and 105.9 and dancing to the music. It always makes me feel at home.

LODGING I've always loved the **St. Regis** [East Side] and the **Four Seasons** [East Side]. The Four Seasons is more modern. It's a scene downstairs, but it's nice—beautiful, clean, modern, with a great spa. The St. Regis is different. It's more conservative and low-key, quiet. The rooms are beautiful. You have your own butler on every floor, who's available twenty-four hours a day. The **Hudson** [Midtown] is the newest, hippest spot. We had the VH1/Vogue Fashion Awards party there. The Hudson is like a party every night.

DINNER Victor's Cafe 52 is a good Cuban spot. It's been around forever. Great Cuban food. This is just home cooking, like you'd get at Grandma's house. I always get the steak or the chicken breasts with white rice, black beans, and sweet plantains. For dessert, don't miss the *tres leches,* which is yellow cake soaked with three milks [whole, condensed, and evaporated]. When you cut into it, the milks ooze out. There's a white cream sauce on top and a cherry.

Saturday

HOW TO LOOK LIKE A LOCAL You have to look like you're not trying. Most people are very casual in New York. It's casual chic: Levi's and a nice sweater—a designer sweater— with sneakers or Timberland boots.

BREAKFAST Good Enough to Eat on Amsterdam and 83rd has great breakfasts. It's not much on atmosphere, but the breakfast is really, really good. They have this strawberry butter that you put on the muffins—it's so delicious. They also have great omelets, waffles, and pancakes, and really good service, but I go just for the strawberry butter. I can't properly describe how good it is; you have to taste it and you'll know why.

SIGHTS Go to the **South Street Seaport.** There's always a lot going on down there, always a lot of energy. The real New York energy is always, of course, at the **Empire**

State Building. That's where you get a sense of what Manhattan is. It's romantic to look out over the city from the observation deck. You can sense the hustle and bustle of New York life. I love **Central Park**—that's where I feel New York the most. You could live in New York your whole life and never see all of Central Park. One day, you're just walking through and you think, *Oh, my God, I've never seen this part of the park!* And they have all of these activities going on there. I also like watching the ice skaters in the **Wollman Rink.**

TRANSPORTATION I grew up in the Bronx in Castle Hill—a regular, lower-middle-class neighborhood, very mixed. It was like . . . have you ever seen that movie *I Like It Like That* with Jon Seda? That was kind of what our upbringing was like. To me the subway really represents New York because I grew up on it, going from the Bronx to Manhattan, which is why I named my album *On the 6.* You see everybody on the 6, from the lowest of the low to the highest of the high. It's a no-hassle way to get into the city—no traffic, no parking. That train is where I started my journey, going into Manhattan to practice and audition. I'd always get on the train at the Castle Hill Avenue stop and take it up to Phil Black's studio, near 51st and Lexington, where I used to take classes. It's now a tae kwon do center. That was a special place to me.

LUNCH I love having lunch at **Cipriani Downtown.** The best part is they have outside seating, and because it's right on West Broadway, you see a lot of interesting people walking by. I always get the artichoke salad—delicious. They also have their famous pasta in cream sauce with ham. And how can I forget the calamari? Everywhere I go, I order calamari if it's on the menu, but Cipriani Downtown has some of the best in New York.

SHOPPING My favorite shops in New York? Downtown, in SoHo and Tribeca, there are so many great shops you could spend all day—all weekend—down there. Furniture stores, clothing stores, record stores—all along the streets. There's also the usual Gucci, Prada, and Versace, but what's unique is a store like **Jeffrey New York,** which sells hot little T-shirts and all kinds of different boots. It's a really cool, hip store in the meatpacking district. **Aedes de Venustas** at 15 Christopher Street sells beautiful candles and perfumes. The areas in the Bronx where I would shop are Southern Boulevard and Fordham Road, where you can get two T-shirts for about $10. Everybody walks around there on the weekends.

SPA The spa at the **Peninsula Hotel** is the best. It's on the roof. They have every treat-

Lotus, New York

ment that you can think of, and it's all about tranquility and quietness and serenity—and all of that is important in a city like New York, where everything's really crazy. They really pamper you at the Peninsula. They make you feel like you're special. I love the facials and the body scrubs. They loofah you everywhere and then pour moisturizers and oils all over, which leaves your skin so soft—you're baby-smooth for weeks.

IF YOU CAN EAT ONLY ONE THING For me, New York represents my culture, which is Puerto Rican. So when I think of going home, I think of home cooking, like rice and beans and chicken and things like that, which you can get at any *cuchi frito* spot. *Cuchi frito* basically means "fried food." They're little Spanish restaurants. Also **Brisas del Caribe** is the most down-home Puerto Rican cooking you can get. It's really, really good. Divey and cheap, but great food.

DINNER I go to **Mr. Chow** for the Chicken Joanna. It's breaded breasts of chicken with amazing sauce. Their chicken satés are so good. For an added treat, you have to order the crispy beef. I don't know what they do to it. It's sweet, but also a little spicy. There's always a Hollywood scene at Mr. Chow. The scene is great, but the food is even better. I go to **Nobu** for the rolls. That's what I get every time.

NIGHTLIFE My favorite club of all time is **Lotus,** a cool restaurant/club where they have

---

My favorite club of all time is Lotus, a cool restaurant/club where they have good food.

good food. There's a downstairs, and the upstairs has a real nice dance floor and stage. I've performed with other dancers at **Limelight**, which is a crazy club in an old church. [Limelight changed ownership and is now named **Avalon**; same location and hip atmosphere.] There's a swing in the middle of one of the dance floors that you can get on. People hop on and try to swing with you. It's a great mix of people, and it's open all night into early morning.

Sunday

WINDOW-SHOPPING On Sundays, when I'm not working, I love to window-shop up and down 5th Avenue. Some of my favorite stores are on that street. The window displays on 5th are fantastic. I love to peek in the windows at **Fendi** for the new bags and shoes. I love looking at the new clothes in the windows at **Saks** and **Henri Bendel.** But my favorite thing is window-shopping at **Tiffany's.** Sure, Tiffany's is closed on Sundays, but I'm window-shopping anyway. Why? Because a girl's gotta dream.

Jennifer Lopez's New York City Essentials

LODGING
Four Seasons Hotel New York, $$$$, (212) 758-5700
57 East 57th Street, East Side

Hudson, $$$, (212) 554-6000
356 West 58th Street, Midtown

The St. Regis, $$$$, (212) 753-4500
2 East 55th Street, East Side

DINING
Brisas del Caribe, Puerto Rican, $, (718) 794-9710
1207 Castle Hill Avenue, the Bronx

Cipriani Downtown, Italian, $$$$, (212) 343-0999
376 West Broadway, downtown

Good Enough to Eat, American, $, (212) 496-0163
483 Amsterdam Avenue, Upper West Side

Mr. Chow New York, Asian, $$$$, (212) 751-9030
324 East 57th Street, East Side

Nobu, new Japanese, $$$$, (212) 219-0500
105 Hudson Street, Tribeca

Victor's Cafe 52, Cuban, $$, (212) 586–7714
236 West 52nd Street, West Side

SIGHTS
Central Park, 843-acre park, (212) 310-6600

One Great Night in New York

I had a big surprise birthday party at Lotus for my thirtieth birthday, and it was really cool. I had been working on my movie *Angel Eyes* and came home to New York to spend my birthday with my family. I could have gone anywhere for my birthday—to Miami or back to Los Angeles or to some island where I could have just been by myself to relax. But instead I decided to go home, and it was the best thing, because I got to share it with everybody. It turned out that Puff [recording artist Sean "Puffy" Combs] had planned this big party for me at Lotus. I walked in and I thought we were going to somebody else's party, but all of New York was there. Not just my family, but everybody in New York who means something to me. Tito Nieves sang "Happy Birthday" to me with his band. *NSync was there. My whole family, friends, people I work with. It made me feel incredible—it made me feel like there's no place like home.

Empire State Building, (212) 736-3100
350 5th Avenue, Midtown

South Street Seaport, shopping district, (212) 732-7678
Fulton and South Streets, Pier 17, lower Manhattan

Wollman Rink, ice skating, (212) 439-6900
830 5th Avenue, Central Park

SHOPPING

Aedes de Venustas, cosmetics/skin care, (212) 206-8674
9 Christopher Street, West Village

Fendi, designer accessories, (212) 759-4646
677 5th Avenue, Midtown

Henri Bendel, department store, (212) 247-1100
712 5th Avenue, Midtown

Jeffrey New York, women's clothing (212) 206-1272
449 West 14th Street, West Village

Saks Fifth Avenue, department store, (212) 753-4000
611 5th Avenue, Midtown

Tiffany & Co., jewelry/gifts, (212) 755-8000
600 Madison Avenue, Midtown

NIGHTLIFE

Avalon, nightclub, (212) 807-7780
47 West 20th Street, downtown

Lotus, nightclub, (212) 243-4420
409 West 14th Street, West Village

SPAS

The Peninsula Spa at the Peninsula New York,
(212) 903-3910, 700 5th Avenue, East Side

New York City

A New York City cab driver is responsible for Brooke Shields's becoming a model. She said, "I was not even a year old, and my mother and I were in a cab heading uptown, when the cab driver said to my mom, 'You've got a beautiful baby, she should model.'" Then the driver pulled out some pictures of his own kids modeling to show her how easy it was. Soon after, the cab driver's prophecy became true. At age three she took her first walk down the modeling catwalk; at nine she landed her first movie role; at twelve she became a movie star, playing the preteen prostitute in *Pretty Baby*. Owing allegiance to the city where the cabby predicted her future, Shields has never left for long, not when she became a familiar face on magazine covers and in myriad movie and TV projects, not even as the star of NBC's hit sitcom *Suddenly Susan*, for which she won a Golden Globe for Best Actress in a Comedy Series, or more recently, when she became a best-selling author and mother of two daughters. Here's a weekend with the self-confessed city slicker, who grew up napping on restaurant banquettes and shooting pool in downtown billiard parlors—in the city that never sleeps.

Lorenzo Agius/Exclusive by Getty Images

Friday

LODGING There's the **Lowell Hotel** [Upper East Side]. That's where a friend of mine stays.

DINNER There are two ways that I would go. The first is this restaurant called the **Candle Café** [Upper East Side], which is completely macrobiotic—a granola type of a place where they serve lots of tofu and soy. But I've taken people there that are not vegetarians, and they

love it because it's so tasty. It has many little candles and crystals, and it's very earthy. I do the "Pick Five"—you pick five things.

If I'm in a celebration mood, we go to a restaurant I grew up going to when I was a little girl, **Il Campanello** [between Avenue of the Americas and 7th Avenue]. It's a really great Italian restaurant without pretension—hardcore Italian food. You leave full and the wine is unbelievable. From beginning to end, you're eating way too much. The bar is fabulous. I used to sleep on the banquette when my mom and all her friends were at the restaurant.

NIGHTLIFE The **Blue Note** [between Avenue of the Americas and MacDougal]. has Ella Fitzgerald–style music and that kind of thing. The **B Bar** [SoHo] is a good place to go for drinks.

Saturday

BREAKFAST Coffee and a bagel—that's your sort of staple in New York. You get very possessive of who makes the good coffee and who doesn't. There's one newsstand that I go to religiously—right on 2nd Avenue between 62nd and 61st. It's that down-home type of a feeling where they see you coming and they know you want *The News* and *The Post* and they already have your change ready.

SIGHTS All my dance classes and theatrical areas were sort of the Upper West Side, but I

Andrew F. Kazmierski / istockphoto.com

never left a radius of about twenty blocks from 52nd up. I was always sort of an Upper East Side girl. I grew up on 52nd Street, on the far East Side. My landmarks? I would have to say **Central Park** for sure, even though that's at the West Side, where the Alice in Wonderland statue is, to the reservoir, which is right by the **Guggenheim Museum.** That's where my mom used to take me in my little stroller. We would go to the little park there. Once I come over the G. W. Bridge, I get on East River Drive [now Franklin D. Roosevelt Drive] and once I see the ASPCA, the animal shelter, then I know I'm in New York. Oh, all my animals have come from there, except for one little dog that we bought. But all my cats for the past thirty years have come from the ASPCA. I love the **Metropolitan Life Building** at the end of Park Avenue. During Christmastime, they have beautiful lights on it. Then the **Empire State Building** and the **Statue of Liberty**—those are the two things that you feel possessive about in New York.

LUNCH My mom, before having me, used to go to **P. J. Clarke's** [Midtown] all the time. And when I was born, she brought me in there and used to put me on the bar—because I was a little baby. Then when I got too big for the bar, you know, age twenty-eight—just kidding—they got me a high chair. They still have my high chair downstairs. It's the best burger in New York; they serve it on an English muffin.

My landmarks? I would have to say Central Park for sure.

EXERCISE AND SPAS I'll run up to the park and enter at the Guggenheim Museum on 81st and go to the reservoir, run around the reservoir, and then run back. The reservoir itself is only about a mile and a half, and then every twenty blocks is a mile. I'm not really a runner, but this city allows you to be at any level. I like to get a massage at **Kimara Ahnert.** They do everything from makeup to waxing to massage to facials to collagen. And also **Bliss 49** [Midtown]—the name says it all.

CULTURE I love the **Whitney Museum of American Art** [Upper East Side]. It's not too large, and yet I can really delve into one part of it and not feel like I'm just so overwhelmed. They'll do retrospectives and I can digest it all. I like the **Museum of Modern Art,** too—MOMA's definitely up there—but at the Whitney I feel I can be inconspicuous. It feels personal to me.

SHOPPING **Gourmet Garage** [multiple locations] took over a garage, and they've got the best produce and healthy vine-ripened tomatoes and any type of organic food. The fruit is amazing—there's such a selection. I love **ABC Carpet** downtown. It's four floors of the most amazing furniture and rugs and carpets and beds and antiques and tchotchkes and everything you can imagine for a house. And then **Kate's Paperie** [SoHo] is one of my favorite places to go and get new diaries and beautiful books to make scrapbooks from.

SNACK You have to talk about the Heaven-D-Lite obsession this city has. Do you know what that is? It's a frozen dessert, but they have them at these candy stores, **World of Nuts and Chocolate,** and they are sprinkled all through the city—West Side, East Side, Uptown, Downtown, Midtown. It's frozen yogurt, but it's not really a yogurt culture; it's a frozen dairy, all-natural thing. People are obsessed with it here. Sometimes I'll skip lunch and I'll have a large one and it feels really decadent, except it's fat-free. I like peanut butter myself, and vanilla is a staple. You watch women go in there, and it's like your flavor choice shows your personality—it's like a *Seinfield* episode.

DANCE CLASSES I hesitate to say this, but I'm an addict for the dance classes at the **Broadway Dance Center.** They've just moved after fifty years on Broadway and 55th—twenty years of which I was a patron. They've got three floors. Different lessons, different levels, everything from tap to ballet to flamenco to modern to every possible dance that you can imagine. The classes are completely professional and are unbelievably good. Ann Reinking used to teach there and you've got everybody from [the late] Gregory Hines to the *Bring in the Noise* team. The cast of *Chicago* takes all their classes there. There's also an exercise class. It's what New York really prides itself on. It's a place where professionals can go and be anonymous and where nonprofessional beginners can go and not feel at all intimidated.

DINNER I just adore being able to go to the **Post House** [Upper East Side] and get really clean food, really clean fish. It's a bright atmosphere; it's beautiful, with tiled floors and waiters that have worked there for twenty years. They take it all very seriously. If you're a meat eater, they have huge cuts of beef and great pieces of swordfish. It has a very old feel.

Another really sexy restaurant is **Raoul's** [SoHo]. It's a late-night dining spot. It's the kind of spot where you can go in the back and sit there and have steak au poivre or some chicken dish and fabulous pommes frittes and really good wine and stay there for hours.

I've been going to the **21 Club** since I was a little girl; they still know what kind of salad I like. The best hometown Southern cooking is found at a place called the **Pink Teacup** [West Village]. It's the best, least pretentious place I've ever been as far as Southern cooking is concerned.

THEATER You try to consume theater in New York, whether you're going to Broadway, or you're going to the **Atlantic Theater Company** [between 8th and 9th Avenues], or you're watching **Lincoln Center** theater. You know, I went to **Shakespeare in the Park** yesterday, and it's one of the most tremendous things. Anybody who comes to New York should see as much theater as they can, because it doesn't get any better than this. The **Eugene O'Neill** [theater district] for me holds a very

special place. It was the first time I had performed on Broadway [as Rizzo in *Grease*]. I got to know the feeling of it, the smell of it, the weight of the stage door, where my windows were. There's such history. You can go to the **Barrymore Theater** [theater district] and you look up and the architecture and the sculpture are staggering. I just love to be able to look up and see balconies and the carvings in the ceilings and imagine how it was many years ago when theater had a sense of protocol to it and a sense of real respect.

Sunday

WORSHIP I would start a Sunday by going to mass, probably **St. John the Baptist** or **Our Lady of Peace** [East Side]. I had my first of everything there at St. John—my first St. Patrick's recital, my first communion. They have a very sweet little midnight mass as well.

BRUNCH I like **Sarabeth's,** which is on the Upper West Side, for brunch or breakfast. You can get breakfast or great fresh salads and sandwiches, and good coffee.

One Great Day in New York

I went to P. J. Clarke's once with my mom when I was two, and Jackie and Aristotle Onassis were sitting at the corner table, in the first section not the back section, and my mom said, "That's Jackie Onassis and she has a little boy your age." It was always a running joke—because he was so cute—that I was going to grow up and get to meet him. I went over to her [Jackie's] table and I introduced myself. This is a mystery to me—I wish I was as confident now as I was then. At that time, they had the individually wrapped sugar cubes, and the big game that I used to play was how many you could stack up and hold between your thumb and your pinkie. And I took it upon myself to go and teach her that. I told her that I was going to grow up and marry her son, and that I had to teach her how to hold the sugar cubes. I did meet him [John Kennedy Jr.] but never told him that story.

SHOPPING Barney's [East Side] is just divine. It's the most exclusive, decadent experience to go in there and go from floor to floor and just appreciate the Kiehl's cosmetics counter and having all that at your fingertips. During the holiday season, they have the most innovative, brightly done, divinely designed windows. I'll always spend some time in the antique jewelry section.

FLEA MARKETS I love going to the **Flea Market** on 6th Avenue [Chelsea] on Saturday and Sunday. You have to get there at seven in the morning, but it's great to go down there and spend the good part of the morning. It's all outdoors and it's only in the summer. But there are two sides: one side is where it's free to get in, and then on the other side it's a dollar to get in. You'll see everything from unbelievable beautiful linens and furniture, to all sorts of pottery and silver and jewelry and old clothing, to old oil paintings.

WALK Once you are out of the hospital range on York, right by where Gracie Mansion is, walk on the river right there. It's very relaxed and beautiful, and with the sparkling moon it shines. You literally can see sparkling from the city lights on the streets. You get a sense of tradition because there are still cobblestone streets. I remember once flying back from somewhere and I was saying to my mom, "Oh, I can't wait to get back and sit in the backyard and just look at the trees and just be quiet!" And someone said, "Excuse me, but where do you live?" I said, "Manhattan." They thought I was crazy, but I believe that at night any street you pick— because of the glass that's been crushed into the cement for the city blocks— they sparkle. They literally sparkle.

Brooke Shield's New York Essentials

LODGING
The Lowell Hotel, $$$$, (212) 838-1400
28 East 63rd Street, Upper East Side

DINING
21 Club, American, $$$$, (212) 582-7200
21 West 52nd Street, Midtown

Candle Café, vegetarian, $, (212) 472-0970
1307 3rd Avenue, Upper East Side

Il Campanello Ristorante, Italian, $$$, (212) 695-6111
136 West 31st Street, Midtown

Pink Teacup, American, $$, (212) 807-6755
42 Grove Street, West Village

P. J. Clarke's, American, $$, (212) 317-1616
915 3rd Avenue, Midtown

Post House Restaurant, steak house and seafood, $$$, (212) 935-2888, 28 East 63rd Street, Upper East Side

Raoul's Restaurant, French, $$$, (212) 966-3518
180 Prince Street, SoHo

Sarabeth's, American, $$, (212) 496-6280
423 Amsterdam Avenue, Upper West Side

World of Nuts and Chocolate, candy shop, (212) 769-1006 (for Upper West Side location, 2578 Broadway), multiple locations throughout Manhattan

SIGHTS
Central Park, 843-acre park, (212) 360-3444
Manhattan

Empire State Building, (212) 736-3100
350 5th Avenue, Midtown

Metropolitan Life Building, (212) 578-3111
1 Madison Avenue, Midtown

Museum of Modern Art, (212) 708-9400
11 West 53rd Street, Midtown

Statue of Liberty, (212) 363-3200
Liberty Island, New York Harbor

Whitney Museum of American Art, (212) 570-3600
945 Madison Avenue, Upper East Side

SHOPPING
ABC Carpet & Home, home furnishings, (212) 473-3000
888 Broadway, downtown

Annex Antique Fair and Flea Market, shopping district,
Avenue of the Americas, Chelsea

Barney's New York, clothing, (212) 826-8900
660 Madison Avenue, East Side

Gourmet Garage, gourmet grocery, (212) 535-6271
multiple locations throughout Manhattan

Kate's Paperie, paper products, (212) 941-9816
561 Broadway, SoHo

NIGHTLIFE
B Bar, (212) 475-2220
40 East 4th Street, SoHo

Blue Note Jazz Club, (212) 475-8592
131 West 3rd Street, Greenwich Village

THEATER
Atlantic Theater Company, (212) 691-5919
336 West 20th Street, Chelsea

Ethel Barrymore Theater, (212) 239-6200
243 West 47th Street, theater district

Eugene O'Neill Theater, (212) 239-6200
230 West 49th Street, theater district

Lincoln Center for the Performing Arts, (212) 875-5000
140 West 65th Street, Upper West Side

Shakespeare in the Park, (212) 539-8500
Central Park

SPAS/EXERCISE
Bliss 49, (212) 219-8970
541 Lexington Avenue, Midtown

Broadway Dance Center, dance and exercise classes,
212-582-9304, 221 W. 57th Streeet

Kimara Ahnert, massage, cosmetics, (212) 452-4252
1113 Madison Avenue, Upper East Side

WORSHIP
Our Lady of Peace, (212) 838-3189
237 East 62nd Street, Upper East Side

St. John the Baptist Roman Catholic Church,
(212) 564-9070, 210 West 32nd Street, Midtown

New York City

I'm a New Yorker to the end," declared Denzel Washington. And while he's divided his time between Manhattan and L.A. for many years, the images in his mind remain New York stories. The son of a preacher and a beautician, he still remembers every train ride from his home in Mount Vernon, New York, from where he can still count off the interminable stops on his way to his classes at Fordham University. He remembers winning the audition for his first professional acting job, an NBC telefilm called *Wilma*, in which he played the boyfriend of Olympic runner Wilma Rudolph, appearing with his future wife, Paulette Pearson. "I was so happy and unbelievably ecstatic I was just running down Madison Avenue, running and screaming and jumping for joy," he said. He first gained fame with an off-Broadway production of the Pulitzer Prize–winning *A Soldier's Play*, which led to his being cast in the NBC TV series *St. Elsewhere*. Washington is now, of

course, among the top tier of actors with his Oscar-winning performance in *Glory*, his Oscar-nominated turn in the title role of *Malcolm X*, his supporting role as Tom Hanks's attorney in *Philadelphia*, and his Best Actor Oscar for 2001's *Training Day*. But no matter whom he's playing, behind the character is Denzel Washington's favorite role: New Yorker.

Friday

LODGING The **Trump International Hotel** is right there on the West Side. It's right on the park and you get a nice view—during the spring and fall when the trees are all red, in winter when the park is white from snow. As a young man in college, I walked around Lincoln Center and saw these buildings and imagined myself being in them one day. Now, when I stay in the Trump International Hotel, it's the same place in such a different set of circumstances. The Trump International has a great restaurant, **Jean Georges.** I also like staying in SoHo at the **Mercer Hotel.** That was kind of interesting staying down there. The Mercer has more of a downtown, funkier, artsy kind of vibe.

DINNER Jezebel is where I always go. Alberta Wright, a friend of mine, owns it. It's a great restaurant on 45th and 9th, and it's beautiful. She used to be an antiques dealer and she has all these great antiques. It's just a very unique place—sort of Southern cuisine, but just nicely done. I can go there and feel like it's home. One of my favorite dishes that they make is a goat cheese salad. It's an excellent, excellent salad. I don't know what she puts in it, but it's really spicy food. When we're not at Jezebel, we always have sushi down at **Nobu** in Tribeca. That's another watering hole of mine.

ENTERTAINMENT There's always great theater. Theater Four down on 54th Street, now the **Julia Miles Theater,** is a favorite of mine because I did a play there, *A Soldier's Play,* which won the Pulitzer Prize, became an Academy Award–nominated movie, and really sort of launched my career. It's just a little old theater down there on 54th between 10th and 11th. I also like the **Cherry Lane Theater** downtown and the **Roundabout** and the **Manhattan Theater Club.**

Saturday

SIGHTS When I think of New York, I definitely think of **Central Park.** I love walking through the park. I always walk up to around 72nd Street. Between 72nd and maybe 60th, there's a beautiful little walkway before you get to the fountains. The trees are just beautiful there, and the benches are really nice and quiet—it's a peaceful feeling. What I love about the park is that there's all kinds of stuff going on. You come up on one section and you've got all your roller skaters, and you go to another section and you've got the guys playing the drums. You go to another section and every-

Jezebel is where I always go. Alberta Wright, a friend of mine, owns it. It's a great restaurant on 45th and 9th, and it's beautiful. She used to be an antiques dealer and she has all these great antiques.

Jezebel, New York

body is boating, and of course, you've got your serious runners up by the reservoir. I used to walk around the park to learn my lines when I was doing *Longfellow*, and I would walk the whole park because I had a lot of lines to learn. I was going over and over and over them and would walk up Central Park West and sometimes I would walk along the horse paths. People would look at me like I was crazy. I was a senior in college.

SHOPPING There was always good shopping around 42nd Street and Times Square. Also, we would go down to Delancey Street and Orchard Street to shop. That's where my mother used to take us. She could get the biggest bargains—still can. I remember my mother bargaining with this guy back and forth over twenty-five cents and she was like, "Well, you know, we've got to catch the train and we don't have the money . . ." I'm like, "Ma, I've got twenty-five cents." And she gave me a look. You can still get bargains on Orchard and Delancey.

But if I'm doing any shopping in New York, usually it will be in those boutiques down in the SoHo area. I like some of the Japanese designers, **Yohji Yamamoto** [SoHo] and **Issey Miyaki** [Tribeca]. My wife is a pro shopper. I'm good for about half an hour and then I'm looking for a seat by the changing room. My wife always stops in **Bergdorf Goodman** [Midtown], that's for sure. It's a great store and you can always find good pieces there. I found some Zegna suits, really nice stuff. Most of the time I come to New York, I go by the **Gap,** because I usually didn't bring enough, so I get a couple of pairs of jeans and a couple of black T-shirts. That's all I need.

LUNCH When I come to New York, I want to make sure I get a hot dog off the street, and I've got to make sure I get a good slice of pizza down at **John's Pizza**—really excellent pizza right there in the Village. I took my son to **Famous Ray's.** I guess there are nine thousand Famous Ray's Pizzas now, right? But the one on Avenue of the Americas at around 11th Street—that's the original Ray's with the heavy, heavy cheese. There was no food better than those hot dogs or those tuna sandwiches from the deli. Where do you go now for a great sandwich? The **Carnegie Deli** [Midtown] or the **Stage Deli** [Midtown].

SNACK I'll tell you one thing I always get in New York. My wife loves these almost sweet, honey toasted or something, peanuts. You've got to get them. She loves them—I'll taste one or two, but she loves them. She's got to have those peanuts. For some reason, there's always a guy right around 57th Street near Carnegie Hall. So, I always make sure to bring her ten bags of these roasted peanuts when I come back.

ARCHITECTURE I love Aldwyn Court, where **Petrossian** [Midtown] is now. It's got terra cotta dragons and everything else all over it. Petrossian is a place for caviar; I've never actually eaten there, but I remember walking by and seeing the people in the window. Very interesting. I've always loved the **Dakota** and the sister building to the Dakota, the **Graham Court** up in Harlem, which is a beautiful building. The Plaza Hotel was done by the same architect.

My favorite street in the city? Wow, that's a tough one because I still love the Upper West Side. I love West End Avenue. 42nd Street. I can't even pick a favorite. I love the Village, I love Canal Street, I love Houston Street, I love 42nd Street. I still like looking at all the buildings on West End Avenue. I don't know—I just love them all. I love New York.

CULTURE I grew up going to the **American Museum of Natural History** [Upper West Side]. I was in the Boys Club—well, now they call it the Boys and Girls Club—and we used to make trips to the museum and to the **Hayden Planetarium.** The planetarium was always one of my favorite buildings. I remember as a little kid my mom taking me down to see the Mona Lisa when they brought the Mona Lisa to the **Museum of Modern Art.** But mostly I remember the dinosaurs at the Museum of Natural History and all the different animals from different parts of the world. The bones, you know, that command the room and the giant elephants, the mammoths.

DINNER I love **Chanterelle.** We met the owners, Karen and David Waltuck, who are just nice, nice people. It's in Tribeca and it has a very good wine list and great, great food. The other place we go to there is **Montrachet.** It's a little more country feeling, but, again, very, very good food. **Primola** is a little Italian restaurant that we always go to on 2nd Avenue between 65th and 64th Streets. Excellent chicken scarpiello. They chop chicken in little pieces and do a nice chicken dinner, as well as really good pasta. I was doing a show on Broadway back in '88, and the real estate agent of the building I was staying in took me downstairs and showed me what was in the neighborhood, and said, "Oh, you've got to go to Primola.

They'll take care of you." She introduced me to the owners and I've been going ever since.

ENTERTAINMENT For jazz, we've been to the **Village Vanguard** [Greenwich Village].

Sunday

LUNCH I always like the pasta at **Cipriani.** The pasta and the people in there—always interesting. It's the old kind of East Side "see and be seen," the rich and famous. It's like being in Italy. Excellent risotto. It's in the Sherry Netherland Hotel on 5th Avenue. You would usually go there for long lunches, you know. I would get there first and leave last. Watch the show. They have their famous drink, the Bellini, that's why you end up staying there a long time.

EXCURSION As a kid I used to love to go up to **City Island,** up in the Bronx near Orchard Beach, a nice little ride out of town. Any New Yorker would know it. **Sammy's Fish Box** is out there where you can get fresh clams and fried fish—very inexpensive. Then up in New Rochelle, really Pelham, there's a place we used to call Greasy Nick's. It's just a funky joint. They do hamburgers and clams and corn on the cob that they serve in these little pie tins. It's actually Jay Leno's uncle's place. When I did Jay's show, I said, "Hey, I've been up to Greasy Nick's." It's called **Leno's Clam Bar,** but we used to always call it Greasy Nick's. I don't know why.

DESSERT I left out Brooklyn! The best cheesecake is in Brooklyn at **Junior's.** That goes without saying. That's the best cheesecake on the planet on Flatbush Avenue, and it's called Junior's. Excellent, excellent, excellent cheesecake. We shot a film a couple of summers ago in Coney Island, and my favorite hot dogs are **Nathan's Famous,** which started on Coney Island. I remember waiting in line to get on the rides at Coney Island, and then suddenly I'm there making a movie.

Denzel Washington's New York Essentials

LODGING
The Mercer, $$$, (212) 966-6060
147 Mercer Street, SoHo

The Trump International Hotel and Towers, $$$$, (212) 299-1000, 1 Central Park West, Upper West Side

DINING
The Carnegie Deli, American, $$, (212) 757-2245
854 7th Avenue, Midtown

Chanterelle, French, $$$$, (212) 966-6960
2 Harrison Street, Tribeca

Harry Cipriani, Italian, $$$$, (212) 753-5566
781 5th Avenue, Midtown

Jean Georges, French, $$$$, (212) 299-3900
1 Central Park West, Upper West Side

Jezebel, Southern, $$$, (212) 582-1045
630 9th Avenue, Hell's Kitchen

John's Pizzeria, pizza, $, (212) 243-1680
278 Bleecker Street, Greenwich Village

Junior's, American, $$, (718) 852-5257
386 Flatbush Avenue, Brooklyn

Leno's Clam Bar, seafood, $$, (914) 636-9869,
755 Pelham Road, Pelham, New Rochelle
(open summer only)

Montrachet, French, $$$$, (212) 219-2777
239 West Broadway, Tribeca

Nathan's Famous Hot Dogs, American, $, (718) 946-2202
multiple locations throughout New York City

Nobu, Japanese, $$$$, (212) 219-0500
105 Hudson Street, Tribeca

Petrossian, French, $$$$, (212) 245-2214
182 West 58th Street, Midtown

One Great Night in New York

I worked at the **Metropolitan Opera House** as an usher during their ballet season back in 1976. The Met is absolutely beautiful. Big sweeping stairs that come down and burgundy seats inside. And they had these private boxes where the Rockefellers and other very wealthy people would sit, and we would always buy some extra cookies for them to nibble on while they were watching the show. It was great because I got to watch Baryshnikov dance every night. The Met is right next to Fordham University, where I went to school. So I could finish a class at 6:00 and be to work at 6:05. What was interesting was to come back to the Met fourteen or fifteen years later when we had the premier for the movie *Glory* that I won an Academy Award for. The dinner after the premier was at the opera house and was a star-studded night. My mom was there, most importantly. I remember riding up in the elevator with her, saying, "Did you ever imagine this?" Just going in there and thinking, *Wow, I used to sit people down and work in here making fifty or sixty dollars, whatever I was making, so I could study to become an actor. And now here I am . . .* Not in my wildest imagination would I think that I would be going to be back to the Metropolitan Opera House one day for a film premier. Going up in the elevator, I remember thinking, *Man, this is like really coming full circle.* It was a magical night.

Primola, Italian, $$$, (212) 758-1775
1226 2nd Avenue, Upper East Side

Ray's Famous Pizza, pizza, $, (212) 243-3010
multiple locations, original is on 11th and Avenue of the Americas

Sammy's Fish Box, seafood, $, (718) 885-0920
41 City Island Avenue, City Island, Bronx

The Stage Deli, delicatessan, $$, (212) 245-7850
834 7th Avenue, Midtown

SIGHTS
The American Museum of Natural History,
(212) 769-5100, 79th Street and Central Park West, Upper West Side

Hayden Planetarium, (212) 769-5920
81st Street and Central Park West, Upper West Side

The Metropolitan Opera, (212) 362-6000
140 West 65th Street, Lincoln Center, Upper West Side

Museum of Modern Art, (212) 708-9400
11 West 53rd Street, Midtown

SHOPPING
Bergdorf Goodman, clothing, (212) 753–7300
754 5th Avenue, Midtown

The Gap, clothing, (212) 674-1877
multiple locations throughout New York City

Issey Miyake, clothing, (212) 226-0100
119 Hudson Street, Tribeca

Yohji Yamamoto, clothing, (212) 966-9066
103 Grand Street, SoHo

THEATER
Cherry Lane Theater, (212) 989-2020
38 Commerce Street, Greenwich Village

Julia Miles Theater, (212) 757-3900
424 West 55th Street, Midtown

Manhattan Theater Club, (212) 399-3000
311 West 43rd Street, theater district

The Roundabout Theater Company, (212) 719-1300
231 West 39th Street, Suite 1200, theater district

The Village Vanguard, jazz club, (212) 255-4037
178 7th Avenue South, Greenwich Village

Oahu

I f you're hungry for Oahu, you couldn't have a better guide than Kelly Preston. One-eighth Hawaiian, her middle name is Kamalelehua, meaning "garden of *lahuas*," the *lahua* being the flower that according to legend will shower rain on the part of the island from which it is plucked. The name fits because Kelly Preston's Oahu is truly a garden, her much-adored hometown where she finds her family, her favorite foods, and all manner of fun. At the time of our interview, Preston was dividing her time between her residence in Los Angeles and homes in Florida, Hawaii, and Maine. At her side were her husband, John Travolta, who pilots their airplanes, and their two children.

But wherever she is, she carries Hawaii with her in her heart. It was on Oahu where, at sixteen, with only TV commercial credits, she was pulled out of her PE class and flown to Los Angeles to audition for *The Blue Lagoon*. Although the role went to Brooke Shields, Preston's future was set. She attended UCLA drama school and soon began appearing in movies, garnering early raves as the ambitious and aggressive fiancée of the sports agent played by Tom Cruise in *Jerry Maguire*. Here's a weekend in Kelly Preston's garden of Oahu delights.

Friday

LODGING I love the Kahala Hotel and Resort [Honolulu]. Growing up, it was the Kahala Hilton, and it's still a beautiful hotel. They've redone it gorgeously and it's got dolphins that you can watch in a small show. It's got a really great beach for kids, with very little waves. Also, the Halekulani in Waikiki has gorgeous rooms, a beautiful pool, and a gor-

geous hula dancer, Kanoe Miller, who does one of the most beautiful hulas ever. She's got beautiful hands and very sensuous beautiful movements. Even if you're not staying there, you can go to the Halekulani for a cocktail and watch the sunset and watch her doing the hula.

DINNER Okay, I am very particular with my food. I have to hit all the hot spots where I used to eat when I was growing up. A lot of them are not fancy restaurants. For dinner, I would probably go to Keo's in Waikiki. It has vibrant colors, beautiful paintings on the wall, because the owner, Keo Sananikone, has an extraordinary art collection. They have a fabulous mai tai that will knock your socks off, and the food is just delicious—really, really fine Thai cuisine. Roy's in Hawaii Kai is just great, tasty, sort of island-Asian food. The appetizers are insane—blackened ahi with this mustardy soy butter sauce, and the coconut shrimp. They have superior *pupus* [appetizers], except that they've got great dinner, too. So don't stuff yourself on *pupus*.

ENTERTAINMENT I love watching Ceclio and Kopono, two guys who play the most beautiful Hawaiian music out in the Waikiki Shell,

Hotels & Resorts of Halekulani

which is an open-air amphitheater in Kapiolani Park right down at the base of Diamondhead. They are kind of jazzy Hawaiian, with a little bit of soft rock. You could also go to Aloha Tower Market Place, which is wild and fun. Lots of different bars, younger people hanging out. One time I heard Willie K there. He's so awesome. He's like a rock-and-roller with a Hawaiian edge, so he can sing beautiful Hawaiian ballads, but he also gets down and funky.

Saturday

BREAKFAST Every trip that I'm there, I never miss driving out to the North Shore. I might start with going to Leonard's Bakery [Honolulu]. Leonard's Bakery has what's called a *malasada*, which is a Portuguese donut. It has no hole, it's super soft, and just melts in your mouth. If you ever thought you had a donut, you've never had a donut until you've had a *malasada* from Leonard's Bakery. It's insane! You have to eat them hot. You can't take them home and expect them to be great. You see people in the parking lot eating *malasadas*, or you eat them in the car on the way home.

BEACHES Drive out the North Shore highway [Hwy. 83]. Start early. I like to stop at different places. The first fruit stand, which is my favorite, is on the right, just after you pass

The Halekulani in Waikiki has gorgeous rooms, a beautiful pool, and a gorgeous hula dancer, Kanoe Miller, who does one of the most beautiful hulas ever. She's got beautiful hands and very sensuous beautiful movements. Even if you're not staying there, you can go to the Halekulani for a cocktail and watch the sunset and watch her doing the hula.

Chinaman's Hat. It's the main fruit stand and the sign says, "Cold Coconuts." You can get cold coconuts out of the cooler that she'll chop for you right there and you can drink the milk. You can see my whole life revolves around food. Before you start your drive, you've got to get some crack seed, which is dried fruit made really super tiny with the seeds inside. There are thirty different flavors. My mouth is watering. Then keep driving. There are tons of beaches. I like to go to the tide pools at Pupukea Beach Park [North Shore]. It's an area that's surrounded by tons of coral. You can go swimming, but there are lots of *wana,* which are sea urchins, you know, the pokey things? So you have to be careful, but it's fun for kids because it's shallow and protected. Ehukai Beach Park [North Shore] has Sunset and Pipeline—those beaches are exciting, but you have to be a really strong swimmer and really good to swim there unless it's kind of a mellow day. You can just go watch surfers. Another great beach is Waimea Bay [North Shore].

LUNCH By now I would probably be starving, so I would go to Haleiwa, the very cute funky town, and I would go to Kua Aina Sandwich Shop, which has the best hamburgers you ever had in your whole life. They also have mahi-mahi burgers and chicken sandwiches. But I always think, *I'm going to splurge and have myself a cheeseburger.* The French fries are insane, but the cheeseburgers—enormous, dripping. It's very tiny, just maybe three little tables, some outdoor tables, but it's always packed. Mostly you can get a table or you take it in the car, but you don't care at that point because the cheeseburger is so good.

DESSERT Then go across the street because you've maybe got an ounce of room left in your stomach and get shave ice at Matsumoto. It's pure deliciousness. They've got all the greatest flavors, but I love *lilikoi*. A lot of times, I'll get a mixture of *lilikoi*/strawberry or *lilikoi*/mango or something like that.

SHOPPING I love Haleiwa on the North Shore. It's got cute, fun shops to go into. But even before that, actually, you have to stop off at the side of the road and get the sweet Kahuku corn. You could eat it raw, it's so good—it's like sugar. There are three stands on the Kamehameha Highway and you'll see the sign, "Sweet Corn—Sweetest Ever." It's the best sweet corn, ever, ever, *ever*. Right after you hit the corn are great antique stores. You can get antique hula dolls, glass balls, you know, from off the ships—toys, all sorts of great, great antiques.

EXERCISE Now you're so full! Sometimes I'll go to the beach again in Haleiwa to jump in the ocean and try to kick around and get some of it off. Oh, a great thing to do is to go out skydiving. I've done it four times. I went skydiving on the North Shore and it's right past Haliewa. It's a great place called Pacific Skydiving. You can go tandem skydiving. I did it with my girlfriends. Actually, my mom, Linda, went skydiving with me the third time I went. So that's the North Shore tour. Now, you can go back to the other side of the island.

MORE BEACHES, FAMILY FUN, HIKING Makapu'u Beach is a gorgeous beach. It's past Sandy's Beach. Sandy's Beach is awesome, too, but the undertow is really intense so you have to really be a strong swimmer. That side of the coast is really beautiful and if it's whale-watching time, you can stop at one of the little lookout places and look at the whales out in the ocean. Sea Life Park is out there, which is really great for the kids. It's a Marineland-type thing. They've got a great Hawaiian show with dolphins and this hula dancer girl who goes out to an island and then she misses her love and the lover comes riding on the dolphins and they do tricks. They've got sea lion shows and you can feed the sea lion fish. A great place to go hiking is Waimea Falls. Wet, moist rainforests set into the valley. It's not a difficult hike at all, anybody can do it. Kids can do it. You hike in and there's a glorious huge waterfall there.

SNACK By this time, you might be hungry again. So this is where I'll get into the it's-nothing-fancy food at Zippy's, which has "fast food," Hawaiian-style. They've got something called Plate Lunch, which is on a paper plate. Two scoops rice and macaroni salad—the best macaroni salad you ever had in your entire life. I crave it. Anybody I've introduced to it craves it. They'll say, "Aren't we going to Zippy's to get the mac salad?" If you're a local, you're always eating at Zippy's.

CULTURE Bishop Museum [Honolulu] is the famous Hawaiian museum. Just really great history, old Hawaii. If you're curious about Hawaii, they've got it all—the great feather cloaks from the kings and queens, all the tools, and koa bowls, and beautiful pieces of art, and things from their court. Just glorious. It's a terrific museum. The Contemporary Art

Museum and the Honolulu Academy of Arts are both good.

SUNSETS At the New Otani Kaimana Beach Hotel [Waikiki] you can have a cocktail in the courtyard area before dinner. Another great place for sunset is to drive up Mount Tantalus. It's a big, gorgeous mountain with homes on it. You drive up this windy road and then there's this state park up there that's gorgeous and you can go hiking and it's just a beautiful, beautiful place. You see wild ginger growing on the sides of the roads. They have a lookout on top.

DINNER Oh, the best Hawaiian food: Ono [Honolulu]. It's a real dive, a supreme dive. And it's open all the time. It's always been good. We get the works. We get *lau-lau, lomi-lomi* salmon, which is like a tomato-salsa type of thing. You've got to get *poi.* You've also got to get Kahlua pig, which is shredded pork, highly seasoned, delicious, delicious, delicious. You've got to get *haupia.* It's a coconut Jello-y–type thing that's so tasty-yummy. There's also Hoku's in the Kahala Mandarin. They've got great fried rice that has a little bit of *lup chong,* which is a Chinese sausage. It's the best fried rice ever and it's a beautiful setting. At any of the hotels, like the Kahala Mandarin, you can sit outside and watch the sunset. Anywhere you can see the sunset is where I like to be on Saturday nights.

Sunday

BREAKFAST In Chinatown, they have things called *manapuas,* which are white doughy buns stuffed with *char siu* pork, sweet and sour pork diced up with some vegetables and onions. You can get *manapuas* and rice cakes. Delish.

THE ISLANDS All of the islands are good. Maui has great waterfalls and scuba diving at a place called Molokini. Kauai I love because it's lush and so untouched, and just gorgeous. Lanai has a great place to scuba dive called the Cathedrals, because when you're down, way deep, it looks like you're diving through church cathedrals. The light shines through these natural coral cathedrals that are just glorious. The islands are the greatest. When you step off the airplane, there's the richness and the scented air. It's warm and there's a light breeze, and it just envelops you. Everybody is very relaxed. If you say you're going to be somewhere at 6:00, don't be surprised if they're not there until 6:20 or 6:30. Even television programs are on Hawaiian time. Even normal shows like *ER* and things like that start late here. That is one of my favorite things about Hawaii. Immediately, you relax. You don't have a care in the world and everything just sort of drains away. You are home.

Kelly Preson's Oahu Essentials

LODGING

Halekulani, $$$$, (808) 923-2311
2199 Kalia Road, Waikiki

Kahala Hotel and Resort, $$$$, (808) 739-8888
5000 Kahala Avenue, Honolulu

New Otani Kaimana Beach Hotel, $$$$,
(800) 356-8264, 2863 Kalakaua Avenue, Waikiki

DINING

Hoku's, Asian/Hawaiian, $$$$, (808) 739-8780
5000 Kahala Avenue, Honolulu

Keo's, Thai, $$$, (808) 951-9355
2028 Kuhio Ave, Waikiki

Kua Aina, sandwiches/burgers, $, (808) 637-6067
66 Kamehameha Highway, Haleiwa

One Great Day in Oahu

I brought John home to meet the whole family, which I'm sure was a little overwhelming because I've got about twenty of them. Johnny had flown us in the Gulfstream II. On the way, I told him that I've got a really great, loving, close family that's lots of fun. I told him about the stuff that we would do and the beaches we would go to. We had been together about a year, but we weren't engaged. He had flown to Hawaii before, so that wasn't a big deal, but at the private airport they greet you with leis and they give you a warm welcome and a kiss. My mom was there and took us back to her house and Hawaiian music was playing and my Uncle Bob was playing guitar. And Aunt Stephanie was there, and all my cousins and everybody. It was really great because in Hawaii, it's very family oriented; your *ohana*, your family, is the basis of everything. It was a family dinner—hanging out in the backyard.

John was probably a little overwhelmed, but he was wonderful. The whole family embraced him and we had a great time. We had a barbecue. Grilled mahi-mahi, teriyaki chicken, rice, which is the staple of every meal, salads—very local food. Oh, it all revolves around food. We were staying at the Halekulani Hotel. I, of course, had to introduce John to my favorite Hawaiian breakfast, which is rice with a fried egg over easy with spicy Portuguese sausage. The next morning he told me that he loved my family. And I was like, "Oh, whew, thank God!"

Leonard's Bakery, bakery, $, (808) 737-5591
933 Kapahulu Avenue, Honolulu

Matsumoto Shave Ice, shave ice, $, (808) 637-4827
66 Kamehameha Highway, Haleiwa

Ono Hawaiian Foods, Hawaiian, $, (808) 737-2275
726 Kapahulu Avenue, Honolulu

Roy's, Hawaiian fusion, $$$, (808) 396-7697
6600 Kalanianaole Highway, Hawaii Kai

Zippy's, Hawaiian fast food, $, (808) 733-3730
multiple locations throughout Hawaii

SIGHTS

Bishop Museum, (808) 847-3511
1525 Bernice Street, Honolulu

Cathedrals I and II, diving, Lanai, south coast

Contemporary Art Museum, (808) 526-0232
2411 Makiki Heights Drive, Honolulu

Ehukai Beach Park, seven miles northeast of Haleiwa
Kamehameha Highway, North Shore

Honolulu Academy of Arts, (808) 532-8700
900 Beretania Street, Honolulu

Makapu'u Beach Park
41-095 Kalanianaole Highway, Waimanalo

Molokini Crater, diving, (877) 873-4837, Maui

Mount Tantalus
Tantalus Drive, North Honolulu

Pacific Skydiving Center, (808) 637-7472
Dillingham Airfield, Haleiwa

Pupukea Beach Park, tide pools, seven miles northeast
of Haleiwa, Kamehameha Highway, North Shore

Sandy's Beach, 8808 Kalanianaole Hwy, Oahu

Sea Life Park, (866) 365-7446
41 Kalanianaole Highway, Waimanalo

Waimea Bay, North Shore

Waimea Falls Park
59-864 Kamehameha Highway, North Shore

SHOPPING

Haleiwa, fun shops, North Shore

North Shore Highway, fresh corn, antiques

NIGHTLIFE/ENTERTAINMENT

Aloha Tower Marketplace, shopping, dining, events,
(808) 528-5700, 1 Aloha Tower Drive, Honolulu

Waikiki Shell, open-air amphitheater, (808) 591-2211
777 Ward Avenue, Kapiolani Park, Waikiki

Philadelphia

The star of such iconic films as *Apollo 13, Sleepers, JFK, Footloose,* and *Diner,* Kevin Bacon is himself an icon. He's such a prolific screen presence that an Internet game tracked how his career intersected with practically every other actor on the planet, calling him the cen-ter of all things in the film universe. But returning home to Philadelphia before our interview several years ago, Bacon was "knee-knocking" nervous. He was going onstage for the first time to perform with the Bacon Brothers, the band he and his older musician brother, Michael, assembled to play a hometown benefit for a family friend. "I was terri-fied," he remembered. When the audience responded enthusiastically, the Bacon Brothers went on the road and into the recording studio. In 1997, they released their first album, whose title *Forosco* is a summation of their musical style, a combination of folk, rock, soul, and country. But no matter how far they go, the Bacon Brothers will never for-get where they started: Philadelphia, where Kevin grew up among five siblings, the son of the late, great architect and veteran city planner Edmund Norwood Bacon, who is credited with saving many local architectural wonders. Here's Kevin Bacon's ode to his hometown.

Friday

LODGING I stay at the **Rittenhouse** [Center City], which is right on Rittenhouse Square. You can get a great room that looks out on the square, which was kind of like my backyard when I grew up. Philadelphia was built in a grid with a series of parks. William Penn designed the city and he put, I guess, four or five parks surrounding the center of the city and Rittenhouse Square is one of them. It's really beautifully planted, and there's winding paths that go through it, and an old fountain in the middle. The Rittenhouse is a great hotel. It's got a great gym—I mean, a health club. It's much bigger than what you would normally get in a hotel, and it's got an indoor pool and mas-sage and facials. The hotel has really good restaurants. They take good care of me there and I love it.

DINNER Around the corner from where I used to live there's **Friday, Saturday, Sunday** [Center City], which was just a small neighborhood place that's also excellent. My dad used to take me to Rococo. [This restaurant in Society Hill is now called **Cebu**.] It's in a building that my father saved from being demolished through urban renewal in the fifties because he especially liked the funny British clock tower in the top. There's a great bar and a nice bar scene.

ENTERTAINMENT The place that [the Bacon Brothers] played most is **Theater of the Living Arts (TLA)** down on South Street. South Street is a real kind of happening fun part of the city—a lot of clubs, a lot of nice little restaurants, inexpensive places to eat. TLA has sort of come full circle. Before I left Philadelphia, I was working on a play there, and my brother had written the music for a play there, and it was an avant-garde theater. Now, it's pretty much a music venue. They put seats in sometimes; they take them out other times. But it's a great venue. The reason that we put our band together is because the family of Harry Spivak—my best friend in the world—owns and runs TLA.

Saturday

BREAKFAST Brunch at the **Four Seasons** [Center City] is nice. It's a gorgeous Four Seasons, down on the Parkway. When we were

kids, if we were driving around all night and staying out late, we would end up at this place called the **Melrose Diner** [South Philadelphia], which was a great breakfast place. On the napkins they used to say, "Everybody that knows goes to the Melrose" or something like that. It's just a classic, "Whaddya want, hon?" place. Good for eggs and bacon. Very much like the diner in the movie *Diner*."

SIGHTS Well, let's see. The **Liberty Bell** is still here; it's still got a crack in it. That whole area is called **Independence Mall.** It's the birthplace of our nation and it's really fascinating. There are amazing tours that you can take and, historically, it's really pretty incredible. All those guys in those powdered wigs? You can still feel their ghosts down there—Philadelphia feels like a very historical city.

There's been a lot of great architectural preservation. You have houses that span from

P. Wei/istockphoto.com

The Liberty Bell is still here; it's still got a crack in it. That whole area is called Independence Mall. It's the birthplace of our nation and it's really fascinating.

precolonial times to the 1800s and on and on. They've been able to maintain a lot of the artistic architectural integrity of the town. Having lived in New York for so many years, Philadelphia seems like a very small-scale city, a bunch of real great small neighborhoods that are kind of tied together into one big city. It's got its share of skyscrapers, but a lot of what the city is built around are neighborhoods with three- or four-story row houses. There's a really strong neighborhood feel in each of these. There's Center City where I grew up. Then, it's West Philly, North Philly, and South Philly, and Kensington and . . . You have Italian neighborhoods and Polish neighborhoods, and there's a real sense of neighborhood pride.

ARCHITECTURE My father was a city planner in Philadelphia. He's made waves and fought battles and woken people up about what's happening, changing, and shaping the city. He was very instrumental in the creation of a neighborhood called **Society Hill,** which is a great neighborhood to see. There's also **Headhouse Square,** which was like an old open-air market in the 1700s. Now it's all cobblestone streets and a lot of restaurants. All around that area are beautiful houses and beautiful little parks and some new houses, but a lot of restored buildings that they just wanted to tear down. My father was real instrumental in making that neighborhood come alive. One of the battles that he lost was trying to put a height limitation on the buildings of all of downtown Philadelphia, that none of them extend above William Penn's hat, which is on the top of City Hall. He lost that one. There are a lot of big skyscrapers.

CULTURE The **Franklin Institute** [Logan Circle] is a great science museum that is also a lot of fun. They have a gigantic replica of the heart that you can walk through. I remember as a kid that was the most amazing thing to do. I would just beg my parents to take me over so I could walk through this gigantic heart. It was always very eerie and you could hear the pulsing of it. It would probably seem tiny now—I would bump my head, I'm sure, if I went through it. But it felt huge when I was a kid. I also like the great **Please Touch Museum** [Logan Circle], the children's museum. If you've got your kids, that's something that is definitely worth doing. The **Philadelphia Museum of Art** [Museum District] is fantastic. And from the steps of the art museum, you can see a straight shot down to City Hall and standing up on the roof of City Hall is William Penn. Even if you don't make it inside, just running up the Benjamin Franklin Parkway and up the steps and pretending you're Rocky Balboa is worth it. Remember?

LUNCH **Pat's Steaks** [South Philadelphia] is great for lunch. The secret of a good Philadelphia cheese steak is after you have had it, you feel like you have to take a shower. It's a long Italian roll with rib-eye steaks, melt-in-your-mouth steak sliced really thin. On top of that is American cheese, and then if you want to start getting creative, you can go pizza steak or cheese steak hoagie—and then lettuce and tomatoes with either sweet peppers or hot peppers. I don't really know what makes cheese steaks great in Philadelphia. Some people say it's in the bun. But, boy, they are really good. You follow it up with a Tastykake, a Philadelphia brand of cakes and pies. My favorite is the peanut butter. They also make these things called Jelly Krimpets. In theory, you're just supposed to bite into it and get a bite of jelly inside the cake, but if you're as experienced and skilled as I am, you can actually gently pull the crumpet apart and end up with a perfect little jelly ball to eat separately.

SHOPPING Reading Terminal, an old train terminal, is now a big, open-air market where people hock their wares—fresh fruits and produce and all sorts of things. **Bassetts,** a Philadelphia ice cream shop, is there. It's very good ice cream, very rich and very creamy. There's also **Antique Row,** a great row of antique stores on Pine Street. It's one antique store after another—a lot of different kinds of antiques. I got a little nice painted end table there. The guy said it was Dutch or something like that. I'm not that great with antiques, but it was really, really pretty and not real expensive.

LANDMARKS The **30th Street Station** is one of my favorite buildings. It's a great old train station that has been the same since it was built. It holds a certain importance to me in my life because it was where I first packed my bags and decided to set off for a new life up there in Manhattan. I still take the train back and forth between Philadelphia and New York. The station represents leaving and coming home. There's this very beautiful statue of an angel picking up a fallen soldier that I remember as a kid it was just amazing to look up and see. It's just a big, big kind of wide open-air train station. There are six kids in my family and sometimes, when it was a rainy day, my mother used to take us up there and let us run around just to burn off steam.

DINNER Old Bookbinder's [Society Hill] is a famous lobster house. It's probably the oldest restaurant in the city; it began in 1865. It's great, a classic sit down, strap on a bib, and have lobster. We would go there on very, very special occasions. It was always saved for something really monumental.

ENTERTAINMENT The Rittenhouse Hotel has a bar called the **Boathouse.** They have peanuts and you can throw the shells on the floor, which I always liked. I don't know why. After our gig at TLA, everybody we knew came back to the Boathouse Row Bar and we hung out. It was a great night. There's a row of boathouses that line the Schuylkill River, where all the rowing teams row out of, and at night they are lit up with lights framing them. The Boathouse bar is not on the Schuylkill River, but it's a theme kind of restaurant built around that.

Sunday

EXERCISE Fairmont Parkway is a beautiful place to run or to take a walk. It runs along the Schuylkill River, where you'll see the guys from the university rowing teams—sculling, as it's called. So you can see them out there racing up and down. I think **Fairmont Park** is the biggest municipal park in the world—it's massive. There's a lot to do out there. **Penn's Landing** is another series of parks. In the summer they have concerts down there, which is on the other river. Philadelphia is bordered by the Delaware River and the Schuylkill River and all the way on the other side of the river is Penn's Landing.

SIGHTS On Sunday, I would walk out on the street, go around the corner to Van Pelt Street where I grew up. My friends would be there and we would have a game of stickball or stoopball or football or something along those lines. You have to be very inventive when you don't have a playground. It's a tiny little street, almost an alley. I don't think two cars could even go down it at the same time. Philadelphia is a great walking city—I would walk down to South Street from my house and there would be a lot to see on the way. Chestnut Street is actually closed to traffic. It's a main artery for the city and they closed it for about ten or twelve blocks and made it into sort of a pedestrian shopping street, so there's always a lot going on.

Kevin Bacon's Philadelphia Essentials

LODGING

The Rittenhouse Hotel, $$$$, (215) 546-9000
210 West Rittenhouse Square, Center City

DINING

Bassetts, ice cream, $, (215) 925-4315
1211 Chestnut Street, Reading Terminal

The Fountain Restaurant at the Four Seasons,
continental, $$$, (215) 963-1500
1 Logan Square, Center City

Friday, Saturday, Sunday, $$, (215) 546-4232
261 South 21st Street, Center City

Melrose Diner, American, $, (215) 467-6644
1501 Snyder Avenue, South Philadelphia

Old Original Bookbinder's, seafood/steak, $$$$, (215) 925-7027, 125 Walnut Street, Society Hill

Pat's King of Steaks, American, $, (215) 468-1546
1237 Passyunk Avenue, South Philadelphia

World Fusion (now called Cebu), international, $$$, (215) 629-1100, 123 Chestnut Street, Society Hill

One Great Day in Philadelphia

My brother Michael came up playing in bands in Philadelphia and was a singer-songwriter. I was involved in music to a certain extent. But I put it aside and decided to become an actor. Then, my best friend in the world, [Theater of Living Arts owner] Harry Spivak, who I've known since I was six, called me up and said, "Why don't you and Michael come down and do a Bacon Brothers concert down at TLA?" It was our first time to play in front of an audience; we had only played on the radio. The marquee said "The Bacon Brothers." There's a great cheese steak shop right across the street from TLA and we got steaks before the concert just to bring the whole thing full circle. Probably a big mistake—it's hard to sing on a cheese steak. I got on stage and I was terrified. It's just the most frightening thing in the world, because you see a sea of—well, in this case not a sea, but a pond—of faces and you stand up there with your guitar and you're going to play songs that you've written from your heart and you're going to sing them. I've been a performer for a long time and I've done a lot of stage acting and movies, but I've never felt more naked, really, than I did that first night. I mean, knees knocking together, nervous as anything. We made it through and came out the other side, and when I got off stage I just said to myself, *I've got to do this again. This was too fun.* And from there it just took off and we kept playing and playing and playing.

SIGHTS

30th Street Station, train station, Market at 30th Street

Chestnut Street
pedestrian blocks are between 8th and 18th Streets

Fairmont Park System, municipal parks, (215) 683-0200
62 neighborhood parks throught Philadelphia

The Franklin Institute Science Museum,
(215) 448-1200, 222 North 20th Street, Logan Circle

Headhouse Square
2nd Street between Pine and South Streets

Independence National Historic Park, (215) 965-7676
free tours available from Independence Hall

Liberty Bell, (215) 965-2305, Market Street, between
South 5th and South 6th Streets, Independence Park

Penn's Landing Park System, municipal parks,
(215) 928-8801, multiple locations throughout Philadelphia

Philadelphia Museum of Art, (215) 763-8100
2600 Benjamin Franklin Parkway, Museum District

Please Touch Museum, children's museum,
(215) 963-0667, 210 North 21st Street, Logan Circle

Society Hill, neighborhood bounded by Lombard, Walnut,
2nd, and 7th Streets

SHOPPING

Antique Row
Pine Street, between 9th and 13th Streets

The Reading Terminal Market, shopping center,
(215) 922-2317, 12th Street between Filbert and
Arch Streets

NIGHTLIFE

Boathouse Row Bar, (215) 546-9000
210 West Rittenhouse Square, Rittenhouse Hotel

Theater of the Living Arts (TLA), music venue,
(215) 922-1010, 334 South Street

Phoenix/Scottsdale

He's a *Saturday Night Live* alum who's graduated to movies and TV series. When I interviewed him, he was in the middle of his long-running prime-time TV series, *Just Shoot Me*, in which he starred as a sarcastic office manager who attempted to date every model who passed through the offices of *Blush Magazine*. But when work is done, David Spade leaves the lights of Los Angeles for his hometown of Phoenix/Scottsdale, Arizona. Spade's journey to fame began on the streets of Scottsdale, in whose environs he's lived since he was four, arriving with his family from the snows of Birmingham, Michigan. At a "fighting weight of ninety-eight pounds," the one-time bully magnet dropped out of local community college, took a job in a skateboard shop and began doing stand-up comedy on the side. In 1990, he rose to the comic pinnacle: a regular job on *Saturday Night Live*. After creating a host of memorable SNL characters, he moved on to film, becoming a comedic staple of both movies and television. Here's David Spade on the city that rises regularly in both his past and present life—his hometown of Phoenix/Scottsdale, Arizona.

Friday

HOTEL The **Phoenician** [Scottsdale] is this big, gorgeous resort. It's got golf. It's just really pretty—always written up. There are great pools, a great spa, and it's right in the heart of everything. I love that place. The funny part is I used to wash golf carts there. I always wanted to save my money so I could play, but they weren't crazy about having the cart washers play. The **Arizona Biltmore** [Phoenix], which was designed by Albert Chase McArthur, a colleague of Frank Lloyd Wright, is a great place, too. That's kind of lower, one or two stories, but laid out flat all over the place. It totally looks Arizona, gray stone, kind of a sixties look. It's got a lot of history. And there is the **Princess,** which is a gorgeous hotel. It's way out in North Scottsdale where everything's being built.

DINNER Royal Palms, which is a hotel that's really cool, has a very nice restaurant called T Cook's. The hotel is totally Arizona looking. It's tucked away on Camelback Road, up from the Phoenician. It's a smaller hotel, but great looking—great restaurant. They have a fireplace in the bar area or you can sit outside. I went there once for Thanksgiving. That place is gorgeous.

Saturday

BREAKFAST I'd go to the Eggery [Phoenix] and the Good Egg. They're a little more casual. I'll have some breakfast with my dad who lives in town.

SIGHTS Phoenix is definitely still that outdoor type of town. Everybody's got tans and everyone wears casual clothes. A lot of Mercedes SL500s, which I felt was odd—once I found out how much they cost. I thought, *How are these people paying for this?* But there's a lot of money there. It's kind of a good laid-back feel—Scottsdale and that whole area where I grew up, Paradise Valley. There's Squaw Peak [Phoenix], which is a great place to run or hike or just hang

out. Echo Canyon [Phoenix] is a great place to hike. There are little holes in the rocks where you can stop and eat a picnic lunch, but you really have to climb and pay attention and know what you're doing. It's real pretty. The Boulders is a really interesting area: mountains and red rocks in way North Scottsdale, where a lot of people like to drive out to. It's very expensive—starts at about a million a house. The Boulders is also the name of a very nice hotel—which also has two golf courses. Of course, even Jack-in-the-Box has a golf course in Phoenix.

SHOPPING There's Scottsdale Fashion Square, which is pretty monstrous. It started out small when I grew up, but then they put a roof on it and extended it an extra block. Now, it's like the Superdome or bigger; there are almost a hundred shops. I went there for Christmas and it was nuts, but it was really fun. They've got everything that you could ever want. Everything under the sun—yogurt, sausages, bookstores, luggage stores, Neiman Marcus, Dillards, Gucci. Old Town Scottsdale, which is called "the West's most Western town," was the big shopping area in the fifties and sixties.

The Arizona Biltmore, which was designed by Albert Chase McArthur, a colleague of Frank Lloyd Wright, is a great place.

Photo by Mike Wilson

It's four small blocks with wooden sidewalks, mom and pop stores, and smaller operations. When Fashion Square opened nearby and got so big, these places did not close down, which is great. A lot of people like Old Scottsdale better. It's fun because you walk along outside and check out all the little stores and Indian jewelry and places. That's for a certain type of people—especially people who have lived there for a long time. It's kind of touristy, which is nice.

LUNCH On a Saturday, sometimes I do the Houston's [Scottsdale] drill. There's one close to me that's fast and easy and I go there. There are some places in Old Scottsdale where you can sit outside. Sitting outside in Old Scottsdale is good and relaxing. If you sit outside, some of the restaurants have misting systems. Even at night it's so hot you still need them. A lot of people will tell you when they go to a restaurant or bar, "Go to this one. They have misters." It's kind of enticing. They're little poles set up with beams across the top, set up in a cage format in the backyard and they spray a tiny, fine mist that you can barely see. It drops the temperature about ten to fifteen degrees. But then you go home damp and humid.

GOLF I play Grayhawk. It's a great golf course in North Scottsdale, designed by Tom Fazio, next to one of my friend's houses. We go and they really take care of us. It's a desert course—a lot of grass, but around that is all desert. When you think of golf normally, it's beautiful grass and big trees on the side and you're trying to avoid the trees and you've got your sand traps. But a desert course is basically beautiful grass and anything that's outside of that is out of bounds. Sometimes the first fifty yards is desert, rock, and cactus, and you have to hit over that into the grass. You have to stay within bounds, because if you get out it's really hard to hit out of the rough, when the rough is a tarantula hole. Grayhawk is a pro course. Tiger Woods played there over Christmas. He had his invitational challenge there. The courses more north I've played are Gold Canyon, which has great views of the Superstition Mountains. I go to the Biltmore a lot; they have two eighteen-hole PGA courses. A lot of people—Michael Jordan, Charles Barkely—play at the Biltmore when they're in town.

CULTURE I remember as kids we'd go to the Heard Museum [Phoenix]. It's Southwestern and Indian art. We'd go there on field trips and my mom would try to take us there and make us smart, but it never quite stuck with me. Now that I'm a flashy superstar I've really gotten shallow; I don't do as much of that as I used to. The Phoenix Zoo—I went there my last trip. Someone wanted to see the alligators or the bears. We went when it was closing, which was great. It's pretty wide open, so we just walked the whole place. I went there to see the animals, so I blended in and checked out everything. The animals are outdoors, so you can get close to them. You want to get in there and pet them all, but they're not crazy about that.

SPORTS I go to the heart of downtown Phoenix to go to the new Chase Field. It's Phoenix's first big major overhead dome, retractable roof. They have the **Arizona Diamondbacks** baseball team. The Cardinals do not play there. Then, I go to see the **Phoenix Suns** at **US Airways Center.** There's a lot going on in downtown Phoenix, including **Arizona Center,** a huge downtown shopping and restaurant center, and the **Arizona Science Center.**

DINNER **Tomaso's** [Phoenix] is an Italian place with just nice old-school Italian. They give you huge portions, great dinners. You can get anything Italian you want there. They'll give you what's on the menu or there are a lot of specials. It's a great atmosphere, a great hang-out, and really nice stuff. Great service—the maître d' comes over and all the waiters are all over you. I don't even think you have to be on a TV show; I think they're just nice anyway. I also like **Morton's,** which is a steak house.

NIGHTLIFE I spent a lot of time in Tempe and all those bars by Arizona State University. I used to do that drill for a while. Tempe's just a little college town by ASU and it's a whole different feel. It's younger and all these little bars are packed and everyone goes to a couple little bars at Mill and University on the corner. Anywhere around there you're in good shape to see college people. I like to go into Tempe and tell the girls that I still go to college there.

Sunday

SPA When I have friends come to town, I tell them to stay at the **Phoenician** and check out the spa. I always get rave reviews about that

place. It's got everything you need from mas-sages to whatever else.

WESTERN LORE **Rawhide** is a cool place to hang out. It's in North Scottsdale and it's an Old West town. It's got covered wagons and it's deserty with the old jail and the old steak house. We used to go there as kids and that was fun for us. They have shootouts in the streets and all that. You just walk around and look at the whole city and hunt for fool's gold. It's a whole theme setup. That's still out there so that's cool—I like things that are "still there."

EXCURSION You can drive out to **Carefree** or **Sedona,** which everyone loves. Everyone who knows I'm from Arizona in L.A. talks about Sedona. It's about two hours up from Phoenix and it's a lot cooler weather. It's a gor-geous, very kind of a spiritual, earthy, crystals kind of hangout. Everyone goes there to get juiced up on energy. And it's got red rocks, it's in the mountains, and it's green up there. You don't see that where we're from in Phoenix, so it's pretty close to have a getaway. There's a lot to do—a lot of walking and little tiny restau-rants, more intimate places that are cool. It's a little romancy up there. Sometimes, I take a girl and we pull off the side of the road and I'll make her watch me shoot squirrels.

David Spade's Phoenix/Scottsdale Essentials

LODGING
Arizona Biltmore, $$$$, (602) 955-6600
2630 East Camelback Road, Phoenix

Boulders Resort, $$$, (866) 397-6520
34631 North Tom Darlington Drive, Carefree

The Fairmont Scottsdale Princess, $$$, (480) 585-4848
7575 East Princess Drive, North Scottsdale

The Phoenician, $$$$, (480) 941-8200
6000 East Camelback Road, Scottsdale

Royal Palms Resort and Spa, $$$$, (602) 840-3610
5200 East Camelback Road, Phoenix

DINING
The Eggery, American, $, (602) 263-8554
50 East Camelback Road, Phoenix

The Good Egg, American, $, (602) 248-3897
multiple locations throughout Phoenix/Scottsdale

Houston's, American, $$, (480) 922-7775
6113 North Scottsdale Road, Scottsdale

Morton's, steak house, $$$$, (602) 955-9577
2501 East Camelback Road, Phoenix

Tomaso's, Italian, $$$, (602) 956-0836
3225 East Camelback Road, Phoenix

T Cook's, Mediterranean, $$$, (602) 808-0766
5200 East Camelback Road, the Royal Palms, Phoenix

SIGHTS
Arizona Diamondbacks at Chase Field, baseball,
(888) 777-4664, 401 East Jefferson Street, Phoenix

Arizona Science Center, (602) 716-2000
600 East Washington Street, Phoenix

Carefree, recreation, 15 miles northeast of Phoenix

Echo Canyon Recreation Area, (602) 261-8318
5950 North Echo Canyon Parkway, Phoenix

The Heard Museum, (602) 252-8848
2301 North Central Avenue, Phoenix

Phoenix Suns at US Airways Center, (602) 379-SUNS
201 East Jefferson Street, Phoenix

Phoenix Zoo, (602) 273-1341
455 North Galvin Parkway, Phoenix

Rawhide, Old West town, (480) 502-5600
5700 West North Loop Road, Chandler

Sedona, recreation,
110 miles north of Phoenix

**Squaw Peak (now called Phoenix Mountains
Park and Recreation Area),** (602) 262-7901
2701 East Squaw Peak Lane, Phoenix

SHOPPING
Arizona Center, (602) 271-4000
455 North 3rd Street, Phoenix

Old Town Scottsdale, (480) 421-1004
East Main Street, Scottsdale

Scottsdale Fashion Square, (480) 990-7800
7014 East Camelback Road, Scottsdale

GOLF
Arizona Biltmore Country Club, (602) 955-9655
2400 East Missouri Avenue, Phoenix

Gold Canyon Golf Resort, (800) 624-6445
6100 South Kings Ranch Road, Gold Canyon

Grayhawk Golf Club, (480) 502-1800
8620 East Thompson Peak Parkway, North Scottsdale

Kate Capshaw

St. Louis

The Kate Capshaw who walked into the Santa Monica café on a sunny California morning seemed different from the glamourous woman you see at the Oscars, sitting beside her husband, perennial Best Director Steven Spielberg. Dressed in boots and slacks, she seemed worlds away from the star who lit up the screen in films like *Indiana Jones and the Temple of Doom, Black Rain,* and *The Love Letter.* The Kate Capshaw who walked into the café is a wide-open, friendly native of the suburbs of St. Louis, where she became a high school department store model, then received a master's degree in special education from the University of Missouri. She taught elementary and high school for two years before heading off to New York to pursue an acting career and eventually landing in Los Angeles. "Both of my parents were from Illinois," she said. "I was born in Fort Worth, Texas, and we moved from Fort Worth to Springfield, Illinois, for about five minutes, then headed straight to St. Louis where my father worked for American Airlines at Lambert Field." But on the day of our interview she was just a laid-back woman in a café, conjuring up images of home. Here's a weekend with Kate Capshaw in the capital of the "show-me" state, St. Louis, Missouri.

Friday

LODGING I think that you have to be downtown if you go to St. Louis. Since I still have family there, it's been a really long time since I've stayed in hotels in St. Louis. But the **Adam's Mark** is a beautiful old hotel right downtown. I can't remember what we were in St. Louis for. I think we were there with the family and my mother hadn't moved into her "bigger home." She was in a very small apartment that couldn't hold all of us, so we ended up staying at the Adam's Mark. It's an old-fashioned hotel—very beautiful. The hotel is very high, so it's nice to get a room up high so you can see the whole city. You can walk pretty much everywhere.

DINNER I love going to restaurants on the Hill, which is an Italian community—a very, very tiny, tiny Italian working class community with probably the city's best restaurants. The

Hill is where Joe Garagiola and Yogi Berra grew up. I like it because it feels a little like—I'm sure people there will hate this or maybe they'll love it—but it feels a little like Queens or Brooklyn in New York. The houses are very small, they are very close together, they all look alike, and you know that the community and the neighbors all know each other and help raise each other's children. It's a real old-fashioned neighborhood feeling. One of my favorite restaurants on the Hill is **Dominic's**—gorgeous food. All the Italian restaurants feel really Italian. Dominic's is more traditional, old-fashioned. It's what we think of as an Italian restaurant, which is dark booths, low ceilings, great wine list.

ENTERTAINMENT There's a great jazz music world going on. My girlfriend Patti Gabriel is a St. Louis–based photographer who works commercially photographing people where they live and work. When I go to St. Louis, she'll take me someplace. I just get in the car and she takes me to clubs—**Jazz at the Bistro** [Grand Center] is really the place for jazz. Her husband is a musician who plays reeds and usually knows what's going on in town, jazz-wise. In an area called the Loop, where the college kids from Washington University hang out, there's **Blueberry Hill,** a restaurant and bar featuring memorabilia from the fifties and live contemporary music.

GAMBLING Go downtown, have a good meal, or go on the boat and gamble. They have gambling boats, most of which don't move, but you can gamble on the boat. I went on the boats when I was in high school, because that was a fun thing to do. A lot of times you would go to a dance, and then you would end up on the boat downtown.

Saturday

BREAKFAST Well, you have to start at **Krispy Kreme Donuts.** I could just go on a Krispy Kreme Donut fest in St. Louis. That's *Krispy* with a *K.* Oh, my God, they are unbelievable. You could be addicted to them. They are these juicy, unbelievable glazed donuts. They have a cream filled . . . Oh, I can't even think about it, they are so good. They are cool little places because you can watch the donuts being made.

SIGHTS You have the **Mississippi River** and you have the **Arch.** The Arch was being built when I had just started school. I remember them asking us to draw crayon pictures of it. So maybe I have something at the foot of the Arch, you know, one of those time capsule things. And they built that and there was nothing down there. It was just downtown. I don't want to say

> The Arch was being built when I had just started school. I remember them asking us to draw crayon pictures of it. They brought the Arch in, which brought a lot of tourist attention.

Lewis Portnoy

there was nothing, but it hadn't been renovated, so it was kind of a tired old St. Louis. They brought the Arch in, which brought a lot of tourist attention. Then they began over the last two decades to build up that area. They've completed the **City Museum**—everything in the museum is made from recycled materials. Then I would go to **Central West End.** That's *the* area. That's where the jazz clubs will be. There are art galleries, photography galleries. I would walk around there all day and sit outside and have an ice cream. **Laclede's Landing,** the riverfront, is an area that's been built up a lot. It's a cobblestone, streetlamp type of area with lots of restaurants and bars.

PARKS The main park in St. Louis is **Forest Park,** which borders the Central West End. Forest Park is where the World's Fair was. That whole area I find particularly interesting because it's really the heart of Old St. Louis per se. The homes that they built for the World's Fair in 1904 were all built there, and they're turn-of-the-century gorgeous. I mean, real seriously beautiful architecture. Those houses are still there. They are so beautiful with the stained glass windows—really, really gorgeous. The **St. Louis Zoo** is wonderful. That's in Forest Park. You can get the zoo, the art museum, the **Jewel Box,** an art deco greenhouse, and more in Forest Park. The park is pretty full service. There's also the **Missouri Botanical Gardens** [the Hill], one of the best in the country. My most positive memories are just sitting outside on a spring day. Missouri in the springtime is so beautiful with all the flowers and the trees blossoming; there are all these beautiful parks in St. Louis where you could sit and think. St. Louis is

a very relaxing place for me—it was relaxing growing up, and when I visit it's relaxing. Even with all the kids, it's just a quieter pace.

LUNCH I didn't go to the Hill while I was growing up because when you live in the suburbs, you don't leave the suburbs. In the suburbs, our night out was **Steak and Shake,** which is like McDonald's. For me, it's closely associated with growing up. But, that was our treat—to go to Steak and Shake. It's still there, although it's not drive-through now, but go-in. Steak and Shake is huge through the South and the Midwest. It was my dream to work there as a carhop. I didn't, but I wanted to when I was ten. I thought that would be so cool to run around in that black-and-white uniform and take orders. The hamburgers were really yummy. You could go there and get chili three ways. They put chili on top of spaghetti. They may have hot dogs, but they didn't when I was growing up. It was hamburgers and chili and chocolate sundaes. Now, of course, the menu includes salads and probably some idea that they are offering a lower fat diet. Steak and Shake is excellent.

SHOPPING The Frontenac area is beautiful. That's where **Plaza Frontenac** is, a mall with Neiman Marcus and Sak's Fifth Avenue. It's more upscale. You would probably find Eddie Bauer, and if there's a Gucci in St. Louis, that's where you would find it. The Ladue-Clayton area is where the rich people live. There are nice houses, shopping, and lots of little restaurants. You get your hair done in Clayton; you know you're going to get a good haircut. Famous-Barr [now **Macy's**] was a beautiful department store, really like Bloomingdale's. Back then, all I did was shop at Famous-Barr and I modeled there. It was my first job. I was thirteen and you could try out to be a model at Famous-Barr's. You went downtown—it's probably one of the first times I remember going downtown on a mission not to visit my aunt. I went downtown and tried out with probably five hundred other girls to be a model. And if you got the job, you worked on Saturdays modeling clothes in their tearoom. So that was exciting for me. There's **Union Station** [downtown], the train station that was recently renovated. They have some nice restaurants and shops. It's a beautiful structure.

CULTURE I think you have to go to Forest Park. They have a beautiful museum—the **St. Louis Art Museum.** It's a gorgeous museum and there are tons of things there. There are the *Water Lilies* by Monet, the Degas sculpture. Usually, museums have an architectural stamp that can be pretty strong. In my mind's eye, I don't have an image of it being an unusual looking building, but it is a beautiful museum, and it's very old.

HISTORY The **Lewis and Clark Center** [St. Charles] is interesting. St. Louis is where they started [their trek from the Mississippi River to the Pacific Ocean in 1804]. You have to remember that St. Louis was one of the most thriving cities of the Midwest, because it's where everyone moved when they left the East Coast. They came to St. Louis because of trading. You know, it's on the river, it was a big stop on the railroad to the West, and it was the last stop in some ways before you got to California. Not only does it have an urban feel, but St. Louis, at its best, is as exciting as New York City—it's just not as dense. It's beautiful because you have a diversity of people and cultures.

SIGHTS Do you know what's funny? You go to the **Anheuser Busch Brewery** [downtown] as a field trip when you are in grade school. They have the horses. You know, the Clydesdale horses. It's also a really beautiful brewery because it's very, very old; it's a beautiful building. The Clydesdales are stabled at the brewery. You'll see them pulling this coach. They're so famous—if you go to a football game and Anheuser Busch has anything to do with it, the Clydesdales are there. It's their trademark. The stables—that I remember. All this stuff you do when you're little and it's all still there and it's all still as beautiful.

SPORTS The **International Bowling Museum and Hall of Fame** [downtown] is in St. Louis. I made my friend Tom Hanks laugh one time so hard because I told him that in our high school, bowling was actually part of our PE program. Yes it was! Bowling! You should mention bowling. Bowling is very big. Why would it be so big in St. Louis? I don't know. Because it's cold and it's got long winters, you go to bowling alleys. It's the only form of exercise there is in the winter. We don't have ice hockey.

VIEW Go up in the Arch. Of course, I did. I went up when I was little, I went up when I was in high school, I went up one more time as a grown-up with my oldest daughter. Well, it's cool. I mean, you're in a capsule. It's sort of like being in a Ferris wheel, but you're enclosed.

There are no windows until you get to the top, and then when you get to the top, it's a pretty small area up there. You can get out. You go up over six hundred feet. You're inside and then it goes up, and of course, because the Arch is an arch, it's always adjusting, so you sit upright as you go up. It's a beautiful view; it's the "Gateway to the West."

DINNER I love **Bar Italia,** a great, little tiny café, almost like a bistro, very local in the Central West End. But you can go in and get beautiful, amazing meals. It's very casual, but something like Formica-top tables and leather chairs. I love going there because it is casual and, of course, Italian. I could take a couple of kids there, easily. I could go there very, very late with girlfriends. It has a great energy. I want to say it feels young—it has a younger crowd that comes, because it's not super expensive. There are lots of artists and photographers and architects. **Tony's** [downtown] is one of the best restaurants in St. Louis. Tony's is big, open, with a beautiful, modern feeling—beautiful paintings, gorgeous plates. Tony's has a beautiful wine list too. You get really serious meals at Tony's. It has a very modern, new interior—very fancy.

ENTERTAINMENT The Muny is fabulous in the summertime. They call it the Muny—it's short for the **Municipal Theater** [Forest Park]. It's the country's oldest and largest outdoor musical theater. Well, let me tell you, we went there several times every summer. That was a huge treat. It was outdoors, so you would pray it wouldn't rain. Meanwhile, St. Louis summers are about as hot and humid as they get,

so it's not very pleasant, but it's so exciting to sit there and have these live musicals going on in front of you. Then, there's the **Fox Theater** [Midtown]. Years ago, my mother worked as an usher at the Fox. I love this—they call it the "Fabulous Fox" theater. Well, it's old, 1929, and it's St. Louis's largest and most magnificent theater. I saw *Gone with the Wind* at the Fox. Because my mom worked there as an usher, she could get tickets to all of the shows.

Sunday

SNACK There's **Ted Drewe's Frozen Custard,** a great ice cream place where you can buy a "concrete." A concrete is a milk shake that when you turn it upside down it doesn't fall out, it's so thick. It's a great ice cream place.

BASEBALL If you're in St. Louis, you've got to go to a baseball game at **Busch Stadium** [downtown], and watch the **Cardinals.** They are awesome—they rock. I don't know how they are going to do this year, and I don't know how they did last year, but you've got to root for the Cardinals. Mark McGwire was, of course, a Cardinal—and Stan Musial. Cardinal games are fun. You get a hot dog and I never went when I was old enough to have a beer, but I imagine that's a cool thing to do.

WALK We rarely went downtown when I was growing up. I had an aunt that lived downtown, and when we went downtown, as a child, it was perceived as possibly being dangerous. I grew up in Florissant, a suburb in North County. There's an old Florissant, which is frequently referred to as "Historic Old Town Florissant, an early French settlement." It's pretty. None of these areas are going to be dense. You can walk through **Old Town Florissant,** which is very tiny. It's very Midwestern—it's very much like a farming community.

EXCURSION Go north, to Hannibal. Mark Twain was not from St. Louis, but he was right there in Hannibal, Missouri, only an hour and a half away. He based *The Adventures of Tom Sawyer* in Hannibal. If you have a feel for Midwestern simplicity, if you're interested in how rural America meets a kind of intelligence and how that plays out, then going to St. Louis and then taking a trip to Hannibal is a lovely thing to do. It's not like going to New York City and going to a Broadway show. It's a whole other trip. It's very quiet. Missouri has some beautiful rolling hills, but in this area, it's not so rolling. It's pretty flat. I'm sure you can stop along the side of the road anywhere and get some taffy. Then, there are the **Meramec Caverns.** [Part of the world's largest single cave formation, these caverns in Stanton were a hideout for Jesse James and his gang.] Those are wild. It's huge and it's wet and it's dark and it's chilly. We would go to Meramec Caverns and go in these caves. Of course, now you wouldn't be able to get me in a cave, but back then, it was like being in another world.

Kate Capshaw's St. Louis Essentials

LODGING
Adams Mark Hotel, $$, (314) 993-2326
315 Chestnut Street, downtown

DINING
Bar Italia, Italian, $$, (314) 361-7010
13 Maryland Plaza, Central West End

Dominic's, Italian, $$$$, (314) 771-1632
5101 Wilson Avenue, the Hill

Krispy Kreme, donuts, $,
multiple locations throughout St. Louis

Steak and Shake, American, $, (314) 447-0478
multiple locations throughout St. Louis

One Great Day in St. Louis

It was pretty exciting to watch the Arch being built. Truly, it started out as two aluminum columns, these huge squares that came up from the ground far apart in a park that was being developed. We watched over the course of two years. It was so forward, so modern. You would drive up to it and the reflection of the sun would hit you in the eyes. It was exciting to watch, but being young, of course, you couldn't understand how an architect could take these two very far apart squares and build them up and make them thinner and thinner and thinner and thinner and turn them and twist them and curve them where they would meet at the top. It seemed unfathomable. It's the same kind of thing as, How do jets get up in the air? How do you build a bridge? How do you get the tops of the Arch to touch, to connect? But, of course they did, and as it got closer and closer and closer, it became quite the attraction. You would drive from the suburbs an hour into the city and watch, and as it got closer and closer, depending on your view, it truly looked like they weren't going to connect. It looked like somebody made a big mistake and it was going to miss, but of course, it connected! And then, the first opportunity that we had to go up in the Arch, we did. Of course, that was the big thing in high school: to go underneath the Arch and kiss.

Ted Drewe's, frozen custard, $, (314) 481-2652
6726 Chippewa Street, Route 66

Tony's, Italian, $$$$, (314) 231-7007
410 Market Street, downtown

SIGHTS

Anheuser Busch Brewery, tours, (314) 577-2626
13th Street, downtown

Central West End, arts district,
west of Midtown, along the central corridor

City Museum, recycling museum, (314) 231-2489
701 North 15th Street, downtown

Forest Park, municipal park downtown

Gateway Arch, (314) 982-1410
707 North 1st Street, downtown

Hannibal, I-70 West to Highway 61 North

International Bowling Museum and Hall of Fame,
(314) 231-6340, 111 Stadium Plaza, downtown

The Jewel Box, art deco greenhouse, (314) 531-0080
Wells and McKinley Drive, Forest Park

Lacledes Landing, shopping/dining district,
(314) 241-5875, Riverfront

Lewis and Clark Boathouse and Nature Center,
(636) 947-3199, 1050 Riverside Drive, St. Charles

Meramec Caverns, tours, (800) 676-6105
I-44 West, Stanton

Missouri Botanical Gardens, (314) 577-9400
4344 Shaw Boulevard, the Hill

Old Town Florissant, historic district,
Florissant, downtown

St. Louis Art Museum, (314) 721-0072
1 Fine Arts Drive, Forest Park

St. Louis Cardinals, baseball, (314) 345-9600
Busch Stadium, downtown

St. Louis Zoo, (314) 781-0900
1 Government Drive, Forest Park

SHOPPING

Macy's, department store, (314) 726-1810
multiple locations throughout St. Louis

Plaza Frontenac, upscale mall, (314) 432-0604
97 Plaza Frontenac, Frontenac

Union Station, shopping complex, (314) 421-6655
1820 Market Street, downtown

NIGHTLIFE

Blueberry Hill, live music, (314) 727-4444
6504 Delmar Boulevard, The Loop

Fox Theater, live performances, (314) 534-1678
527 North Grand Boulevard, Midtown

Jazz at the Bistro, live music, (314) 534-3663
3536 Washington, Grand Center

The Municipal Theater, outdoor musical theater,
(314) 361-1900, Forest Park

San Diego

Annette Bening was an Academy Award nominee for her roles in *American Beauty* and *Being Julia*. The wife of Warren Beatty and mother of four children, she stars with the likes of Michael Douglas (playing the president's love interest in *The American President*), Harrison Ford (*Regarding Henry*), and Robert DeNiro (*Guilty By Suspicion*). In the beginning, however, Bening was a mall girl, a dive boat fry cook, and a walk-on wannabe actress at the Old Globe Theater. She was, in short, a child of San Diego, one of a million from someplace else (born in Topeka, Kansas), at one with the whales, the ocean, and the constant Southern California sunshine. From the San Diego suburb of San Carlos, she was accepted by the American Conservatory Theater in San Francisco, appearing in summer Shakespearean festivals and regional productions before moving to New York and appearing on Broadway. Her star turned in *The Grifters*, which won her the first of three Academy Award nominations. And while you'll surely see her walking across the stage at the Oscar ceremonies, here's a walk down the beaches where Annette Bening's star first shone.

Friday

LODGING Well, of course, there's the **Del Coronado,** which is on Coronado Island and is just beautiful. Now they have added on quite a bit to the hotel, so it's no longer just what it originally was, but *Some Like It Hot* was shot there. The hotel is really pretty and it sits right on the beach. If you remember, there are some scenes in *Some Like It Hot* where they are sitting out in their little cabanas. The hotel has an old-fashioned sort of feeling about it. For me, it also brings back memories of proms and things. When I was a kid growing up, they only had a ferry that went back and forth across the harbor. It was really fun. Now, there's a stunningly beautiful bridge that goes across to Coronado. It's a great ride as well as a great hotel.

DINNER One of my favorites is the **Bali Hai,** which sits right on the harbor. The food is Polynesian, I guess you would call it. It's kind of one of those corny theme restaurants, but it's nice. You can watch the boats going in and out. The harbor activity in San Diego is stunning. I worked on a boat that went out of Shelter Island when I was a kid. I started scuba diving and then I worked as a cook on a scuba diving boat, and Bali Hai is in the part of the harbor that we went out of. If you go to the Bali Hai, you can sit and watch the harbor, which is really beautiful. **Mr. A's** is downtown in a high-rise building. It's called Mr. A's, as in Alessio, because that was one of the old families of San Diego, and it's a restaurant that sits way up on top of downtown at the top of the hill. You have a view of the entire city and that's also a really special fun place to go. The food is fish and steak. For the newer kind of hipper cuisine there's a place called **California Cuisine** [Hillcrest].

ENTERTAINMENT I would have to give the **Old Globe Theater** a plug. It's a regional non-profit repertory company in **Balboa Park,** which is the enormous park and recreation area right in the middle of San Diego. The Old Globe Theater is one of the oldest regional theaters in the country. Every summer they do a Shakespeare Festival and they have an outdoor theater, and then they also have an ongoing season all year round. A wonderful man named Jack O'Brien runs it. When I was in college, I got a walk-on in one of the "pre-show" entertainments for one of the Old Globe's plays. I literally walked across the stage. I tried out for plays there, but I never got a part. I hope to someday go back and do a play there.

Saturday

BREAKFAST There was a place on College Avenue, just a little coffee shop. I was thinking about it the other day because I had a boyfriend at the time who I was so impressed with, and I remember he took me there and showed me how to put salt in the tomato juice and I thought that was so cool. The place isn't there now, but the **La Valencia Hotel** in La Jolla is good for breakfast. It's one of the older, classier hotels in the San Diego area, very Spanish looking, and it sits up on a block overlooking the ocean. You can look over **La Jolla Cove,** the famous cove where people go diving.

SIGHTS Of course, the **San Diego Zoo** [Balboa Park] is this famous, famous zoo—a

Lowell Davies Festival Theatre; photo by Craig Schwartz

I would have to give the Old Globe Theater a plug. It's a regional nonprofit repertory company in Balboa Park, which is the enormous park and recreation area right in the middle of San Diego. The Old Globe Theater is one of the oldest regional theaters in the country.

really great zoo, a stunningly beautiful zoo. It's the kind of zoo you can go to and not be depressed for the animals. One of their most famous exhibitions is the orangutans and the gorillas. They have it set up where there's a glass partition and you can get real close to the gorillas. They come down and sit and you can watch them. There's also an extraordinary aviary that you can walk into and see all these wonderful exotic birds. Oh, the other thing that was always really fun was the seal show, and they have a wonderful reptile house. They have a children's zoo where you can feed the animals and pet them.

BEACHES We spent a lot of time at **Ocean Beach,** although I don't really know how Ocean Beach is anymore. **La Jolla Shores** is a great beach, the main big beach in La Jolla. It's a big stretch with lots of parking, big lifeguard stations, lots of snack bars and restrooms. Really clean. You can rent the little rafts and boogie boards and all the stuff that you need to go swimming. There you'll find La Jolla Cove, which is just a smaller enclosed cove that's a nice place to swim. The **La Jolla Beach and Tennis Club** is right on La Jolla Shores beach and it's a great hotel, very fancy.

LUNCH Harbor Island, which is across the road from the airport, is a long, skinny peninsula and a really nice place to stroll. There's a restaurant there called **Tom Ham's Lighthouse** that's really cool. It sits right on the harbor. We don't go there because of the food; we go because of the spot. You can sit there and watch the boats go by. At night it's really pretty because it's all lit up. And you can see the

Coronado Bridge, which I mentioned is a very beautiful bridge, and you can look at the aircraft carriers and sit across the harbor on the other side, because the other side, of course, is Coronado Island, which is mainly a naval base.

SHOPPING I was a mall girl—we would go to the shops and hang out. There's a big one, the **Fashion Valley Center.** La Jolla is a really good place for shops. It has really eclectic and more high-end shopping. You could also wander the beach streets of Ocean Beach and find funky little shops that have wonderful things as well. **Horton Plaza** is a shopping and restaurant area downtown, which has been revitalized and cleaned up. Then there's **Old Town,** which is the old historical part of the city that has been preserved, and it's mainly Spanish in feel. There are a lot of places to walk around to buy souvenirs. You can get great food there, there's lots of music, lots of mariachis, lots of shops, and lots of history. That's the oldest part of the city and near the **Cabrillo Mission,** which is where the first of California's missions were built [the old, orignal Spanish churches that stretch along the coast].

CULTURE All the museums are in Balboa Park: the **Art Museum,** the **Automotive Museum,** the **Aerospace Museum,** the **Spanish Village Art Center,** the **Timken Museum of Art**—and more. Balboa Park is, of course, a very spacious, twelve-hundred-acre park. There's lots of green grass, lots of open areas. There's lawn bowling, there are people jogging, and the Laurel Street Bridge that goes over one of the highways and is fun to walk across. In La Jolla, a very posh high-end beach community, there's the **Museum of Contemporary Art.** They have works from Warhol, Rauschenburg, Stella, a lot of California artists. If I only had time to go to one museum, it would be that one. You can go to the **La Jolla Play House,** which has been around for a long time. It's a very hot, very contemporary, well-funded theater. They do a lot of stuff there that eventually moves to New York.

SPORTING You can hike **Cabrillo National Monument** on Point Loma [a monument to the first European expedition to set foot, in 1542, on what would later become the west coast of the United States]. The end of Point Loma is a peninsula into the ocean next to the harbor, and you can drive out to the end of it. There must still be a lighthouse out there. You can walk around the monument and hike around. Or you can go into the **Anza-Borrego Desert State Park,** which is on the other side of San Diego, and look at the stars. I went camping there as a kid. Anytime you go way out into the ocean or way out into the desert, you can see the stars much better.

COCKTAILS There's a wonderful bar and restaurant at the **La Jolla Beach and Tennis Club** that's famous for high tide. The waves come crashing up on the windows. It's really fun. My parents went there again the other day for their anniversary. That's a really nice place to stay, as well. But if you have a drink or a meal and you want to sit by the ocean, go at high tide, when the waves will crash right onto the glass.

DINNER Anthony's Fish Grotto, right on the harbor, is one of the old, established, great restaurants. It sits next to one of the tourist attractions that's been there forever—the *Star of India,* which is this old schooner with sails that they've refurbished and you can run around on it.

Sunday

NATURE Torrey Pines is the beach community directly north of La Jolla. It's very beautiful. There's a kind of tree called the Torrey Pine and they are an extremely rare native pine tree. There are only something like six thousand Torrey Pines in this area. Some of them grow fifty feet tall on the cliffs. There's a hang gliding port there. You can drive out to these huge cliffs on the north side of La Jolla in Torrey Pines, where they literally put the hang glider on and then jump off of the cliff over the ocean. There's the **Torrey Pines Municipal Golf Course,** a really beautiful golf course, which is surrounded by Torrey Pines.

WHALE WATCHING When I was working on the boat, we'd go to the **Coronado Islands,** which are about thirty miles off of San Diego. They're Mexico-owned, but you can dive there. During the whale migration, the big gray whales come in between the mainland and Coronado Island. On some days two hundred whales pass the San Diego coast. It's amazing! They are really, really beautiful animals and they migrate all the way down to Scammon's Lagoon in Mexico, where they give birth. During the right season, you will see lots of whales. I was sitting on Ocean Beach once and saw a whale go by. They have to come up to breathe, so you can always see them as they are traveling down the coast. It's an amazing sight.

Annette Bening's San Diego Essentials

LODGING
Hotel Del Coronado, $$$$, (619) 435-6611
1500 Orange Avenue, Coronado

DINING
Anthony's Fish Grotto, seafood, $$$, (619) 232-5105
1360 North Harbor Drive, Harbor Island

Bali Hai, Polynesian, $$$, (619) 222-1181
2230 Shelter Island Drive, Point Loma

California Cuisine, California, $$$, (619) 543-0790
1027 University Avenue, Hillcrest

La Jolla Beach and Tennis Club, American, $$$,
(858) 454-7126, 2000 Spindrift Drive, La Jolla

La Valencia Hotel Restaurant, California, $$$,
(858) 454-0771, 1132 Prospect Street, La Jolla

Mr. A's, American, $$$$, (619) 239-1377
2550 5th Avenue, Baker's Hill

Tom Ham's Lighthouse, American, $$$, (619) 291-9110
800 Harbor Island Drive, Harbor Island

SIGHTS
Anza-Borrego Desert State Park, (760) 767-4205
200 Palm Canyon Drive, Borrego Springs

Cabrillo Mission, www.nps.gov/cabr

Cabrillo National Monument, (619) 557-5450
1800 Cabrillo Memorial Drive, Point Loma

Coronado Bridge, www.coronado.ca.us/bridge

Coronado Islands, diving and whale watching,
www.coronadovisitors.com

La Jolla Cove, diving, (888) 525-6552, 1100 Coast
Boulevard

La Jolla Shores, beach, 8200 Camino del Oro

Museum of Contemporary Art, (858) 454-3541
700 Prospect Street, La Jolla

Ocean Beach, 1950 Abbott Street

San Diego Aerospace Museum, (619) 234-8291
2001 Pan American Place, Balboa Park

San Diego Art Institute, (619) 236-0011
1439 El Prado, Balboa Park

San Diego Automotive Museum, (619) 231-2886
2080 Pan American Place, Balboa Park

One Unforgettable Day in San Diego

I was a cook on a scuba diving boat. I was a very mediocre cook. I would make scrambled eggs and toast and bacon and sausage and grilled cheese sandwiches and hamburgers. Usually, we would go to San Clemente Island, which is an island about sixty miles off the coast of San Diego. But once we were hired by the Bureau of Land Management to take a bunch of scientists on a trip to a place called Tanner Banks, which was an area hundreds of miles out. The scientists wanted to record the life that was there. We were supposed to be there for about five days, but after we dropped anchor, a big, big, big storm came up and the skipper was a little confused about what to do. We were basically just hanging on. We were all in the pilothouse, the poor passengers down below. The most dangerous thing that can happen to you in a storm is to get sideways. That's when you can tip over. So it was very dramatic. The nose of the boat would go into the water, and the water would completely cover the boat and then the boat would come up back out of the wave and again, pull, pull, pull on the anchor chain, and then slam back down into the water. It did that over and over for quite a long time until the anchor chain snapped, and . . . We got through being sideways safely and then we basically just got out of there. It was like the biggest surf ride I had ever had in my life.

San Diego Zoo, (619) 231-1515
2920 Zoo Drive, Balboa Park

Spanish Village Art Center, (619) 233-9050
1770 Village Place, Balboa Park

Timken Museum of Art, (619) 239-5548
1500 El Prado, Balboa Park

SHOPPING
Fashion Valley Center, mall, (619) 688-9113
7007 Friars Road, Mission Valley

Horton Plaza, mall, (619) 239-8180
324 Horton Plaza, downtown

Old Town San Diego, shopping area, (619) 291-4903
San Diego Avenue at Twiggs Street, Old Town

THEATER
La Jolla Playhouse, live theater, (858) 550-1010
2910 La Jolla Village Drive, La Jolla

Old Globe Theater, Shakespearean theater,
(619) 234-5623, 1363 Old Globe Way, Balboa Park

GOLF
Torrey Pines Golf Course, (800) 985-4653
11480 North Torrey Pines Road, La Jolla

San Francisco

He may have left his heart in San Francisco, but these days Tony Bennett is all over the map. The entertainer that Frank Sinatra called "the best singer in the business" has completely reinvented himself. Bennett—an Italian immigrant grocer's son, originally christened Anthony Dominick Benedetto—got his stage name in 1949 from a suggestion by Bob Hope, according to Bennett's autobiography, *The Good Life*. He's become as popular with the MTV crowd as with those who grew up with his music. But there is yet another side to Bennett: he's also an artist who paints daily, even while touring. Whenever he's ready to return to his spiritual home, he trades his songbooks for his artist's easel and returns to the "Paris of the United States" that gave him his first hit. Here's a weekend with the crooner in the City by the Bay.

Friday

LODGING I like either the **Mark Hopkins** [Nob Hill] or the **Fairmont Hotel** [Nob Hill], but there are so many great ones—the **Ritz-Carlton** [Nob Hill] is beautiful also. My niece was the interior decorator for the **Sheraton** and she did a spectacular job. The best romantic hotel I know is the **Inn at the Opera** [Civic Center]. Very small, very elegant. There's a small beautiful restaurant and intimate, quaint, delightful rooms—like a touch of Paris. All the great classical musicians stay there. I usually paint in the Sutter Suite in the Fairmont. There is a magnificent view of **Coit Tower** [Telegraph Hill] and the **Golden Gate Bridge,** and also beautiful views of the rolling hills and the downtown buildings.

ENTERTAINMENT *Beach Blanket Babylon* [North Beach] is a show that's sold out for years and years. I love it. The crew is always original and they do satires on everything: society personalities, show business, and political personalities. They have big, giant hats—like the Golden Gate Bridge on top of their heads. It's always fresh, it's always new, and they've got a great crew. It's amazing to me that this one theater has never had anything but sold-out seats every single night. The tourists love it, the people in town love it, and they are very famous in San Francisco. They do satires on very bizarre kinds of things that make everybody cheer and laugh.

Saturday

BREAKFAST Sear's is a famous little breakfast place right near the St. Francis Hotel. On a Sunday or Saturday, there are lines waiting to get in—it's very famous in San Francisco. The owners and the waitresses and waiters are so friendly to everybody, and they give you the best breakfast that you could ever have anywhere in the world. It's not quickies—it's food very, very well served; the cooking is extra special. Anything they have in there is very delicious.

SIGHTS I love to paint different places in San Francisco. I like the hills. I like the way the beautiful buildings look. I'm always looking for the light and there's so much of it there—the sailboats in the day and the Golden Gate Bridge and **Coit Tower** [a 210-foot cylindrical column completed in 1924 at the top of Telegraph Hill], which was given by Mrs. Lillie Coit to the firemen that saved so many people during the earthquake in the early 1900s. In San Francisco, Coit Tower is like the Statue of Liberty. I can paint these places over and over again. I've painted the **Japanese Gardens** many times. They remind me of Kyoto, Japan, which is the most spiritual

place in the world. I've done **Lombard Street** on Russian Hill, the crookedest street in the world. It's beautiful, filled with flowers. I've painted **Fisherman's Wharf.** I painted the workers as they take their shovels and put the big heaps of fish into big pails.

I like the cable car that goes right down to Fisherman's Wharf, where the cable cars turn around. I usually would start right at the top of **Nob Hill** and go all the way down. On the cable cars you'll see tourists, but also the natives who live there. They are so proud of their city and not in an artificial way. They just think it's the greatest place they could ever live in and welcome any excuse to have a parade or a celebration. It's almost comparable to the natives of Rio de Janeiro. Any excuse to have a little party or to have a celebration, everybody shows up—all the politicians, the mayor, the chief of police, and the cable car executives.

Beach Blanket Babylon is a show that's sold out for years and years. I love it! The crew is always original and they do satires on everything: society personalities, show business, and political personalities. They have big, giant hats—like the Golden Gate Bridge on top of their heads.

David Allen/Larry Merkle

SHOPPING I like **Macy's** right downtown. I just like the whole atmosphere of it. But **Wilkes Bashford** [Union Square] is my favorite. They have beautiful clothes there, European. They have Brioni suits and everything top of the line. They treat you great and you can't get better clothes. I just bought a beautiful cashmere jacket for the fall. It's so mellow. I can't believe it's so smooth; it's cut just right.

LUNCH The **Big Four** restaurant in the Huntington Hotel is called the Big Four for the four men who founded Nob Hill. It's a beautiful room—very dark and clubby with a fire always going. The service is great and it's wonderful quality food. In the bathroom, they have a wraparound picture of San Francisco before the earthquake. Sometimes I go to Fisherman's Wharf, where all the boats and great restaurants are. At the outdoor fish stands you'll see big, giant lobsters and great Dungeness crabs. Just go from stand to stand, listening to all the guys selling all their wares. You can have a good picnic right on the wharf

CULTURE I love the **Asian Art Museum**— that's fantastic. My great late friend, Cyril Magnin, a very philanthropic man, gave them two rooms full of green Chinese jade. There's unbelievable artwork in that place. It's especially memorable to me because I used to love hanging out with Cyril.

EXERCISE Walking is great because you gotta go uphill, which is really a tremendously exhilarating experience—very aerobic. [According to the city archivist, San Francisco has forty-two hills; the two steepest, at a 31.5 percent gradi-

ent, are Filbert Street between Leavenworth and Hyde, and 22nd Street between Church and Vicksburg.] I like to walk around the top of Nob Hill. There's **Huntington Park** right on the top of Nob Hill. I go there and sketch a lot. Watching the little kids on the swings and playing in the sand—it's all very enjoyable to me. Under the Golden Gate Bridge, there's a wonderful, wonderful walk; it's right by the ocean, the boat basin. But the Fairmont has the best facilities. I play tennis all the time. I go to the **San Francisco Tennis Club** [Nob Hill] and the Fairmont downstairs has the best workout room that I've ever seen. It's state-of-the-art, all the equipment that really works—the bicycles and the weight presses.

DINNER There's the famous garlic restaurant, the **Stinking Rose** [North Beach]. Go there for fun—it's garlic supreme! You get garlic on any sort of menu item you want. The Stanford Court Hotel has the restaurant, **Fournou's Ovens** [Nob Hill], where they have an open kitchen and they grill everything. Then there's the **Fior d'Italia** [North Beach], a restaurant with a little Tony Bennett room for me with all my gold records and paraphernalia—pictures of me singing with Judy Garland or standing with Ed Sullivan. [The room has since been reduced to the Tony Bennett booth.]

THEATER There are a lot of theaters that have legitimate plays. I saw *The Trials of Oscar Wilde* at **Theater on the Square** with the most amazing cast. They were all American actors that imitated British people. Usually it's the British who do a good job of imitating Americans, but this was flawless—it didn't once sound phony. One of my favorite theaters is the **Masonic Auditorium** on the top of Nob Hill. I like it because it's just so intimate. It's big, but you get on the stage and you feel like everybody has a front row seat.

ENTERTAINMENT The **Fairmont Hotel** has great jazz, famous jazz musicians. Of course, there are jazz and pop rooms everywhere. Whenever I see that hotel, I remember what Johnny Mathis's father said to me. I met him at the bottom of San Francisco and he said, "Where are you playing?" I said, "The Fairmont." He said, "In our town, if you play the top of Nob Hill, you've hit the top." The **Louise M. Davies Symphony Hall** [Civic Center] is a tremendous concert hall. I did a command performance there for the queen and Prince Philip. It's San Francisco's Carnegie Hall. Then there's the **Great American Music Hall** [Polk Gulch]—a lot of great jazz and folk music in that place.

There's the **Plush Room** [downtown], which is like the Algonquin Hotel in New York.

Sunday

WORSHIP Grace Cathedral [Nob Hill] is gorgeous, very special and very well built, and one of the great things to look at. At night, when they light the stained glass windows up, it looks like the aurora borealis. All those beautiful colors in the stained glass.

LUNCH Right over the Golden Gate Bridge is an artists' colony called **Sausalito.** Sculptors, painters, graphic artists—they live there. It has magnificent views of the city, looking back on San Francisco. The weather there is magical. Whenever it's a foggy day in San Francisco, you just go over that Golden Gate Bridge and 98 percent of the time you get to Sausalito and the sun will be out. For lunch in Sausalito, I like the

One Great Night in San Francisco

It was early 1961 when I first sang "the song" in San Francisco during a two-week engagement at the [now defunct] Venetian Room in the Fairmont Hotel. I was completely unknown in town. I had been warned that it was a very cold city—if they don't know you, you have a tough time with the audience. The room was packed. It was right about one quarter through the show before I sang it. I mentioned Douglas Cross and George Corey, who wrote the song. I mentioned that they were native San Franciscans and said, "They wrote this song about your great city." As soon as I finished singing, the place exploded. The recording representatives came running up to me at the end of the show and said, "You must record this song!" I thought it was going to be a local song. I had no idea it would become an international hit and become my signature song for the rest of my life. It's made me a world citizen, being commissioned to sing it in six command performances, for seven American presidents. The best kick is to hear it in the karaoke bars in Asia, the song everybody sings when they're learning English in South Korea, Kuala Lumpur, and Bangkok, dreaming of coming to America. The greatest moment for me was when the *New York Times* mentioned that at the end of the Vietnam War the homesick soldiers were sitting around the campfire singing "I Left My Heart in San Francisco."

Alta Mira. It's very famous and almost ancient at this point. It's been there almost a hundred years. Wonderful food, wonderful atmosphere. You sit out in the sun on a beautiful day and watch all the boats go by.

Tony Bennett's San Francisco Essentials

LODGING
Fairmont Hotel, $$$$, (415) 772-5000
950 Mason Street, Nob Hill

Inn at the Opera, $$, (415) 863-8400
333 Fulton Street, Civic Center

Mark Hopkins Inter-Continental, $$$$, (415) 392-3434
1 Nob Hill, Nob Hill

The Ritz-Carlton, $$$$, (415) 296-7465
600 Stockton Street, Nob Hill

Sheraton Fisherman's Wharf, $$$, (415) 362-5500
2500 Mason Street, Fisherman's Wharf

DINING
Alta Mira, continental, $$$, (415) 332-1350
125 Buckley Avenue, Sausalito

The Big Four, continental, $$$$, (415) 771-1140
1075 California Street, Huntington Hotel, Nob Hill

Fior d'Italia, Italian, $$, (415) 986-1886
2237 Mason Street, North Beach

Fournou's Ovens, California, $$$$, (415) 989-1910
905 California Street, Stanford Court Hotel, Nob Hill

Sear's Fine Foods, casual, $$, (415) 986-0700
439 Powell Street, Union Square

The Stinking Rose, Italian, $$, (415) 781-7673
253 Columbus Avenue, North Beach

SIGHTS
Asian Art Museum, (415) 581-3500
200 Larkin Street, Civic Center

Coit Tower, (415) 362-0808, 1 Telegraph Hill

Fisherman's Wharf, Mason and the Embarcadero

Golden Gate Bridge, (415) 921-5858, Highway 101

Huntington Park, Nob Hill

Japanese Tea Garden, (415) 668-0909
Golden Gate Park

Lombard Street, Russian Hill

Sausalito, artists' colony,
across the Golden Gate Bridge from San Francisco

SHOPPING
Macy's, department store, (415) 397-3333
170 O'Farrell Street, Union Square

Wilkes Bashford, designer clothing, (415) 986-4380
375 Sutter Street, Union Square

NIGHTLIFE/ENTERTAINMENT
Beach Blanket Babylon, live performances,
(415) 421-4222, 678 Green Street, North Beach

Great American Music Hall, live music, (415) 885-0750
859 O'Farrell Street, Polk Gulch

Louise M. Davies Symphony Hall, live music,
(415) 864-6000, 201 Van Ness Avenue, Civic Center

Nob Hill Masonic Center, live performances,
(415) 776-4702, 1111 California Street, Nob Hill

The Plush Room, live music, (415) 885-2800
940 Sutter Street, downtown

Theater on the Square, live performances,
(415) 433-9500, 450 Post Street, Union Square

TENNIS
San Francisco Tennis Club, (415) 777-9000
645 5th Street, Fairmont Hotel, Nob Hill

WORSHIP
Grace Cathedral, (415) 749-6300
1100 California Street, Nob Hill

Ashley Judd

San Francisco

Ashley Judd spent part of grade school in the Bay Area with her mother, Naomi, and sister, Wynonna, who later became the dynamic country-singing duo known as the Judds. But it was her grandmother's long-time house in the city's beloved Pacific Heights area that made Ashley a spiritual San Franciscan.

Judd is a rare combination of brains and beauty—a Phi Beta Kappa nominee and honors graduate of the University of Kentucky, with a major in French and four minors. But the city of San Francisco speaks more to her soul than her intellect. She returned to the city to film *Someone Like You*, a romantic comedy costarring Greg Kinnear. Back then, romantic comedy was something of a departure for Judd, who had starred in thrillers like *Double Jeopardy* opposite Tommy Lee Jones, *Eye of the Beholder* with Ewan McGregor, and *Heat* alongside Robert De Niro, Al Pacino, and Val Kilmer. Judd's informal acting training began in childhood. While her mother and sister put their energies into music, Ashley turned toward the world of books, spending her childhood playing the literary characters in her mind. She attended a dozen different schools in Kentucky, Tennessee, and California before the Judds became country-western superstars.

After college, she set aside her dreams of joining the Peace Corps and followed her sister's suggestion to move to L.A. to become an actress. After some midlevel TV fare, she entered the mainstream movie world with the hit independent film *Ruby in Paradise*. But here's a weekend where a piece of Ashley's heart will always remain—San Francisco.

Friday

LODGING I love the **El Drisco Hotel** because it's in Pacific Heights. There are majestic views of the bay and the bridge and the hills of Marin County. Pacific Heights is terrific for getting some exercise. You can walk at a leisurely pace, or you can turn it up a notch when you go up and down those hills. Pacific Heights is aesthetically one of the most pleasing cosmopolitan neighborhoods in America, and the El Drisco is a great big wonderful old home that's been converted into a luxury hotel. The prices are not prohibitively expensive. It's very charming and very sweet and has this incredible bonus of being close to Fillmore and Union streets, which have my favorite poking-around shopping. Another really good hotel is the **Renaissance Stanford Court** [Nob Hill]. They really took great care of me. We were shooting at night and I needed to sleep during the day. It was quiet and room service was really delicious and very fast. They had great towels and slippers—all the stuff that you look for. It's also within walking distance of all the nice shops.

DINNER On a Friday night I would go to **Florio.** It's on Fillmore and it's terrific French [now Mediterranean]. Of course, they've got the required steak pommes frites. The people at Florio were always cool. They would let me sit in the window, which was not really part of the restaurant, so my pups could come in and lie on the floor. We would pretend to be in France.

Saturday

SIGHTS I love the **Marina,** which has free parking—another indication of what a terrific city San Francisco is. It's so geared toward a genuinely easy quality of life. You just go down to the Marina and hop out of your car and you can join a spontaneous game of volleyball or touch football on the Marina Green. Or you can walk out to the base of the **Golden Gate Bridge** and you've got the beautiful city skyline behind you. Then there are the hills of the Marina, with very little development. There's **Sausalito,** where you can see a little bit of the Marina and can see some of the houses built on the hills in

Tiburon. So much of that area is still untouched. It is constantly reminding us, I think, of the balance that we should strike between development and preserving our wide-open spaces. They're doing a big restoration project at the moment on the Marina, where they are encouraging a healthier and stronger natural habitat. I love it down there.

SHOPPING A little home furnishings store is **Sue Fisher King** [downtown]. I bought a fantastic woven tote bag there and it was only eighteen bucks. It's in such a high-end neighborhood, but they are not absurd in their pricing. A place that gave me a lot of pleasure in San Francisco is called **Ixia** [Upper Market], which is a florist. I spoke with them on the telephone and I described what my apartment was like. They never saw the interior of it, and every single week they sent over arrangements that were perfectly suited to my style and taste. **Union Square** is great for shopping. We were shooting at night, I was sick, I didn't have an assistant, and I still managed to get all my Christmas shopping done on Maiden Lane, which radiates out of Union Square. They have all the nice shops. I thought that the **Prada** store had a particularly good selection. A lot of Prada is ubiquitous, but they had stuff that I had never seen before, which is really saying something. Everybody is really down-to-earth in San Francisco. Nobody is snooty. **Wilkes Bashford** [Union Square] is a great store. They've got a terrific buyer—a very eclectic mix. It's men's and women's.

HIKING My entertainment consisted of hiking in **John Muir Woods.** It's just unbelievable how accessible and beautiful everything is. One time I went into the bottom of Muir Woods, where they've built platforms because there are so many people who go there that it's as populated as a shopping mall. But there was something wonderfully spirited about it because you knew that all these folks were going to be around these extraordinary old trees and breathe the fresh air. You can hike to the beach or you can do something more challenging by going up all the wonderfully marked and very educational trails. When you're among those one-thousand-year-old redwoods, you feel liberated and you feel a sense of awe. I think it definitely encourages a sense of responsibility to living more peacefully and less aggressively with our resources.

LUNCH If I could only eat one thing in San Francisco, it would be the fried-egg pizza at **Rose's Cafe** [Cow Hollow]. Rose's has outdoor seating, and they have little dog treats on the menu. I always start with a little dish of olives because I love good black olives, and they make a polenta. It's a little bit like a breakfast polenta with slightly spicy tomato sauce on top of it, so it's like a cross between Cream of Wheat and a polenta dinner entree. But go for the fried-egg pizza. It's a super-thin, wood-fired pizza with fontina cheese and fried eggs and strips of ham—and, of course, I have to pour olive oil all over the whole thing, too. For some reason when I'm there, I always want Coca-Cola. I do not drink soda pop, but something about the saltiness of the olives and the polenta makes it a Coca-Cola kind of day. The **Balboa**

My entertainment consisted of hiking in John Muir Woods. It's just unbelievable how accessible and beautiful everything is.

Cafe [Cow Hollow] is always great for lunch. They've got two different kinds of burgers—the Balboa Burger that comes on a baguette, or the Bar Burger, which comes on a homemade bun. It's a bit like a brasserie with a lot of good comfort food. You definitely get full.

BOOKS City Lights Booksellers and Publishers [North Beach] is so cool—funky and fabulous. I love it. You definitely get in touch with your inner fire to help change the world there. Sometimes all the books in the window are so negative. You have to be careful about how much of that stuff you expose yourself to at one moment. I love to go in and buy leftist magazines and get all fired up. I'm into reading the *Nation* every week. They have a huge magazine section.

HERBS AND ELIXERS Chinatown is great. I actually got really sick with bronchitis

National Park Service

while we were filming, and my makeup artist went to Chinatown and talked to a man who put together packages of herbs and roots. She boiled it for me and I drank these very pungent potions to get better; I'm certain it helped. Herbal shops are all around Chinatown. I sort of say the older the person, the more credible the establishment. The older and more wizened the owner's appearance, the more likely he is to have good advice and profound experience with herbs and roots. I don't recommend that people take the herbs wantonly. They have very strong medicinal effects.

DINNER PlumpJack Cafe [Cow Hollow], owned by the same folks who own the Balboa Cafe, is another San Francisco institution. It's small, with really nice, attentive service. It's a pretty calm, soothing atmosphere. I particularly love the salads. They mix them up with different kinds of nuts and dried fruit, and you could make a very good meal out of a salad and a light entree. PlumpJack has a terrific wine list. The owners also own a wine store, so if you're in the mood for a certain kind of burgundy, but you want to be adventuresome and maybe try something that you've not had before, you can have a conversation with them about it. I made it a policy while in San Francisco never to spend more than thirty dollars on a bottle of wine in a restaurant, and we always had the most delicious stuff.

Sunday

EXCURSION For Christmas I gave my sister and her boyfriend two nights at the **Post Ranch Inn** in Big Sur [about 150 miles south of San Francisco]. It's fantastic. It's really expensive, though—the most expensive hotel in America that we've ever stayed at, so we don't go there that much. You literally have individual free-standing rooms that are built into the cliff overlooking the Pacific Ocean. One night that we were there, there was a lightning storm out at sea. God put on a pretty fantastic show. We stayed there once in 1991 or 1992. My family, my mom, and my sister and Pop and everybody,

One Great Day in San Francisco

An amazing thing happened in **Presidio Park,** which is really beautiful. On Thanksgiving Day, I joined some childhood friends from Kentucky for a touch football game. It's like a Saturday game that the same group of people get together to play. I met so many nice young people. A lot of young married people, people who were about to start families, which was a great environment for my fiancé and me to be in, since we were in a parallel situation in our personal lives. I woke up and thought, *You know, that's a really American thing to do on Thanksgiving. Go to a beautiful public park and just get rowdy playing touch football with a bunch of strangers.* Then one day when we took the pups down to the Marina and walked out to the bridge, we ran into two different people that we had met at the touch football game on Thanksgiving Day. It's just that kind of a city where it's open and friendly—it's accessible. Everyone is so oriented to the outdoors. It's in the most beautiful, natural setting of any American city, and I'm just always happy there—San Francisco makes me happy.

and I took a motorcycle trip from the Bay Area down Highway 1 to Malibu. I rode on the back of my sister's Harley. When we got to Post Ranch Inn, I crashed her bike in the parking lot right in front of the whole welcoming staff. I showed up there sometime after that and the guy was like, "You been riding your bike any?" I was so embarrassed that they remembered.

Ashley Judd's San Francisco Essentials

LODGING
El Drisco Hotel, $$$, (415) 346-2880
2901 Pacific Avenue, Pacific Heights

Post Ranch Inn, $$$$, (800) 527-2200
Highway 1, Big Sur

Renaissance Stanford Court Hotel, $$$, (415) 989-3500
905 California Street, Nob Hill

DINING
Balboa Café, American, $$$, (415) 921-3944
3199 Fillmore Street, Cow Hollow

Florio, French, $$$, (415) 775-4300
1915 Fillmore Street, Pacific Heights

PlumpJack Café, Californian, $$$$, (415) 563-4755
3127 Fillmore Street, Cow Hollow

Rose's Café, Italian, $$, (415) 775-2200
2298 Union Street, Cow Hollow

SIGHTS
Chinatown, Grant Avenue

Golden Gate Bridge, www.goldengatebridge.org,
Highway 101

Presidio Park, national park, (415) 561-4323

Muir Woods, national park, (415) 388-2596

Sausalito, artists' colony,
across the Golden Gate Bridge from San Francisco

SHOPPING
City Lights Booksellers and Publishers, (415) 362-8193
261 Columbus Avenue, North Beach

Ixia, florist, (415) 431-3134
2331 Market Street, Upper Market

Prada, designer clothing, (415) 391-8844
140 Geary Street, Union Square

Sue Fisher King, home furnishings, (888) 811-7276
3067 Sacramento Street, Presidio Heights

Wilkes Bashford, designer clothing, (415) 986-4380
375 Sutter Street, Union Square

San Juan, Puerto Rico

It's been nothing but starring roles for Benicio Del Toro since his Oscar-winning turn in Steven Soderbergh's 2000 masterpiece, *Traffic*. But when it comes to artistic influences, Del Toro points not merely to his formal dramatic training, but to the childhood days he spent in San Juan, Puerto Rico. Born in the Santurce section of the city, Del Toro, dressed in shorts, would jump off a local bridge into the sea dozens of times a day, entertaining the tourists, and in the process, becoming a performer. When he enrolled at the University of California in San Diego, he planned to become a lawyer like his father, but a freshman acting class led him back to the stage. Thus began an increasingly prestigious series of appearances, first on television shows like *Miami Vice*, then in films like *The Usual Suspects* and *Snatch*, before striking Oscar gold in *Traffic*. Here's a weekend with Benicio Del Toro in his hometown of San Juan, the sunny capital of Puerto Rico.

Friday

LODGING El Convento, which used to be a convent, is in Old San Juan. It's a good hotel. If you want something larger, there's the **Wyndham El San Juan.** It has a big casino and a great beach, on Isla Verde. I like the **Condado Plaza.** It's right on Condado Beach, which is one of the most famous beaches in the Caribbean. **Numero Uno** [Ocean Park] is an old guesthouse turned into a hotel. It has a restaurant called **Pamela's.** It's right on the beach and the food is very good. If you want to be mellow, there's the **Horned Dorset Primavera Hotel** [Rincon]. That's more European. There's no casino and the rooms have no phones, but they have really good service and a terrific restaurant. If you're going for golf, the **Hyatt Dorado Beach Hotel & Country Club** has two great eighteen-hole courses.

SIGHTS I like the inside of the island. **El Yunque,** forty-five minutes from San Juan, is beautiful. My dad has a little house in El Yunque, where I like to go and kick back. El Yunque is a rainforest on this little island, just green and tropical, junglelike. There are all kinds of paths where you can hike. There are hundreds of different tropical trees and the *coqui*, a small frog. It's protected national forest. You can also go to **Rio Camuy Cave Park** [Arecibo], which is hundreds of acres of caves. It's pretty impressive.

DINNER There's the **Parrot Club** in Old San Juan. It has what they call new Latino cuisine. It's funky. It's loud. But really good food. It's a mixture of locals and tourists. The guy who owns it also has **Dragonfly,** an Asian-Latino place, right in front of the Parrot.

NIGHTLIFE There's a bar called **Maria's,** which is fun. They make great banana daiquiris. It's on Calle del Cristo, where there's always some kind of nightlife. Old San Juan is pretty small. You can go from place to place and hear live music.

Saturday

SIGHTS All of Old San Juan was once a walled city. Every corner of it is interesting; it's got history. **El Morro,** the old fort, is pretty impressive. I don't think there's a fort in mainland U.S.A. that big, that old. So it's a good sight to see. There's a church, **Porta Coeli,** in San German, which is one of the oldest churches in the New World. And there's **the capitol,** which is modeled after the one in Washington, D.C., but this one's right near the ocean.

CULTURE The **Museo de Arte,** in a former hospital, is a great little museum. They show local art and they have shows from outside, too.

There's a restaurant in the museum that's fantastic. There are a lot of art galleries in Old San Juan. On the first Tuesday of every month, they have open galleries where people can go in at night and see all the galleries. You just go from gallery to gallery. There are a lot of people on the street, and it's throbbing with energy.

LUNCH There's a hill in Santurce, where I grew up, called Miramar. There's a hotel there called the Excelsior that has a good restaurant downstairs, called **Augusto's.** It's an upscale, dressy kind of place.

BEACHES I like the beach at **Ocean Park.** That's where everybody used to hang out. It's the one I know. I could walk from my house to there in no time. But any beach on Puerto Rico is beautiful, and the water is quite warm.

SHOPPING There are a lot of shops in Old San Juan. But when I need clothing, I go to **Monsieur** in Condado, which is a good men's store. **Plaza Las Americas** is probably the biggest shopping mall in the Caribbean. It's huge and has everything.

DINNER **Via Appia** is a good place to have pizza and a beer. It's in Condado, near the beach, where you can watch people go by. Right in front of Via Appia is **Zabo,** this old house they turned into a restaurant. The food is good and the atmosphere is really nice. They serve Puerto Rican food, but they get creative with their cuisine.

All of Old San Juan was once a walled city. Every corner of it is interesting; it's got history.

NIGHTLIFE I went to the casinos a little. There's the Condado Plaza Casino. The El San Juan hotel has a good casino, probably the biggest on the island.

Sunday

BREAKFAST I like going to **La Bombonera** [Old San Juan]. It's been around for a hundred years, maybe longer. For breakfast, it's really packed. A lot of locals. You can get anything, but I like the *mallorcas,* which are bread and cheese with sugar on top. It's a type of donut that's terrific. You'll get fat quickly, but it's good. Anyone who goes to San Juan should try one of those.

EXCURSION The island of **Culebra** is really great. It's untouched, undeveloped. I went scuba diving there and it was beautiful. The beaches are quiet and there's fluorescent water. It comes from microbes in the water, which if you stir, light up like fireflies. You have to go when there's no moon. It's about an hour ride on a ferry. **Vieques** is beautiful, too. It's more isolated. There's also **Mona,** which is sort of like the Galapágos Islands. There are species of animals that are only from that place. There's an iguana from Mona and you can only find it on that tiny, deserted island, where you go to swim and see the animals. They have ferries going there. It's a trip, but it's pretty impressive.

Benicio Del Toro's San Juan Essentials

LODGING
Condado Plaza Hotel & Casino, $$, (787) 721-1000
999 Ashford Avenue, Condado Beach

TexPhoto/istockphoto.com

Hotel El Convento, $$–$$$, (787) 723-9020
100 Cristo Street, Old San Juan

Horned Dorset Primavera Hotel and Villas, $$–$$$$,
(787) 823-4081, Apartado 1132, Rincon

Hyatt Dorado Beach Hotel Resort & Country Club,
$$–$$$$, (787) 796-1234, Highway 693, Dorado

Numero Uno Guest House, $–$$, (866), 726-5010
1 Santa Ana Street, Ocean Park

Wyndham El San Juan Hotel and Casino, $$–$$$$,
(787) 791-1000, 6063 Isla Verde Avenue

DINING
Augusto's Cuisine, international, $$$, (787) 725-7700
801 Avenue Ponce de Leon, Excelsior Hotel, Miramar

Dragonfly, Asian-Latino, $$$, (787) 977-3886
364 Calle Fortaleza, Old San Juan

La Bombonera, Puerto Rican, $, (787) 722-0658
259 Calle San Francisco, Old San Juan

Pamela's Caribbean Cuisine, Caribbean fusion, $$$,
(866) 726-5010, 1 Santa Ana Street, in Numero Uno,
Ocean Park

The Parrot Club, Latino, $$$, (787) 725-7370
363 Calle Fortaleza, Old San Juan

Via Appia, Italian, $$, (787) 725-8711
1350 Avenue Ashford, Condado

Zabo, Caribbean/Pacific Rim, $$$, (787) 725-9494
14 Calle Candina, Condado

SIGHTS
Culebra, island, (787) 742-3521 ext.441,
www.islaculebra.com

El Capitolio, historic building, (787) 724-2030 ext. 2472
Puerta de Tierra

El Morro, old fort, (787) 729-6777, www.nps.gov.saju
501 Norzagaray St.

El Yunque, rainforest, (787) 888-5646,
www.elyunque.com

Mona, island

Museo de Arte, museum, (787) 977-6277
299 De Diego Ave, Santurce

Ocean Park, beach

Porta Coeli, church museum, San German

Rio Camuy Cave Park, Route 129, Arecibo

Vieques, island, www.vieques-island.com

SHOPPING
Monsieur, men's clothing, (787) 722-0918
1126 Avenue Ashford, Condado

Plaza Las Americas, mall, (787) 767-5202
525 Roosevelt Avenue

NIGHTLIFE
Maria's, bar, (787) 721-1678
204 Calle del Cristo, Old San Juan

How My Acting Career Began in San Juan

I never really acted in Puerto Rico. I did all my acting on the street. I just had a kitsch, you know. "I'll jump from the bridge! I'll jump from here." I know there's someone who has a picture of me jumping from the bridge, which is called the Bridge of Two Brothers, that connects Old San Juan to Condado. People jump from that bridge into the ocean. Kids still do it and I always stop and watch them jump. I was probably eleven, twelve back then. There would be tourists, and I'd be going, "Here I go! Watch me!" I was just playing the clown. I'd do it for the tourists, and I'd do it for me, just to get those butterflies in my stomach. You could do it maybe twenty, thirty times a day. People would take pictures and say, "Jump again!" Subconsciously, my desire to become an actor began in Puerto Rico.

Santa Barbara

When Jeff Bridges and his wife, Sue, were shaken awake in their Los Angeles home on January 17, 1994, by the Northridge Earthquake, they soon began voicing a two-word mantra: Santa Barbara. "We had a house in Malibu that burned down before the earthquake, and then we lost our other house to the earthquake, and so we finally took a hint and said 'Okay, we're out of here!'" A venerable star who's been nominated for four Oscars, Bridges spent some time in Santa Barbara in the early eighties, filming a movie called *Cutter's Way*. He stayed at the Rancho Encanto and shot scenes in and around the harbor. *Gorgeous place,* he thought. But he was an L.A. kid, born and bred, the son of the actor Lloyd Bridges. Santa Barbara, however, known as the American Riviera because of

its Mediterranean-style setting and Spanish-Moorish architecture, quickly won his heart. Here's a weekend with Jeff Bridges on the streets, hills, and beaches of Santa Barbara, California.

Friday

LODGING There are so many good ones here. You have the **Biltmore,** which is right on the ocean, a wonderful old hotel. It was a ranch at one time. I don't think they have riding there anymore, but it's got small low-type buildings, and they are ranch style. It's got a great history and great architecture, and it's right across the street from the beach. It also has a restaurant that, among other things, has a terrific Sunday brunch. There's the **San Ysidro Ranch,** which is where the Kennedys, John and Jackie, spent their honeymoon; that's a very quaint, inn-type place to stay in Montecito. **El Encanto** is

another great place to stay, very lush and up in the hills.

DINNER One of my favorites in town, on State Street, is a restaurant called **Piranha,** which serves exotic sushi. It has special rolls and it's not your run-of-the-mill sushi bar. It's a high-tech sushi bar. You know, you sit up on high stools, they have little tables, and, of course, you can sit at the sushi bar as well. You would see pretty much a cross-section of all kinds of people. But I'm usually not looking at people as much as the fish when I go in there—and the wonderful dishes that they're serving.

NIGHTLIFE Are you familiar with State Street? It's a great street to just stroll on and watch people and window-shop. They have all kinds of small boutique stores on State. I don't do too much clubbing these days. But I've seen some wonderful shows at the Santa Barbara County Bowl, which is the great theater. It's a miniature version of the Hollywood Bowl, except the parking hassle is so much less and you're outside and overlooking the Pacific Ocean. I've seen Jackson Browne and David Crosby, Michael McDonald and Bonnie Raitt there. It's so convenient and easy and laid back. I find I go there a lot. The Granada, an old movie theater, is quite unique. The interior looks like the exterior. It's almost like you're outside, but you're inside. I don't know how you describe it. The inside is like you're outside in a patio almost. It's a large movie theater, the kind where the first-run movies would play.

Saturday

BREAKFAST I don't know if I want to give this away, but the East Beach Grill is a little outdoor café on the water at East Beach. It's a great locals' spot.

SIGHTS Almost every day I thank my lucky stars that we ended up in Santa Barbara, because it's so beautiful. You think of the coast of California as facing west, but Santa Barbara really faces south, so the weather hits the land in different patterns and keeps everything lush here. It feels very different than Los Angeles for that reason. Just the architecture of the town is really beautiful and it has been really respected. The courthouse is something to behold. It's a gorgeous piece of architecture, an old Spanish-style building. The main street that goes along the ocean is Cabrillo Boulevard. Probably one of the main things to see is the Old Mission, which is one of the original missions and is known as the "queen of all missions." Father Serra came up the coast to California dotting missions all along the way, and this is a particularly beautiful one, with a beautiful rose garden in the front. It's a quite spectacular location. From here, you can see the mountains. It's your typical mission architecture. There's quite a history. It's been refurbished over the years; there are some parts that are original. I've taken my kids to it and it's a wonderful thing.

THE BEACH The great attraction of Santa Barbara is the water. There's sailing and whale watching and fishing and surfing—some of the best surf on the coast is here. Rincon Point is a great place to surf. When the swell is right, the surfing is really good all up and down the coast.

I've seen some wonderful shows at the Santa Barbara County Bowl, which is a great theater. It's a miniature version of the Hollywood Bowl, except the parking hassle is so much less and you're outside and overlooking the Pacific Ocean. (© 2003 AArthurFisher.com, printed with permission)

My favorite beaches? There's **Butterfly Beach,** which is right in front of the Biltmore; that's a wonderful public beach for walking. We take our dogs down there. If you bring your dogs, make sure that you bring a little plastic bag so you can clean up after them. That's important—put that in there. There are big cliffs. There are people surfing and you can watch. You see a lot of ocean life. I mean, you're very likely to see dolphins and seals just about every time you go out in the ocean. Maybe you heard in the news, but our pier, **Stearns Wharf,** burned down in 1998. [It has since been rebuilt and is now Santa Barbara's most visited tourist attraction.] I was going to say that was another great thing to do in Santa Barbara—to take a walk on the pier. There are some nice restaurants and you can watch the surfers and fish and all that.

SHOPPING There's a place called **Wendy Foster's** that my wife, Sue, really favors; that's in Montecito. Whenever I need to get her a gift, I know I'm pretty safe by going there. They have all kinds of unique jewelry, interesting dresses, and all different sorts of designers. I couldn't give you the names, but I know that they have beautiful clothes. There are, of course, shops up and down State Street. It's chock full of all kinds of restaurants and clubs. You know, Santa Barbara is quite a college town, so there are a lot of young guys and gals here. There are a lot of clubs and coffee shops and antique stores, clothing and boutique-type stores. And there are two very large mall-type complexes called the **El Paseo** and the **Arcada.** Again, those are done in the old Spanish architecture. The El Paseo is the oldest; it was built around an original adobe house from the 1800s.

LUNCH The Mexican restaurant, **Super-Rica,** is on the funky side. It's almost like a stand. You go for lunch and wait in line and place your order at a window. There's usually a line—it's that good. People really will wait. Either you can take it out or you can eat there. The food is really unusually good—authentic Mexican food. I usually ask them at the window what they recommend, but there are all kinds of great foods there. They have tables and a patio. It's not a real big place. Like fifteen to twenty tables. Anybody who knows Santa Barbara knows about this place. It's a locals' favorite. There are some nice restaurants in Montecito that are neighborhood places. **Mollie's** has probably the best pizza that I've ever tasted. Wonderful homemade crusts. **Pane e Vino** is another Italian restaurant in Montecito.

STROLLING **Lotusland** is a wonderful botanical garden in Montecito. It was the private residence of a woman named Madam Ganna Walska back in the twenties or maybe even before then. You have to make reservations, [far in advance; tours are only given from mid-February through mid-November], but it's really worth visiting. Over the years, she just created incredible world-class gardens of rare plants. People come from all over the world to visit it. The **Santa Barbara Botanical Gardens** are also really worth seeing.

EXERCISE The mountains are filled with hiking trails, which is another great thing to do with your family. In the spring and summer months, the waterfalls are very lush. Cold Springs is a wonderful hike. There's a trail that goes up into the mountains. East Camino Cielo Road and trail runs all the way across the tops of the mountains and gives you spectacular views of the ocean. You can hike farther than you would probably ever want to go. Rattlesnake Canyon is another great place—another trail head. They're dotted all around. There are just incredible trails. You think you're in another country.

CULTURE There's a great Natural History Museum here. There's a Music Academy that gives concerts as well. That's something the family might enjoy doing.

EXCURSION The towns of Ojai and Solvang are just inland from Santa Barbara. Solvang is like a Shaker village; it's almost like Disneyland's Frontier Land. There are a lot of lakes—Cachuma Lake is inland from us. Ojai has beautiful horses and horse ranches, wonderful riding and that kind of thing for families to check out. There is some lovely wine country around here too. I'm not really into it as much as my brother, who loves to go on wine tours, but there's the Fess Parker Winery in Los Olivos. Ojai is a small town, but it's also a wonderful valley. Krishnamurti, an Indian philosopher back in the thirties and forties, had a spiritual community out there. Beatrice Wood, the famous potter, used to live out there. It's really a wonderful, wonderful place.

DINNER Stella Mare's is almost like eating in someone's home. It's a converted old house. I would say it's international cuisine, I guess maybe being more California cuisine. It's light-tasting, healthy. It's halfway between town and Montecito. It's right by the big water reserve, almost by the bird refuge. Another wonderful place to eat is the Wine Cask—very good food. The Wine Cask has a wonderful wine list and great California food. It has a European feel, almost like you're in a chateau or something. It's just really gourmet food there, and it's right across from the wonderful old theater, the Lobero Theater.

ENTERTAINMENT The Lobero Theatre is the place where you see stage productions and concerts. Eating at the Wine Cask and going across the street to the Lobero Theatre is typical of what living here is like. We had a wonderful evening where we went to the Wine Cask and then just strolled across the street about ten minutes before the curtain went up, just sauntered in and saw Shawn Colvin. I think it might be the second oldest, if not the oldest theater in California, and seeing someone on the level of Shawn Colvin, in solo concert, was just great. My wife and I looked at each other and said, "Isn't this great? Look how easy!" Shawn Colvin, who that year had won the Grammy for the best album. The Lobero is a great theater. The acoustics are so terrific—it's a place that performers love to play.

Sunday

BRUNCH The Biltmore has a Sunday brunch that's really spectacular. Well, it's just really a feast for your eyes, as well as your palate. They have every kind of breakfast you can imagine.

Guys cooking pancakes, making omelets, and lox and bagels. The normal breakfast there is wonderful too. You could also go to the Montecito Inn. Charlie Chaplin used to have a studio here and he built a hotel, the Montecito Inn, in the Lower Village of Montecito. There used to be quite a film industry here. The Montecito Inn is filled with history of Charlie Chaplin. It's not really a museum, but I think they've probably got some literature on him. The hotel is white and old-fashioned looking. Charming.

SIGHTS The Santa Barbara Zoo is a wonderful thing to do with the kids. It's a smaller version of the zoos that you might find in San Diego or Los Angeles, but it's very well kept up, very clean, not very crowded. It's a wonderful place to bring kids and stroll around. It's right off the beach between Montecito and Santa Barbara, which are almost joined. It's pretty easy to get around here.

EXCURSION Montecito is a small community just south of Santa Barbara. There's an upper village and a lower village, where there are some shops, and those are very nice, but it's mainly a residential area. It was once an old Indian village, and the Chumash Indians must have had a wonderful life here. They used to make canoes and go to the Channel Islands. Another thing that you can do is take a boat to the Channel Islands and spend the day seeing those islands. They are really beautiful and quite pristine. There's no building allowed. If you go by motor boat, it takes a couple of hours. Depending on what time of year you go, it could be foggy, but once you get over there, it's quite spectacular. There are big caves, and there's wonderful kayaking. You can actually go quite a way into the caves. You see all kinds of sea life and sea lions. There's great whale watching around Santa Barbara. The Santa Barbara Sailing Center will take you out. You can also rent boats; they have sunset cruises, too, which are a lot of fun, especially on the big catamaran.

A Great Day in Santa Barbara

The day I taught my three daughters how to surf was a sunny day. They had a friend coming up to visit and we thought, *Let's go!* We got one of those new foam boards that are pretty gentle. If it hits you in the head, it won't kill you. So we got our wet suits on and went to the backside of Rincon, which is just north of the point break. I've been surfing since I was twelve or something, and I've gotten so much pleasure out of it that I wanted to turn them on to it. I'd taught them in the pool a couple of times, too—getting them to paddle and stand up in the water. They were a little apprehensive about it. Once they got going, once they stood up and saw that they could do it, they were okay. To teach somebody to surf, you don't push them. You get them out and teach them how to hold the board, first giving them some lessons on the sand, and then taking them out to the ocean and holding the board for them and letting them stand up a couple of times and fall down when a wave comes. Then just push them on a wave and they stand up and off they go. Oh, it was thrilling! Once they started to have fun and stand up, they were all pretty good. They really took to it. On that day, they became California surfer girls.

Jeff Bridge's Santa Barbara Essentials

LODGING

El Encanto Hotel and Villas, $$$, (805) 687-5000
1900 Lasuen Road

The Four Seasons Biltmore Hotel, $$$$, (805) 969-2261
1260 Channel Drive

The Montecito Inn, $$$, (805) 969-7854
1295 Coast Village Road, Montecito

San Ysidro Ranch, $$$$, (805) 969-5046
900 San Ysidro Lane, Montecito

DINING

East Beach Grill, American, $, (805) 965-8805
1118 East Cabrillo Boulevard

La Super-Rica, Mexican, $, (805) 963-4940
622 North Milpas Street

Mollie Trattoria Restaurant, Italian, $$, (805) 565-9381
1250 Coast Village Road, Montecito

Pane e Vino, Italian, $$, (805) 969-9274
1482 East Valley Road, Montecito

Piranha Restaurant and Sushi Bar, Japanese, $$$,
(805) 965-2980, 714 State Street

Stella Mare's, Californian, $$$, (805) 969-6705
50 Los Platos Way

The Wine Cask Restaurant, Californian, $$$,
(805) 966-9463, 813 Anacapa Street

SIGHTS

Butterfly Beach, walking, Santa Barbara, right across the
street from the Biltmore Hotel

Cachuma Lake, recreation area, (805) 686-5054
Santa Barbara

Channel Islands National Park, (805) 658-5730
1901 Spinnaker Drive, Ventura

The Courthouse, (805) 962-6464, 1100 Anacapa Street

Fess Parker Winery, (800) 841-1104
6200 Foxen Canyon Road, Los Olivos

Lotusland, botanical garden, (805) 969-9990
695 Ashley Road, Montecito

Ojai Valley Inn Ranch & Stables, horseback riding,
(805) 646 5511 ext 51

Old Mission Santa Barbara, (805) 682-4713
2201 Laguna Street

Rincon Beach, surfing, Ventura County

Santa Barbara Botanic Garden, (805) 682-4726
1212 Mission Canyon Road

Santa Barbara Museum of Natural History,
(805) 682-4711, 2559 Puesta Del Sol

The Santa Barbara Zoo, (805) 962-6310, 500 Ninos Drive

Solvang, town, (800) 468-6765, www.solvangusa.com

Stearn's Wharf Trading Company, (805) 962-4118
2178 Stearn's Wharf, Cabrillo Boulevard

SHOPPING

El Paseo Mall, 800 block of State Street

La Arcada, mall, 1100 block of State Street

Wendy Foster, clothing and jewelry, (805) 565-1506
516 San Ysidro Road, Montecito

THEATER/ENTERTAINMENT

The Granada Theater, movies, (805) 899-3000
1216 State Street

Lobero Theatre, live theater and concerts, (805) 963-0761
33 East Canon Perdido Street

Music Academy of the West, concerts, (805) 969-4726
1070 Fairway Road

The Santa Barbara County Bowl, performance venue,
(805) 962-7411, 1122 North Milpas

HIKING/SAILING

Cold Springs Trail, goes up into mountains

East Camino Cielo Road, trail runs across tops of
mountains

Rattlesnake Canyon Trail, Las Canoas

The Santa Barbara Sailing Center, (805) 962-2826
133 Harbor Way

Seattle

S itting in his Bel Air home, surrounded by his Grammys, his Emmy, his Oscar, and his memories, Quincy Delight Jones Jr., known world-round simply as "Q," contemplated the city where it all began. A king of American entertain-ment, Q has been a ubiquitous player in every era of the second half of the last millennium: bebop (performing with Charlie Parker and Dizzie Gillespie); big band (a member of both Basie and Hampton's orchestras); jazz (conducting for Miles Davis); sixties croon (his arrangement for Sinatra's "Fly Me to the Moon" was played by astronaut Buzz Aldrin on his 1969 lunar landing); pop/rock (producing Michael Jackson at his height, including conducting the "We Are the World" sessions); rap (producing Ice T and many others). He coproduced with Steven Spielberg *The Color Purple*, which won eleven Oscars and marked the film debuts of Whoopi Goldberg and Oprah Winfrey; launched Will Smith in NBC's hit series *The Fresh Prince of Bel Air*; and has been nominated for more than seventy-seven Grammys. Here, Quincy talks about his first stage, the city of Seattle, where as the son of a navy shipyard worker, he found his future when he picked up his first trumpet at age twelve.

Friday

LODGING The **Woodmark** is out there near Microsoft in Carillon Point, right on Lake Washington in Seattle's Silicon Valley. When I lived in Seattle, that was like a—I don't want to say "swamp," because they didn't have swamps in Seattle, but it wasn't anything like it is since Microsoft and all those things have happened. It's another Seattle now, but it's beautiful. The Woodmark must be almost twenty years old. It's a beautiful hotel. It's very romantic, has a nice ambience, and it's right on the water.

DINNER Well, the first night I would have to go to my brother's house—Richard Jones. He's the superior court judge up there and he is a cooking maniac. He cooked some for Oprah one night and it was fantastic. So I would have to stop there first. They're in meat and potatoes country up there in Seattle because it's cold and rainy. The **Metropolitan Grill** [downtown] has the best steak in the world. Oh yeah—the best steak on the planet. They have one up in Vancouver, too. We went two weeks ago. It's just awesome—aged New York steaks and sirloins and T-bones.

ENTERTAINMENT I have a lot of family in Seattle. We would probably go to the **Jazz Alley** [downtown] the first night. It's a jazz club, live jazz. Seattle is a big jazz city, and Jazz Alley is one of the nicest jazz clubs in America. These clubs didn't exist when I was living in Seattle. I played during the war with Charlie Taylor's band and with Bumps Blackwell's band. Bumps Blackwell eventually found Sam Cooke and Little Richard. He's from Seattle—he was like our guru then. He had a taxi cab chain, he had worked in a butcher shop, he worked in a jewelry store downtown, he worked at Boeing. We played with Billie Holiday when I was fourteen years old and we played with Billy Eckstein. We played with Ray Charles at the Elks Club. We would start out at seven and play

Seattle Theatre Group

dinner music with white cardigans and bow ties and cut-mute trumpets at the Seattle Tennis Club. Very subdued—dinner music. Then we would play the black clubs at ten. We played with Billie Holliday at the Eagles Auditorium.

Saturday

BREAKFAST We might go to the **Salish Lodge Dining Room,** which looks out over Snoqualmie Falls, which is beautiful, gorgeous. It's in Snoqualmie, Washington, about thirty minutes from Seattle. The lodge is famous for its great view of the falls. I would go there for breakfast. Again, it's Northwest food.

SIGHTS You have to remember, I go back to Seattle when the Smith Towers were the biggest things in town. Just like when I first worked at Vegas, we worked there with Sinatra and Basie at the Sands Hotel when it was eight stories high. It's the same with Seattle now—there's all this beautiful, amazing architecture. Like the **Space Needle,** the six-hundred-foot tower built for the '62 World's Fair, is always great to see. Seattle still has the purest water and no pollution. You take a breath of air up there and it's just like an oxygen tank. But the Seattle I remember, during World War II, was probably the hottest city in America. All the military was there and all the party players—the club people—were there, because that's where the soldiers were: army, navy, Marines, everything. They took off from there to go to Japan.

A place that's close to me, where we used to play all the time, is the Paramount Theatre. It's a real classic with deco and all the thirties interiors.

I was raised there since I was ten years old, coming from Chicago. We went to Bremmerton first—which is an hour from Seattle on the ferry—and my father worked in the Bremmerton navy shipyard. I have a friend up there, Dennis Washington, who is the king of the Northwest now, probably the "copper king" of America, big railroad owner. We used to shine shoes together during the war—ten years old—at Matriarch City in Bremmerton. Dennis Washington and I went back two years ago to find the YMCA right next door to the Fauntleroy Ferry dock where we shined shoes. We had paper routes with the *Bremmerton Sun*, and we went to Navy Art City Grade School together, and we shined shoes for the sailors.

RECREATION **Mount Rainier** is south of Seattle and absolutely beautiful. On a clear day you can see it from the city. **Whistler,** one of the great ski resorts in America, isn't too far away. But there's so much water around Seattle, naturally you want to be very connected with the water. That's what I like about it. Great fishing, especially salmon. We went up with Paul Allen [Microsoft cofounder] last year. We went with Dennis Washington year before last. He's got a fantastic fishing boat and a refurbished tugboat. In Seattle, you've got all of these bays, like Lake Union, which is near the University of Washington. I've been there on Dennis Washington's boat. The houses of all the computer barons are on Lake Union and Evergreen Point and Hunts Point on Lake Washington.

CULTURE A very good friend of mine, Dale Chihuly, is one of the greatest glass artists on the planet. I just saw him at one of Paul Allen's events at Kingdome. It's always interesting to see any of his exhibits. There's the **Seattle Art Museum** [downtown], and the **Museum of History and Industry** [McCurdy Park], which tells the story of the city through various exhibits. Jacob Lawrence, a great African-American artist, is from Seattle too. His exhibits are at the **Henry Art Gallery** at the University of Washington and the Seattle Art Museum. He also has some exhibits in his old neighborhood—in the Central District at the **Francine Seders Gallery.**

LUNCH The **Palisade** restaurant on Elliott Bay has a piano bar, and there's a little bridge with live fish swimming underneath it. They have a lot of lobster and crustaceans. It's a Polynesian restaurant with a big saltwater pool filled with Pacific Northwest fish. The best fish are always from cold water, deep cold water, and that's why there's such great fish in New England and New Zealand, Long Island, Washington, and Alaska. Seattle has some of the best fish in the world. And then there's the **Ponti Seafood Grill** on Lake Union—a canal runs past it. It's classic Northwest, a place to eat outside.

SHOPPING There's no place in the world like **Pike Place Market,** the oldest farmer's market in the country. They have probably the sweetest Dungeness crab in the world. It's so good. They're the really big crabs and, oh boy, they know how to do it. The market is famous; you've probably seen the pictures of the vendors throwing the fish back and forth. When I was growing up in Seattle, I couldn't afford the Pike Place Market. We would eat at the old Father Divine's, a restaurant where you could go in the door and say "peace" and eat for fifteen cents—and I mean incredible food. We used to eat there all the time.

SNACK We used to eat at **Ivar's Acres of Clams.** They're still there, three locations, the original on Pier 54 on the Seattle waterfront. Make sure you got those good thick juicy clams—razor clams, Manila clams, and little necks. I remember as kids in Bremmerton we used to run over the oysters. In those days, we didn't eat oysters. At Acres of Clams, they're just hard-core. They'll fry them for you or steam them, however you want them. You put the horseradish and lemon and vinegar and hot sauce on to really get it just right.

DINNER Canlis [West Lake Union] always impresses me because they have an amazing wine cellar, probably the largest wine cellar in Seattle. They have wine tastings and everything else. It's big stuff. My idols are food and wine people all over the world. What you learn if you're really a food junkie, which I am, you learn to know the choice produce of each area. Canlis is on the scale of the world's great restaurants because they're dealing with superior produce. Canlis has great steaks and the Northwest seafood. Seattle also has a great **Chinatown,** one of the largest Chinatowns outside of San Francisco. We'd go to all of the places on Jackson Street.

ENTERTAINMENT A place that's close to me, where we used to play all the time, is the **Paramount Theatre** [downtown], which is Ida B. Cole's Microsoft baby. Ida B. Cole is a former Microsoft marketing executive. She spear-

Three Great Days in Seattle

I wanted to find a way to divert the attention from my fiftieth birthday. It was traumatic. I heard they had taken state funds away from our high school, Garfield. I used to live right across the street from Garfield, which is where Jimi Hendrix and Bruce Lee went. So I decided to go up there for three days and really give back to Seattle, because Seattle gave me a lot, really a lot. On the first day, we had all the city fathers and the Chamber of Commerce and Civil Air Patrol, which I wrote a theme song for when I was fourteen or fifteen years old. The mayor and the senators and congressmen and everybody were there. We raised the money for the school at that particular event.

Then the next night we did a black tie event at the Paramount Theater for $250 a head and we took the Seattle symphony. We had just done *The Wiz*, so we had a choir and we did "Brand New Day" with the symphony orchestra. We hired Patty Austin and James Ingram. We had a reunion of the band we had thirty-eight years ago—Ray Charles came and the Bumps Blackwell band and Ernestine Anderson. Alex Haley came and Hank [Henry] Mancini came up, just for the birthday. The next day we played at the former Seattle Civic Auditorium where I used to play as a kid. The third night we did a regular rock concert with my band. We had a couple of hits out then. All three nights were very successful and we donated that money to Garfield High. It was so much fun. It was awesome. I got to see all of the people and, oh, that special place. Hey, man, that's your roots, right? It was a great way to turn fifty.

headed a group of investors and bought the Paramount and changed it into a real state-of-the-art theater for Broadway shows. She does *Phantom of the Opera* and all that there. They do filming and state-of-the-art television production. Everything is in there. It's a real classic with deco and all the thirties interiors.

Sunday

LUNCH What you remember about Seattle is the seafood, with one exception: **Ezell's Fried Chicken.** It's really serious, great, great, great take-out fried chicken cooked in a special process that keeps the oil out and the juices in. It's so good that Oprah flew them to Chicago to cook for her birthday and sometimes has the chicken sent to her by overnight mail. Out front, there's a sign, "Oprah's Favorite Chicken." It's fantastic.

WHALE AND EAGLE WATCHING I love to go to the **San Juan Islands,** an archipelago of islands, that you get to by a thirty-minute ferry from Anacortes, a town an hour north of Seattle. My friend Dennis Washington has a private lodge on Stuart Island. There's a Robert Trent Jones Golf Course up there—it's awesome. This place is God's country. You can see eagles and whales all over the place.

Quincy Jones' Seattle Essentials

LODGING
The Woodmark Hotel, $$$, (425) 822-3700
1200 Carillon Point, Kirkland

DINING
Canlis, continental, $$$$, (206) 283-3313
2576 Aurora Avenue, West Lake Union

Ezell's Fried Chicken, American, $, (206) 324-4141
501 23rd Avenue, Central District

Ivar's Acres of Clams and Fish Bar, seafood, $$,
(206) 624-6852, multiple locations throughout Seattle

Metropolitan Grill, steak house, $$$$, (206) 624-3287
820 2nd Avenue, downtown

The Palisade, seafood, $$$$, (206) 285-1000
2601 West Marina Place, waterfront

Ponti Seafood Grill, seafood, $$$, (206) 284-3000
3014 3rd Avenue North, Fremont

Salish Lodge Dining Room, American, $$$,
(425) 888-2556, 6501 Railroad Avenue SE, Snoqualmie

SIGHTS
Chinatown–International District
South Dearborn Street and 4th Avenue South

Francine Seders Gallery, (206) 782-0355
6701 Greenwood Avenue North, Central District

The Henry Art Gallery, (206) 543-2280
15th Avenue Northeast, University of Washington

Mount Rainier, www.nps.gov/mora

The Museum of History and Industry, (206) 324-1126
2700 24th Avenue, McCurdy Park

Pike Place Market, giant indoor/outdoor market,
(206) 682-7453, Pike Street, downtown

San Juan Islands, accessible via Washington State
Ferries, in Seattle (206) 464-6400

Seattle Art Museum, (206) 654-3100
100 University Street, downtown

Space Needle, (206) 905-2100
400 Broad Street, Seattle Center

NIGHTLIFE
Dimitriou's Jazz Alley, live music (206) 441-9729
2033 6th Avenue, downtown

The Paramount Theatre, live music/theater,
(206) 467-5510, 911 Pine Street, downtown

SKIING
Whistler BC Ski Resort, (604) 932-0606, (877) 932-0606

George Stephanopoulos

Washington, D.C.

George Stephanopoulos serves as lead anchor for *This Week with George Stephanopoulos*, an ABC network Sunday morning staple where he discusses politics and current affairs with fellow pundits like Cokie Roberts and George Will. That is a long way from July Fourth in 1981, when Stephanopoulos took his very first trip to Washington, D.C., from his

home in Cleveland, carrying with him what most people carry to Washington: a sense of awe. A Rhodes Scholar and son of a Greek Orthodox priest, Stephanopoulos's first Washington job was as a congressional intern. That position launched him on a journey that would eventually take him all the way to the White House, where as key strategist in both Clinton presidential campaigns, he became the young face—and most eligible bachelor—of the Clinton administration, eventually serving as senior advisor to the president for policy and strategy. Although he now lives in New York with his wife, actress Alexandra Wentworth, a piece of Stephanopoulos's soul remains in the nation's capital. Here's a weekend with George in Washington, D.C.

Friday

LODGING The new **Ritz-Carlton** is in a perfect location, right between Georgetown and Dupont Circle downtown. It's pretty central—only a few blocks from the White House, a couple of blocks from the Kennedy Center, near everything. It has access to Sports Club/ LA, the best gym in D.C. It has friendly service and it's huge, with every possible machine,

squash courts, basketball courts, pool—and it's brand-new.

DINNER A.V. Ristorante Italiano [downtown] is straight out of the Rat Pack—1950s Italian food, lots of red sauce, little fireplace in the back, jukebox.

NIGHTLIFE Blues Alley is a jazz supper club in Georgetown. It's intimate and all the headliners go there. It's been there forever. You can also go to **Nathan's** in Georgetown for a drink. It's at the crossroads of M Street and Wisconsin, so it's in the heart of the action. It's run by a woman named Carol Joynt, a longtime CNN reporter and producer, so a lot of people hang out there.

Saturday

BREAKFAST When I had my first job on Capitol Hill back in the early 1980s, I would go to the **Eastern Market.** It's about seven blocks south of the Capitol. It's a farmer's market, a great big old warehouse with butchers and cheese makers and people coming to set up their stalls with produce. In the back corner, there's a breakfast bar. You just walk up, get a paper plate, and they have the best homemade pancakes and sausage, egg, and cheese sandwiches on homemade bread. It's probably been there thirty or forty years. It's real down-home. For a Tex-Mex brunch, go to **Austin Grill** [Georgetown]. They have great migas and fresh tortillas. It's straight out of Austin.

SIGHTS You can walk from the Eastern Market to the Capitol. That's still the most impressive sight in Washington—the **Capitol dome** on a clear day. It's the highest point in D.C. From the Capitol, you can walk right down the **National Mall.** You'll quickly hit the Smithsonian and the National Air and Space Museum. If you want art, you have the National Gallery of Art with the East and the

Go to anything at the Kennedy Center. There are always three or four different things going on.

West buildings on the right. My favorite is the East Building, which has great Mark Rothkos, Picassos—a terrific collection. Then, as you keep walking down the Mall, you'll hit the Reflecting Pool, the famous site of all the marches, where Martin Luther King gave his famous "I Have a Dream" speech. On your way, you could go to the Jefferson Memorial and see the cherry blossoms, which usually bloom in late March or early April. You've got to have great timing. They last about two to three weeks, but it's worth making a trip if you hear the blossoms are about to bloom. The pool around the Jefferson Memorial looks like it's surrounded by cotton candy.

CULTURE In Dupont Circle, go to the **Phillips Collection.** It has a lot of Bonnard and twentieth-century collections—Milton Avery, Georgia O'Keeffe. It has a real homey feel because it was once a private home. If you still feel like walking after all that, you can walk up Massachusetts Avenue, which is **Embassy Row,** and see all the embassies. There's the British Embassy with the famous Churchill

Photo by Carol Pratt

statue, which people might remember from when Princess Diana died. A lot of people left flowers there. There's also the **Islamic Center,** the most elaborate mosque in D.C. You'll see, too, the **Greek Orthodox Cathedral** and the **National Cathedral.** It's some of the best architecture in Washington.

LUNCH If you were doing the Mall on Saturday, you would end up toward Dupont Circle. I would have lunch at **Kramerbooks & Afterwords Cafe,** the best bookstore in America. You've got books in the front and a café in the back. They often have music Wednesday through Saturday nights. They have a great lunch and the world's most friendly and fascinating manager, Michael Sean Winters. He knows everyone in town and he'll sit down with White House aides, with gallery owners, with journalists. If you want something more casual, try **Pizzeria Paradiso** on P Street. There's always a line, but it's worth it. My favorite is the four cheese. Don't worry about the calories—get Gorgonzola, Parmesan, fontina, and mozzarella all in one.

EXERCISE Washington is a great walking city. The city is divided into four different quadrants, but it doesn't feel congested. In Georgetown, you can walk along the towpath on the canal, where Jimmy Carter used to jog. It's a great dirt track. You can go for miles on the towpath. As you head toward Georgetown University, there are these narrow steps that go almost straight up by the towpath to Georgetown. Those stairs are famous from *The Exorcist,* the scene where someone tumbles down them. When I first moved to Washington,

I was in much better shape than I am now and I used to run up those steps.

DINNER For Saturday night, go to the **Palm** [downtown]. That's the power restaurant, heavy on the political crowd. It's always filled with cabinet members. The power brokers hang out at the Palm. There are two things to get—steak and lobster. I usually go for the steak, but my wife likes the lobster. It's a lot of heads turning, people trying to figure out who's saying what to whom at which table—and a lot of fun. It's a loud, happy place.

NIGHTLIFE Go to anything at the **Kennedy Center** [Foggy Bottom]. There are always three or four different things going on. You have the National Symphony Orchestra, and several times a year they'll have the Washington Opera. There are always first-run theater performances, plus the American Film Institute does their classic films there. They're always having different festivals. There's nothing like the view from the terrace of the Kennedy Center overlooking the Potomac on a nice night—it's just gorgeous.

Sunday

SIGHTS On Sunday, after you've watched *This Week* on ABC, the best place to go is **Dumbarton Oaks.** It's hidden away, way up above Georgetown. It was an old mansion that belonged to former ambassador Robert Woods Bliss and his wife, Mildred. They gave it to Harvard in 1940; it's a museum that specializes in Byzantine and pre-Columbian art. But even more spectacular is what's behind the mansion:

lovely formal gardens, which you can walk through on Sunday afternoon. It's quiet and it feels like it's just been plucked out of another century.

EXCURSION In the fall, take a drive out Skyline Drive into the Virginia Hills. It's wonderful. If you're ambitious, it's nice to drive out to **Monticello,** Jefferson's home. The most memorable time was when Clinton was first inaugurated. We drove into D.C. on a bus and stopped off at Monticello on the way. At Monticello you see Jefferson's genius—he was the architect. You see his wine cellar, his plans for the grounds, a great collection of his writings. It's special. It's been meticulously restored—an exquisite place.

George Stephanopoulos's Washington, D.C Essentials

LODGING
The Ritz-Carlton, $$$$, (202) 912-4100
3100 South Street Northwest, Georgetown

DINING
Austin Grill, Tex-Mex, $$, (202) 337-8080
2404 Wisconsin Avenue Northwest, Georgetown

A. V. Ristorante Italiano, Italian, $$$, (202) 737-0550
607 New York Avenue, downtown

Kramerbooks & Afterwords Cafe & Grill, American, $$, (202) 387-1462, 1517 Connecticut Avenue Northwest, Dupont

Market Lunch (in Eastern Market), American, $, (202) 547-8444, 225 7th Street, Capitol Hill

Palm Restaurant, American, $$$$, (202) 293-9091
1225 19th Street Northwest, downtown

Pizzeria Paradiso, pizza, $$, (202) 223-1245
2029 P Street Northwest, Dupont

SIGHTS
Dumbarton Oaks, mansion/museum, (202) 298-8402
2715 Q Street Northwest, Georgetown

Embassy Row, Massachusetts Avenue, from Dupont Circle toward the National Cathedral

The Islamic Center of Washington, D.C.,
(202) 332-8343, 2551 Massachusetts Avenue NW

Phillips Collection, art, (202) 387-2151
1600 21st Street Northwest, Dupont

One Great Day in D.C.

My summer internship was in the summer of 1981. I was a junior in college. I arrived on July Fourth weekend—always a great day in Washington, with thousands and thousands of people on the Mall. I had never been to Washington before. I remember walking around the Mall all day long and then sitting up by the Capitol that night for the fireworks display, and having so much fun and feeling like I was part of a big patriotic celebration. Then, on the following Monday morning, I took the subway into work for the first time. I came out of the subway and saw the Capitol dome lit up against a perfectly blue sky. It inspired me. From the moment I started as an intern—getting coffee and making copies and doing research for my local congresswoman, Mary Rose Oakar, and walking through the marble halls with the other interns—I knew it was the place I wanted to be. Washington is a center. It's a magnet. The whole country comes to Washington; it's where the country's business is done. From that first day, I was hooked.

National Cathedral, (202) 537-6200
Massachusetts and Wisconsin Avenues, Northwest

National Mall, www.nps.gov/nama

Monticello, (434) 984-9822
Charlottesville, Virginia., 125 miles from Washington, D.C.

Saint Sophia Greek Orthodox Cathedral, (202) 333-4730, 36th Street and Massachusetts Avenue

U.S. Capitol, (202) 225-6827
545 Seventh Street SE

NIGHTLIFE

Blues Alley, jazz supper club, (202) 337-4141
1073 Wisconsin Avenue, Georgetown

The John F. Kennedy Center for the Performing Arts, (202) 467-4600, 2700 F Street Northwest, Foggy Bottom

Nathan's, bar, (202) 338-2000
3150 M Street Northwest, Georgetown

International Destinations

Berlin

N ot a single head turned when Jodie Foster blasted into the outdoor café at the Farmers Market in Los Angeles. No eyebrows rose when she sat down at a table in the middle of a packed alfresco dining patio and I pulled out a tape recorder for our interview. Not one eye stared as she began taking me through an hour-long journey into one of her favorite cities: Berlin. It seemed strange that one of the most famous actresses of her generation could blend into a midday lunch crowd, with not one person, not to mention paparazzi, taking notice. But, then again, maybe it's not so strange at all.

Foster has always disappeared into her characters, from her Oscar-winning turns in *The Silence of the Lambs* and *The Accused* to the airborne psychological drama, *Flightplan*. On this sunny day, she could have just been another young L.A. woman with energy to burn, all of her considerable life force focused on the city that has become such a passion that she said she has in her bedroom "a very famous photograph of the Russians planting a flag on the Reichstag when they took over Berlin."

Foster returned to Berlin to film parts of *Flightplan* after numerous visits in the past. "I have to say it is actually the most exciting city in Europe," she said. "I'm a big fan of Paris, and I've spent a lot of time in Rome, but Berlin's got something going on. It's this new excitement about the future and possibility. I love the city—I could blab on about it forever." And with that, she took me through Berlin without taking a breath, oblivious to the oblivious world around her.

Saturday

ATTRACTIONS: THEN AND NOW
The first time I went, the Berlin Wall was still up, and I was a kid. My mom took me to **Checkpoint Charlie,** and we went to East Germany, and we went to the opera and to this beautiful, old, old, old coffeehouse, and then kind of toured around East Germany. At that time, there was no regular lighting. Everything was only lit by neon. There were no signs anywhere in East Germany. So many of the places

had been destroyed by the war, and they didn't really bother to fix them. It was just a completely different place. Then I came back as the wall was coming down, which was really exciting. All everybody wanted to talk about was politics, social issues, and moral ideas, and all that kind of stuff. Then I went just after the wall came down, and it was a city of cherry pickers and cranes! When you looked through the Brandenburg Gate, where the wall used to be, it was nothing but cranes and construction sites. The most construction sites I have ever seen in one place. Today, Checkpoint Charlie apparently is one of the most visited sites in the world. There's a tiny little white building that looks like an outhouse, and there is a **Checkpoint Charlie Museum,** where they have all the artifacts from the wall and some of the artifacts from Checkpoint Charlie, from people who tried to scale the wall, or tunnel, or

tried to get in. Now, it's like the moneymaking thing there, where they have the T-shirts and the buttons and the "I went to Checkpoint Charlie!" mug. It's become like a souvenir shop.

FAVORITE NEIGHBORHOOD East Berlin is the coolest place to live. It's beautiful. The best restaurants are there, the best shops, art galleries. People are walking in the streets. There is all this new, new architecture that was brought into East Germany because they dumped so much money into it. It was so amazing to see the transformation of all those years. You have two pieces of really old architecture, and you're able to put a modern structure right in the middle, because it was bombed out. There is no place in Europe where you can do that. In Paris, you'd never be able to because of the codes. We shot *Flightplan* all over the place, but one of our locations was **Charlottenburg,**

© Jewish Museum Berlin; photo: Jens Ziehe

which is a really pretty part of West Berlin—really cool shops, beautiful old apartment buildings with hardwood floors and high ceilings, good little restaurants.

CULTURE I said, "Well, I'll go to the **Jewish Museum** [designed by architect Daniel Libeskind] for a couple of hours, then I'll go shopping for a couple of hours, and then I'll go to work." I was at the Jewish Museum for four and a half hours. At the Jewish Museum, you have the feeling of being put on a train and being shipped away to a camp. So the way the building is designed, you have these long, long, long corridors that are almost like a train station. Then you see these stories of the families. Then you get to the end of this corridor, and you walk into a room, and they only let in five people at a time. This room is completely dark. It's all concrete and at the top there are two slits, and you can hear Berlin beyond, but you can't see it. It's sort of like being in a train. You'll hear fire engines going by and things happening, but you're completely blocked out of it.

ART **Pergamon** is the ancient-civilization museum. The Germans bought the ancient city of Pergamon from Turkey and hauled it back, block by block by block. They took out the ancient site and rebuilt it inside the museum. If you love antiquities and all the BC stuff, it's just amazing. What I love is the **Bauhaus Museum.** I went there the first time, the second

I said, "Well, I'll go to the Jewish Museum for a couple of hours, then I'll go shopping for a couple of hours, and then I'll go to work." I was at the Jewish Museum for four and a half hours.

time, the third time, the fourth time. I always go there. It has photographs, art pieces—all from the Bauhaus school. It's in a building that was the original Bauhaus building, built by a famous architect. That's definitely worth seeing. It's just a small museum.

HISTORY I went around the city, and I remember seeing the **Reichstag,** the outside clearly. The Reichstag is fabulous now. It was the seat of parliament. Before Hitler came to power, there was a fire at the Reichstag, and he blamed it on the Communists. That was his excuse for getting rid of parliament [and firmly establishing Nazi rule]. Parliament never met there again. The Reichstag remained empty. During the war, it was bombed and destroyed, then it was used throughout the 1960s, when the wall was up, for demonstrations and things like that. No one had ever been inside. Right before they renovated, Christo and Jeanne-Claude wrapped it in silver in 1995—they did one of those installations—and it was pretty fabulous. The renovation on it, which is amazing, was finished in 1999. It has the fabulous view of all of Berlin, because there really wasn't anything built much higher than it.

LUNCH When I was a kid, my mom took me to beer gardens. But, you know, beer gardens are only good in the summertime. I found a great lunchy coffee bar called **Einstein Café** that was really good and had music.

SHOPPING One of the things I've been doing since I was a kid is going to **Ka De We.** It's basically like a department store you'd find anywhere, like Harrods. Then on the top they have the food halls, like they do at Harrods. They have prosciutto from Italy, chocolate, the best you can imagine, and then they have food halls, including this whole area that's only fish. You can get clam chowder, every kind of fish you can think of. They make the food right there. Then you get a little glass of all the different wines—a different Riesling or Prosecco. I always get the schnitzel—veal that's fried, your traditional German meal. I always have schnitzel and a Riesling.

In West Berlin, the famous shopping street is called the **Kurfurstendamm.** They do the most spectacular Christmas lights there in the wintertime. It goes on and on and on, and then they do these big sculptures of animals and Santas. At the end of the Kurfurstendamm, they have the coolest night market at Christmas. The **Kaiser Wilhelm Memorial Church** there was bombed, but they left it that way, so it's kind of a monument to having been bombed. They built a really modern church around it, so it's almost like an amazing modern sculpture with this tower sticking out. On that plaza is the best of the night markets—the crowds and the sledding and the hot dog stands and all that kind of stuff.

NIGHT SHOPPING The night markets are a funny German tradition that happens at Christmastime. As soon as the sun goes down, around five or six o'clock, there are these night markets all over the city that have lights and they have different stands. They have all these wursts, like the hot-dog-wurst-sausage places where they have curry dogs, currywurst, and all these different types of sausages. The night markets have tons of things for kids. I wish I had taken my

kids, actually. I didn't think there was going to be anything for them to do in the wintertime. I thought it was going to be dark and difficult.

DINNER I went to one of the best restaurants I have ever been to in my life: **Restaurant Vau.** It's like one of those meals that people have in Paris that they talk about their whole life, where it's all the different little courses of a half partridge with grapefruit and so on, and each thing is served with the perfect wine to go with it. We decided to do the tasting thing, so we were there for hours. It is in the central part of Berlin. Vau is beautiful, with almost a Viennese touch but still really contemporary design on the inside with wood paneling. You wouldn't have found that in Germany ten years ago. It was the best meal I've had in one hundred years. I also went to a place I really liked called **Lubitsch,** like the director. It's in Charlottenburg. It's German food with a Euro slant to it. Almost like a German version of a French brasserie.

NIGHTLIFE I'm not a nightlife person, but a couple of nights we went looking for fun. We couldn't find any because we were always off so late. We'd get off work at three in the morning, and we'd go driving around the city, saying, "What about this place, and what about that place?" Nobody would be in there. We did find two good places, **Maria am Ostbahnhof** and **Sage Club.**

Sunday

SAUSAGE One day when we were shooting scenes in the subway, I was starving. We were at Alexanderplatz. There was this big, ugly, horrible, International-style building—it was like their version of the Virgin Megastore—and they have every European record you could think of. I went there with this girl from the crew who had a nose ring and bleached-white hair, and she'd been in a band and she wore really cool clothes. I was like, "I want some German music to take home. It's going to be great." I spent three hundred euros or something like that, and I bought all these records. By the time I got back, there was no food left, and then everything was closed. They always outfit me with these bodyguards, and the German bodyguards are my favorites because they're very polite, nice German guys. I said to them, "I'm starving and what I really want is sauerkraut, wurst, and a beer," and they went—well, I don't know where they went. They went and brought back fantastic sauerkraut, fantastic beer—and there were potatoes, those funny potatoes they have. There I was, in the subway, wearing my big old coat, sitting on the ground, having my wurst and my beer and my sauerkraut. It was great.

Jodie Foster's Berlin Essentials

DINING

Einstein Café, Austrian, $$,
011-49-30-261-50-96, Kurfurstendamm 58

Lubitsch, German, $$$, 011-49-30-882-37-56
Bleibtreustrasse 47, Charlottenburg

Restaurant Vau, International, $$$$, 011-49-30-20-29-730
Jagerstrasse 54/55

SIGHTS

Alexanderplatz Bauhaus Museum,
011-49-30-254-00-20, Klingelhoferstrasse 14

Allied Museum, Checkpoint Charlie,
011-49-30-25-37-250, Clayallee 135

Jewish Museum Berlin, 011-49-30-259-933-00
Lindenstrasse 9-14

**Kaiser Wilhelm Gedächtniskirche
(Memorial Church),** 011-49-30-218-50-23
Lietzenburger Strasse 39, Breitscheidplatz

Pergamon Museum, ancient civilization,
011-49-30-20-80-50, Am Kupfergraben

Reichstag, 011-49-30-22-73-21-52, Platz der Republik

SHOPPING

Ka De We, department store, 011-49-30-2121-0
Tauentzienstrasse 21-24

Kurfurstendamn, shopping district, western city center

NIGHTLIFE

Maria am Ostbahnhof, 011-49-30-21-23-81-90
Strasse der Pariser Kommune 8-10, Friedrichshain

Sage Club, 011-49-30-27-89-830, Köpenicker Strasse 76

Michael Douglas

Bermuda

Everybody knows Michael Douglas, son of movie legend Kirk Douglas and star of films including *Fatal Attraction, Wall Street,* and *The American President.* But you may not know that Douglas's mother, Diana Dill Darrid, hails from a family that can trace its Bermudan roots to the 1630s. Douglas and his brothers have made annual pilgrimages to Bermuda since their childhood, getting to know this green archipelago of islands dotted with seventy-nine national parks as well as they knew Los Angeles. When I interviewed him, Douglas was regularly returning to Bermuda for both business and pleasure, having completed a $5 million renovation of the Dill family's forty-five-year-old Ariel Sands, a fourteen-acre, fifty-room resort.

"My first cousin, Seward Johnson, the sculptor who does those lifelike bronze sculptures, and another first cousin, Elaine Wold, put some money into and refurbished it, and it's having a new life," Douglas said. "So I got into the hotel business." Here's a gull's-eye view of Michael Douglas's Bermuda.

Friday

LODGING My mother is Bermudan, and basically the Dills like to think they're a credible old family. I think there were some pirates involved back then, and they inhabited the parish of Devonshire. One of the things they had was this property on the South Shore with this beach that they built into a cottage colony in the early fifties called Ariel Sands [Devonshire Parish]. A cottage colony is basically a hotel but made up of individual cottages. Some are two bedroom, some are one bedroom, or more. What makes it so unique is it has a real lovely beach, and it's probably one of only two or three places on the island where you can actually eat dinner right there on the beach. It's got some saltwater pools, and now it's got a nice spa and exercise center. But it's a real peaceful, restful spot with a great restaurant, family run / family owned, with a lot of pictures up on the walls of my family members and me from different movies in the past.

SIGHTS Well, you know, Bermuda is a tiny island. It's only about twenty-two miles long, and about a mile and a half wide at its widest spot. The island is surrounded by this reef—

turquoise water all around you. So the views are spectacular. Every angle has this great unique color scheme that goes with these houses painted different pastel colors with white limestone roofs. The greatest thing going for Bermuda now is the security and safety issue. It was England's first and last colony. It's out there, isolated. The main towns are Hamilton and St. George's. The South Shore is probably the nicest side. On the far end are the dockyards, where the British served in the war and based their ships. It's a little world unto itself now. They've beautifully refurbished a lot of stores. There's a great craft mart, and there's a great little pub, the Frog and Onion [Royal Naval Dockyard]. It's like a time warp. You think you're in England. It's a total little English pub that's sitting out there. The Somerset/Dockyard Ferry will take you from the dockyards up around back into Hamilton. It's a really beautiful ride. It takes you across the bay on the Somerset Bridge, the world's smallest drawbridge. One of the things that's so staggering about Bermuda is the strong culture. Very few of the Caribbean islands, except maybe Jamaica, have a strong sense of their own culture. But in Bermuda you really feel it.

DINNER There's a little restaurant, down by the airport, called Dennis's Hideaway [St. George's Parish]. It's just home cooking. It's one of the best places I've ever had shark. He makes a shark hash—shark with herbs and spices—and you spread it on crackers like a dip. They've got hogfish, snapper, shark hash, and conch fritters. Dennis Lamb, the cook/owner, is a fisherman and a restaurateur, and he's just great. He's got all kinds of stories and he's a lot of fun. Dennis's is down by St. George's, which is a whole other world. It's a very charming place. The irony is that the island is small, but it takes a long time to get around because the speed limit is twenty miles per hour.

NIGHTLIFE The Swizzle Inn [Bailey's Bay] is named after that famous drink there, the Rum Swizzle. But the real Bermudan drink is called a Dark and Stormy. That's ginger beer with rum.

Ariel Sands resort

What makes Ariel Sands so unique is it has a real lovely beach, and it's probably one of only two or three places on the island where you can actually eat dinner right there on the beach. It's got some saltwater pools, and now it's got a nice spa and exercise center. But it's a real peaceful, restful spot.

The Swizzle Inn, that's in Hamilton. Yeah, it's a little dining place. It's fun. They've got something called Bermuda Gold, which is fairly unique—a slightly sweet after-dinner liquor that's made in Bermuda.

Saturday

BEACHES Horseshoe Bay is one of the really nice beaches, and there are a number of beautiful beaches in Paget, including Elbow Beach. They are all public beaches. Cambridge Beach is a lovely area way up near the tip. The sand is white talcum, a fine, fine, fine sand. Because of these offshore reefs, the beach doesn't just drop off. It's got this great azure water going way, way far out. There used to be a little place called the Flats, where Tucker's Point is now. At the Flats, the tide is so strong, you could spot where all the water rushes out through this narrow opening. I used to go down there and tie ropes off the bridge and water ski, or slalom ski just from the pressure of the water running out. Trying to water ski without a boat, just right off the bridge.

LUNCH Tom Moore's Tavern [Bailey's Bay] was named after the old Irish poet, Tom Moore. Truly fabulous eating—in an eighteenth-century house. It's right next to a nature reserve, so it's just gorgeous. The nature reserve has all of these caves where you can go swimming, so bring a swimsuit. We used to have family reunions at Tom Moore's Tavern. I remember the first time one of my relatives dived into this pool, and he didn't come up. I got so hysterical. He knew that there was this little tunnel where you could hold your breath and go through the tunnel and come out in another pool on the other side. But he tricked me pretty good.

GOLF I'm a golf fanatic. I started playing about twelve years ago—now I'm so gone it's ridiculous. In Bermuda, I'm a member of a club called the Mid Ocean Club [Tuckers Town], which is a stunning, stunning golf course, redesigned by Robert Trent Jones. They have days of the week where the public is allowed to play. The Mid Ocean has been there for a tremendously long time. They hold a lot of tournaments there, including the Maryland Shoot-out and some other PGA events. The other great course is Tucker's Point [Tuckers Town]. Probably one of the greatest public courses is called the Port Royal Golf Course [Southampton Parish]. What makes the golf here so great? Well, they've got Bermuda grass and the views are unbelievable.

SIGHTS Tourists can't drive on Bermuda. Part of the reason is to keep the number of cars down. There is only one car allowed per family. So what you do is rent Mopeds. I would take a Moped on the ferry from Hamilton and go across to the Bermuda Maritime Museum [Royal Naval Dockyards], a great museum. It's basically the history of Bermuda maritime life, when the British were there in the very beginning and leading right up to World War II. The museum is in the dockyards, where you can go shopping. Then, you would take the Moped, not on the ferry, on the back roads along the south shore. You can go to this place called Church Bay. It's a great place to go swimming. Another lovely spot on the south shore is the Edmond Givens Gardens, an eighteen-acre park now called Palm Grove. Bermuda has a lot of nature reserves. It's a beautiful spot to go hiking around. It's got a couple of saltwater ponds. Actually, the thing that's really surprising is right next to it is a dairy, which is really bizarre.

EXERCISE They used to have a railway line on Bermuda. It's now a hiking trail, called the Bermuda Railway Trail [Devonshire]. It's really cool—a footpath and a bicycle path. It's eighteen miles of trails. It goes through the most beautiful country and it runs along the coast, a public right-of-way that just meanders around this incredible country along the coast for a while, with great views from the cliff tops. Bermuda has a lot of biking, a lot of runners, and then of course, boating. It's the center of yachting. They've got a tremendous big harbor, Hamilton Harbor. You can rent a boat. They rent and sell a lot of sea kayaks, which is a big workout. There's a lot of diving, parasailing, windsurfing, scuba diving, and swimming—obviously, all the swimming in the world. Great night swimming, too, which I really enjoy.

SHOPPING Bermuda is known for its silver and wools, things you might have to go over to England to find. Astwood-Dickinson [Hamilton] is a jeweler. They've got a lot of Bermuda crafts, things that are actually designed in Bermuda. A store called Walker Christopher [Hamilton] has beautiful sterling silver, even some Christmas ornaments. It's the best place for buying jewelry.

DINNER I think you would have to go to Port O' Call [Hamilton], which I like a lot. It's a really nice restaurant. The overriding feeling of the whole place is English. Very charming—kind of rustic. There are a lot of little restaurants on Front Street in Hamilton, and they look right out at the bay. There's a restaurant called Little Venice [Hamilton], which I like. It's a little more informal.

NIGHTLIFE There are a lot of places in downtown Hamilton. Fresco's Wine Bar [Hamilton] is a charming place that has entertainment. It's down a little alleyway, in a cellar. It's got the vaulted brick ceilings and a great chef who wins all the awards. There are a lot of clubs in Hamilton. I haven't been doing that for a while.

Sunday

LUNCH The Ariel Sands has a great restaurant called Aqua [Devonshire Parish]. It's right on the beach. It's a real popular place for lunches, because it's like a beach club. After lunch, you could go to a fun place called Rock Island Coffee. That's a locals' place just outside of Hamilton. It's a cottage that my family used to own. It used to be an old Bermuda cottage where my grandfather and my uncle used to have their law offices. Rock Island Coffee has a lot of mixtures of coffees and teas. It has a lovely garden out the back. Very peaceful, tranquil with a beautiful view of Hamilton Harbor and the shore.

SIGHTS My relatives live all over Devonshire. It's just beautiful, like a little bit of England with all these lovely cottages. You should really take a look at Old Devonshire Church, which has been there since 1716. St. Peter's Church in St. George's at the far end of the island is the oldest Anglican church in the Western Hemisphere. That's a whole world unto itself. But the Devonshire church is really close to Ariel Sands, and my whole family, the Dills, are all buried there. My Uncle Lawrence, who was a classical organist, used to play the organ for years and years in the Devonshire Church. It gives me a great feeling of solace and security to go down to places and see where my mother's family has been worshiping for 350 years.

Michael Douglas's Bermuda Essentials

LODGING
Ariel Sands, $$$, (441) 236-1010, 1-800-468-6610
34 South Shore Road, Devonshire Parish

DINING
Aqua, International, $$$, (441) 236-2332
34 South Shore Road, Devonshire Parish

Dennis's Hideaway, Bermudan, $$, (441) 297-0044
Cashew City Road, St. George's Parish

Frog and Onion Pub, English pub, $$, (441) 234-2900
The Cooperage, Royal Naval Dockyards

Little Venice, Italian, $$$, (441) 295-3503
32 Bermudiana Road, Hamilton

Port O' Call, seafood, $$$, (441) 295-5373
87 Front Street, Hamilton

Rock Island Coffee, café, $, (441) 296-5241
48 Reid Street, Hamilton

Tom Moore's Tavern, continental, $$$$, (441) 293-8020
Walsingham Lane, Bailey's Bay

SIGHTS
The Bermuda Maritime Museum, (441) 234-1418
Pender Road, Royal Naval Dockyards

Bermuda Railway Trail, Devonshire

Cambridge Beach, Somerset

Church Beach, Southampton

Elbow Beach, Paget

Horseshoe Bay, Warwick

Old Devonshire Church, Middle Road, Devonshire

Palm Grove Garden, formerly Edmund Gibbons Gardens, Devonshire, South Shore

Somerset Bridge, near the Heydon Trust Estate, Middle Road

Somerset / Dockyard Ferry, (441) 295-4506
Hamilton, Dockyards

One Great Day in Bermuda

Most of my anecdotes fall around my mother's family, and they are a pretty eccentric group. There were the times we went out sailing together. There were enormous beacons out in the middle of the bay for airplanes. They're two stories tall and have bright flashing strobe lights for airplanes. Our boat captain was my Uncle Tommy, who is not with us anymore, and he was singing some crazy ditty about wearing kilts and things tied around the ribbon. It was pretty crazy stuff. He put the boat, this little ketch, right into that beacon and wrapped the whole sail around that enormous strobe light. I was blinded by this incredible light, and we were trying to get the sail removed from it. We couldn't believe he did that—I thought he did it on purpose. Uncle Tommy was legendary. Once we landed on a reef and we all had to swim back in to shore. He would be wild. I don't know what his drink of choice was, but it was a lot. He would start having a good time, singing all these old sea ditties, knocking back a couple, and we would just go, "Whoop, here we go!"

St. Peter's Church, York Street, St. George's

Hamilton Harbor, water sports, www.bermuda-online.org

SHOPPING
Astwood Dickinson, jewelry, (441) 292-5805
83 Front Street, Hamilton

Bermuda Botanical Society Visitor's Center,
(441) 236-5291

Dockyards, on the South Shore

Walker Christopher, jewelry, (441) 295-1466
9 Front Street, Hamilton

NIGHTLIFE
Fresco's Wine Bar, bar, (441) 295-5058
Chauncery Lane, Hamilton

Swizzle Inn, pub, (441) 293-1854
3 Blue Hole Hill, Bailey's Bay

GOLF
Mid Ocean Club, golf, (441) 293-0330
1 Mid Ocean Drive, Tuckers Town

Port Royal Golf Course, (441) 234-0974
Middle Road, Southampton Parish

Tucker's Point Golf Course, (441) 298-6915
Tuckers Town

Buenos Aires

In *Under the Tuscan Sun*, Diane Lane played a book critic who quits the rat race, moves to Tuscany, buys an old house, and finds a new love. Yet even though the film, based on Frances Mayes's best-selling novel, is set in the Italian countryside, it's apropos for Lane's discussion of Buenos Aires, because Lane made a similar journey to the Argentine capital. She left her job and her family, and while she didn't find true love, she did fall hard for the city itself. A veteran traveler and actress, she has journeyed far and wide, especially in her career, which has been a slow and steady trip to the top, with the expected ups and downs. At fourteen, she was on the cover of *Time* (in a story about child stars on the rise). She soared again with breakout roles in hits like the *Lonesome Dove* miniseries, *A Walk on the Moon,* and *The Perfect Storm*. She garnered an Oscar nod for her steamy portrayal of a philandering wife in *Unfaithful*. Here, she turns in a genuine performance as a bon vivant in Buenos Aires.

Saturday

PROPER ATTIRE Argentina is below the equator, so their summer is our winter and vice versa. You have to think about that when you go there. Bring a sweater and tie it around your waist. You want to stay casual, even though it's a cosmopolitan city. At night, people do dress up. You want to bring comfortable shoes for daytime, for sightseeing and shopping, but you want to bring something dressier to go out in the evening. You'll fit in more and feel less like a tourist if you make the effort. It's part of immersing yourself to dress up at night.

LODGING The Alvear Palace Hotel is the greatest. It's just Old World, built in 1932. Their breakfast is extraordinary. They have a whole spread of native fruits, nuts, pastries, meats, cheeses, and eggs, and of course, *dulce de leche*. It's a sweet cream, usually served with pastry, the specialty of the house. You want to dine on the sunny side of the hotel's restaurant, called L'Orangerie. The hotel's lobby is so great. I just remember all the antique chairs, chandeliers, and the curved spiral staircase coming down. You feel like you're in Paris or Budapest or someplace.

DINNER There was a place called Cantina La Placita on the Plaza Julio Cortazar, in the Palermo Viejo section. It serves traditional Argentinean fare, but it has an Italian flavor to it. You want to start with the antipasto plate: cured mixed olives and marinated red peppers. They have a fabulous pasta puttanesca. Their filet mignon melts in your mouth. It's all local people there; it's not really a tourist place.

NIGHTLIFE You've gotta see a live tango show. There are many places and there are a lot that cater to tourists. There's also the Plaza Dorrego, where they dance the tango outside, and El Viejo Almacén, once an old general store in a San Telmo colonial house, where the show starts at 10 p.m. The tango is so dramatic, and these people are so comfortable in their skin. It's effortless. It's extraordinary. It's like watching a bullfight without any bulls getting killed.

Saturday

SIGHTS You must visit the Recoleta Cemetery. I photographed it like crazy. I'm still car-

rying the pictures around with me and hoping to paint them one day. The prominent families of Buenos Aires all have mausoleums there. There are generations of family members who are interred. And it's where Eva Peron is buried. You just walk those paths and the monuments are so dramatic, haunting, and beautiful. It's a very peaceful experience—it's out of this world. It's like an outdoor museum.

LUNCH Almost every great meal I had in Buenos Aires was under twenty-five dollars. One of the great things there is the abundance of places to eat that are extremely reasonable—like El Obrero. I heard that when U2 played Buenos Aires they asked to be taken to a traditional place and El Obrero is where they were sent. It's an old restaurant, traditionally Argentine, run by a Spanish family, serving both pasta and traditional dishes.

CULTURE One of my favorite places is MALBA, the Museum of Latin American Art of

One of my favorite places is MALBA, the Museum of Latin American Art of Buenos Aires. The building is architecturally great and the museum houses twentieth-century masters. It's a no-brainer—you gotta go there.

Malba—Colección Costantini

Buenos Aires. The building is architecturally great and the museum houses twentieth-century masters like Diego Rivera and Antonio Burney. It's a no-brainer—you gotta go there. Then there's Casa Rosada. It's the equivalent of our White House. It's pink and its color comes from an old tradition of mixing oxblood with the plaster. The upper left balcony of Casa Rosada is the immortalized balcony where Evita gave her speeches.

SHOPPING There's high-end shopping around the Alvear Palace. And there's Calle Florida, a pedestrian street that has lots of shops and lots of bargains. Leather is the specialty and you can get some of the best at a store called Casa Lopez. You can walk from place to place on Calle Florida. Frankly, Buenos Aires is a town that you can walk in and you don't need a taxi all the time. It's not like Los Angeles; it's a lot like Rome. Then, of course, there's Avenue 9th of July, which is best known as the widest street in the world.

ANTIQUES The antiques flea market in the San Telmo district, which is held every Sunday in Plaza Dorrego, is just fabulous. It's not as famous as the flea market in Paris, but there are bargains and beautiful European antiques brought over decades ago by Spanish and Italian immigrants. There are coffeehouses on the plaza and lots of boutiques and galleries. I fell in love with some pieces of furniture over there and I still have them. You can truly find great things. I also got all this wonderful glass, Lalique and Galle and another famous artist in crystal and glass. They were sitting there like gems waiting for people to stumble upon them and take them home. I bought this little lamp that was so strange and wonderful, made by hand, with all these encrusted jewels that look like dripping grapes. It's in my daughter's bedroom now. I had to get the wiring changed for the plug to fit in a U.S. socket, but it was worth it. Oh, and I got a gorgeous armoire, very obviously hand-inlaid. It might even be as old as 1790. I had it shipped here and it just rippled like bacon because it's so dry in L.A. Buenos Aires is a very humid place, like being in the Philippines or something.

DINNER There's an area called Puerto Madero, the refurbished docks on the river. There are a lot of grill houses there called *parillas*. One that I love is Estilo Campo, where they have incredible Argentinean beef. But the best-tasting steak I've ever had was at a restaurant called Cabaña Las Lilas, a traditional place whose owners have their own cattle ranch.

NIGHTLIFE It seemed like it was endless and there was no wrong turn you could take. The food, it's so competitive. There's so much pride in the cooking that it pretty much eliminates any lousy food as long as you are eating what the locals are eating. People like to have a good time. But when you eat that late, you've got to burn it off. You can't just go home with a belly full of beef. You go out, dinner lasts a while, and you go home at like three in the morning. Two popular places are Central, a bar and late dinner place in the Palermo Hollywood area, and Milión, a locals' stop in an old French three-story house.

Sunday

BEVERAGE *Mate* is the traditional Argentine nonalcoholic tea. It was made popular by the gauchos, and it's served in those silver-rimmed, hollowed-out gourds. Every antiques store offers these cups for sale, and you sip it through a silver strawlike strainer. The straw itself is the strainer for the tea. It's served in coffee shops and in large mugs. Usually one cup is passed from person to person. That's just the way they do it. It's really a nice way to unwind after a long day of sightseeing. A nice place to have *mate* is Cumana, a restaurant on Rodriquez Peña.

SPORTS The local [soccer] team is the Boca Juniors, and they play in a stadium called Estadio Boca Juniors. Going to a game there is an unforgettable experience.

GREAT OUTDOORS There are great beaches just a few hours away. Uruguay's Punta Del Este, called the Hamptons of South America, isn't too far away. The best hotel there is the Conrad, which is right on the beach and has a casino. Nearer to Buenos Aires is a little town called Tigre, where people live on the inland waterways. It's similar to North Carolina or Florida. Not swampy, but laden with waterways. It's very humid and you get more into that jungle thing. In the main part of Tigre, there's a little area like Coney Island. You can take an inexpensive boat up one of the waterways and have lunch at one of the nice restaurants that can only be reached by boat. It can be really magical when you look back and see the sunset reflected off the Buenos Aires skyline in the distance.

DINNER A place called Sucre, which means "sugar" in French. And then there's Bar Uriarte, where the chef creates a new and exciting spin on traditional dishes. Sucre is a big, modern room with wood-burning ovens and rotisseries, and you can watch the chefs roast meats and assemble dishes. The crowd is younger and hipper. Dinners start late in Buenos Aires and last for hours. A restaurant will be empty at ten at night but full at midnight. That's kind of fun.

DESSERT One of my favorite places is Persicco, where they make the best ice cream in the whole world. There are many locations for it now. You want to find Persicco early in your visit because you'll want to go back, the ice cream is so unforgettable. It's a cheerful place, but pretty spartan.

THE PEOPLE The people are the best part of Buenos Aires. They are just so warm, open, and funny. They are very well-read people. They are very helpful. They're also very opinionated, which is refreshing. The economy has been terribly depressed in the past few years and the government is always in upheaval, but the people are very optimistic and resilient. One would think the economy would engender a lot of strife and misery, but these people are so . . . I don't know what it is. They are just so contented in a way I haven't seen in any other culture. They are a warm, generous, comforting type of people. They love to laugh and display affection. Your heart opens when you go there.

Diane Lane's Buenos Aires Essentials

LODGING

Alvear Palace Hotel, $$$$, 011-54-11-4808-2100
Avenida Alvear 1891

Conrad Resort & Casino Punta del Este, $$$$,
011-598-4249-1111, Avenida Barritz y Artigas, Parade 4,
Punta del Este, Uruguay

DINING

Bar Uriarte, Italian/Argentine, $$,
011-54-11-4834-6004
Uriarte 1572

Cabaña Las Lilas, steak house, $$$,
011-54-11-4313-1336
Avenida Davila 516, Puerto Madero

Cantina La Placita, Italian/Argentine, $$,
011-54-11-4832-6444, Serrano 1636, Palermo Viejo

Cumana, Argentine, $$, 011-54-11-4813-9207
Calle Rodriguez Pena 1149

El Obrero, Italian/Argentine, $, 011-54-11-4362-9912
Agusti R. Cafferena 64

Estilo Campo, steak house, $$, 011-54-11-4312-4546
Alicia Moreau de Justo 1840, Puerto Madero, Capital
Federal

L'Orangerie Restaurant, international, $$$,
011-54-11-4808-2100, Avenida Alvear 1891,
Alvear Palace Hotel

Persicco, ice cream, $, 011-54-11-4808-0888
Salguero 2591, Palermo

Sucre, French/Latin, $$, 011-54-11-4782-9082
676 Sucre, Belgrano

SIGHTS

Casa Rosada, Argentina's "White House,"
011-54-11-4344-3600, Hipolito Yrigoyen 219

Cementerio de la Recoleta, cemetery,
011-54-11-4804-7040, Junin 1790, Recoleta,
Capital Federal

Estadio Boca Juniors, sports stadium,
011-54-11-4309-4700, Brandsen 805

Museum of Latin American Art of Buenos Aires,
011-54-11-4808-6500
Avenida Figueroa Alcorta 3415

Punta del Este, beach,
Uruguay, 50-minute flight from Buenos Aires

SHOPPING

Casa Lopez, leather, 011-54-11-4311-3044
Marcelo Torcuato de Alvear 640, Capital Federal

San Pedro Telmo flea market,
Defensa 1000, Capital Federal Plaza Dorrego

San Telmo district, antiques, 011-54-11-4312-5550

NIGHTLIFE

Central Tango, bar, 011-54-11-5236-0055
Rodriguez Pena 361

El Viejo Almacén, dance club, 011-54-11-4307-6689
Independencia and Balcarce

Milión, bar, 011-54-11-4815-9925
Parana 1048

Caribbean Tour

I 've always looked at life as a voyage—with a thousand ports of call behind me and, I hope, a thousand more to see," wrote singer/songwriter Jimmy Buffett in his best-selling autobiography *A Pirate Looks at Fifty*. Parrotheads, as Buffett's band of global groupies are called, have reason to rejoice, as he continues to perform: his double CD *Live at Fenway* is the singer's thirty-sixth release. Few performers epitomize their geography better than Jimmy Buffett does the Caribbean. Born in Mississippi, he did a stint in Nashville, but didn't find his voice—or his audience—until he moved to Key West, Florida, in the early seventies. As Buffett's star rose, his sails opened and he began living his songs, captaining all manner of

boats throughout the Caribbean and piloting the *Albatross*, a ten-passenger Grumman seaplane. So doff the tie and ditch the wristwatch. It's time for an island-hopping weekend with Jimmy Buffett in the Caribbean.

Friday

LODGING One of my favorite hotels in the whole Caribbean is in Haiti—the **Oloffson** in Port-au-Prince. From Lillian Hellman to Graham Greene, it has an incredible literary history. To me, it's the Caribbean of the thirties. In Nevis you can either stay in a big, fancy resort like the **Four Seasons,** or you can get into

Hurricane Cove, near the airport. It has verandas and palm-lined beaches. [On Harbour Island in the Bahamas] I have some friends who run the **Pink Sands Hotel,** which I like. On Jamaica I stayed over at **Strawberry Hill,** which is one of Chris Blackwell's Island Outpost hotels. I also stay at **Goldeneye,** which was Ian Fleming's house. Goldeneye is a wonderful spot; it's like being in a James Bond movie. If you want action, go to St. Barts. I owned a hotel there, which was more of an all-night bar than it was a hotel, but it burned to the ground. Now my favorite hotel there is the **Eden Rock.**

MUSIC I took my kids to the **Bob Marley Museum** in Kingston, Jamaica. If you're a Bob Marley fan, you should go there. It's a funky little place, but worth going to. The great thing about the Caribbean is the diversity of the music. I have made it my business to collect CDs from the islands. Calypso, reggae, soca, zook—you name it, I like it.

DINNER I always liked **Papillote** underneath Trafalgar Falls in Dominica. It serves "mountain chicken," which is large frogs. Of course, everything tastes like chicken, but they're great. There's a hot waterfall and a cold waterfall up at the falls. They'll take you from the airport and drop you at this little restaurant, and then you can hike to the falls and come down and have a meal.

Randy Gurley, Maya's Restaurant

NIGHTLIFE I've always wanted to do "The Jimmy Buffett Ten Best Bars in the Caribbean" as a show—just get in my seaplane and play these bars. I'd start in Bimini at the **Compleat Angler,** where Hemingway lived and which influenced *The Old Man and the Sea*. Then the **Staniel Cay Club** in the Bahamas and **Happy People Marina.** Happy People has a great dance floor and Staniel Cay's got a great dinner. Then I would go to **Kaye's** on Rum Cay, which is down at the end of the Bahamas. It's a very remote, very beautiful island. From the Bahamas, I'd stop at the **Turtle Cove Inn** in Providenciales, which I would put as one of my top-ten seafood restaurants in the world. They do the best fresh conch dishes there. I'd then go to the **Anegada Reef Hotel** and play there. After that, **Le Select** in St. Barts, where I let them use the Cheeseburger in Paradise trademark for the restaurant and I get to eat and drink free for the rest of my life. If I was heading south from there, one of my other little spots would be the **Admiral's Inn** in Antigua. It's where all the yachties go. And there's **Frangipani,** a great little French hotel with a great restaurant in Bequia.

Saturday

BREAKFAST I eat breakfast at Eden Rock on St. Jean Beach in St. Barts. I like the view because I used to live in St. Jean. I wrote a couple of books and albums there, and I used to rent a room at the Eden Rock. It was kind of my office.

If I could pick anywhere for dinner in the Caribbean, it would be Maya's on St. Barts.

BEACHES The most deserted beaches I've ever seen are on **Long Island** in the Bahamas. There are a couple of little hotels there and this incredibly long pink sand beach. The beaches in **Barbuda,** off of Antigua, are absolutely beautiful, too. The reefs have some of the best diving in the world.

FISHING Up-island in the Bahamas, I'd have to say **Harbour Island.** You can fish there, and there are nice restaurants and a marina. Just look up "Bonefish Joe" Cleare, and he'll take you fishing. I think every island has a Bonefish Joe, but he's probably the best one.

MOUNTAINS There are beaches in Jamaica, but I go for the mountains. I really like islands with mountains. It's that incredible rivers-meet-the-ocean kind of thing. Dominica is probably my favorite, and Jamaica as well. I like the **Cockpit Country** up in the Jamaican mountains. Tropically lush plants. And it just smells good. You get away from the heat of the beach and get into altitude, and there are farms up there and beautiful rolling hills and mountains and rivers, and you can see the ocean.

LUNCH I like to eat at my own restaurants in Jamaica. **Margaritaville** in Montego Bay, and **Marguerite's,** which is the restaurant next to it. Marguerite's is the best restaurant in MoBay, and not just because I happen to be in business with them. It's kind of a combination of jerk and Cajun, and it's really nice there. Then there's a little hotel and restaurant called the **Caves** in Negril, which is a great spot. It's just basic Jamaican—beans and rice and jerk. It's also a great place to stay because the rooms are carved out of caves.

SHOPPING Here's what I bring back from the islands: King, the great grapefruit drink that you can't get in America. I will shop for wine in St. Barts. I love blush wines. Everything is exorbitantly priced in St. Barts, but one of the great bargains is the rose wines. The other thing is this great coconut oil from Nevis that they press down there. Of course, there's no sunscreen in it whatsoever, but it's the best coconut oil around. I collect hot sauces from all the islands. Naturally, each island thinks it has the best peppers. My favorites are Matouk's from Trinidad and Pickapeppa from Jamaica.

DINNER First, I'd go to **Le Select** in St. Barts and have a Ti Punch. If I could pick anywhere for dinner in the Caribbean, it would be **Maya's** on St. Barts. Maya's is right on the water and they have great French-Creole cuisine. After that, I'd go to **Bete A Z'ailes,** a great place for music on the harbor, and I'd finish my night at **Le Ti-St. Barths.**

Sunday

HIKING There's this incredible hike from Cap-Haïtien, a city down on the water in Haiti, up into the old fortress of Henri Christophe, who was the first king of Haiti. He built these palaces that were based on Versailles and San Souci right there in the jungles of Haiti. They're all ruins now, but it's amazing to take the walk up the road they built to this fortress. Last week, I took my son over to **Brimstone Hill** in St. Kitts, which is the fortress that's called "the

Gibraltar of the Indies." It has an incredible history of the Amerindians that the French were fighting. The fort has monkeys climbing all over it. You can take a cab ride from the airport in St. Kitts. It's worth a day trip.

Jimmy Buffett's Caribbean Essentials

LODGING

Eden Rock, $$$$, 011-590-590-29-79-99, 1-877-563-7105, Baie de St. Jean, St. Barts

Four Seasons, $$$$, (869) 469-1111, Pinney's Beach, Nevis

Goldeneye, $$$$, (876) 975-3354, Oracabessa

Hotel Oloffson, $, 011-509-223-4000, Port au Prince, Haiti

Hurricane Cove, $$–$$$$, (869) 469-9462 Oualie Bay, Nevis

Pink Sands Hotel, $$$$, (242) 333-2030 Harbour Island, Bahamas

Strawberry Hill, $$$$, (876) 944-8400 New Castle Road, Irish Town

DINING

The Caves, Jamaican, all inclusive, $$$, (876) 957-0270 Light House Road, Negril

Eden Rock, French, $$$, 011-590-590-29-79-99 Baie de St. Jean, St. Barts

Le Ti-St. Barths, eclectic dining, $$$, 011-590-590-27-97-71, Pointe Milou, St. Barts

Margaritaville, Caribbean, $$, (876) 952-4777 Montego Bay, Jamaica

Marguerite's, Caribbean, $$, (876) 952-4777 Montego Bay, Jamaica

Maya's, eclectic, $$$, 011-590-590-27-75-73 Rue de Public, Gustavia

Papillote, Caribbean, $$, (767) 448-2287 Trafalgar Falls Road, Dominica

Turtle Cove Inn Hotel, seafood and bar, $$, (649) 946-4203, 1-800-887-0477 Suzie Turn Road, Providenciales

SIGHTS

Barbuda beaches, beaches and diving

The Bob Marley Museum, (876) 927-9152 56 Hope Road, Kingston, Jamaica

One Hungry Day in the Caribbean

I can tell you how "Cheeseburger in Paradise" got written. It was probably 1974 and I was on my very first boat, a thirty-three-foot sailboat. We had gotten into some weather and had to go into Ponce in Puerto Rico to get fixed. We sailed from Ponce with a rigged-up bow sprit that was broken, and it was a rough passage. We sailed into Roatán, got off the boat, and were starving. We were dying for a cheeseburger after being at sea for ten days eating fish. And there, like an oasis, was this brand-new restaurant at the Village Cay Marina. We went in and just started gobbling cheeseburgers and drinking piña coladas because we were so glad to be on land. We had about three cheeseburgers each. For some reason, as I was walking out I looked and saw a package in the kitchen and the label was written in French: *Cuoderrie Produit de Cheval.* Do you know what *cheval* is? Horse! I went back to the guy and said, "This will never do. You've got a good idea here, but you've got to take the horse meat off the menu." We went back the next day and the owner was very proud that he'd gotten real hamburger from Puerto Rico, and we sampled the cheeseburgers again. I wrote the song right there: "Cheeseburger in paradise, heaven on earth with an onion slice."

Brimstone Hill, fortress, (869) 465-2609,
www.brimstonehillfortress.org, St. Kitts

Cockpit Country, mountains, www.cockpitcountry.com
Jamaica

Harbour Island, fishing, www.harbourislandguide.com
Bahamas

Long Island in the Bahamas, beach,
www.geographia.com/bahamas/bsliin

NIGHTLIFE
Admiral's Inn, bar, (268) 460-1027, (268) 460-1153
English Harbour, Antigua

Anegada Reef Hotel, seafood, (284) 495-8002
Providenciales

Bete A Z'ailes, live music, 011-590-590-29-74-09
Gustavia, St. Barts

Compleat Angler, bar and live music, (242) 347-3122
Alice Town, Bimini

Frangipani, beach club, (784) 458-3255
St. Vincent, Bequia

Happy People Marina, lounge, (242) 355-2008
Staniel Cay Coast, Bahamas

Kaye's, bar and grill, no phone,
Rum Cay, Bahamas

Le Select, bar, 011-590-590-27-86-87
Gustavia, St. Barts

Staniel Cay Yacht Club, Bahamian cuisine,
(954) 467-8920, Exuma Cays, Bahamas

Anthony Hopkins

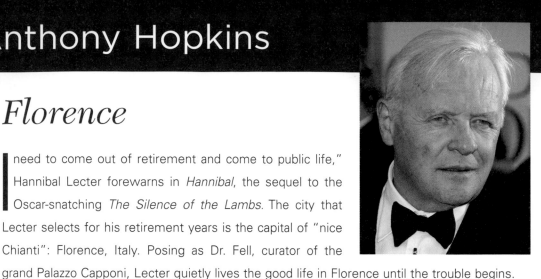

Florence

I need to come out of retirement and come to public life," Hannibal Lecter forewarns in *Hannibal*, the sequel to the Oscar-snatching *The Silence of the Lambs*. The city that Lecter selects for his retirement years is the capital of "nice Chianti": Florence, Italy. Posing as Dr. Fell, curator of the grand Palazzo Capponi, Lecter quietly lives the good life in Florence until the trouble begins.

Sir Anthony Hopkins, who won a Best Actor Oscar for his original performance as the cannibalistic psychiatrist, spent several months living and filming in Florence. Hopkins and the cast and crew of the big budget sequel, which included Julianne Moore and Gary Oldman, became well-known temporary Florentines, constantly trailed by paparazzi. Although he spent more time in character than he did sightseeing, Hopkins said he "enjoyed the whole experience of being there."

The experience represented one more total immersion into a role for the son of a baker, born on New Year's Eve 1937, in Port Talbot, Wales. At seventeen he wandered into a YMCA amateur theater production and knew he'd found his place in the world. In 1965, he auditioned for Sir Laurence Olivier, then director of the Royal National Theater of Great Britain at the Old Vic, and eventually became understudy to the master. But it was Hopkins's work in more than ninety films that placed him among the ranks of the finest living actors. Hopkins now lives full time in Los Angeles. But when he was on the the set in Florence as the notorious Hannibal Lecter, here are the places where he raged.

Friday

LODGING Grand Hotel Villa Cora is just on the outskirts of the city. It's a beautiful old villa with large grounds and gardens. It's just up from the Piazzale Michelangelo and the Boboli Gardens and Forte di Belvedere. In twenty minutes, you can be in the center of the city. I found that very pleasant and took many pleasant walks. It's very crowded with tourists in Florence, like most Italian cities today. But Villa Cora is a small, quiet hotel. The **Hotel Lungarno** is a charming, smaller hotel with good food, service, and vicinity to all our locations. It's right on the river Arno overlooking Florence and the famous Ponte Vecchio. They also have apartments adjacent to rent. The **Westin Excelsior Hotel** is a beautiful hotel, also farther down the Arno, recently redone.

DINNER I went to one trattoria called **Quattro Leoni** [Piazza della Passera], "The Four Lions." It was just a trattoria and I ate the same thing every night—a bit of fish and tomatoes and onions, and that's about it. I don't vary my diet. I sat at the same table every night and had my meal and went home. I like it because it was available; you can always get a table there and it was good food.

NIGHTLIFE The nightlife in Florence is actually surprisingly active. All the locals enjoy a stroll after dinner—they eat quite late—and congregate in the many piazzas, particularly the **Piazza della Repubblica.** As it was originally an ancient Roman forum, then became the central market until the end of the nineteenth century, it has always been a magnet for people. Many a café is open, with tables and chairs practically filling the huge piazza. Music is always present and one can sense everyone took this special time to enjoy his or her life a bit more.

Saturday

BREAKFAST The Westin Excelsior Hotel has a buffet breakfast, but it tempts one to eat too much. The favorite Italian breakfast is, of course, a cappuccino and *cornétto*, or croissant. Florence has plenty of cafés for quick espressos and cappuccinos.

SIGHTS We shot on Florence's oldest bridge, the Ponte Vecchio. Lots of crowds, lots of sightseers, lots of shops selling gold. Giancarlo Giannini, the great Italian actor, shot some scenes there. There are scenes where I'm walking along the riverbank, near the Ponte Vecchio, which we did the first day. I went to the **Palazzo Vecchio** a great deal. It's been the seat of Florentine government for nearly one thousand years and a monument to the rule of the Medici family, whose patronage led Florence to become the leader of the European Renaissance. One day we had an exclusive tour, which included seeing the suspended ceiling above the Salone dei Cinquecento, designed four hundred years ago by the brilliant architect and artist, Giorgio Vasari. Even today, architects from all over the world come to study from this master. We were also taken into the private studio of Francesco I de' Medici, where he collected his art and practiced alchemy. There was even a small room, where he secretly dissected humans for study. We were led into the very private corridor, Corridoio Vasariano, a wedding present from Francesco de' Medici to his wife Giovanna D'Austria. The corridor connects the Palazzo Vecchio with the **Uffizi Gallery,** where they had their offices. It also passes over the Ponte Vecchio, so they could go to their other residence, the Palazzo Pitti, without being seen by the public. This raised, covered "street" is chock-full of valuable art and history.

CULTURE In the film, Hannibal is curator of the Capponi Library and lives in the grand **Palazzo Capponi.** It's still there, a great big library full of manuscripts that go back to the twelfth, thirteenth centuries. Fascinating place. It's a big house, full of books and manuscripts. The owners have letters from Dante and popes from centuries past. All kinds of letters preserved from ancient kings of England and France when the wars and the great troubles were going on. Some of the descendants of the Capponi family still live there to this day. Hannibal Lecter becomes the curator of that museum. So in the story, that's where I live.

SHOPPING In the film, I'm seen walking around marketplaces at night, stalking people. Tourists flock to Florence all year long to admire the monuments and art treasures, but they also come to taste the everyday life and buy the goods unique to Florence. Leather goods, sold in fine shops or in the street markets of Il Mercato Nuovo or in the Piazza San Lorenzo or along the Ponte Vecchio, are the best to be found. Tuscany also has fine linens and the centuries-handed-down art of *ricami,* or embroidery. The finest store in all of Italy is that of **Loretta Caponi** [Piazza Antinori], whose family has done linens for the tables, boudoirs, and palaces of the kings and queens of Europe for the past centuries.

LUNCH The production organized a location as the permanent site for our catered lunch inside the five-hundred-year-old Villa Corsini. Imagine sitting amongst cavernous frescoed walls, water-damaged from years of the flooding waters of the Arno, and where one of the most important Florentine families held court. An exclusive *Hannibal* trattoria with never a bad meal, of course. We were also entertained at an eighteenth-century, fully restored villa between town and the Piazzale Michelangelo, rented by

Dino and Martha De Laurentiis's favorite restaurants include the famous Gelateria Vivoli.

the producers Dino and Martha De Laurentiis. The De Laurentiis's favorite restaurants include **Osteria de' Benci** [Piazza Santa Croce], **Caffè Rivoire** in the Piazza Signoria, and **Gilli** in the Piazza della Repubblica, as well as the famous *gelaterias,* **Gelateria Vivoli** [Piazza Santa Croce] and **Gelateria Ermini** [Duomo].

ART I did go around the Uffizi Gallery. That was pretty interesting, because of how big it is and seeing Botticellis and the Giottos. The Medici collected great wealth in art, housed in the Uffizi: from Botticelli's *Primavera* and *The Birth of Venus,* Giotto's *Ognissanti Madonna,* Leonardo's *Annunciation,* Paolo Uccello's *The Battle of San Romano,* Raphael's *Madonna of the Goldfinch,* and Michelangelo's *Tondo Doni,* to the many grotesques and the painted ceilings of the Gallery—all giving testimony to the splendor of the Italian Renaissance. The art in the Palazzo Vecchio alone could consume several days of viewing. From statues of Donatello, massive murals of Vasari, and murals depicting Florence's battle and victory against Pisa. The **Pitti Palace** [Piazza Pitti], with its splendid gardens, is a centerpiece of art objects, statues, and restored rooms of the family. We visited many a

Gelateria Vivoli

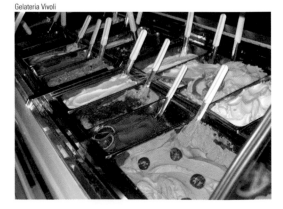

church full of statues, frescoes, and paintings depicting the ideals and facts of the centuries of politics and religion so vital to the Italian Renaissance. Of course, the masterpiece of Michelangelo, the magnificent statue of David at the Gallery of the Accademia with his different versions of Pietà is astonishing. I tried to buy Michelangelo's David, but they wouldn't sell it to me.

DINNER The crew's favorite restaurant was **Coco Lezzone** [Piazza Santa Trinita], a quick walk from the Hotel Lungarno, a family-style trattoria, with the best steak *fiorentina*. They make a great *fiorentina pappa di pomodòro*, thick tomato soup, and pastas with tartuffi. Across from the Hotel Lungarno is another trattoria, **Mamma Gina** [Ponte Vecchio], where the crew ate quite often and where our production team frequently stopped for a quick meal together. Their grilled veal chops and Tuscan *fagiolini* [white beans] were the crew's favorites.

Sunday

LUNCH/EXCURSION Italians center their activities around food—and the Sunday noon meal, which is usually buffet-style, with grilled vegetables, cheeses, fresh pizza bread, prosciutto, omelets, tomatoes, and salads. There was always the temptation on Sundays to visit the great art and treasures of Siena, which are a little more than an hour's drive, or the Roman theater in Fiesole. Since we were in Florence before it got too hot, the weather was splendid.

SIGHTS Other sites featured in the film are the **Pharmacy of Santa Maria Novella,** one of the oldest perfumery-pharmacies in the world, established in 1221. The opera sequence in *Hannibal* was shot in front of the Pazzi Chapel, in the courtyard of the church of the Santa Croce. The Pazzi family had organized the assassination of one of the Medicis on the steps of this chapel. A descendant, Renaldo Pazzi, was one of our lead actors in the script. It

One Memorable Day in Florence

We filmed inside the Palazzo Vecchio—very grand, very big, very oppressive. As Lecter, I killed two people inside the Palazzo Vecchio. I sliced a cop named Pazzi's throat out, disemboweled him, and threw him out the window into the Palazzo Vecchio, which was very nice. I enjoyed that. Thomas Harris [author of *Hannibal*] visited while we were shooting. He'd lived with these characters so long that to see the sequence of Lecter throwing Pazzi to his death was something he relished. We were on the balcony of the Palazzo Vecchio, where a member of the original Pazzi family, Francesco, was executed during the uprising, the rebellions. There was a lot of butchery back in the fifteenth, sixteenth centuries. Terrible things happened there. How did I feel? Kind of depressed, because a lot of people were burned at the stake in Florence in the sixteenth century. We were standing at a place where Savonarola [the fifteenth-century religious leader] was burned at the stake. They just roasted these people alive and the mobs cheered. It was a pretty brutal time. Florence is a beautiful city to walk around. But it's pretty haunted, built on a huge mountain of bloodshed and horror. But it's still an interesting, beautiful city.

was a coincidence we would be shooting this pivotal scene there.

Wherever the camera turned, the backdrop and vistas of Florence were rich: whether we were shooting in the loggia of the Uffizi Gallery, with the long cinematic corridors; to the statues featured in the Piazza della Signoria in front of the Palazzo Vecchio; to the exterior steps of the Spedale degli Innocenti [the Orphans' Hospital] with grand arches and the famous discs in terra cotta decorated by Andrea della Robbia; to the corridors along the Piazza della Repubblica; to the Mercato Nuovo, where the famed statue Fontana del Porcellino, the wild boar that, legend has it, can ensure a return to Florence by throwing a coin into the basin and rubbing his nose.

Anthony Hopkin's Florence Essentials

LODGING
Grand Hotel Villa Cora, $$$$, 011-39-055-229-8451
Viale Niccolo Machiavelli 18

Hotel Lungarno, $$$$, 011-39-055-27264000
Borgo San Jacopo 14

Westin Excelsior Hotel, $$$$, 011-39-055-27151
Piazza Ognissanti 3

DINING
Caffè Rivoire, Italian, $$, 011-39-055-214-412
Piazza della Signoria 5

Coco Lezzone, Italian. $$, 011-39-055-287-178
Via del Parioncino 26, Piazza Santa Trinita

Gelateria Ermini, gelato shop, $, 011-39-055-244-464
Via Gioberti 125, Duomo

Gelateria Vivoli, gelato shop, $, 011-055-292-334
Via Isole delle Stinche 7, Piazza Santa Croce

Gilli, Italian, $$$, 011-39-055-213-896
Piazza de Repubblica 3

Mamma Gina, Italian, $$$, 011-39-055-239-6009
Borgo San Jacopo 37, Ponte Vecchio

Osteria de' Benci, Italian, $$, 011-39-055-234-4923
Via de Benci 13, Santa Croce

Quattro Leoni, Italian, $$, 011-39-055-218-562
Via dei Vellutini 1, Piazza della Passera

SIGHTS
Palazzo Capponi, library, Via de Bardi 6

Palazzo Pitti, 011-39-055-238-8614, Piazza Pitti 1

Palazzo Vecchio, 011-39-055-276-8224
Piazza della Signoria

Pharmacy of Santa Maria Novella, perfumery/pharmacy, 011-39-055-436-8315, Via della Scala 16

Uffizi Gallery, 011-39-055-238-8651
Loggiato degli Uffizi 6

SHOPPING
Loretta Caponi, handmade linens, 011-39-055-213-668
Piazza Antinori 4

NIGHTLIFE
Piazza della Repubblica, town square
heart of old town Florence

Hong Kong

In *Rush Hour 2*, the sequel to his 1998 hit, Jackie Chan once again played a Chinese police inspector forced to buddy up with an LAPD detective played by Chris Tucker. But while the original was set in America, *Rush Hour 2* unfurled on Chan's home turf, where he was named Chan Kong-sang, which means "Born in Hong Kong Chan." Chan had already starred in more than one hundred films in Asia before exploding on to the scene in the U.S. with 1996's *Rumble in the Bronx*, followed by *Rush Hour*, *Shanghai Noon*, and *Jackie Chan's First Strike*. It's been a long climb to stardom for the son of parents who worked as cook and house-keeper for the French ambassador to Hong Kong. His parents enrolled him at seven in the Beijing Opera Academy, where he trained from 5 a.m. to midnight daily in the martial and performing arts. In 1971, he became a stuntman in Bruce Lee's *Fists of Fury*. Like Lee, Chan performs all his own stunts, which, he claims, has resulted in breaking practically every bone in his bionic body. "Everything from the top of my head to the bottom of my feet," he said. One thing has remained unbroken: his abiding love for his hometown. Here's a weekend with the action hero in Hong Kong.

Friday

LODGING The **Hotel Inter-Continental** [Kowloon] and **The Peninsula** [Kowloon] are both big hotels. But sometimes I recommend that my friends not spend so much, and instead save money for shopping by staying at the **Marco Polo** [Kowloon]. From there, you're just two minutes from the main shopping center, one minute from every type of food, one minute from the ferry. The hotel is linked to a shopping mall, theater, everything.

DINNER Felix, at the top of the Peninsula Hotel, is one of the most ultra-modern restaurants in Hong Kong. It's really funky. I don't want to give it away but, well, the toilets are very cool. They also have a beautiful wine bar. You have to get dressed up. You wouldn't be out of place if you wore a tux. But the highlight, especially for me, is when you go to the toilet. From there, you can see the whole harbor. Because the male receptacle is very tiny and is in front of glass, it looks like you're standing out over the harbor. It's an experience.

NIGHTLIFE Nathan Road is open twenty-four hours a day. The discos stay open until five or six in the morning. The main business in Hong Kong is the tourist business, so everything is designed around that. Happy Valley is an area where there's a lot of good karaoke. I love to sing. The old karaoke place is called **Green Box** [locations throughout the city]. I also like the karaoke rooms [now called **Echoes**] at the Emperor Hotel. Sometimes, when I have people in town, we'll all go there and have some drinks, sing karaoke, play pool, hang out.

Saturday

BREAKFAST For breakfast, I like the Whampoa area. There are small shops where they sell bean curd. I like to eat tofu with milk in the morning. I also like to have rice rolls. It's sticky rice, stuffed with shredded pork and chopped green onion. Another breakfast specialty is long, crispy Chinese donuts wrapped in flat rice noodles. It's a Shanghainese thing actually. Very good.

The Peninsula is the oldest colonial-style hotel in Hong Kong.

SIGHTS My favorite thing is to take a tram or bus up to **Victoria Peak.** I like to go to the top, the highest point on Hong Kong Island, and look down. If you're lucky and it's not foggy, it's a beautiful view. You see the skyscrapers and the eight mountains of Kowloon. You see the streets, the people, and the neon everywhere. Victoria Peak has a park and the Peak Tower, which has restaurants, shops, and amusement park rides. I also like to take the **Star Ferry** to Kowloon, which is the heart of the new Hong Kong, home to its nightlife and artistic community. People say everything's for sale in Kowloon. You can go to the streets of Tsim Sha Tsui, Kowloon's commercial center, whose alleys are always full of sounds and smells: fresh cut flowers, skewers of roasting meat, perfume, laughter, music, heated conversation, and whispers.

Murphy O'Brien Public Relations

SHOPPING I have my own clothing line. It's called **Blanc de Chine,** and it's also a store on Pedder Street, in central Hong Kong. Another line is called Bleu de Chine. It's a more casual line—younger, modern Chinese stuff. Hong Kong has lots of markets. There's the **Stanley Street Market,** where a lot of foreigners go to shop for cheap clothing, T-shirts, souvenirs, paintings, prints, everything. There's the **Ladies' Market,** which has clothing, not only for ladies but everyone. **Temple Street** has a mile-long market that is best at night; you can buy everything from clothing to electronics and it's a show in itself. There's also **Hollywood Road,** which is all antiques. I collect antique teacups and saucers. I have more than a thousand. I've found many of them on Hollywood Road.

LUNCH Yan Toh Heen is the Chinese restaurant in the Hotel Inter-Continental. The restaurant isn't fancy, but classy. If you want just typical Hong Kong food, you have to go to the stalls in Mongkok. They have the women's pantyhose tea. They put tea leaves inside pantyhose and then pour hot water through the hose and make tea. It's very good, very traditional. I love to go to the little noodle stalls in the Dai Pai Dong region on the new territory side of Hong Kong. It's Chinese-style fast food: noodles and sandwiches. *Dai pai dong* is the proper name for all the stalls. That's what it means— "street stall." They're everywhere. You can't miss them.

EXCURSION Lantau is an island off of Hong Kong. The Big Buddha statue is on Lantau Island. It's this big giant Buddha. You climb stairs up to it. Lantau has Hong Kong's second-highest mountain [and the new airport]. There's a place on Lantau called Taio. It's a little old fishing village, and probably the last place around that's got old-world Hong Kong flavor. They still use little junks to go fishing. You should also see the islands of **Cheung Chau,** which have open-air cafés, clear-water beaches, and temples dedicated to the protector of fishermen.

SOUP BREAK Chinese people love food, especially soups. Chinese soups are very therapeutic. Just like Western people have chicken noodle soup for colds, Chinese people have different soups for everything: "Oh, your eyes look a little pink; I'll get you carrot soup." Chinese people eat everything for their health. Longevity. Health. Beauty. Good fortune. Shark fin soup is supposed to be good for your health. Good shark fins look like huge noodles. And cheap shark fins are little and look like vermicelli. For dessert, I like the green bean soup. It's almost like tapioca, but it's little beans. And, of course, it's also soup.

HIGH TEA Go for the high tea, the classic English high tea, at the Peninsula. The Peninsula is the oldest colonial-style hotel in Hong Kong. They have a beautiful high tea that everybody goes to. There's a harpist playing and you have this beautiful silver tea set—the works.

DINNER I have a chain of fast-food sushi restaurants called **Genki Sushi.** There are about thirty of them. You sit down, then the sushi just starts coming around on a conveyor belt. You pick up what you want. You eat and you run. It's Hong Kong's version of fast food.

NIGHTLIFE The one place you have to go is **Lan Kwai Fong,** the nightspot area right in the heart of the central city. Everyone would surely tell you what a good time they had in this area of clubs, restaurants, pubs, and discos. Whatever your tastes may be, you're surely going to find it in Lan Kwai Fong.

Sunday

BREAKFAST You have to go for dim sum. It's like little dishes, lots of varieties. The famous ones are the shrimp dumplings, called *ha gow* in Cantonese, and *siu mai,* the pork dumplings. The pork buns called *cha siu bao* are also very well known. With dim sum, you drink lots of tea, the popular choices being jasmine and oolong. My favorite is chrysanthemum and jasmine. Many of the good seafood restaurants are open for breakfast, too. Many Hong Kong restaurants are open from morning till past midnight, probably because of high rental prices—entrepreneurs have to make use of every minute!

EXCURSION The colony of **Macau** is probably the best excursion. It's like Hong Kong, but instead of the British taking over, it was the Portuguese, so Macau has a very European flavor. There are temples and casinos and museums and great restaurants. It's like going to an old city in Europe—only an hour by boat from Hong Kong.

OUTDOORS Hong Kong is an island, but there are mountains. It's not grand mountains like the Rockies, but sharp little mountains, very steep. Sometimes I walk or run Repulse Bay, which is an area with nice trails. There are trails that go up to Victoria Peak. You can

One Great Day in Hong Kong

One day when I was seven, my dad, who had never taken me on an outing before, told me we were going on a trip. Excited, I ran and changed into my best outfit: a cowboy costume, complete with ten-gallon hat and plastic six-shooters. I'd never been down to the lower city before, though I'd seen it from Victoria Peak. We boarded the ferry for Kowloon. When I asked where we were going, my dad said, "Somewhere special." On the ferry, I watched the skyline approaching, holding my cowboy hat tight against my head with one hand. The ride across the bay is a short one, and minutes after we'd left, we were told to prepare to land in Kowloon.

Even though it was still early, I'd already decided this was the best day of my entire life. Kowloon was dirtier and more crowded and louder than anything I'd ever seen in my life, and I loved it. I'd never seen so many people. Everyone had a purpose—heading to work after a long night's sleep or home after a long night's play. What, I wondered, was our purpose? My head spun with curiosity, but my father was determined to move on, and I was dragged along in his wake. Finally, one last turn brought us onto a street lined with tenements whose windows were dark and shuttered. "Here we are," he said. The sign before us identified the building as the Beijing Opera Academy, a name that told me nothing at the time, but meant everything for my future as an actor. My father had just taken me to my new school.

actually walk all the way up and down the peak on these paths. Hong Kong also has the MacLehose Trail in the New Territories, which hosts an annual one-hundred-kilometer race. You go in teams of four. It took me twenty-three hours with my team. I think the record is like thirteen or something, and that was by Gurkha soldiers. It's hellish. I cried at the end. At Clearwater Bay, there are both hiking trails and beaches. Stanley Beach is nice as well.

Jackie Chan's Hong Kong Essentials

LODGING
Hotel Inter-Continental Hong Kong, $$$$, 011-852-2721-1211, 18 Salisbury Road, Kowloon

The Marco Polo HongKong Hotel, $$$, 011-852-2113-0088, Harbour City, Kowloon

The Peninsula Hong Kong, $$$$, 011-852-2920-2888 Salisbury Road, Kowloon

DINING
Felix, Asian/Pacific Rim, $$$$, 011-852-2920-2888 Salisbury Road, Peninsula Hotel, Kowloon

Genki Sushi, Japanese fast food, $, 011-852-2722-6689 98 Granville Road (main location)

Yan Toh Heen, Cantonese, $$$, 011-852-2721-1211 Salisbury Road, Hotel Inter-Continental, Kowloon

SIGHTS
Cheung Chau Islands
6 miles southwest of Hong Kong

Lantau Island
outlying island, Hong Kong Islands

Star Ferry, 011-852-2366-2576
Star Ferry Pier, Edinburgh Place

Victoria Peak, 011-852-2849-7654, 1 Lugard Road

SHOPPING
Blanc de Chine, clothing, 011-852-2524-7875
12 Pedder Street, Central

Hollywood Road, antiques,
Sheung Wan on Hong Kong Island

Jackie Chan Designs, 145 Waterloo Road, Kowloon

Ladies' Market, clothing, Mongkok

Stanley Street Market, shopping district,
southern district of Hong Kong Island

Temple Street Night Market, shopping district,
Yau Ma Tei

NIGHTLIFE
The Echoes, karaoke bar, 011-852-2893-3693
Golden Valley, Emperor Hotel

Green Box, karaoke bar,
multiple locations throughout Hong Kong

Lan Kwai Fong, dining/entertainment district,
Lan Kwai Fong

Jamaica

The supermodel sitting in the Plaza Hotel suite in Manhattan isn't exactly what she seems. On the surface she's Naomi Campbell, the emblematic face of global fashion, the first black model to appear on the covers of *Time* and French and British *Vogue*. But there's more to Naomi Campbell than meets the senses.

The "honorary goddaughter" of Nelson Mandela, she has raised more than five million rand for the Nelson Mandela Children's Fund and joined the Dalai Lama in fund-raising efforts to build kindergartens for poor communities worldwide—including one built in her name in her spiritual home—Jamaica. Though she was born in London and presently travels the world, the homeland of her late great-grandmother and grandparents is in her blood. She returns regularly to spend time with her family, including her honorary dad, Chris Blackwell, the Jamaican-based hotelier and founder of Island Records, who first recorded Bob Marley and many other Jamaican entertainers. Here's a weekend with Naomi Campbell on the Caribbean island of wood, water, sunshine, and supermodels.

Friday

ORIENTATION I think out of all the islands I have been to in the Caribbean, Jamaica's the nicest. It's got everything you could want: ranches, farmland, beaches, the highest mountains, rivers, and waterfalls. The main cities are Kingston, the capital between the Blue Mountains and the ocean, and the resort cities of Ocho Rios, Negril to the west, and Montego Bay. Port Royal, now a fishing village that you get to on a twenty-minute ferry ride, was once the biggest trading center, home to the pirates and buccaneers before an earthquake in the 1600s put most of it underwater. When I go to Jamaica, I want to feel the culture. So I love to go to Cockpit Country, where Chris Blackwell has a ranch. It's got horses and pigs and cows and goats. Nothing lavish. Jamaican time, as you'll know, is a lot different from New York time. You're on JA time and everything is very relaxed, and they have a saying that's called "soon come," which means everything will take care of itself soon.

LODGING Well, I'm actually really a spoiled little girl, because Chris Blackwell gave me my twenty-fifth birthday at **Goldeneye,** which is the former home of Ian Fleming, who wrote the James Bond books. His desk is still there. But now Goldeneye is a resort villa near the town of Orcabessa. It's like a little village; there's the main house and these deco huts. Just being there—amid such tranquility and history, knowing what Ian Fleming has created in James Bond—is wonderful. Chris has asked guests who've stayed there to plant trees during their stay. I planted one, as did Quincy Jones, Jim Carrey, Martha Stewart, Christy Turlington, and Harry Belafonte. Mine hasn't grown very much, but I do know that the biggest and tallest tree that I ever saw there was River Phoenix's tree. It is outstanding compared to everybody else's.

Strawberry Hill [Irish Town] is about thirty minutes from Kingston in the Blue Mountains on the cliffs above the sea. It has an Aveda spa in it now, and it's more relaxing. You go to bed a bit earlier, and it gets a little chilly at night because you're in the mountains. Then there's the **Caves** in Negril, about an hour and a half from Montego Bay, a resort set above volcanic caves above the ocean. If you're into to scuba diving and snorkeling, that's the one to go to. Very rocky. Negril is very touristy, like Ocho Rios, whereas Goldeneye and Strawberry Hill are not touristy at all. Montego Bay has the **Half Moon Golf, Tennis and Beach Club,** which has just about everything. I did a shoot for *Harper's Bazaar* at the **Trident** [Port Antonio], an elegant hotel on the cliffs with its own castle. A lot of fashion shoots are done at the Trident.

Island Outpost Properties

Goldeneye is the former home of Ian Fleming, who wrote the James Bond books. His desk is still there, but now Goldeneye is a resort villa.

DINNER Strawberry Hill has a really lovely cozy restaurant, one of the best in Kingston. It has a panoramic view of all Kingston, with the white tablecloths and really fantastic food, which they call New Jamaican Cuisine. They also have a spa menu at lunch, because you have the spa. Strawberry Hill is definitely more for relaxation and taking care of yourself. I tend to go to bed quite early because the air up there is so clean, you pass out quite early.

NIGHTLIFE At night most of the beaches have a sound system playing lots of reggae. It's people getting together on the beach. There are also a lot of dance halls in Kingston—**Asylum** is my favorite. They really get down there. People are dancing—doing the skank and dance hall and rubadub. They have their moves down. I wouldn't want to compete against any of the Jamaican women, because I would lose for sure.

Saturday

BEACHES I love **Frenchman's Cove,** like a Blue Lagoon–type beach east of Port Antonio. There's a rope from a tree that you can swing on. On most of the beaches in Jamaica there's always someone cooking fish on the barbecue and making festival—a dish of flour, cornmeal, and sugar. That's part of the Jamaican tradition. On **Hellshire Beach** near Portmore, there are little stalls with *escoviche* (spicy fish) and fish tea, a soup they boil for hours and hours. It's just so good. But my favorite is the private beach at **Goldeneye.** It's so inviting and private. I'm not the world's best swimmer, but I have no fear when I'm there. The water is

beautiful. Warm. Very clear. They have a sound system. You can play volleyball and go on the jet skis down the coast.

SHOPPING There's a **produce market in Port Maria** where we go for groceries on Wednesdays, when they get all the fresh produce. Port Maria is basically just a little port town where people get their necessities. Then there's an **arts and crafts market in Ocho Rios,** which is brilliant. You get all sorts of stuff there—dolls and beads and everything in between. I buy T-shirts and little red, gold, and green bikinis. There are lots of boutiques in Ocho Rios with Indian fabrics, very good quality and easy to wash. They don't crease. Just great holiday clothes. You can take home the great coconut oil that they make in the house at Goldeneye. They mix it with olive oil and the coconut is so good for your skin. It makes it very soft.

LUNCH I adore jerk chicken, the spicy chicken you can get all over Jamaica. Every place makes jerk chicken. It's made with the special Walker's Wood Jamaican Jerk Seasoning. It's very, very spicy and it's brownish. They barbecue the chicken in that sauce. When I come in from Montego Bay, I always stop at one of the **jerk centers** on the way. They're all good. I take it to go. I eat it in the car driving around. Jerk chicken is one of the things I have that makes me know I'm back in Jamaica. I know I've landed, definitely.

CULTURE There's the statute of Bob Marley in Kingston and the **Bob Marley Museum,** which used to be his home and recording studio. Chris Blackwell owns and maintains **Firefly** [St. Mary], Noel Coward's former home and once the home of Sir Henry Morgan, the buccaneer. It is now a museum about ten minutes from Goldeneye, heading toward Port Maria. The house is more or less the way it was on the day Coward died in 1973. His shirts still hang in the closet. You can see the piece of paper that Noel Coward left in the typewriter. Sophia Loren, Elizabeth Taylor, Richard Burton, Vivian Leigh, Churchill, Katharine Hepburn, and many others visited Noel Coward at Firefly. You can see the towels with his initials, all of his sketches on the wall, and all his paintings. It's a modest house, but it's got the most incredible view you could ever see.

HIKING I went to **Dunn's River Falls,** which is beautiful, a six-hundred-foot waterfall just outside of Ocho Rios. You can climb to the top of the falls or swim in the water at the bottom. Once, I climbed up and I had to climb back down because I wouldn't get into the pools at the top. I was too chicken because I couldn't swim then. But it's so beautiful.

DINNER I've been to **Jade Garden** in Kingston, which is considered the best Chinese restaurant in Jamaica. I have Chinese in my family, in my blood, and there's a huge population of Jamaican-Chinese. My grandmother came from St. Anna's Bay, and she is half Chinese. Her name was Ming before she got married. The other great restaurants are **Heather's** [New Kingston], which is known for kebabs and Jamaican food; **Norma's on the Terrace** at Devon House; the **Blue Mountain Inn** in Gordon Town on the way to the Blue Mountains; and an outdoor place with wonderful salads and curried snapper called **Guilt Trip**

One Great Day in Jamaica

When I was five, I was in Bob Marley's video for the song "Is This Love?" They picked me from my school in London to be in the video. I remember I cried, "Mommy, I don't want to go near him because he's got worms in his hair!" I thought his dreadlocks were worms or snakes. In the video, there's a scene of Bob Marley outside on the street with the kids, and he's holding my hand and a little boy's hand, Paul Metford, a friend of mine from school. We were hopping and dancing in the street with him, and then it goes interior and we are at a party dancing with him. There's a scene where I fall asleep and he covers me up with a blanket. I haven't changed. I look exactly the same.

The night of my twenty-fifth birthday at Goldeneye, I met Bob Marley's mother. The party basically went on for four days. It wasn't big, but it was great. We would wake up and have another birthday cake. Chris Blackwell just kept having birthday cakes until they ran out. Meeting Bob Marley's mother during the birthday, I was truly in awe. She's a wonderful woman. She said to me, "I wish my son was alive to meet you because he would like you." I said, "Well, I met him when I was a child." She was like, "Really?" And I explained it to her. She's an amazing woman—full of strength.

[now called **The Upper Crust**] on the Barbican Road.

Sunday

WORSHIP Sunday, you can go to church. There isn't one that I go to specifically, but there are churches all around Jamaica. The **Church on the Rock** has a choir that sings gospel with reggae tracks. They are very serious about God in Jamaica and on Sundays everyone is in church. But every day in Jamaica is like a Sunday—a day of relaxation, a day of rest. Music is definitely a highlight of all days—on the beach, in the house, everywhere.

Naomi Campbell's Jamaica Essentials

LODGING

The Caves, $$$$, (876) 957-0270, Light House Road, Negril

Goldeneye, $$$$, (876) 975-3354, Oracabessa

The Half Moon Golf, Tennis and Beach Club, $$$, (876) 953-2211, Rose Hall, Montego Bay

Strawberry Hill, $$$$, (876) 944-8400 New Castle Road, Irish Town

Trident Villas and Hotel, $$$, (876) 993-2602 Anchovy, Port Antonio

DINING

The Blue Mountain Inn, European, $$$, (876) 927-1700 Gordon Town Road, Gordon Town

Heather's, Jamaican, $$, (876) 926-2826 9 Haining Road, New Kingston

Jade Garden, Chinese, $$$, (876) 978-3476 106 Hope Road, Kingston

Jerk Chicken Centers, $ multiple locations throughout Jamaica

Norma's on the Terrace, Jamaican, $$$, (876) 968-5488, 26 Hope Road, Devon House

Strawberry Hill Restaurant, New Jamaican cuisine, $$$, (876) 944-8400 New Castle Road, Irish Town, St. Andrew

The Upper Crust, Caribbean, $$$, (876) 977-5130 20 Barbican Road, Kingston

SIGHTS

The Bob Marley Museum, (876) 927-9152 56 Hope Road, Kingston

Dunn's River Falls, waterfall and swimming, Highway A3, Ocho Rios

Firefly, museum, (876) 725-0920 Grants Town, St. Mary

Frenchman's Cove, Port Antonio

Goldeneye Resort, private beach, (876) 975-3354 Oracabessa, St. Mary

Hellshire Beach, Port Royal

SHOPPING

Ocho Rios Craft Park, market

Port Maria, produce market, St. Mary

NIGHTLIFE

Asylum, nightclub, (876) 906-1828 68 Knutsford Boulevard, Kingston

WORSHIP

Church on the Rock Jamaica, Ltd., (876) 924-7620 7 Clifton Drive, Kingston

London/Canterbury

Once upon a time, in the verdant county of Kent, in the city of Canterbury, England, a boy was christened Orlando Jonathan Blanchard Bloom, after seventeenth-century composer Orlando Gibbons. Alas, this Orlando, being from Canterbury, where Geoffrey Chaucer based his famously unfinished tales, would soon take a more dramatic turn with his life. Having excelled in local plays at an early age, he moved to London at sixteen to attend drama school, a journey that not only transformed the boy into a man, but also into a star born for epics on the silver screen. In London, he met the wizard behind *The Lord of the Rings*, who cast Bloom as the elfin Legolas Greenleaf. Soon, our hero was a prince of filmdom, performing alongside the kings: with Viggo Mortensen in the *Lord of the Rings* trilogy, Johnny Depp in *Pirates of the Caribbean*, and Brad Pitt in *Troy*. He starred on his own in *Kingdom of Heaven*, a typically Orlando-esque adventure about a common man who serves a doomed king, falls in love with a forbidden queen, and rises to knighthood. Herewith, Bloom tells the equally captivating story of his own fabled life in Canterbury and London.

Friday

CULTURE In Canterbury, there is a place called the **Canterbury Tales,** which is like a little walk-through museum where you see all the different characters described. The mannequins are all dressed up, and there are even the sounds and smells of the times. It's quaint. Often, I'll dream of walking through streets in England that I used to walk. St. Thomas Hill in Canterbury is one that was locked in my head. It actually led to my old school, and I grew up on that hill. We had a house on St. Thomas Hill. But growing up in Canterbury, the **cathedral** was always right in my backyard, and for different school functions we would go to the cathedral. And at Christmas my mom loved for us to go and sing carols at the cathedral. I think that sort of space instills a sense of awe and history and imagination. All of the history that went along with Canterbury—being brought up there, it became a part of who I was. I suppose it may have had some lasting impression that has inspired me to do the historical, epic kind of stories.

LONDON ORIENTATION I moved to London to finish my studies and go to drama school. My dad drove me up, and I stayed with family friends. On my first night, I put on London radio stations. I remember waking up my first morning and thinking about all my friends in Canterbury who were probably at the same boarding school, and, wow, here I was listening to KISS FM. In Canterbury, it was like invective radio. And I remember thinking, *Wow, this is cool. I'm in London and I'm listening to great music on London radio*. I had dreams of being an actor, and the National Youth Theatre, which is an amateur dramatics company based in London, was something that I joined initially. I also finished my education at the Fine Arts College in North London, did theater, photography, and sculpture—subjects that weren't available to me at school in Kent. I felt that if I wanted to be an actor, London was the best place to start. I lived there for seven years until I left to do *Lord of the Rings*.

SIGHTS I consider London my home. I pine for it. I find myself more often than not in America, predominantly L.A., so I feel homesick for London. I think it's the energy. It was so liberating. Nobody was judging you. You could dress however you liked. You could really just be essentially who you wanted to be. I remember when I was a child we'd occasionally go up to London on the weekend. We'd go to the the-

ater and grab something to eat, or we'd go shopping on Oxford Street or along the Kings Road. So I had a connection with London, because it's only about an hour and a half from Canterbury. I remember going to the **Tower of London** [Tower Hill], too, and seeing the Crown Jewels. They're all there in a case, and then there are the Beefeater men, who are there to guard the jewels.

DINNER When I started drama school, I had a flat in the center of London under the British Telecom Tower, and I always used to think of the tower as my back garden. It was like a beacon for home, because it's so tall and I could always see it flashing. I lived on Hanson Street, and there was a fantastic little greasy spoon there. In the summer we'd sit outside under the BT Tower eating eggs and bacon, tea and toast. On the other end of my street is a restaurant called **Back to Basics.** It's a small fish place with really lovely waitresses from Sweden or Stockholm or somewhere. The food is fantastic, the fish fresh, really well cooked. My good friend whom I lived with in the flat was Swedish, and he loved the food there and recognized the cooking as a taste from home. There was a restaurant next to it called **Silks & Spice.** They have one in Camden, as well. It's got great Thai food.

Saturday

SHOPPING I worked at **Paul Smith** [Covent Garden] when I first moved to London. It was a great place to work. I got a lot of great clothes from there, and I still do. But back then I got a great discount. It kept clothes on my back the whole way through school. Now I'll dress in one of his suits or I'll wear his shirts. Paul Smith's got great British style. There are little details and things that make his stuff stand out. I think what I learned about style from there is to be individual and not to feel like you have to conform. Just wear what feels good and be a little eccentric if you feel like it.

LUNCH I normally lay low when I get to London these days. But I used to go to a pub, the **Old Ship** [Hammersmith], that has beautiful views of the River Thames. There's also the **Cow** [Notting Hill], a pub near the Portobello Road market, which is a great place to go on the weekend. The Cow was always good for a pint of prawns or some oysters and a Guinness. It's got character. When I was younger, I used to go to pubs and bars and hang out with friends and do Soho. But it's been a while. That was before I broke my back [see "One Pivotal Day in London" below].

SIGHTS It's always great to see **Buckingham Palace** [St. James]. Really, if you only have one day in London, for my money, you should walk through **Hyde Park** or **Green Park**

and then walk down to Buckingham Palace. The **Tate Galleries** are great, too. Very inspired. **Madame Tussauds** [Regent's Park] wax museum was always an interesting place to go. I went there when I was very young. They have a planetarium there, as well. And there's the **London Zoo** [Regent's Park]. I actually studied animals at the London Zoo. It was part of a course. We had to go there every weekend, study the animals, come back, and mimic the animals' behaviors. I studied all these fantastic animals, like apes and lions, but I ended up being a lizard. The teacher felt that stillness was something that would be of great use to me later in my career. She said, "It's a lizard for you, young man!" I have to tell you, it was fantastic studying lizards. I learned stillness, composure. You don't have to be doing something to be doing something. Sometimes you can do too much.

HIGH TEA Tea at **Fortnum & Mason** [St. James] is great. You get great fresh tea there. When I say fresh, what I mean is loose tea or tea bags. My cousin's got a big thing for the tea at Fortnum & Mason, so we go and grab tea there and bring it back to L.A. They also have Marmite and bangers and mash and fish and

One Pivotal Day in London

I was visiting friends in Lisson Grove. They had a roof terrace on the landing below their apartment. I got up to the fourth floor and I could see this roof terrace. I could have just jumped straight from the window onto the ledge, but instead I got onto this piece of drainpipe flashing, nothing really substantial, and I fell back and landed on a first floor terrace between some iron railings and an old washing machine. I had a rather miraculous escape from death and the possibility of spending my life in a chair. For four days I contemplated that, having been told by the doctors that I would never walk again. It's something that's actually been a very positive part of my life. It made me appreciate life with a fresh set of eyes. Forced me to slow down, look around, and think a little more.

chips. Fortnum & Mason is very English. Just the packaging of the teas or whatever you're buying and the shop itself is very old-school English.

DINNER I do go home. I still have family there. But I don't go back as often as I'd like. When I'm in Canterbury, I try to go to **Café des Amis,** a Mexican restaurant. I guess I was sixteen when we started going there. It had just opened. The food is outstanding. The best Mexican food you'll eat. Honestly. I've traveled around Mexico, and I still find Café des Amis to be a pretty good match to anything I've had in Mexico. It's in an old building overlooking the river and the West Gate Towers, which are the gates to the city. It used to be a store where they sold odds and ends, brass objects and things. There's also **Papa's Fish Bar** in Canterbury. They have great white bread. I remember that loaf called Mother's Pride, with Marmite.

Guildhall School of Music & Drama

I had dinner recently with Ridley Scott in London at **Cipriani** [Mayfair], a great little restaurant. We were there for Ridley's birthday and the waiter came over and said, "Ah, we had your friend Johnny Depp here last night." It was one of those funny stories, ships passing in the night. I think he was there shooting *Charlie and the Chocolate Factory*. Another place is the **Wolseley** [Mayfair]. It has really good food. More recently, when I've been popping back, I've been having nice meals at **J. Sheekey,** in the West End. Fantastic fish.

THEATER I spent three years at the **Guildhall School of Music & Drama** [Square Mile]. That's where Ewan McGregor studied, and David Thewlis, who is in *Kingdom of Heaven*. And Joe Fiennes. You can see the third-year performances there. It's a great school. I had three fantastic years there. It's next door to the **Barbican.** The Royal Shakespeare Company had productions going on at the Barbican, and we would see productions there. But we had our own productions at school. That was where I learned it was something I really loved.

Orlando Bloom's London/Canterbury Essentials

DINING

Back to Basics, Swedish, $$, 011-44-207-436-2181
21A Foley Street, London

Café des Amis, Mexican, $$$, 011-44-122-746-4390
93 St. Dunstans Street, Canterbury

I spent three years at the Guildhall School of Music & Drama. That's where Ewan McGregor studied, and David Thewlis, who is in Kingdom of Heaven. *And Joe Fiennes.*

Cipriani, Italian, $$$$, 011-44-207-399-0500
23 Davies Street, London, Mayfair

Fortnum & Mason, English, $$$, 011-44-207-734-8040
181 Piccadilly, London, St. James

J. Sheekey, seafood, $$$, 011-44-207-240-2565
28 St. Martin's Court, London, West End

Papa's Fish Bar, seafood, $$, 011-44-122-776-1013
33 Wincheap, Canterbury

Silks & Spice, Thai, $$, 011-44-207-482-2228
27-28 Chalk Farm Road, London

The Wolseley, European, $$$$, 011-44-207-499-6996
160 Piccadilly, London, Mayfair

SIGHTS

Buckingham Palace, 011-44-207-766-7300
Buckingham Palace Road, London, St. James

Canterbury Cathedral, 011-44-122-786-5350
The Precincts, Canterbury

The Canterbury Tales, museum, 011-44-122-747-9227
St. Margaret's Street, Canterbury

Green Park, Royal Parks System,
Piccadilly and Constitution Hill

Hyde Park, recreation area, 011-44-207-298-2100
350 acres in central London

London Zoo, 011-44-207-722-3333
Outer Circle, London, Regent's Park

Madame Tussauds, wax museum, 011-44-870-999-0046
Marylebone Road, London, Regent's Park

Tate Britain, art museum, 011-44-207-887-8000
Millbank, London

Tate Modern, art museum, 011-44-207-887-8888
Bankside, London

Tower of London, 011-44-870-756-6060
Tower Hill, London

SHOPPING

Paul Smith, clothing, 011-44-207-836-7828
40 Floral Street, London, Covent Garden

PUBS

The Cow, pub, 011-44-207-221-5400
89 Westbourne Park Road, London, Notting Hill

The Old Ship, pub, 011-44-208-748-2593
25 Upper Mall, London, Hammersmith

THEATER

Barbican Centre, 011-44-208-638-4141
Silk Street, London, Square Mile

Guildhall School of Music & Drama,
011-44-207-628-2571, Silk Street, London, Square Mile

Kenneth Branagh

London

H e was a green teenager "up from the country like a character in a Dickens novel," arriving in London to attend the Royal Academy of Dramatic Art. One can imagine Kenneth Branagh just off the train, staring open-mouthed into the maw of Europe's largest city. But Branagh did not cower before the royal metropolis. He dived right in, taking in the city's action and attractions in a single nonstop day, a bacchanal of activity that left him breathless. Having conquered London, he eventually did the same thing in his career, seemingly attacking everything at once—forming his own theater company and writing, acting, and directing. To fund his company, he penned the first installment of his autobiography, *Beginning*, at age twenty-eight. He's famous for starring in a multitude of films, ranging from Woody Allen's *Celebrity* to William Shakespeare's *Henry V* to John Grisham's *The Gingerbread Man*. But he's equally renowned as a director, commandeering films such as a star-studded version of *Hamlet,* in which he also starred, and *Dead Again*, in which he not only directed, but played two different roles opposite his then-wife, Emma Thompson. But when the cameras are off and the muses are quiet, you'll find the squire at home just outside of London. Here's Branagh's take on the capital where he came of age.

Friday

LODGING The **Covent Garden Hotel** [Covent Garden] is very nice and right in the center of town. It's a new hotel, but it has an Old World feel to it, without being chichi. In a way, it reminds me a little more of the apartment-style hotels that are in New York now. Very personalized service and a really good place to meet. The hotel has a brasserie that's a good place for an early evening drink, or to have a lightweight meal at lunchtime or evening. It's a good atmosphere—nice long bar. If you have the money to stay in a suite on the riverside, the **Savoy** [West End] is really terrific. I was once taken to the hotel's **River Restaurant**

[presently only open for breakfast] with its wonderful view over the river, by Sir John Mills, who had regaled me with stories about how he ate there with Noel Coward, who stayed at a suite at the Savoy during the blitz of the Second World War. The place is full of memories. It's full of tradition without being imposing.

DINNER Although it's a cliché from someone like me, the **Ivy** [West End] is probably London's top theatrical restaurant. It is much favored by actors and showbiz people. The thing I like best about it, apart from the very friendly service, is the food. It has a wonderful mixture of a European menu and elements of what you might call British comfort food. Like their sticky toffee pudding. I would call that a delicious kind of nursery food. It's the kind of thing that you have memories of as a child, the kinds of things you dreamt about, the sort of treats you had when you had been ill or on the road to recovery. It conjures up images of stickiness and sweetness and sponge and custard and all those things that I associate with Britain and its sometimes terrible diet. The sausages at the Ivy are fantastic. They include mashed potato in various dishes. They do fantastic fish cakes. The Ivy's sister restaurant, **Le Caprice** [Green Park], is just around the corner from the Ritz. The chocolate mousse at Le Caprice is to die for. Also tremendous fish cakes and a very nice bar as well.

NIGHTLIFE One of the things that has happened with London, thank God, is that we have become slightly more of a late-night city. If New York is the city that never sleeps, London used to be the city that never got up. It used to be rather embarrassing to bring visitors from abroad and find that everything closed down. Now there are many more clubs. A lot of places in Soho are staying open late, a lot of places in St. Martin's Lane. People might be interested in going to Notting Hill, which was the title name of a Julia Roberts and Hugh Grant film that celebrates this extraordinary part of London, which also contains Portobello Market. Notting Hill is a very vibrant, very multicultural, very cosmopolitan place.

Saturday

WALK The parks continue to be the lungs to the city. On a Saturday if the weather is good, a great place to go is into **Hyde Park,** where there are a number of places to just sit and have a coffee on the Serpentine, the lake inside Hyde Park. Or **Regent's Park. Green Park** is also a lovely park and so is **St. James's Park.** One of the great things about London, despite also having terrific buses and an underground service, is that you can walk so many places. It was one of the first things that surprised me about London. After about a month, I realized that I didn't have to live by my underground map. I could actually walk places. I was also very surprised at how big the parks are. They are great places to have a coffee on a Sunday morning and buy the paper. In the summer, you can also rent deck chairs, which is a peculiarly British thing to do. I mean, there are lots of park benches around, but they also bring the deck chairs out and you see all those Brits hanging around with handkerchiefs knotted in all four corners over their heads to avoid sun stroke and having their coffee.

I encourage anybody who comes over to not

rely on tubes and buses, brilliant though they are, but don't forget that you can walk your way around London. You can get by the river and walk along the embankment from Chelsea all the way up to the Tower of London and on the way you'll see the Houses of Parliament, you'll see the Globe Theatre, you'll see St. Paul's, you'll see Waterloo Bridge, the National Theatre, the Festival Hall, the Savoy Hotel. But the part of London that I enjoy most is **Trafalgar Square.** Just to see Nelson on top of his column right in the middle of that place and the lions around and see the National Gallery overlooking Trafalgar Square. You'll see what seems like every red London bus in the world traveling around that square. It's a real bit of London which is cheap and easy to enjoy.

LUNCH On a Saturday, I probably would have lunch at the opera pavilion, a marketplace with a balcony just at one end of the piazza in **Covent Garden,** a very bustling market, both outdoors and indoors. From where you sit on

that balcony, you can see the **London Transport Museum,** which is a terrific museum, right in the center of Covent Garden. There's also a lot of street theater. There's the **Dove** [Hammersmith], a pub right on the river. From Hammersmith Bridge, you walk along the river to get to it and you can sit outside. The Dove is very Old World—full of nooks and crannies. You have to bend your head going in so you don't bang it on some great wooden rafter. It feels Dickensian and I'm very fond of Dickens. If you want a real English lunch that leaves you a bit stodgy, but is delicious, fish and chips are the thing to have. You would go to the **Seashell Restaurant** [Marylebone].

CULTURE A favorite museum is the **Imperial War Museum** [Southwark], if, like me, you're interested in the extraordinary history and nature of warfare. It covers the military world full stop. Another one is the **Victoria and Albert Museum** [South Kensington], which is particularly good at exhibitions. A lot of people go to the Victoria and Albert Museum just for the café and the gift shop, because you can get a sense of what's going on from there if you haven't got time to go around the museum.

SHOPPING A shop that I particularly like is **Liberty,** which is on the corner of Great Marlborough Street and Regent Street—a great famous shopping thoroughfare in London. Liberty feels like a throwback, this wonderful

V&A Images/Victoria and Albert Museum

The Victoria and Albert Museum is particularly good at exhibitions.

building full of wooden doors and old-fashioned elevators. The service is wonderful. If you like arts and crafts furniture, which I do, there's much to be found. London is a great place for bookshops. The center for all of that is Charing Cross Road, sort of a book buyer's paradise. There are bookshops on every conceivable subject and one of London's biggest and most famous bookshops, **Foyles.** These are places I haunted in my days as a drama student. Amongst the big and the small, there are lots of secondhand bookshops or secondhand sections, and so it's possible to shop for books cheaply in Charing Cross Road. That's a great way to spend an afternoon.

TEA For a bizarre thing they do in the afternoon, go to the **Waldorf Hotel** [Covent Garden]. Not only do they do a very good English breakfast, but they do a tea dance in the afternoons, which is a bizarre English ritual where at three you have sandwiches and cake and tea and a sort of Palm Court orchestra plays while you dance. It's in a palm-ridden ballroom at the **Aldwych,** and again, there's something very old-fashioned, Old World about it. But I love walking into it—in the middle of a London day that is—if I want to just check out of modern life for a minute.

EXCURSION A place that I find terrifically romantic and inspiring is Greenwich, and particularly from the **Royal Observatory,** which is up on the hill at Greenwich. A great spot from which many people looked back and painted London, because it's quite high and you get a fantastic view. There's also the **National Maritime Museum,** which is a fantastic museum that has a very lively sense of the incredible naval history we have.

DINNER I like eating downstairs at **Alistair Little** in Soho. It's a kind of modernist bistro. One of the things I like to do on a Saturday is to see a movie at four or five-ish. Then have dinner so you don't eat too late. I like the atmosphere at Alistair Little. They have a fantastic cook and the menu is very eclectic. If you don't like huge portions of things, you're all right there without being cheated. I feel as though everybody is in there discussing films. There are so many brilliant Indian restaurants. I think the best one I've eaten in is the **Bombay Brasserie** in Kensington. It's huge. Cavernous. They are particularly fantastic with their Indian vegetarian fare. I was taken there once by Ismail Merchant, the famous Indian producer of the Merchant-Ivory films, and he should know because he makes a mean curry himself.

THEATER Increasingly, the West End has some more serious fare, which I applaud. I also like very much to go to the **National Theatre** [South Bank]. Even if you don't go and see a play at the National Theatre, they are forever having what they call "platform performances," which take place at 6 or 6:30 in the evening, and are sometimes discussions or conversations with people in the plays or about the plays. One company to keep an eye out for is the **Royal Court Theatre** [West End], which has produced several plays that have gone on to Broadway, like Coner McPherson's play *The Weir,* as well as the work of a very promising Irish playwright called Martin McDonough. Another good theater company is **Almeida Theatre** out of Islington.

ENGLISH BREAKFAST If you want a really terrific English Sunday breakfast, I recommend a place called **Maggie Jones** [Kensington]. They have wooden tables and a bit of gingham here and there and bottles of red wine used as candleholders. There's lots of great English food—English puddings, bread and butter pudding, summer pudding in the summer which is delicious, terrific roast beef, and Yorkshire pudding, which is a huge favorite of mine.

EXCURSION I adored working in and visiting **Blenheim Palace.** It's in Woodstock near Oxford, about an hour on the train, and it's open to the public. It has the most extraordinary gardens designed by Capability Brown, a legendary genius of a landscape gardener. That's a name isn't it? It was the home of the first Duke of Marlboro, the birthplace of Winston Churchill, and it's arguably the finest palace in Britain. It does epitomize inequality, but nevertheless, there's something breathtaking about it, and we had the good fortune to film there when we were making our film of *Hamlet*. It's actually quite near Windsor, so if you want to do **Windsor Castle** as well, you can.

DINNER I like a restaurant very much called **Kensington Place** down in Kensington. It's right next to Kensington Gardens. There's a very kind of refreshing, open, light kind of atmosphere. Great food.

Kenneth Branagh's London Essentials

LODGING

Covent Garden Hotel, $$$, 011-44-207-806-1000
10 Monmouth Street, Covent Garden

The Savoy, $$$$, 011-44-207-836-4343
The Strand, West End

DINING

Alistair Little, European, $$$$, 011-44-207-734-5183
49 Frith Street, Soho

One Great Day in London

I came to London when I was just seventeen and a half. I went to the Royal Academy of Dramatic Art. I had come from Reading, which is about forty miles outside London, as green as a green thing. When I first came to London, I had never been in a black taxi, I had never been on the tube, I had never been in a London bus, and generally felt as though I was up from the country like a character in a Dickens novel. So I was once taken on what's called "a real London day" with a couple of friends of mine. We met up for a breakfast and we had a real fry-up—sausage, bacon, eggs, etc. Then we went to see a matinee of *Peter Pan.* Then we went to troll the bookshops in Charing Cross Road, and then went to a place for the most fantastic chocolate eclairs at tea time. We went to see a movie, *La Luna,* by Bertolucci. Afterwards, we had supper at **L'Escargot** [Soho], a marvelous restaurant where you feel like you're going into somebody's house, in Greek Street, where I had my very first snails. I did all that in one day and it was a great day. I ended the day back in my apartment in Clapham Commons after midnight. I just thought, *London is an amazing place,* because as you go through the day, you hear every sound, every accent, see every color. If you've lived in the suburbs until you're eighteen, it's quite a shock to the system.

The Bombay Brasserie, Indian, $$$,
011-44-207-370-4040, 1 Courtfield Close, Kensington

The Dove, English pub, $$, 011-44-208-748-5405
19 Upper Mall, Hammersmith

The Ivy, British, $$$, 011-44-207-836-4751
1 West Street, West End

Kensington Place, British, $$$, 011-44-207-727-3184
201 Kensington Church Street, Kensington

Le Caprice, British, $$$, 011-44-207-629-2239
Arlington Street, Arlington House, Green Park

L'Escargot, French, $$$, 011-44-207-439-7474
48 Greek Street, Soho

Maggie Jones, English, $$$, 011-44-207-937-6462
6 Old Court Place, Kensington

The River Restaurant, English breakfast, $$,
011-44-207-836-4343, Savoy Hotel, West End

The Seashell, fish and chips, $$, 011-44-207-224-9000
49 Lisson Grove, Marylebone

The Waldorf, tea service, $$$, 011-44-207-836-2400
Aldwych, Covent Garden

SIGHTS
Blenheim Palace, 011-44-870-060-2080
Woodstock, Oxfordshire

Covent Garden, cultural center, www.coventgarden.uk.com

Green, St. James's, and Regent's Parks, Royal Parks
System, www.royalparks.gov.uk

Hyde Park, recreation area, 011-44-207-298-2100
350 acres in central London

The Imperial War Museum, 011-44-207-416-5000
Lambeth Road, Southwark

London Transport Museum, 011-44-207-379-6344
39 Wellington Street, Covent Garden

National Maritime Museum, 011-44-208-858-4422
1 Romney Road, Greenwich

National Portrait Gallery, art museum, 011-44-207-306-0055, St. Martin's Place, Trafalgar Square

Royal Observatory, 011-44-208-312-6565
1 Greenwich Park, Greenwich

Tower of London, 011-44-870-756-6060
Tower Hill, London

Trafalger Square & Nelson's Column
Central London

The Victoria and Albert Museum, 011-44-207-942-2000
Cromwell Road, South Kensington

SHOPPING
Foyle's, bookshop, 011-44-207-437-5660
113 Charing Cross Road, Charing Cross

Liberty, department store, 011-44-207-734-1234
Regent Street, West End

THEATER
Almeida Theatre, live theater, 011-44-207-359-4404
1 Almeida Street, Islington

National Theatre, 011-44-207-452-3000, South Bank

Royal Court Theatre, 011-44-207-565-5000
Sloane Square, West Sloane Square

Madrid

I can eat at the same time we do the interview," said Penélope Cruz, ordering lunch at a hilltop hotel in L.A. and encouraging me to do the same. But I could hardly keep up, as in short order she plowed through fried risotto balls and a titanic salad stacked with slices of fried goat cheese. Cruz was deservedly hungry. It had been a morning packed with meetings, yet another day in a

career involving movie after movie since the actress first arrived in Los Angeles. Clad in jeans and a pink Chanel-esque jacket, she was part Audrey Hepburn elegance and all Carmen Miranda energy. Early in our interview, it was clear Cruz knew where she was going—and that she was going there fast.

We were meeting to talk about her hometown of Madrid, where she was born Penélope Cruz Sánchez, the daughter of a merchant and a hairdresser, and a performer practically from birth. She was in ballet class at four and a professional dancer in her teens. By the time she turned sixteen, she was hosting a TV show for kids and auditioning for movies. She became a star first in Spain and then across Europe before coming to America for 1998's *The Hi-Lo Country*. By her midtwenties, with dozens of films under her belt, she began appearing on the big screen with a string of lead-ing men, including Matt Damon (*All the Pretty Horses*), Nicolas Cage (*Captain Corelli's Mandolin*), Johnny Depp (*Blow*), and Tom Cruise (*Vanilla Sky*). But that day in the hotel, she might as well have been back in the city of her birth, which she still visits several times a year. So sit back and get ready for a whirlwind tour through Madrid with Penélope Cruz.

Friday

RETURNING HOME My apartment there is the first thing I ever bought. I sold it to my sis-ter and then bought it back. My mother said, "I don't want your sister to sell it to somebody else. It's the first house you ever bought." I thought, *That's true. It means something. And it's a good investment. I should buy it back.* It's in the Barrio Salamanca, which is a great area. Really nice and peaceful. Near the center of town, but more quiet, with a lot of great restaurants and nice stores, good shopping. My other house is my real house in the countryside, where I live when I'm there.

CHILDHOOD FAVORITES I grew up in a place called Alcobendas, and also San Sebastian de los Reyes, which is twenty minutes outside of Madrid. As a little girl, I would go to Madrid all the time, shopping or going for a weekend. It meant we would have to take the Metro and the bus, and that was a treat for me. I loved going to a big mall or a theater or the movies. There was a park, **Parque de Atracciones,** and going there was like the highlight of the year. It's like our Disneyland. Just go and do the rides and eat all the sugar you can find. The same thing you have here—cotton candy and caramelized apples. You eat all you can get from your parents, do all the rides, and go home crying from all the confusion.

LODGING I very much like the **Santo Mauro.** It's smaller. It has great gardens, great food, great meeting rooms downstairs, and a little bar. It's a very private hotel. Beautiful. It's also near the Barrio Salamanca, where I have the store. The **Hotel Villa Magna** is a big hotel with a Chinese restaurant downstairs. A lot of people go there just to eat at the restaurant.

DINNER I would go to a restaurant north of the city called **Caserón de Araceli.** Or I would order food from there and take it home.

At the Prado you have to see the Goya Room. You have to see one of my favorite paintings ever. You know this painter? He's called Bosh, but in Spanish we call him El Bosco. The painting is called El Jardin de las Delicias.

The food is amazing. They have this black risotto, black rice. You know that? With the ink from the squid? And good clams. Very homey. Old. There's also a place outside of Madrid called **El Escorial.** It's about an hour away. Good things to see there and good restaurants. Some of the best restaurants in Spain, where you can eat something called *fabada*, a Spanish dish prepared with white beans. El Escorial is one of the best places to find it. It takes hours to recover after that. You eat everything. You can't control yourself.

Saturday

SIGHTS At the **Prado** you have to see the Goya Room. You have to see one of my favorite paintings ever. You know this painter? He's called Bosh, but in Spanish we call him El Bosco. The painting is called *El Jardin de las Delicias.* It's sort of a dark painting and can be a little bit disturbing. But it's just incredible that somebody did that. Maybe you can look at it and see what I mean. Some of the flamenco painters are there. There's one I love, but I can't remember his name. There is some Velázquez

in there, but El Bosco's is the painting. You can look at it for hours.

SHOPPING There is one street, Ortega Y Gasset, that has all the boutiques, like **Chanel** and **Dolce & Gabbana.** I love **Max Addict,** owned by Paz Vega, a store specializing in shoes. I like buying in my shop, and I don't give myself a big discount. People laugh at me, but I say, "No, I don't get the right numbers at the end of the month." If I buy, I pay. My shop is in the Barrio Salamanca and is called **Amarcord.** I bought the place and decorated it with a decorator. I had a vision of how I wanted it to be: pink, with all wood, and a little bit of a vintage feeling, but also a fifties feeling. The day I came in before construction was finished was a great day for me, because I had seen it in my head, and we made it happen. The clothes we sell are from designers I've found on my trips. I discovered designers who weren't being sold in Spain—you couldn't find them in Madrid—and others you could only find in a couple of places.

DINNER I would go home, eat at my house. But if I had to go out, I would probably go to **Lucio,** which is probably the best restaurant we have in Madrid. It's a very simple place, a very old restaurant. They do this dish that I also can do because somebody told me their secret. It's broken eggs with fried potatoes, and it's just incredible. They fry the eggs and break them in a particular way with garlic on top of the fries— plus a little secret. But I can't talk about it. They have good Serrano ham. Good wine. Good fish. Great taste.

Café Hispano [Zaragoza] is where I get together with friends like Fernando Trueba, the director of *Belle Epoque*. I've done two movies with him, and we have a group of friends and always go there. They have a room they give us that seats twelve people, and they let us stay there until four or five in the morning. The food is sort of Mediterranean. They have clams with potatoes, a great dish. They also have one of the best *croquetas*, which are fried. They make it with *harina*.

FLAMENCO My sister, Monica, is one of the best flamenco dancers in the world. I love seeing her dance. She was dancing with Joachim Cortez for a long time. Now she has a TV show called *Un Paso Adelante*, which is really good. There are bars in the center of Madrid where you can see dancers. But the best thing is to throw yourself in the street in the south of Spain and look for a group of gypsies who are singing and join them. That's really the thing. You just go and sing with them. I once did a party in Madrid, a party for Tom when we were there for *Vanilla Sky*, and I did a flamenco party. So I called some friends and said, "Okay, bring some of your friends who play drums," and they improvised it. It was magic what we saw. They can play music with a fork, anything. They have it in their blood.

NIGHTLIFE Prince played in Madrid when I was fourteen, and I was fascinated. I was speechless. Speechless! I never dreamed that I would get tickets to that concert, being so young. I just felt very inspired by an artist. I had seen a lot of opera and ballet because I had been dancing since I was four. I'd been a fan of classical music since I was four, too. I would sit in a corner of my house and listen. But this was just one of these days that you remember, that inspires you. We had a party afterward at a discothèque called **Joy Madrid.** That was one of the first times I went out and experienced the nightlife of Madrid. **Chicote** is a good bar. Manolete, the bullfighter, used to go there, and I believe Hemingway did also. It's very old, and you can feel all of that history. They have a lot of pictures. Not of Madrid, but of Spain in general. They have great sangria—wine with *cassera*, which has bubbles.

LATE-NIGHT SNACK If you want to experience a night out in Madrid, you go to dinner about 10:30 or 11. Then you see the sun come up and you eat *churros* with chocolate. That's the big tradition in Madrid. I've only done it once. But it's part of the ritual to end like that, eating *churros* in the morning. Then you go to sleep.

Sunday

OUTDOORS **El Parque de Retiro** is beautiful, our biggest, most famous park. It has a lot of runners, a little lake. It's very near the center of the city. I love to walk around the middle of town. For someone who hasn't been, I would say go to the **Plaza Major.** You will see the spirit of the city. A combination of couples with young kids, magicians in the street, old women together. Good energy. Good people. There are a lot of painters in the street at the Plaza Major.

PAELLA There's one place, **Casa Benigna,** where my friend Fernando Trueba took me. It's also where I met director Stephen Frears for the movie I did with him, *The Hi-Lo Country.* That's where he told me he was going to cast me. It was my first American movie. So I have good memories of that place. It was a good lunch.

Penélope Cruz's Madrid Essentials

LODGING

AC Santo Mauro, $$$$$, 011-34-91-319-6900
Calle de Zurbano 36

Hotel Villa Magna, $$$$, 011-34-91-587-1234
Paseo de la Castellana 22

DINING

Café Hispano, Mediterranean, $$, 011-34-97-622-2161
Avenida de las Torres, 42, Zaragoza

Casa Benigna, paella, $$$, 011-34-91-413-3356
Benigna Soto 9

Casa Lucio Restaurante, Castilian, $$, 011-34-91-365-3252. Cava Baja 35

Caserón de Araceli, Castilian, $$$, 011-34-91-841-8531
Olivar 8

SIGHTS

El Escorial, city near Madrid, 30 miles northwest of Madrid

Museo Nacional del Prado, 011-34-91-330-2800
Paseo del Prado

Parque de Atracciones, park, 011-34-91-463-2900
Casa de Campo

Parque del Retiro, park, Puerta de Alcala

Plaza Major, town square, Plaza Major, city center

SHOPPING

Amarcord, designer fashions, 011-34-91-575-0543
Calle de Claudio Coello 113

Chanel, designer fashions, 011-34-91-431-3036
Jose Ortega y Gasset 14

Dolce & Gabbana, designer fashions,
011-34-91-575-9539, Jose Ortega y Gasset 14

Max Addict, shoes, 011-34-91-521-7240
Augusto Figueroa 3

NIGHTLIFE

Joy Madrid, discothèque, 011-34-91-366-3733
Arenal 11, Plaza Major

Museo Chicote, bar, 011-34-91-532-6737, Gran Via 12

Gwyneth Paltrow

Madrid

When Gwyneth Paltrow was fifteen, she flew to Spain as an exchange student from Spence, a private girl's school in Manhattan. Having always had a "burning desire to go to Spain," she landed in Madrid, then took a bus a half hour south to a tiny village called Talavera de la Reina, where she lived for a month with a pig farmer and his family. At first, she was homesick and unable to understand what anyone was saying. "But a week later," she said, "I never wanted to leave."

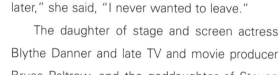

The daughter of stage and screen actress Blythe Danner and late TV and movie producer Bruce Paltrow, and the goddaughter of Steven Spielberg, Paltrow first appeared on-screen in Spielberg's *Hook* in 1991. Eight years later, she took home the Best Actress statuette for *Shakespeare in Love*, and memorable roles followed in a variety of later films. Offstage, the actress lives with husband Chris Martin, frontman for the band Coldplay, in London, with their children, Apple and Moses. We think it's safe to say Paltrow's kids won't be fifteen before having their passports stamped in Spain.

Friday

ARRIVAL I got off the bus in Talavera de la Reina, and my Spanish mother was there to pick me up at the bus station. I couldn't understand a thing she said. She spoke like five-hundred miles per hour. She took me to meet my exchange brother, then I slowly met the rest of the family. I felt like I had been transported to another planet. I was really homesick the first week. But it was such a charming, peaceful town, and we were allowed more freedom than I had in New York. We went to see bullfights, which are pretty unbearable. We would go dancing, and they would try to teach me this very traditional, old Spanish dancing women do, which is amazing. The family is always together. Everybody comes home every day to eat lunch together, and then they all go back off to school or work. Everything is very centered around family. I never looked back, and I did not want to go home. The next time I went I was nineteen, and I have gone basically once a year at least ever since.

HER FIRST VISIT TO MADRID Well, I didn't have any money, really. I can't even remember where I stayed. It was in the old section of Madrid, which is amazing. It was sort of a cross between a hotel and a youth hostel, and it overlooked a beautiful square. I went with some friends and we just walked everywhere. We went to all the museums and all the bars and restaurants. I have always loved it there. Now I go to Madrid and I go south to Talavera to go see my family. My exchange sisters both live in Madrid. They are twins. I'll say, "I just landed. What time are we meeting up?" I always go and see them, or to any wedding, and the rest of my family will go, too, not just me. When my father died, my Spanish mother flew to Rome immediately to be by my side and fly with me to New York. Three more of the family came over for the funeral. We are really tight. I have a plot of land that they gave me from their farm that eventually I will build a house on. They raise *papa negra* pigs, the nicest ham. They have black hooves. They are very special.

LODGING One of my favorite hotels in the world is the **Santo Mauro.** It's this huge mansion built for the Duke of Santo Mauro in 1895 that they have converted. The rooms are phenomenal. The king-size beds are the biggest,

---

One of my favorite hotels in the world is the Santo Mauro. It's this huge mansion built for the Duke of Santo Mauro in 1895 that they have converted.

widest beds you'll ever see in your life. It's one mattress, but it's like the width of two queen-size beds. Downstairs, the Santo Mauro has a big library, a big sitting room. It's the most lovely place. They have a beautiful garden and a restaurant. They serve breakfast in the library, which has super high ceilings and the most beautifully done moldings. One of my favorite things there, which you can get anywhere in Spain, is *chocolate con churros*. It's breakfast food, or for before you go to sleep if you've been out dancing and drinking all night. It's a cup of the thickest hot chocolate and fried dough, and it's amazing. Another nice hotel is the **Hesperia.** I stayed there once and had a fantastic suite. It's very clean and modern, and the suite I stayed in had a Jacuzzi out on the balcony.

DINNER The first thing I always want to do is eat some paella. I think most people think there is only one kind of paella, but that's not really true. When you go to Spain, if you go to a rice

restaurant, you can have all the different kinds. Like there's one with shellfish; there's one that has rabbit and chicken in it. There are a million incarnations. One great paella is at Casa Benigna. It just is not done properly outside Spain. I think it's the saffron, the quality of the rice, and that fresh squeezed lemon over the top. Oh, my mouth is watering just thinking of it!

Satutday

CULTURE The **Prado Museum** is massive and they have the most incredible old master Spanish paintings. Velázquez and El Greco, they are just so full of power. **Reina Sofía** is a more contemporary museum, more modern.

STROLL Just walking, especially in the old section of Madrid, is amazing. They have great shops there, and they have this sort of Main Street [Calle Gran Vía] where they have those stores you would find in any European city or New York. I love walking down that street and just watching all the people shop. There is a big **Starbucks** there that just opened that people are getting into. It is exactly like the ones in L.A. It's a surreal experience, because you're in Spain, and Spain is a country that is really always into itself. For example, they're never really interested in what anyone else is doing fashionwise or foodwise. Everyone else in the world could be wearing boot-cut jeans and they'll be wearing tapered jeans. It takes forever for trends to work their way in. They have an incredible culture—they don't need to really change it. They are all happy people and, for the most part, it is very contented. It's not subject to trendiness at all. You can never find in Madrid

the super-cool, cutting-edge café that you can in Paris or the Lower East Side of Manhattan. It is just a different vibe. Then you go into Starbucks and it's literally like you're in L.A. It's funny.

SHOPPING There's a girl shop called **La Rosa Que No Muere.** It's a small shop in a great little shopping area. They have really cool stuff, like great jewelry and jeans. **El Corte Inglés** is a department store that is everywhere. Those are fun to go into. You can find everything. It's not super expensive, but they are nice. Definitely by Spanish standards, a nice department store.

TAPAS My favorite tapas is basically bread, and then they rub tomato on it to get all the juice, and then they put anchovies on. It is delicious. And the olives they bring, all the little fried seafood stuff they bring, I love. *Gambas ajilo*, which is shrimp with garlic, is a type of fish I love. The best places for tapas are on Cava Alta and Cava Baja streets: **La Tasca de Jesus** and **Juana la Loca.**

DINNER In the old section of Madrid there's a place called **Casa Lucio.** It's old-school Spanish food. There are checkered tablecloths, and they bring you tons of *tapas* before your dinner comes. There's also another place I like called **El Landó.** They have really nice Spanish food there, too. When you go in, there are pictures on the wall of all the famous people who have eaten there. I definitely saw Tom Cruise, some sports people, and a lot of others. Casa Lucio and El Landó are both sort of not-too-fancy restaurants. You are hard-pressed to find a restaurant in Madrid that is super buttoned up.

It's not like France, where every other place is a three-hour meal with waiters and tuxedos. You can find that in Spain, but it's not the norm.

When I get tired of eating Spanish food, I go to this Japanese restaurant called **Tsunami.** It's just a modern, really nice Japanese restaurant with really good food. Then if you want a meal that's not so expensive, there is a chain of places called **Museo del Jamón.** You can have paella and if you eat meat, the *jamón Serrano*, the ham. I like going there for an inexpensive bite to eat. There is a great seafood restaurant in Madrid called **La Trainera.** It's more upscale, but not a foreboding kind of atmosphere. Just delicious.

NIGHTLIFE The great thing about Madrid is that it really gets going every single night. It's not like New York where there is a rope and they won't let you into a club. Everyone can go. There's a place I like called **Fortuny.** It's a disco, and they have a big outdoor area and people are out there just having drinks when it's nice weather. Inside it's cool. There's the dance floor and there are sofas. It has a nice atmosphere. You can see flamenco shows in Madrid, but it's pretty touristy, because it's not really indigenous to that part of Spain. They don't eat until 10:30 or 11 at night. Then they'll go out after that. So if you go to a club at 1 a.m., it's just kind of getting going. They will go home and sleep for four hours or something, and they'll get up and go to work. They'll go home after lunch and have a nice three-hour nap, then they go back to work again. I'm not a big napper, but I definitely like to sit down. My Spanish father, he goes out [meaning to sleep] after lunch. We all sit down and put our feet up, maybe doze off, or maybe just read. It's nice to have that quiet time to digest.

Sunday

ONE PERFECT DAY I would sleep late and then go down to the drawing room of Santa Mauro and have some breakfast. Then I'd walk around, go to museums, walk through the parks. Then visit the Prado or La Reina Sofía. Then meet friends for lunch, which takes a good long time. Then maybe just keep walking. If the weather is good, it is so nice to sit outside in a café and while away the afternoon. The old part of Madrid is really cool for walking around. There are a lot of little alleyways and streets with shops and cafés and tapas bars. Then you go home and rest, take a bath or whatever, and you go out to dinner late. Then you go to a bar, like **Marula Café,** or to a disco, like Fortuny. Spain is really the only country where I go out to a disco still, because I go out with my siblings from my exchange family and there is a big pack of us. They are so full of life. We all go and stay out dancing until four in the morning.

Gwyneth Paltrow's Madrid Essentials

LODGING
AC Santo Mauro, $$$$, 011-34-91-319-6900
Calle de Zurbano 36

Hesperia Madrid, $$$$, 011-34-91-210-8800
Paseo de la Castellana 57

DINING
Casa Benigna, paella, $$$, 011-34-91-413-3356
Benigna Soto 9

Casa Lucio, Castilian, $$, 011-34-91-365-3252
Cava Baja 35

El Landó, Castilian, $$$, 011-34-91-366-7681
Plaza Gabriel Miro 8

Juana la Loca, tapas, $$, 011-34-91-364-0525
Plaza Puerta de Moros 4

La Tasca de Jesus, tapas, $$, 011-34-91-366-6161
Calle de Cava Alta 32

La Trainera, seafood, $$$$, 011-34-91-576-8035
Calle Lagasca 60, Retiro/Salamanca

Museo del Jamón, Spanish, $, 011-34-91-531-5721
Carrera de San Jeronimo 6

Starbucks, coffeehouse, $, www.starbucks.com

Tsunami, Japanese, $$$, 011-34-91-308-0569
Caracas 10

SIGHTS
Museo Nacional del Prado, 011-34-91-330-2800
Ruiz de Alarcón 23

Museo Nacional Centro de Arte Reina Sofía, 011-34-91-774-1000, Santa Isabel 52, Las Cortes

SHOPPING
El Corte Inglés, department store, 011-34-91-379-80-00
Preciados 3

La Rosa Que No Muere, women's shop, 011-34-91-578-3198, Conde de Aranda 4

NIGHTLIFE
Fortuny, disco, 011-34-91-319-0588
Fortuny 34

Marula Café, bar, 011-34-91-366-1596
Calle Canos Viejos 3, Esquina Bailen 27, Bajo Puente

On the Road with Gwyneth Paltrow

What do you never leave home without?

My iPod, a big bottle of water, comfortable walking shoes, and a good moisturizer.

What kind of moisturizer?

There's a woman in London named Amanda Lacey who makes these great oils for your face. So I use those. Cecilia has a really great antiaging moisturizer, too. The anti-aging part really keeps the free radicals and all that off your skin.

Anything you always wear while traveling?

I have a thin cashmere throw that I can keep warm with on the plane or that I wrap around myself when I go out at night. Hermés makes a super thin one and it's nice and big, too.

What do you pack for Madrid?

Since it's a mild climate, lots of jeans and boots and blazers and stuff like that. It can get really warm during the day and chillier at night. It's a pretty casual city.

Unless you're going for a wedding or specific fancy occasion, you don't have to bring anything too formal. At night I'll wear a skirt or some nice trousers and a pair of high heels.

What's always in your carry-on bag?

A couple of books, depending on what I'm interested in.

For example?

Right now they're all baby books: *The Contented Little Baby Book, On Becoming Baby Wise,* and *The Happiest Baby on the Block.* There's another one called *Trees Make the Best Mobiles,* which is a great book about how to raise your child in a cool way. I also have the iPod and a tube of Eight Hour Cream, an old Elizabeth Arden product. It's sort of like Vaseline, but not. You can put it anywhere. It's really good for traveling. And I'll have Bliss, from the spa in New York, but they sell the cosmetics everywhere now. They make a very lightly tinted moisturizer with sunscreen in it.

Mexico City

In his thriller *Original Sin*, Antonio Banderas played a Cuban tycoon recently married to a sexy, dangerous, and unpredictable young bride, scorchingly portrayed by Angelina Jolie. Although the movie's setting mimics 1880s colonial Cuba, the film was actually shot in and around Mexico City. It was there, too, that Banderas filmed *The Mask of Zorro*. Banderas's love of Mexico is undoubtedly tied to the city's similarities to his native Spain, from which he arrived in Los Angeles in 1991, speaking little English, to star in *The Mambo Kings*. He learned his lines phonetically and his performance introduced him as an international star, heir to Rudolph Valentino's "Latin Lover" throne.

Raised in Malaga, he planned to become a professional soccer player until a foot injury and a viewing of the 1979 movie *Hair* derailed his dreams. He promptly enrolled in drama school and traveled across his homeland in his own theatrical company. Meeting quixotic Spanish director Pedro Almodóvar—to whom he presented a Best Foreign Language Film Oscar—Banderas became a star in Spanish cinema. In America, he was soon working with legends such as Tom Hanks in *Philadelphia*, Brad Pitt and Tom Cruise in *Interview with the Vampire*, Madonna in *Evita*, and Sir Anthony Hopkins in *The Mask of Zorro*. He fell in love with Melanie Griffith in 1995 when they costarred in the comedy *Two Much*. They were married in 1996 and had a daughter, Stella del Carmen, the following fall. Banderas remains humbled by the people, art, and architecture of the oldest city in North America, La Ciudad. "I feel like Mexico is part of me—the language and the history," he said. Here's where you can find Antonio Banderas in the city of twenty-three million people.

Friday

LODGING If you want a place with a lot of resources—a gym and massages—and want to be very comfortable and secure, the best place is the **Four Seasons** on the Paseo de la Reforma. I've been staying there since I did *Zorro*. Another hotel is **Casa Vieja,** a little place with only ten rooms. If you are going to Mexico and want a taste of the place, this is the hotel for you. It's a beautiful place, painted in the Mexican style with a lot of color. Every piece of furniture, every painting, is traditional Mexican style. The kitchen may be open the entire night, so you can go in and prepare yourself some food. It is absolutely a space where you feel more at home. You have to make reservations a long time ahead, because it's starting to get famous with a circle of people who book the hotel continuously. Every time I want to go there, I have to call six months before.

DINNER There are two restaurants that I love. One is **La Hacienda de los Morales,** and the other is the **San Ángel Inn.** They are big restaurants with typical Mexican food. Both of them are huge haciendas, historical colonial buildings. Both have patios, beautiful architecture, graceful lawns, good service. San Ángel is a little bit away from the urban center. It's in a

very nice area where rich people live. Even though you're surrounded by huge buildings, you feel like you're in another time, in another place. My thing in Mexico is *sopa del tortilla,* and I love tamales of any kind. I love the hot food. But I have a problem with my stomach, so I cannot eat it. At San Ángel Inn, they have chicken or beef tamales. La Hacienda de los Morales is practically the same thing, but it's in the center of the city. The same type of Mexican food: fajitas, quesadillas, all the resources of the land.

ENTERTAINMENT You'll find mariachis playing at both La Hacienda de los Morales and the San Ángel Inn. But if you go to the **Plaza Garibaldi,** a huge square, you'll find an incredible amount of mariachis, especially in the afternoon and evening. It's almost like a joke. You can find probably a hundred mariachis playing. You can hire them to play anywhere you want—your home, your hotel, a party.

Casa Vieja

Saturday

BREAKFAST The **Majestic Hotel,** with its rooftop terrace overlooking the Zócalo, is famous for breakfast. It's a beautiful view of the historic city. They have the eggs with grilled Mexican salami and grilled sausages. It's pretty American, but with a Mexican touch—like with guacamole. If you get there early, you can see the changing of the flag ceremony and watch the military band, which is very famous.

Casa Vieja is a little place with only ten rooms. If you are going to Mexico and want a taste of the place, this is the hotel for you

SIGHTS I don't want to go over the security thing, because that's not the point. Obviously, you have to keep an eye on what you're doing and the money that you are carrying, but I consider Mexico City a place to walk, because walking in Mexico City is when you're going to feel what the city is all about and what it was five hundred years ago. I walk in the **Zócalo,** in the historic center of the city. I remember seeing a very emotional speech by Vicente Fox, the president, in front of the statue of *El Ángel*, a monument for freedom, in the Paseo de la Reforma. Listening to the new president's speech was a special moment. When I went to Mexico again and was walking in the area, I remembered that speech and the meaning that speech had for anybody like me, who feels Mexico because they speak the language that I do. The new president promised changes in Mexico, which finally becomes a democracy after this last election. He talked about solving problems that have been endemic in the city, like poverty and crime. So I am very hopeful.

CULTURE There are wonderful museums. You have the **Modern Art Museum,** which is very nice. You have the **National Gallery.** But if I have to recommend a specific museum, it would be the museum of **Dolores Olmedo Patiño,** who was a close friend of Diego Rivera and a very close friend of his wife, Frida Kahlo. It's probably the best collection of Riveras and Kahlos together in Mexico City that you can find. It is a wonderful place to go. You can also go to Frida Kahlo's house and Diego Rivera's studio, which is not elaborate. It brings to mind how little you need to create art.

LUNCH Fonda el Refugio is a great Mexican restaurant in la Zona Rosa. What's wonderful about it is that all of the cooks in the kitchen are women. The food is fantastic. If you are out walking, you have to be careful eating from the stalls on the street. When I'm on the street, I just get the tamales. They are so hot—I don't think anything can survive on them. You can get them from little chariots in the park, like hot dogs in New York.

TOUR We were shooting at **Churubusco Azteca Studios,** which is a place you can visit. I remember people coming onto the set who looked like tourists with cameras. Those are the most famous studios in the city. They've been there a long, long time. It's a historical place that has been redone. By the time we were doing *Zorro,* they were in the middle of rebuilding the place, and now it's a very well done studio in which many movies have been shot. *Titanic* did interiors there. *Zorro* was there. The movie that I did with Angelina was shot in there, too. Mexico City cinema is big. Having Los Angeles so close, it's normal that productions go there because they find it cheaper working in Mexico, and the crews are very good.

SHOPPING El Palacio de Hierro is one of those monstrous supermalls where you can find anything. The pink area, **la Zona Rosa,** is probably the best place in Mexico for shopping. It has the best stores in the world, from Armani and Valentino, to antiques stores and boutiques. You'll find whatever you are looking for in la Zona Rosa. That area is a little bit funny at night—you have to be careful. **Mercado de Artesanías** is a huge street market very close to the Zócalo, and there's an antiques market in la Zona Rosa, as well.

DINNER You can go to **Fonda Don Chon,** the famous Aztec restaurant, where you can eat things like fried worms. They taste like potato chips. They fry them, so when they get to you, they don't look like worms, just something very crispy. **La Gruta** is a restaurant in a huge cave where they say people used to hide out close to the pyramids in Teotihuacán. It's Mexican food. The waiters and waitresses have the folkloric dress and there's music.

NIGHTCAP Of course, you can get good tequila at places like the **Bar l'Opera.** I don't drink alcohol, my friend. I am not to be trusted. But *un poquito* of tequila after a beautiful dinner is not going to cause you any damage. And it's good. Also, they have the *mezcal*, with the worm, which is not recommended. It's a little dangerous. It depends on how much you drink.

I mean, water can be very dangerous if you drink the whole pool.

Sunday

THE PARK On Sundays I just walk in the park. Half the population of Mexico City goes to **Chapultepec Park** with their kids to play. I went there with Melanie and the kids. They have boats, little attractions, and museums. I used to pass through there because it was on my way to the studio from the hotel. There is a fantastic roller coaster in Chapultepec Park. It's one of the best roller coasters in the world.

EXCURSION I've climbed to the top of both of the pyramids in **Teotihuacán** and sat there for a while. It's about thirty minutes from the city and it's very worthwhile to go there. The pyramids are called the Sun and the Moon. If you have an imagination and you stop in front of the pyramids and remember that this was

One Great Day in Mexico City

The day that Angelina Jolie won the Oscar, we brought a huge mariachi band—probably fifty guys—to play songs for her. Violinists, trumpet players, guitarists. We were in the middle of shooting when Angelina got the Oscar nomination. She'd won the Golden Globe and had the possibility of getting the Oscar, so the production decided to stop for a couple of days to allow her to attend the ceremony in Los Angeles. I had to go, too, because I was giving the award for Best Foreign Language Film, which I gave to my friend Pedro Almodóvar. We had a party after the Oscars at my home, but since we had to shoot the next day, a private plane was going to be waiting for me at 4:30 in the morning. I was at home, no drinking, no nothing, while everybody was nuts, swimming in my pool. And there were Oscars everywhere. Suddenly, I had to leave. I got on the plane and arrived in Mexico City around 11 in the morning their time. I went straight to the studio and started shooting. Angelina got back around 4 p.m. At around 4:30, the mariachis came. We brought Angelina out of the makeup trailer and they sang for her. It was a beautiful thing. The entire crew was there, and each member gave her a rose—like 150 roses—one by one. At the end, she got a big bouquet of flowers.

once a huge avenue with buildings and houses on the side, you realize the magnitude of what that empire was fifteen hundred years ago. It's impressive. I was expecting just to see two pyramids among the trees, and what I saw was an entire city with houses, with streets, with squares. It's an almost spiritual place to go.

Antonio Banderas's Mexico City Essentials

LODGING
Casa Vieja, $$$, 011-5255-5282-0067
Eugenio Sue 45

Four Seasons Hotel, $$$$, 011-5255-5230-1818
Paseo de la Reforma 500

DINING
Best Western Majestic Hotel Terrace Restaurant,
Mexican, $, 011-5255-5521-8600
Avenida Madero 73

Fonda Don Chon, Aztec/Mexican, $$$, 011-5255-5542-0873, Regina 160

Fonda el Refugio, Mexican, $$, 011-5255-5525-8128
Liverpool 166, la Zona Rosa

La Gruta, Mexican, $$, 011-5259-4956-0127
Peripheral Highway, Teotihuacan

La Hacienda de los Morales, Mexican, $$$,
011-5255-5096-3054, Vazquez de Mella 525

San Ángel Inn, Mexican, $$$, 011-5255-5616-1543
Diego Rivera 50

SIGHTS
Chapultepec Park, public park,
at the end of Paseo de la Reforma

Estudios Churubusco Azteca, movie studios,
011-5255-5549-3060, Atletas 2, Colonia Country Club

Museo de Arte Moderno, art museum,
011-5255-5553-6233, Chapultepec Park, Section 1

Museo Dolores Olmedo Patina, art museum,
011-5255-5555-1016, Avenida Mexico 5843, Xochimilco

Museo Nacional de Arte, art museum,
011-5255- 5130-3410, Calle Tacuba 8

Plaza Garibaldi, between the streets Republica de Peru
and Republica de Honduras downtown

Teotihuacán, archeological zone, 011-5259-4956-0276
30 miles northeast of Mexico City

Zócalo, historic center of the city,
at the intersection of Juárez and 20 de Noviembre streets

SHOPPING
El Palacio de Hierro, shopping mall,
011-5255-5229-3154, Avenida Durango

La Zona Rosa, shopping district,
Insurgentes Avenue

Mercado de Antiguedades, antiques market,
Londres 154, Plaza del Angel Mercado de Artesanías

NIGHTLIFE
Bar l'Opera, bar and restaurant, 011-5255-5512-8959
Cinco de Mayo #10

Celine Dion

Montreal

Named for a song her mother sang during her pregnancy, Celine Dion, the youngest of fourteen children, was literally born to music. She grew up in her parents' piano bar, Le Vieux Baril (the old barrel), in the village of Charlegmagne, "a Little House on the Prairie town where everyone knew everyone," just outside of Montreal. Dad played accordion, mom played violin, and the fourteen kids waited tables, sang, and played every conceivable instrument. One day when she was five, Dion stood up on a table in the bar and sang a song. Pretty soon, the town folk were planning their evenings around appearances of "La Petite Quebecoise" (the little Quebecer). Now, her village is the world and she sings from stages, TV, movie screens, and ten-times-platinum CDs whose sales set worldwide records. Her voice consoled the doomed lovers in the movie *Titanic* in her hit song "My Heart Will Go On," and she's earned her place in the Barbra-Tina-Aretha-Diana-Madonna pantheon of musical divas. But when it comes to Montreal, in many ways she's still the little girl on a tabletop, belting out a song for the locals. Here's a weekend with Celine Dion in the city where she first became a star—Montreal, Canada.

Friday

LODGING I would recommend the **Hotel Omni Montreal.** I know this hotel very well since our wedding reception took place there, and all of our out-of-town guests really enjoyed their stay. The hotel has the advantage of being situated downtown, and most of the major activities in Montreal are only a minute's walk away. The hotel has many rooms with spectacu-lar views of **Mount Royal,** the seven-hundred-foot mountain for which Montreal is named. The Omni has one of the best restaurants in town: **Zen,** an avant-garde Asiatic restaurant.

DINNER When I'm back in town, I'm always anxious to go back to some of my favorite restaurants. On top of the list is **Guy & Dodo** [downtown]. They serve a very nice French cuisine in an elegant and warm atmosphere.

Guy is a gifted chef and Dodo has a smile you don't forget. **Daou** [East Montreal Island], whose Lebanese cuisine—which my husband knows best—is just as good as home. A Lebanese feast awaits you here. It's a family restaurant with great food run by the four daughters of the original owner. I love the *kebe nayeh,* which is similar to steak tartare, and the *koussa,* which is stuffed zucchini, and the meat pies and the stuffed grape leaves. It's so good I have their stuffed zucchini shipped to me while I'm on tour. And **Faros** [downtown] Greek cuisine is tops. *Faros* means "lighthouse" in Greek. It's a small, quaint, family-run restaurant, decorated like a very clean Greek fisherman's tavern. They serve grilled fish, zucchini chips, wonderful salads, and memorable baklava for dessert.

ENTERTAINMENT First, check the **Bell Centre** for a major event like a hockey game or an internationally known big-name concert. I perform there regularly. The city has many multicultural arts complexes—like **Place des Arts** [downtown] and **Théâtre St-Denis** [Latin Quarter]—where there are always exciting musical and theatrical productions. Check in advance for local or international festivals, such as **Just for Laughs** [Latin Quarter], the comedy festival, or the now-world-famous **Montreal International Jazz Festival** [downtown]. They have free entertainment and live concerts, as well as a spectacular series of superstars.

I know the Hotel Omni Montreal very well since our wedding reception took place there, and all of our out-of-town guests really enjoyed their stay. The hotel has the advantage of being situated downtown, and most of the major activities in Montreal are only a minute's walk away.

If you like jazz, **Maison du Jazz** [downtown] is a nice place, founded by Charles Biddle, well known for the music and the ambience he creates in his club. He's a famous jazz bass player from Montreal and his club has live jazz seven nights a week. Mostly traditional jazz—piano, bass, and drums—with a special guest every night. It could be a saxophone, trumpet or singer. Maison is very popular and requires reservations, especially on weekends.

Saturday

BREAKFAST Nickels restaurants are a chain of family-oriented diners my husband and I invested in a few years ago. I supervised the menus, the fifties and sixties decor, the way the waitresses are dressed, and much more. It's named for my lucky number—five. You can get

Hotel Omni Montreal

a second helping of smoked meat or spaghetti at Nickels for only a nickel [after 5:00 p.m.]. I feel at home there—especially because many members of my large family—thirteen brothers and sisters—owned or managed the Nickels diners. So it's the same style as it was at home, when my mother was raising us—simple, warm, good, and clean. For breakfast, I would have fresh fruit, oatmeal with maple syrup, maybe an omelet, toast with peanut butter, and a cappuccino or Earl Grey tea. [Note: Dion founded the Nickels concept but is no longer involved with the chain.]

SIGHTS Montreal is an island in the middle of the St. Lawrence River, thirty-one miles long and ten miles wide. It's connected to mainland Canada by fifteen different bridges. If you catch a sightseeing bus, they'll take you to all of the major attractions. There's **Old Montreal,** the ninety-five-acre historic quarter of old buildings, restaurants, and cafés in the original eighteenth- and nineteenth-century buildings along the St. Lawrence River. It all started there. At the **Old Port,** you can take a short cruise or rent bicycles and Rollerblades to stroll the quaint streets—from the Basilique Notre-Dame, through the small streets in the Old Quarter, then around rue St-Francois-Xavier until you get to place d'Youville—it's like a trip back in time. Along the way, admire the vintage buildings—like the **Centre d'Histoire de Montreal,** the old fire station that's been transformed into a high-tech museum tracing the history of the city, or the **Banque de Montreal**—all restored to their original look. The **Olympic Stadium** funicular is always a joy. In two minutes, you're at the top of the Inclined Tower, which goes up almost nine hun-dred feet. You can see fifty miles in any direction—a breathtaking view of the city.

WALK From the Hotel Omni Montreal, take rue Ste-Catherine to boulevard St-Lawrence and go until rue Notre-Dame, make a left on rue Notre-Dame, and continue until Rue Bonsecour. Make a right on Bonsecour and make another right on rue St-Paul. You'll be at the **Bonsecour's Market,** Montreal's original city hall, which was recently renovated to hold special exhibitions. Then, continue west on St-Paul and go to rue Marche Bonsecour, turn left, then turn right on rue de la Commune. Walk down the street until you get to the **Montreal Museum of Archaeology and History,** which tells the story of Montreal's history and is built on Pointe-a-Calliere, the place where the city's original fifty-three settlers landed from France. Along the way, you'll pass the many restaurants and terraces of place Jacques-Cartier. Afterwards, walk east on rue de la Commune until you get to rue St-Suplice, turn left, and continue until you get to the **Notre Dame Basilica,** where we got married. It's a magnificent church with incredible woodwork carving, fourteen stained glass windows, a vaulted ceiling, and a twelve-ton bell that can be heard from miles and miles away.

SKIING AND GOLF If you like to ski, you can go up north to the Laurentians mountain region—a world-class ski resort area that resembles Switzerland. It's filled with forests, lakes, and mountain villages. My favorite village is **Saint-Sauveur des Monts,** which is an hour away from the city. It's a charming little ski resort, full of lively places to have a lunch or coffee. The village is famous for night skiing on Mont-Habitant and Mont-Christi. It's fun all year long—summering around its lakes, watching the leaves turn red in autumn—but it's especially great in winter, cross-country skiing or relaxing by a crackling fireplace. In the village of Terrebonne, I love to play golf at a great course called **Le Mirage.**

SHOPPING Underground Montreal is the biggest underground city in the world, a temperature-controlled urban center where 250,000 people visit every day. You can start your shopping day by strolling St. Catherine Street, a major shopping area and a great walking street in the center of the city, home to some of the city's most popular restaurants, bars, and shops. Then, you can visit the famous underground shopping malls: **Eaton Center, Place Ville-Marie, Promenades de la Cathedrale, Place Montreal-Trust** [downtown]—all connected through underground tunnels, which makes it easy during the winter. You can literally shop from one mall to another without heavy coats and snow boots.

LUNCH Go to **Schwartz's** [Plateau Mount-Royal] for smoked meat—a Montreal specialty that's very similar to pastrami—and delicatessen. It's one of the most famous delicatessens in the world. Although it's fairly small, it's always busy—a great noisy deli that specializes in smoked meat, which is piled high on sandwiches, and rib steaks. Get there early because the lunch line forms at 11 a.m. every day.

SAILING After lunch, why not visit some of the islands surrounding Montreal, which is, of course, an island itself. Sainte-Helene Island has the **Stewart Museum,** where you can explore Montreal's only fort and relive the early years of the New World. The fort was built over four hundred years ago. On Sainte-Helene, you can visit **La Ronde** and its mega-playground, or the **Biosphere** for the environmentally conscious. When the Biosphere was built by Buckminster Fuller for the Expo 67's U.S. pavilion, it was the largest geodesic dome in the world. Today it's a museum with many interesting environmental exhibits.

CULTURE The **Insectarium** [Hochelaga] is a museum dedicated entirely to the study of insects. It was developed in 1990 by the insect expert, George Brosssard, who donated 250,000 insects from his private collection. You'll see everything from butterflies to cockroaches. The **Botanical Gardens** [Hochelaga] is a collection of theme gardens and greenhouses, a wonderful parklike atmosphere where you can study thousands of types of trees, flowers, and plants or just enjoy the serenity. The **Biosphere** is a huge wonderland with thousands of plants and animals, where you can walk between the environments of North, Central, and South America, then tropical forests and mountain environments like you'll find in the Laurentians, then the marine atmosphere of the St. Lawrence River, then the Arctic. You'll see rodents, raccoons, penguins, beavers, lynx, and bats. It's like traveling the world without ever leaving Montreal.

DINNER Mikado [Latin Quarter], the Japanese restaurant, is a must for sushi lovers. **Moishe's** [downtown] has great steaks. It's been there for sixty years, a dark clublike atmosphere. I love the rib steak with Monte Carlo potatoes, which is like a twice-baked potato with secret ingredients, with a shrimp cocktail or chopped liver to start. For great Italian food, try **Da Vinci** [downtown west], a traditional family-owned Italian restaurant in a 140-year-old Victorian mansion in the heart of the city. I love the fruit plate and the light pastas, like spaghettini primavera. **Barolo** is in Chomedey, a Montreal suburb. It's another family Italian restaurant specializing in pasta, seafood, lamb, and veal.

NIGHTLIFE Hop over to Notre-Dame Island and its world-famous **Casino** for a night of fun or serious gambling. You can dine there or enjoy a show at their cabaret. Make sure you take a peek at the fabulous view the Casino offers of Montreal by night. When you want to go back to town, the Metro will take you there in minutes. You can then go on to St. Lawrence or St. Denis Streets, where hundreds of restaurants, bars, and cafés are there to tickle every fancy. Or you can go up the mountain to Laurier or Bernard Streets, where a chic crowd of locals give it a special atmosphere, much different from the more touristic atmosphere downtown. You will feel like an insider; most of the restaurants on Laurier or Bernard Streets are very good and cozy. Or choose Crescent Street—where boys meet girls at the many bars, restaurants, and terraces, only five blocks from the Hotel Omni Montreal. It's a must!

Sunday

BRUNCH Brunch is very popular in Montreal on Sundays. **Hotel de la Montagne** [downtown] offers an elaborate one. But lots of smaller restaurants have a more relaxed formula, such as **Eggspectation,** which has twelve different kinds of Eggs Benedict, or **Thursday's** [downtown], on the second floor of the famous Thursday's discotheque. There are clowns and magicians to entertain the children. You can get brunch from the buffet or order a la carte.

EXCURSION You can go all the way down to **Quebec City,** a town with a European flavor that's full of surprises and magic. It's located two and a half hours from Montreal. There's so much to enjoy there that you might want to take a side trip. We call it our Belle Provence—the Provence of Quebec. The **Winter Carnival** and **Summer Festival** are two major events. You can find plenty to do there for even longer than three days. One of my favorite places in Quebec City is the area around the hotel, **Chateaux Frontenac.** Built on top of Cap Diamant, the oldest part of the city, now restored in full, the hotel is surrounded by little streets with painters and artists selling their art. A must-see.

Celine Dion's Montreal Essentials

LODGING
Hotel Omni Montreal, $$, (514) 284-1110
1050 rue Sherbrooke ouest, downtown

Le Chateau Frontenac, $$$, (418) 692-3861
1 rue des Carrieres, Quebec City

DINING
Barolo, Italian, $$$, (450) 682-7450
2200 boulevard Cure Labelle, Chomedey

Daou, Lebanese, $$$, (514) 334-1199
2373 boulevard Marcel

Eggspectation, continental, $, (514) 842-3447
multiple locations throughout Montreal

Faros, Greek, $$$, (514) 270-8437
362 Fairmount Avenue West, downtown

Guy & Dodo Morali, French, $$$, (514) 842-3636
1444 Metcalfe Street, downtown

Hotel de la Montagne, Sunday brunch, $$$,
(514) 288-5656, 1430 rue de la Montagne, downtown

Mikado, Japanese, $$$, (514) 844-5705
1731 rue St-Denis, Latin Quarter

Moishe's, steak house, $$$$, (514) 845-3509
3961 boulevard St-Laurent, downtown

Nickels, diners, $, (514) 333-6544
multiple locations throughout Montreal

Ristorante Da Vinci, Italian, $$$, (514) 874-2001
1180 Bishop Street, downtown west

Schwartz's, deli, $, (514) 842-4813
3895 boulevard St-Laurent, downtown

Thursday's, French, $$, (514) 288-5656
1445 Crescent Street, downtown

Zen, Asian, $$$$, (514) 284-1110
1050 rue Sherbrooke ouest, Omni Hotel, downtown

SIGHTS

Banque de Montreal, (514) 877-6810
119 rue St-Jacques, Old Montreal

Biodome (Biosphere) de Montreal, environmental
museum, (514) 868-3000, 4777 avenue Pierre-de-Coubertin

Centre d'Histoire de Montreal, (514) 872-3207
335 place d'Youville, Old Montreal

Montreal Museum of Archaeology and History,
(514) 872-9150, 350 place Royale, Old Montreal

Insectarium, insect museum, (514) 872-1400
4581 rue Sherbrooke est, Botanical Garden

La Ronde, amusement park, (514) 397-2000
22 chemin Macdonald, Montreal Islands

Montreal Botanical Gardens, (514) 872-1400
4581 rue Sherbrooke est, Hochelaga

One Great Day in Montreal

When I was twelve, my mother wrote a song for me called "Ce N'etait qu'un Reve" ["It Was Only a Dream"]. One of my brothers and I recorded a cheap demo tape of the song at home and sent it to Rene Angelil, a music producer and manager. After listening to the tape, Rene called and asked my mother and me to come to his office in Montreal. He gave me a pen and told me to pretend it was a microphone and that I was onstage looking at balconies and people. He cried while listening to me sing and said he would work with me. He had to mortgage his house to pay for the production of my first album. Fourteen years after we met, Rene and I got married on December 17, 1994, at the Notre Dame Basilica in Montreal. We all arrived at the Hotel Omni Montreal, formerly the Westin Mont-Royal, the night before. We had dinner in my suite, all the girls together with my mother. It was like a farewell to my younger years, when most of my sisters were like second mothers to me. I was not allowed to go on the second floor where the reception was to be held. It was meant to be a total surprise. The whole second floor was converted for the reception: a grand hallway, an English library with a huge Christmas tree, a Casino-type of bar, a *Saturday Night Fever* discotheque, and a forties supper club. Real magic, indeed! Nature was also at the rendezvous since it started snowing early that Saturday—by the time I got to the church, the ground was all covered with this beautiful white carpet. It was incredible. And it stopped just as we were coming out. It was like a gift from heaven—and from Montreal.

Mount Royal Park, (514) 843-8240
1260 Remembrance Road, Montreal Island

Notre Dame Basilica, (514) 842-2925
110 rue Notre-Dame ouest, Old Montreal

Old Montreal, (514) 873-2015, Saint Lawrence Waterfront

Old Port, (514) 496-PORT, 333 rue de la Commune ouest

Olympic Stadium and Inclined Tower, (514) 252-8687
4141 avenue Pierre-de-Coubertin, downtown

Stewart Museum, (514) 861-6701
20 Tour de l'Isle Road, Montreal Island

SHOPPING

Bonsecours Market, shopping district, (514) 872-8477
350 rue St-Paul est, Old Montreal

Le Centre Eaton, shopping center, (514) 288-3708
705 rue Ste-Catherine ouest, downtown

Les Promenades de la Cathedrale, shopping center,
(514) 849-9925, 625 rue Ste-Catherine ouest, downtown

Place Montreal Trust, shopping center, (514) 843-8000
1500 McGill College, downtown

Place Ville-Marie, shopping center, (514) 861-9393
1 place Ville-Marie, downtown

NIGHTLIFE/ENTERTAINMENT

Bell Centre, hockey/concerts, (514) 932-2582
1260 rue de la Gauchetiere ouest, downtown

Casino de Montreal, (800) 665-2274
1 avenue du Casino, Notre Dame Island

Festival International de Jazz de Montreal,
(514) 523-3374, (888) 515-0515
multiple venues, downtown

Just for Laughs Comedy Festival, comedy festival,
(514) 845-3155, multiple venues, Latin Quarter

Maison du Jazz, jazz club, (514) 842-8656
2060 rue Aylmer, downtown

Place des Arts, live music, (514) 285-4200
175 rue Ste-Catherine ouest, downtown

Théâtre St-Denis, live theater, (514) 849-4211
1594 rue St-Denis, Latin Quarter

SKIING/GOLF

Club de Golf le Mirage, golf course, (450) 477-7280
3737 chemin Martin, Terrebonne

Saint Sauveur des Monts, ski resort village,
45 minutes north of Montreal

Kate Hudson

Paris

Kate Hudson had one hour and one condition: If her months-old baby boy, Ryder Russell Robinson, awakened, she had to run. We were talking about Paris, which Hudson called "my favorite subject." The actress first visited Paris as a child with her mother, Goldie Hawn. Since then, she's starred in many movies, including her breakout roll as a rock-and-roll groupie in *Almost Famous*. But the film that took her back to Paris was *Le Divorce*, which filmed for three months in the City of Light, a dream for Francophile Kate. So, here we go, whisked away to Paris with Kate Hudson, who promised to keep talking as long as her own little one stayed fast asleep.

Friday

LODGING We stayed at the **Plaza Athénée.** A beautiful hotel—really nice. There's a fun bar and the service is excellent. The Plaza Athénée is very friendly, too. My other favorite hotel is the **George V.** It's beautiful and classy and big, and it's got all the amenities you need. The **Ritz** is also beautiful, but very expensive.

DINNER L'Amis Louis is one of the best restaurants I've ever been to. It's very small and very hard to get in to; you have to make reservations almost a year in advance, but it's our favorite. And the *côte de boeuf*, it's ridiculous—incredible. And they have a wine list you would travel six thousand miles for. It's just a great vibe. I get their foie gras and their potatoes and spinach.

Saturday

STROLL You have to walk. Paris is a walking city. You walk, you take the Metro. That's how you have to experience Paris—even if you end up walking for miles. That's where you have your romantic moments. Even if you're alone, you know. You'll look back on Paris and say, "Remember that day I walked for an hour to get to that little coffeehouse? Or that little place where I had croissants?" That's what Paris is to me. At whatever hotel you're at, ask them: "What's the best creperie?" A *galette* is what they call it; it's a different kind of crepe. It's buckwheat, and I get eggs in it and ham and it's so yummy.

ART You've got to go to the **Louvre,** even if it's just that every time you go back you say, "I'm just going to do one room." That way, eventually, you'll have seen the whole thing. You have to see the Mona Lisa, and then the **Picasso Museum.** The best is **Monet's Gardens** in Giverny, if you're there in the spring or summer. You have to check that out because it's just insanely beautiful. You realize how inspired this man was by his surroundings. Sometimes that's everything, you know.

SNACK After the Louvre, I'd probably go get a hot chocolate at **Angelina's.** It's right down the street, and it's a must-do. It's like drinking cake through a straw. It's the most amazing concoction of hot chocolate that you'll ever taste in your life. The amazing thing about it is that it's really thick, and when you try it without the *crème fouettée*, it's bitter. But then you put the *crème fouettée* on it and, well, it's a sort of ritual. They bring it to you in a pitcher, with the *crème fouettée* on the side, and you put it together to your own liking. And when you put the *crème fouettée* on it, it sweetens it. So it's sort of this amazing alchemy of chocolate and cream. Together it's the most sensational thing you'll ever have. Afterward, you might as well check yourself into the nearest hospital—because it's overload. They also have really good pastries. It's very touristy, but worth it.

I'd go to stores you can't go to anywhere else—like Colette. That's my favorite store in Paris.

LUNCH I'd go to **Chez Janou** for lunch. It's a little more laid-back restaurant, a little more hip. It's just outside the Marais. The food is Provençale, and it's amazing. You have to get the chocolate mousse when you're there, because it comes in this big tub, a big bowl, and you just scoop out the mousse, and, oh my goodness, it's so yummy! It's on a fabulous street corner, and it feels like you're in a real neighborhood—we love that. They have wonderful stuffed peppers, and their rabbit is excellent if you eat meat.

SHOPPING I'd go to stores you can't go to anywhere else—like **Colette.** That's my favorite store in Paris. Then there's **L'Eclaireur** in the Marais. It's like Maxfield's in Los Angeles, with local designers, some Dries Van Noten, and beautiful things I'd never seen before. The Marais is the best place to go shopping; it's the most young and hip area.

MUSIC I'm not a club person, but my husband and I did go hear some music. We went to see jazz pianist Ahmad Jamal at that beautiful con-

Colette, Paris

cert hall. Oh, it's a famous one; it's really high up. There are a lot of balconies. When you walk in, it's almost like a circle and the balcony kind of circles up. But the best was the **Zenith,** where we went to see Bob Dylan. The Zenith is more like an arena. It's not the most charming. It's not like the Paradiso in Amsterdam, you know, where I went to see the Black Crowes. But it was amazing because it was Bob and he's always amazing.

DINNER There's **404.** It's a Moroccan restaurant that's really fun. My favorite drink is there, and it's called a 404 Cocktail. It's sort of like a *mojito* with vodka. They have it in London as well, at a place called Momo's. It's the same owner. Really good, really fun, and really good couscous. The seating's pretty low, very bohemian, a little more funky. There's also a wonderful Italian place called **Stresa.** I love it. I always get the pasta with caviar—just a flat pasta with butter and caviar. That's my favorite. And then a scoop of vanilla ice cream with a shot of espresso over it. As you can tell, food is a big part of my time in Paris. Oh, then there's **Bofinger,** the brasserie that has all the big platters of seafood. It's a famous place. It's two floors . . . Uh-oh! There goes my baby. My baby needs me, so I've got to go.

Kate Hudson's Paris Essentials

LODGING
Four Seasons George V, $$$$, 011-33-1-49-52-70-00
31 avenue George V

Plaza Athénée, $$$$, 011-33-1-53-67-66-65,
1-866-732-1106, 25 avenue Montaigne

The Ritz, $$$$$, 011-33-1-43-16-30-30
15 place Vendome

DINING
404, Moroccan, $$$, 011-33-1-42-74-57-81
69 rue des Gravilliers

Angelina's, tea salon, $$, 011-33-1-42-60-82-00
226 rue de Rivoli

Bofinger, Alsatian brasserie, $$$, 011-33-1-42-72-87-82
5 rue de la Bastille, near Bastille Opera

Chez Janou, Provençale, $$$, 011-33-1-42-72-28-41
2 rue Roger Verlomme

L'Amis Louis, café, $$$$, 011-33-1-48-87-77-48
32 rue Vertbois

Stresa, Italian, $$$, 011-33-1-47-23-51-62
7 rue Chambiges

SIGHTS
The Louvre Museum, 011-33-1-40-20-53-17
34 quai du Louvre

Monet's House and Gardens, 011-33-2-32-51-28-21
Rue Claude Monet, Giverny

Picasso Museum, 011-33-1-42-71-25-21
5 rue de Thorigny

SHOPPING
Colette, hip department store, 011-33-1-55-35-33-90
213 rue St. Honore

L'Eclaireur, clothing, 011-33-1-48-87-10-22
12 rue Mahler

NIGHTLIFE
The Zenith of Paris, live music, 011-33-1-42-08-60-00
211 avenue Jean Jaures

Paris

H ere's Elizabeth Hurley's secret for maximizing a long-distance airplane flight: "I put on my own pajamas, socks, and lots of moisturizer. Then I have a glass of champagne and pass out." The woman needs her rest—especially if she's flying to Paris, her favorite destination, in which, as you'll soon discover, she's a nonstop blur. A London-based actress-turned-model-turned-actress-again-turned-businesswoman, with her own swimsuit/clothing line, Hurley pierced the global consciousness in 1994 in a black Versace safety pin gown, on the arm of her then significant other, Hugh Grant, at the premier of his *Four Weddings and a Funeral*. In record speed, she became a star on three fronts: modeling (representing Estée Lauder in its worldwide campaigns), movies (including *Austin Powers*), and, with Hugh Grant under their Simian Films banner, producing (*Extreme Measures*, *Mickey Blue Eyes*, among others). Currently living in London, she's within easy flying or Chunnel distance from Paris. Here's where you'll find her.

Friday

LODGING Paris is brimming over with ravishing hotels, but nothing beats the **Ritz.** I love the Ritz, I dream about the Ritz, and—like Coco Chanel—could happily live at the Ritz. The rooms are to die for, the service is impeccable, and the food is guaranteed to turn the most abstemious supermodel into a glutton. If I were to be sent to the electric chair, my last meal would have to be the Ritz's spaghetti Bolognaise. I order it as soon as I arrive, no matter what time of day—and wolf it in seconds. I don't know what they put in it, probably about eight pounds of butter, but who cares? It's France!

STROLL I rarely unpack properly in hotels and normally just yank things out of suitcases when I need them, but at the Ritz I unpack beautifully, put on my prettiest clothes, and go for a stroll in the **Tuileries Gardens.** Here, you'll see lovers entwined on park benches, old men playing boules, and more dog poop than you could believe exists. I deftly avoid stepping in this and sit down at a little café in the middle of the park where I order a Coca-Cola. Nothing remarkable in that, you may say, except I never, ever drink sodas of any description as I think they're appallingly bad for you. But French Coca-Cola—in a glass bottle of course—tastes so different and so delicious that I can't resist it.

DINNER Dinner would be at the **Costes Hotel.** Not only is the food good—I love the bizarrely named dish Le Tigre qui Pleur—The Tiger Who Cries—don't ask, it's steak—but there are masses of interesting people to stare at. Last time I was there, Roman Polanski and Harrison Ford were at the next table. It's quite a hip hotel with a very sexy bar all done up in scarlet velvet and, best of all, it's only a short walk from the Ritz. Therefore, you can avoid being humiliated by a taxi driver, who traditionally has to pretend not to understand a word of one's English.

NIGHTCAP Then it's back to the Ritz, a quick Kir Royale in the **Ritz Bar,** and up to my room for a heavenly soak in the enormous bathtub and the best sleep—window wide open, of course.

I love the Ritz, I dream about the Ritz, and—like Coco Chanel—could happily live at the Ritz. The rooms are to die for, the service is impeccable, and the food is guaranteed to turn the most abstemious supermodel into a glutton.

Saturday

BREAKFAST I never set an alarm in Paris, because I'm so excited about breakfast that I leap out of bed alarmingly early. I ring down for the papers, put on a huge fluffy bathrobe, and spy out of the windows on to the Place Vendome, to see what's happening in Gay Paree. I swoon when breakfast arrives—the bacon and eggs seem like a gourmet feast and the coffee is so strong that you feel barking mad for a few hours. I rarely eat fruit because it makes me nauseous. But in France I'm frequently tempted by the luscious peaches. How can they taste so good?

Hotel Ritz, Paris

SHOPPING Saturday is shopping day as most shops are shut on Sundays. Every shop is tempting, but first stop is always **Sabbia Rosa,** the sexiest underwear shop in the world. It's fiendishly expensive as everything is handmade, but it is so pretty and special that it's worth working 24/7 to get your hands on a few pieces. Everything is altered for you and delivered to your hotel in a few hours. They also have a riveting guest book in which I was fascinated to spot Woody Allen and Soon Yi! Next, it's off to **Diptyque,** the best candle and soap shop. I buy masses of Figuier and Baies and wonder how in God's name I'm going to carry them home. Then it's my favorite department shop in the world—**Le Bon Marche.** Every nice thing known to man rests smugly on these heaving shelves, including my own range— Elizabeth Hurley Beach—and I buy everything from hair products to lampshades. Clothes range from designer to extremely cheap and very stylish.

LUNCH A spot of lunch at the **Brasserie Lipp** sounds tempting by now. This landmark restaurant serves the most delicious food and it takes forever to choose. My French friend Julie always has Andouillettes, a rather terrifying dish consisting mostly of pig's innards, but I usually settle for oysters and steak tartare.

AFTERNOON TEA You must have tea in **Angelina's** on the Rue du Rivoli. This is a very famous *salon de thé* where you can sip vervain tea and eat the most unbelievable cakes and tarts whilst you gloat over your purchases. Alternatively, you could buy the best bread in Paris at **Poilane** on the Rue de Cherche Midi,

or visit the best cake shop, **Mulot,** on the Rue de Seine and buy madeleines or croissants.

DINNER Back to the hotel for a nap and a bath, and then out for dinner! Even though you are guaranteed a *crises de foie* [crises of the liver], I feel compelled to go to **L'Amis Louis,** a tiny, expensive, dietitian's nightmare. There are only a few things on the menu: foie gras, beef, chicken, lamb, French fries, salad, and fruit. But I swear on everything I hold sacred, that you will never, ever have tasted food so good! The meat is unbelievable, the portions massive, and the ambience superb. You're not really fit for anything after such feasting, but if you're feeling strong, you could stagger to **La Closerie des Lilas,** a brasserie with a piano bar, for a drink. It's cozy, sexy, and fairly discreet and quiet.

Saturday

MORNING My *crisis de foie* is normally rampaging by now so I skip breakfast and sit weakly on the Ritz terrace and drink Badoit water. This and a quick swim in the magnificent swimming pool usually revives me and I go for a walk in **Parc Monceau.** Prepare to be sickened by the sight of exquisitely dressed French women and their sinisterly well-behaved children. Ignore them, and buy a tiny shot of espresso and maybe nibble on a Petits Oursous, a little marshmallow bear.

CULTURE After yesterday's capitalist bonanza, today is our day of culture, so I visit my favorite museum, the **Jacquemart-Andre.** Situated in a converted very grand house, there's an eclectic mixture of beautiful paintings, statuary, furniture, and Roman stone. It's very calming and civilized and reminds me slightly of the Frick in New York.

LUNCH On my way to lunch I insist on passing my favorite bridge, the **Pont Alexandre Third.** It's very pretty and grand and you die to be kissing someone on it. Lunch in the famous **Café de Flore** is a must—very French and delicious, full of lovers and chic older people. An omelet and salad will never have tasted so good.

SIGHTS Afterwards, a trot around the gorgeous **Luxembourg Gardens** [Left Bank] and then on to Le Marais—the very beautiful, ancient district. Wonder at the elegance of Place des Voges, avoid the tourist shops, and head for the **Picasso Museum.** Afterwards, wander round the enchanting streets, peer into intriguing courtyards, and grab a coffee or chocolate at **Ma Bourgogne.**

ONE LAST STOP By now, I'm ready to drop, so back to the hotel for a snooze and the nightmare of cramming everything into suitcases and heading off for the airport. Whatever you do, don't miss the final, very important stop. The food shops in the airport are fantastic, so buy cheese, pâté, wine, and chocolate, and sink into your plane seat feeling fat and poor, but amazingly happy.

YOU CAN'T LEAVE PARIS WITHOUT . . . You can't visit Paris without buying gorgeous, inexpensive children's clothes, so I do a whirlwind shop for various nephews, nieces,

and godchildren. **Du Pareil au Meme** and **Petit Bateaux** are everywhere and excellent. **Colette** is a fabulous boutique. They must have a very smart buyer because there's not one thing in there that you don't want to take home: clothes, hair ornaments, soap, etc. Everything is gorgeous!

Elizabeth Hurley's Paris Essentials

LODGING

Hotel Costes, $$$$, 011-33-1-42-44-50-00
239 rue St. Honore

The Ritz, $$$$$, 011-33-1-43-16-30-70
15 Place Vendome

DINING

Angelina's, tea salon, $$, 011-33-1-42-60-82-00
226 rue de Rivoli

Brasserie Lipp, Alsatian brasserie, $$$,
011-33-1- 45-48-53-91, 151 Boulevard St. Germain

Café de Flore, café, $$, 011-33-1-45-48-55-26
172 St. Germain, 6th Arrondissement metro

Hotel Costes Restaurant, French, $$$,
011-33-1-42-44-50-25, 239 rue St. Honore

L'Amis Louis, French, $$$$, 011-33-1-48-87-77-48
32 rue Vertbois

Ma Bourgogne, French, $$$, 011-33-1-42-78-44-64
19 place des Vosges

SIGHTS

Jacquemart-Andre, museum, 011-33-1-45-62-39-94
158 Boulevard Haussmann

Luxembourg Gardens
62-acre park on Paris's Left Bank

Picasso Museum, 011-33-1-42-71-25-21,
5 rue de Thorigny

Parc Monceau, along Boulevard De Courcelles

Pont Alexandre III, historic bridge
8th Arrondissement

Tuileries Gardens, municipal park, Central Paris

SHOPPING
Colette, hip department store, 011-33-1-55-35-33-90
213 rue St. Honore

Diptyque, candles and soap, 011-33-1-43-26-45-27
34 Boulevard Saint Germain

Du Pareil au Meme, children's clothing,
011-33-1-46-33-87-85, multiple locations throughout Paris

Elizabeth Hurley Beach, online shop for beachwear,
www.elizabethhurley.com

Gerard Mulot, bakery, 011-33-1-43-26-85-77
76 rue de Seine

Le Bon Marche, upscale department store,
011-33-1-44-39-81-00, 22 rue de Sevres

Petit Bateau, children's clothing, 011-33-1-45-00-13-95
multiple locations throughout Paris

Poilane, famous bakery, 011-33-1-45-48-42-59
8 rue du Cherche-Midi

Sabbia Rosa, lingerie, 011-33-1-45-48-88-37
73 rue des Sts-Peres

NIGHTLIFE
La Closerie des Lilas, brasserie, 011-33-1-40-51-34-50
171 Boulevard du Montparnasse

Ritz Bar, English-style pub, 011-33-1-43-16-30-70
15 Place Vendome, at Hotel Ritz

Paris

Philippe Starck is the world's most irreverent architect and designer. He calls himself a "creator of fertile surprises" and sees his work as nothing less than to "reconstruct a world." During our interview, he sat inside one of his creations, Mondrian, the Sunset Boulevard hotel that captures the Los Angeles spirit of sun and hip sensibility. In the Mondrian, Starck was not some anonymous architect, but a wiry-haired, black-attired star, shaking hands and signing autographs. His work is already exhibited in museums in several international cities. His cutting-edge designs have pushed the limits of imagination everywhere, from the Asahi Building in Tokyo to the late French president Francois Mitterrand's Elysée Palace apartment to his own fanciful lines of furniture, lamps, toothbrushes, kettles, clocks, bathrooms, pasta, boats, eyeglasses, motorcycles, television sets, ashtrays, and much more. But there is one place Starck wouldn't even dream of redesigning—the city that was his birthplace and now serves as his sanctuary: Paris, France. So abandon your preconceptions and clean your spectacles. Here's a weekend in Philippe Starck's Paris.

Friday

LODGING The **Hotel Rafael** [Champs Elysées/Arc de Triomphe] is not so small, but it's a chic hotel. Yeah, and it has a very good bar. Small, charming, warm, good barman, ultra *classique*. It's where I would stay.

LUNCH I love **Relais Plaza,** the restaurant in the Plaza Athénée Hotel. It's small and very fun. Very nice, beautiful lighting, beautiful decoration—very art deco and very rich. I always eat a club sandwich.

SIGHTS Paris is the Seine, the river. That's where I have my house. It's just at the limit of Paris. It's a small island called Isle St-Germain, where there is a very huge famous picture of Jean du Buffet. On this island, we have our house, which is like a wood lighthouse with a quay and a boat. My favorite place on the Seine is a tunnel underneath Place de la Bastille and Place Stalingrad. It is a tunnel for boats, **Canal St-Martin.** When you're on a boat, it's all black and there are holes in the ceiling and you can see the sky from the boat. It's a beauty. My favorite bridge is the **Pont Neuf,** the oldest stand-in bridge in Paris, because there is a small bench, and people can sit on the Pont Neuf as in Valencia and Florence. There were shops and vendors on the Pont Neuf back in the Middle Ages. At night, the **Bateaux Mouches** are an interesting way to see the river. It's a good trip. Now we have a boat, but before, I rented a boat to go with my friends, take a fiesta, or take an aperitif at the sunset. We'd go from Isle St-Germain to Bercy. You see everything. You go through Paris.

COCKTAILS There is a Mexican bar I love on Rue Biron called **La Perla**—very classy, very Mexican. I like the low-design classic restaurant; I hate the trendy restaurant. I drink frozen margaritas, without salt, and we eat plain cheese nachos with a lot of jalapeños.

DINNER There is a fantastic Indian restaurant, **Ravi.** It is very small—one, two, three, four, five tables. Very, very luxurious. Very well done. With fantastic food. Best Indian food of Paris and the most beautiful table and decoration you can imagine. The owner is Mr. Ravi.

NIGHTLIFE My daughter plays drums almost every night on **la Passerelle des Artes,** a very thin metallic pedestrian bridge in front of l'École des Beaux-Arts. It's a meeting place of the people who play drums. At night, everybody comes, from one to one hundred or two hundred—every night. It's great! It's for young people.

BREAKFAST Café de Flore [6th Arrondissement St-Germain] is always good at night, or for breakfast. Sometimes, when I arrive very early by the plane, I take a breakfast at Flore. I have Welsh rarebit. I love that when I arrive from the plane, and then we go to the flea market.

SIGHTS In the **Musée National des Arts Africains et Oceaniens** there is an aquarium for crocodiles, which is very, very theatrical, very strong. It's very mysterious and the feeling is very wet and heavy. There are crocodiles in the water. And there is something fascinating— the **Place de Bastille**—the drawing of the old fortress. When you walk, if you can with all the cars on the Place de la Bastille, you have the design on the ground of the architecture blueprint of what it was before. But there is the design on the ground, stones of different colors that make up the blueprints of the designer. It's incredible to walk in a virtual castle that has disappeared.

LUNCH I like many of the old restaurants, like **Bofinger** [Bastille]. It's an old brasserie, art nouveaux. It's a good place, very good for every day, very well done, very correct. Very good for lunch.

ARCHITECTURE I was born in Paris on a very strange street, **rue Mallet-Stevens.** Robert Mallet-Stevens was a famous architect of the twenties and thirties and he has a street completely built by him. He was a famous designer. I was born on this street. Very strange, huh? The street is a masterpiece of architecture. You see almost all of the houses of Mallet-Stevens.

SHOPPING Edifice is a shop that has a lot of my products. My shoes come always from **Paraboot**—the best shoes in the world. My jacket always comes from **Agnes B.,** but custom made. She does this only for a happy few. In Paris, every gift always comes from **Hermès.**

VIEWS The **Observatoire de Paris** is a beauty. Sometimes, I make a party there. Sometimes, when we want to present something to the press, we rent it out. There is a very old telescope there. I love it! I love astronomy. I love science.

NIGHTLIFE The most trendy place for the night is called **Le Cabaret.** It's close to the Champs-Elysées. La Cabaret is the hottest place today in Paris. It's a very small, old nightclub, but with hot customers.

Sunday

SIGHTS The only place that really inspired me is le Rocher de Vincennes. It's a rock of Vincennes in the **Parc Zoologique Bois de Vincennes.** There is an artificial mountain for the deer or for the wild animals, in the park of Vincennes. It's like a dream; it's like a Jules Verne story. A fake mountain in the center of Paris—incredible.

There is a beautiful park in the northeast of Paris called Parc des Buttes-Chaumont.

EXCURSIONS Fifty kilometers outside of Paris in the forest is **Chateau de Rambouillet.** It is huge, very beautiful, because it was designed for Louis XIV. It's a theater set—it's completely done like a Japanese garden. It's incredible. Also, there is a beautiful park in the northeast of Paris called **Parc des Buttes-Chaumont.** It's a beauty, because one more time you are in the book of Jules Verne.

DINNER La Maison du Valais, close to la Madeleine, is a very nice restaurant where you eat fondue—something from the mountains. It looks like a chalet from the mountains.

VIEWS I don't walk in Paris—I drive a motorcycle. Once more, I love to ride along the quay close to Pont Neuf at night. Riding along the

highway of the quay, the Voie Georges-Pompidou, you pass along the Seine. You have the feeling that Paris is one of the most beautiful cities in the world. Because it's like a theater set, it's perfection. It's not a city—it's theater.

Philippe Starck's Paris Essentials

LODGING
Hotel Rafael, $$$$, 011-33-1-53-64-32-00, 17 avenue Kleber, Champs Elysées/Arc de Triomphe

DINING
Bofinger, Alsatian brasserie, $$$, 011-33-1-42-72-87-82 5 rue de la Bastille, Bastille

Café de Flore, café, $$, 011-33-1-45-48-55-26 172 boulevard St-Germain, 6th Arrondissement St-German

La Maison du Valais, Swiss, $$$, 011-33-1-42-60-22-72 20 rue Royale, close to la Madeleine

La Perla, Mexican, $$, 011-33-1-42-77-59-40 26 rue Francois Miron

Le Relais Plaza, French, $$$, 011-33-1-53-67-64-00 25 avenue Montaigne, Plaza Athénée Hotel

Ravi, Indian, $$$, 011-33-1-42-61-17-28, 50 rue de Verneuil

SIGHTS
Bateaux Mouches, boat tours, 011-33-1-42-25-96-10 pont de l'Alma

Canal St. Martin, senic waterway, rue Lafayette

Chateau de Rambouillet, 011-33-1-34-94-28-79 Rambouillet, 31 miles from Paris

La Passerelle des Artes, pedestrian bridge, quai du Louvre, place de l'Institut

Musée National des Arts Africains et Oceaniens, museum, 011-33-1-44-74-84-80, 293 avenue Daumesnil

Observatoire de Paris, 011-33-1-40-51-22-21 61 avenue de l'Observatoire

Parc des Buttes-Chaumont, park, 011-33-1-40-71-74-00 northeast part of Paris on rue Botzaris

Parc Zoologique Bois de Vincennes, 011-33-1-44-75-20-10, 53 avenue de Saint-Maurice

Place de la Bastille, intersection of boulevard de la Bastille and boulevard Beaumarchais

Pont Neuf, historic bridge, connects Paris's Left and Right Banks, across the river Seine

Rue Mallet-Stevens, 16th Arrondissement

SHOPPING
Agnes B., clothing, 011-33-1-42-33-04-13, 3 rue du Jour

Edifice, housewares, 011-33-1-45-48-53-60 27 boulevard Raspail

Hermès, clothing, 011-33-1-40-17-47-17 24 faubourg St-Honore

Paraboot, shoes, 011-33-1-76-93-88-00, 6 rue du Bourg l'Abbe

NIGHTLIFE
Le Cabaret, nightclub, 011-33-1-58-62-56-25 2 place du Palais Royal

One Great Day in Paris

One night for my birthday, I rented a boat to make a fiesta with my friends. We were on the Seine, almost in front of my house, although it wasn't my house yet at the time. For one minute I gave the wheel to somebody else. It was a big boat and the man turned too short of the Isle St-Germain and glug, glug, glug—the boat, on the 18th of January at three in the morning, *sank!* What did we do? We swam! Forty of us with bottles of champagne. I love this sort of thing—it's funny. But the boat? It was finished. Afterwards, we continued the party, completely frozen and wet, on the bank of the Seine. That story tells me you can make everything in Paris. You can even play the *Titanic* in the Seine.

Rome

More than twenty years ago, actress Susan Sarandon went to Rome and experienced a miracle. Arriving to film *Mussolini & I*, she was already a star from her performances in *The Rocky Horror Picture Show, Pretty Baby,* and *Atlantic City.* Born and raised in New Jersey, she started life as Susan Abigail Tomalin. Yet in Rome she was reborn, falling in love not only with the city, but also a Roman, who fathered her first child. "I just fell in love with the light and the people and the food," she remembered of her first visit. "The fact that there's so much history. It's reassuring that when you have evidence of the past, it somehow makes you feel there could be a future."

She returned to the U.S. and broke through the film actresses' normally dreaded age-forty barrier with a series of strong, sexy roles, including *The Witches of Eastwick, Bull Durham,* and *Thelma & Louise.* Then she won the Best Actress Oscar for her role in *Dead Man Walking.* Though Sarandon now lives in New York with actor Tim Robbins and their children, she will always remain in part a citizen of Rome. Here's a weekend with Susan Sarandon in the Eternal City.

Friday

LODGING The De La Ville Inter-Continental Hotel is at the top of the Spanish Steps. It's smaller, which I love. It's actually where I got pregnant, which was like a miracle for me. It's one of those hotels that have little tiny balconies. If you're in the front, you overlook the whole city, and if you're in the back, you overlook one of those strange, magical little views of everybody's laundry hanging out. I stayed in the room where Lennie Bernstein had stayed. There was this amazing light and the birds were all singing. It's just idyllic.

DINNER Quinzi & Gabrielli is still the best, most fabulous seafood restaurant. The best fish you could ever imagine and the best oysters. It's in the old part of the city, very close to the Pantheon. You can't get any better than that.

Another great fish restaurant, almost on the level of Quinzi, is **Alberto Ciarla**. In Rome, the restaurants don't change like they do in New York or L.A. About ten yards from Quinzi is **La Rosetta**. That's also fish. Then, we have the old showbiz places like **Dal Bolognese** on Piazza del Popolo. When I was doing *The Tempest*, John Cassavetes brought everyone there to eat.

NIGHTLIFE Of course, everybody just walks around. Go to the **Piazza Navona,** which has a medieval circus atmosphere with performers all year round. I remember going there to people-watch on those nice, balmy nights. The **Fontana dei Fiumi** is the fabulous fountain in the middle of the piazza, where all the kids run around late at night. If you're with kids and not dieting, you can get great gelati, ice cream in all sorts of flavors. **Tre Scalini** on the Piazza Navona is famous for the tartufo chocolate dessert. Somehow, you can eat and eat in Italy and you never gain weight. **Piazza Santa Maria della Pace,** "Square of the Peace," is a

La Dolce Vita kind of place where everybody goes. It's full of paparazzi and bars like **Bar della Pace**. The **Trattoria Pizzeria della Pace** [now called **Zio Ciro**] is also there, a great hangout. Try the pizza bianca.

Saturday

ESPRESSO There's nothing like getting up in the morning and having one of those incredible espressos. In Rome, there isn't such a thing as what you think of as breakfast in America. You get a croissant and cappuccino at the local bar. But you can sit and people-watch at the **Raphaël,** a really old, tiny hotel, which is lovely.

SIGHTS I love the **Colosseum,** and so do my kids. All of these cats used to live there. The Colosseum is a very dramatic sight. You can get books that have a plastic sheet that shows the city the way it used to look before it was in ruins. Then you pick up the sheet and see the ruins. You get a rush from being inside these old buildings, which have such a strong presence, such resonance. And then you go nearby and there will be somebody dressed in a gladiator costume, an actor, getting a bottle of water in his Spartacus outfit.

MUST SEE I saw the **Sistine Chapel** before and after it was renovated, and I have to say it was so bright when they finished painting it. That's a must, but it's very difficult because of the wait—especially during the tourist season.

The De La Ville Inter-Continental Hotel is at the top of the Spanish Steps. It's smaller, which I love. It's one of those hotels that have little tiny balconies.

Intercontinental Hotels

There are a number of other chapels that have amazing paintings—lots of very ornate angel happenings all over the place—that are lesser known. The **Galleria Borghese Museum** is in the middle of the seventeenth-century Villa Borghese park. Then, of course, you have the **Vatican Museum,** which is sort of the Disneyland of Rome. There are lines around the block.

LIVING LIKE A ROMAN The trick with Rome is just to get brave and start wandering around. You come around a corner and you're in some fabulous piazza. And every view you get when you look out your back window—and I've lived in a number of apartments there—is just enchanted. Between the light and the food and everyone seeming to be in love, it's just a magical place. It's a good antidote to the lives we have in the busy cities, because you really can't get anything done, even if you wanted to. Everything closes down for hours during lunch. I've always joked that if it said One Hour Photo, you'd have to figure out which was the one hour where you could actually get anything processed.

LUNCH You'll find the real Rome, as opposed to the tourists' Rome, in the upscale neighborhood Parioli, which has several fantastic restaurants. One is **Celestina,** which is the hip, trendy place where all the soccer players and everybody go. It's hard to get a table, but it's really worth it. If you want to have an American meal, there is **Jeff Blynn's,** named for a former top male model who owns it. It's like Morton's in L.A.—great traditional American food.

SHOPPING **Campo de' Fiori** is wonderful. When I was living in Rome that was the marketplace where I went. There's a day you get your chicken, a day you get your flowers, a day you get your bread. It's on one of the most beautiful little squares, which at night is the most popular place for young people. There are three wine bars, one better than the next, all on the square. All of the great designers are on the **Via del Corso, Via Condotti**, and **Via della Croce**—the Fifth Avenue and Rodeo Drive of Rome. But I prefer the little stores in and around Piazza Navona. Many of them are on a charming street, **Via del Governo Vecchio,** which has little antiques stores, boutiques, and mom-and-pop shops. That street is like a time capsule. **Antica Officina di Santa Maria Novella** has been around forever. It's a really old pharmaceutical company from Florence, which makes something called Poivere per Bianchire le Carni, which means something like "the dust to whiten your skin." It's the most amazing face mask. From this, they built an empire of natural products. Also, **Pineider** is probably the oldest stationery store in Italy. They did stationery for the Medicis.

TRANSPORTATION Going in and around the older parts of the city on a motorcycle is the best. It's hard to get around in a car. With a bike, you can break all the rules and get places much quicker—going down stairs and through one-way streets. I did it on a motorcycle in the romantic summer of my pregnancy—up and down all the little streets the wrong way. I must say that the parking rules are crazy. You park up on sidewalks. It's just a free-for-all. Parking is impossible, and with a car you're stuck in traffic. You really do better on foot.

DINNER The hottest place in town is Gusto near Piazza Augusto Imperatore. It's a very successful L.A./New York–style trendy restaurant. It's quite big, with tables right under the columns of this modern-looking square. We used to go to the Tuscan restaurant Nino with Gore Vidal. It's right at the bottom of the Spanish Steps. We would sit there all night long and have a fabulous dinner, and then everybody would start singing. There are a lot of places where you never see tourists, where the Romans live: Prati, a residential area comparable to the Upper West Side of Manhattan, which has Cesare, a really, really wonderful Tuscan fish and meat place. Il Matriciano is a very special place, one of the top five restaurants in town.

The owner, Alberto, and his sister, Rosetta, know everything about everybody. If you want something known, you go to the restaurant and tell them about it. A week later, everybody will know.

NIGHTLIFE Goa is a great club in the Ostiense area. One of my favorite areas, besides the old part of the city, is Trastevere. It's very much like the SoHo of Rome. There are galleries and pubs, and it's funky and quite international. But the real Roman rite is to get a pizza after the theater or the movies. One of my favorite pizzerias is Nuova Fiorentina in the center of Prati. Amazing pizza, amazing food—not too big, not too small, just right—and you're sure to run into writers or intellectuals or someone you know from television or the movies.

One Miraculous Night in Rome

In the summer of 1984, I was working on a film in Italy with Bob Hoskins and Anthony Hopkins and an international cast. It was eventually shown as a TV movie in the U.S. called *Mussolini & I.* I played Mussolini's daughter. I met up with Franco Amurri, who's now a writer/director still living in Rome. Franco was working for Leonard Bernstein, translating his opera, which was being done in Italy. I was with another friend and I ran into him and we started dating. I was all over Italy that summer—Lake Como, Verona, everywhere, filming this thing about Mussolini and spending time with Franco in Rome. We basically did Rome on a motorbike. That was the magic summer when I conceived my daughter. When I tell people that she was conceived on the Spanish Steps, they always have this image of us actually prone on the Spanish Steps. But in fact, it was in a room at the De La Ville hotel atop the Spanish Steps. It was more than magical. It was a miracle, because I was told I couldn't have children. Eva was born in March 1985. I stayed in Italy, living right off the Piazza del Popolo, and then near the Piazza Navona once my baby was born. I always tell people who have been trying to conceive but haven't that they should just go to Rome and eat and drink and be merry, and miracles will happen. I wasn't looking to get pregnant, and I wasn't supposed to be able to get pregnant. What does that tell you about Rome? If you want to start a family, that's the place to go. If you want to start your life in any way, I recommend Rome.

Sunday

EXCURSION The Appian Way is incredible. Just outside of the city, it becomes an old paved Roman road just the way it was during the gladiator era. You'll find the same landscape as you'd see in movies like *Spartacus*. The ruins and the catacombs line both sides of the street. If the Colosseum gives you a feeling of ancient Rome, the Appian Way makes you feel that you're still in ancient times.

Susan Sarandon's Rome Essentials

LODGING
De La Ville Inter-Continental Roma, $$$$,
011-39-06-67331, Via Sistina 67/69

Hotel Raphaël, $$$$, 011-39-06-682831
Largo Febo 2, Piazza Navona

DINING
Alberto Ciarla, seafood, $$$, 011-39-06-5818668
40 Piazza San Cosimato

Celestina, Italian, $$$, 011-39-06-8078242
Viale Parioli 184

Cesare, Tuscan, $$$, 011-39-06-6861227
Via Crescenzio 13

Dal Bolognese, Italian, $$$, 011-39-06-3611426
Piazza del Popolo 1-2

Gusto, Italian, $$$, 011-39-06-3226273
Piazza Augusto Imperatore 9

Il Matriciano, Italian, $$$, 011-39-06-3212327
Via dei Gracci 55

Jeff Blynn's, American, $$$, 011-39-06-8070444
Viale Parioli 103C

La Rosetta, seafood, $$$$, 011-39-06-6861002
Via della Rosetta 8/9

Ristorante Nino, Tuscan, $$$, 011-39-06-6795676
Via Borgognona II

Quinzi & Gabrielli, seafood, $$$$, 011-39-06-6879389
Via della Copelle 6

Ristorante Pizzeria Nuova Fiorentina, pizzeria, $$,
011-39-0637516181
Angelo Brofferio 43

Tre Scalini, Italian, $$, 011-39-06-709-6309
Dei Santi Quattro 30

Zio Ciro, pizzeria, $$, 011-39-06-6864802
Via della Pace 1

SIGHTS
Appian Way, scenic Roman roadway,
runs from Rome to Brindisi

Fontana dei Fiumi in Piazza Navona, town square,
Piazza Navona

Galleria Borghese, museum, 011-39-06-32810
Pizzale del Museo Borghese 5

Roman Colosseum, 011-39-06-672-3763
Piazzale del Colosseo

Santa Maria della Pace, church, 011-39-06-686-1156
Vicolo del Arco della Pace 5

Sistine Chapel, www.vatican.va
Viale del Vaticano, Vatican Palace

Vatican Museums, 011-39-06-6988-3333
Viale Vaticano

SHOPPING
Antica Officina di Santa Maria Novella, cosmetics,
011-39-06-6872446, Corso della Rinascimento 47

Campo de' Fiori, open-air market, Piazza Campo de' Fiori

Pineider, stationery, 011-39-06-6878369
Via dei Due Macelli 68, Spanish Steps

NIGHTLIFE
Bar della Pace, café/nightclub, 011-39-06-6861216
Via della Pace 3/7

Goa, nightclub, 011-39-06-5748277
Via Libetta 13

Owen Wilson

Rome

To say, 'I lived in an apartment right next to the Palazzo Fernese that Michelangelo designed,' reminds me of the opening line in *Out of Africa*: 'I had a farm in Africa, at the foot of the Ngong Hills,'" said Owen Wilson in his signature Texas twang before suddenly jolting from his daydreams of Rome and back to reality. "But . . . what was I saying again?" He was saying that he became so enamored of the Eternal City while filming *The Life Aquatic with Steve Zissou*, costarring Bill Murray, Willem Dafoe, and Cate Blanchett, that he "had to call American Airlines" to extol its virtues once he got home. We were sitting in Wilson's house in Santa Monica, situated on a leafy glen off a major California thoroughfare, which the actor had decorated with black-and-white photographs, books, and a boar's head. But for all practical purposes, he was back in Rome. He ran up and down his stairs to bring pictures, documents, evidence, if you will, that he, the lanky Texan who rode a crazy grin and broken nose to big-screen stardom, really was, from September 2003 to February 2004, a citizen of Rome. He'd had the trip arranged in his mind before he even got on the plane. His college buddy and longtime writing partner, director Wes Anderson (the pair cowrote the underground hit *Bottle Rocket*, as well as *The Royal Tennenbaums*), had told him he'd written a script for a movie, to be filmed in Italy, called *The Life Aquatic*. In this film Wilson didn't have the major role, which suited him just fine. "I thought it was nice because it gave me a lot of downtime to explore the city," said Wilson.

Friday

LODGING I rented an apartment that I stayed in for almost the whole time. [Wilson ran upstairs and returned with a photograph taken from his third-floor apartment window.] But because the movie went over, I also stayed at the **Hotel de Russie,** which is the best hotel there, I think. It's right near the Piazza del Popolo. I also stayed at the **Hotel Eden,** which is really nice, but I prefer the Hotel de Russie. It has a good gym and a terrace and outdoor area that are really beautiful. The sheets in both hotels were linen, which was like sleeping on napkins. I think of good sheets as being really soft, and these are almost rough, but then you get used to them. That was my experience with Italy in general, that they've perfected the art of living. So anything they did that you think, *Well, I prefer it this way, that's what I'm used to,* if you give it a chance over there, it usually turns out better the way they do it. I'd go into a little dive and have some *penne arrabiata* and it'd be better than anyplace in L.A., where you pay an arm and a leg. You hear all this stuff about diets and staying away from carbs and pasta, but there you eat pasta all the time. Everybody does and everybody looks pretty trim. [He paused, as if forgetting something.] I remember the *American Way* thing is that you're supposed to say where you go on Friday night, the hotel you stay in, etc. Is there a questionnaire I fill out, or have you changed the format?

DINNER Should I just start reeling off places? Right near the Hotel de Russie is a great place called **Dal Bolognese.** It's kind of fancy. They have great art on the wall from artists who've gone there. Then right down the street is **Beltramme Fiaschetteria,** which is run by this guy, Cesare. It's casual and you can just walk in. They have this *cacio e pepe* pasta dish, a cheese-and-pepper spaghetti, that's a Roman specialty.

Saturday

SIGHTS You just can't believe the **Colosseum** has been there as long as it has. Growing up in Dallas, you're used to, well, "That 7-Eleven has been there since 1972. That's a landmark."

Then you go to Rome, and you're talking about something that's like two thousand years old. I went to the **Sistine Chapel.** It's something you need two days to explore. I always associate the **Trevi Fountain** with that scene in the Fellini movie where Anita Eckberg is dancing in the fountain and looks really sexy. I didn't see her in the fountain, unfortunately. You do see a lot of people throwing coins in, though, and it sort of takes your breath away.

LUNCH I'd go to **Gina's** for lunch a lot and get this great salad with avocados and mozzarella. They also had great desserts there. I'm not a big dessert eater, but for some reason I'd eat dessert with every meal over there. The stuff was just so good. **Ciampini** was my favorite place for gelato. Over near the Trevi Fountain is **San Crispino,** which was written up in the *New York Times* as having the best gelato in Rome. I liked San Crispino, but when I found Ciampini, I felt it was the best. I liked the coffee ice cream and the yogurt.

CULTURE I don't think of myself as a huge museum-goer. I'm somebody who goes so I can tell people I went, rather than really wanting to go. I get kind of tired as soon as I walk into a museum. I'd rather be outside, you know, throwing a football. But in Rome, I felt like it wasn't like seeing it in a museum setting, and I was able to appreciate it more. I guess the churches had all this money and they commissioned all these artists to do these great works. The **Contarelli Chapel** near Piazza Navona has three Caravaggios. Then, of course, you could ride your bike over to **St. Peter's,** near where the pope lives. In the evening, they ring the bells, which are kind of ominous sounding. It sent a shiver down my spine just listening to it.

BIKING During the film shoot Willem Dafoe got a motor scooter, and I think Bill had one, too, but I had a bicycle. It was the best way to see the city because you could get around so quickly. Bill and Willem were on the scooters, so they had to follow the traffic. But on a bike, I would just go the wrong way down a one-way street so I could go more as the crow flies. I actually had three bikes, so when my brother Luke was visiting me and when another friend from Texas came, the three of us would tear over to the Colosseum and the adjacent spot where they filmed the *Ben-Hur* chariot races.

FILM HISTORY Cinecitta (the Roman movie studio) is where Fellini shot a lot of his movies. I'd been there a couple of years before, when they were filming Martin Scorsese's *Gangs of New York*. Scorsese had said some nice things about *Bottle Rocket*, the first movie I worked on, so I arranged to visit the set and was able to shake hands with him and watch them filming. Sometimes when

we were filming there you'd have an early call to be on set at like six in the morning and they'd be making their fresh bread for the day. The best place in Rome to get bread is called Il Forno. It's really old and it opens early.

DINNER Nino's is famous for its white beans marinated in olive oil. I'm a guy who likes to get a routine down, so I'm not super-adventurous about trying new places. I find something I like and then hit it every day.

NIGHLIFE La Maison is part of a cluster of clubs near the Abbey. Everybody smokes there, so that's a bit of a drag. But it's offset by the way people there are so elegant. Sometimes in the States the music scene is too loud. There it seemed more tasteful. At clubs in Rome, you'd see a doorman outside of what looked like this thousand-year-old building, and then you'd go inside and it'd be kind of modern.

Sunday

OUTDOORS I had a great driver, Francesco, and he'd take us up to this big, beautiful park, Villa Borghese. One of the things that happened in Villa Borghese is that I met this girl and her mother. Her father was the Spanish ambassador to the Vatican. The Palazzo di Spagna is this incredible building where the pope comes

Norman Walsh

I always associate the Trevi Fountain with that scene in the Fellini movie where Anita Eckberg is dancing in the fountain and looks really sexy. I didn't see her in the fountain, unfortunately. You do see a lot of people throwing coins in, though, and it sort of takes your breath away.

every December 8 to recognize Spain, and the girl's family invited me to go there. So I got to see the pope. I had taken one suit with me, and I only did that as an afterthought. But I was lucky I did, because I ended up having to wear it a lot. Another night, I got to go to a party at the French Embassy, which is normally closed to the public, and you had to wear a suit. There's also this cool night in Rome every fall called the White Night, where everything stays open until four in the morning. And the museums are open till midnight. There's a great energy in the city then.

SOCCER Romans are soccer fanatics, and I went to see a couple of games. It was fun and I got back into the sport while I was over there. I had a friend who visited, and we were kicking a soccer ball around in the piazza one night, at like two in the morning. We had gone out to a club and came back to give my dog some exercise and he was chasing the ball back and forth, and the police guarding the French Embassy were watching us, and my friend and I were thinking, *Are these guys gonna kick us out?* But they started getting into it and started kicking

the ball around with us. It was a great moment, having my dog there in the shadow of a building designed by Michelangelo and kicking a soccer ball at two in the morning with Italian cops.

ITALIAN STYLE Even though Italy is known for its fashions I didn't shop much, but I did wear a scarf. [He ran upstairs and returned with a blue cashmere number.] You just throw it around your neck and knot it. I was thinking scarves are so cool, so great. I got back to Dallas and wore one out and felt kind of self-conscious. I felt a little too foppish, like a dandy, so I stopped wearing it. It's one of those things that's only good for Rome, I guess, because you can dress with a little more pizazz there.

Owen Wilson's Rome Essentials

LODGING
Hotel de Russie, $$$$, 011-39-06-328-881, Via del Babuino 9, Piazza del Popolo

Hotel Eden, $$$$, 011-39-06-478-121, Via Ludovisi 49

DINING
Beltramme Fiaschetteria, Italian, $$, no phone, Via della Croce 39

On the Road with Owen Wilson

What do you always take with you when you're traveling?

Running shoes. Running is a great way to see a city when you get jet lag and wake up at five in the morning. Also, good music. And I always carry my dopp kit and a change of clothes. I never check my bags. I keep things pretty small. It's a little bit trickier when you're traveling with a girlfriend, though, because they can take more stuff.

So how did you do it when you went to Rome for six months?

I packed up two huge bags with baseball gloves and a football and photographs I like to take if I'm going to be somewhere for a long time. Stuff to remind me of home.

Ciampini, gelato, $, 011-39-06-678-5678
Viale Trinità dei Monti

Dal Bolognese, Italian, $$$, 011-39-06-361-1426
Piazza del Popolo 1-2

Gina's, Italian, $$$, 011-39-06-678-0251
Via San Sebastianello 7A

Il Forno di Campo de' Fiori, Italian, $,
011-39-06-6880-6662, Piazza Campo de' Fiori

Il Gelato di San Crispino, gelato, $,
011-39-06-679-3924, Via della Panetteria 42

Ristorante Nino, Italian, $$$, 011-39-06-679-5676
Via Borgognona II

SIGHTS
Basilica di San Pietro (St. Peter's)
011-39-06-6988-3712, Piazza di San Pietro

Contarelli Chapel, 011-39-06-688-271
San Luigi dei Francesi

Fontana di Trevi, off Via del Tritone

Roman Colosseum, 011-39-06-700-5469
Piazzale del Colosseo

Sistine Chapel, 011-39-06-8530-1758
Viale del Vaticano, Vatican Palace

Spanish Steps, www.piazzadispagna.it
Trevi Fountain

Villa Borghese, park, 011-39-06-488-991
Piazzale Flaminio

NIGHTLIFE
La Maison, clubs, 011-39-06-683-3312
Vicolo dei Granari 4

GUIDE/DRIVER
Franceso Magnarelli, 011-39-338-817-0577

Sydney

I t was something of a culture shock," Naomi Watts said of her move at age fourteen from gray, proper Sussex, England, to sunny, anything-goes Sydney, Australia. "All these beaches and beach cultures, and the kids were very different— free-spirited and a bit mischievous—from where I had been going to school. It was very liberating." Gone were her proper British boarding school aspirations and predictable life. She modeled, became an assistant at a Sydney fashion magazine, and went to auditions, where she met actors like Nicole Kidman and Thandie Newton. The three would eventually appear together in an Australian film called *Flirting*. In the early nineties, she took another leap, moving, with nebulous contacts and no guarantee of work, from Sydney to L.A., taking with her the strong work ethic shared by her fellow Aussie actors. "There's a sense of needing to survive," Watts said. "We're not afraid to get our hands dirty

and work hard. You know, we're the underdog. I suppose everyone who comes out of Australia has this same work ethic and is there for the right reasons."

The budding actress was soon winning bit parts in movies and roles on American TV, but it wasn't until she shook the scenery in David Lynch's dark 2001 film *Mulholland Drive* that Watts gained major recognition. Her star continues to rise, but her roots remain firmly planted in the Down Under capital where it all began.

Friday

ORIENTATION That Sydney is voted one of the world's best cities doesn't surprise me at all, because it's very progressive. It's influenced by other countries, but it's still very pure and its own place as well. It's very unique. I must say that from the time I arrived, it really has changed quite a lot. It has gotten much better. I lived in the Mossman area, in a beautiful place called Cremorne Point, which lies on the North Side. Sydney is surrounded by water, and we were right there on the harbor. We didn't have a view of the **Sydney Opera House** or anything like that, because we were looking in the opposite direction. Nevertheless, it was a beautiful view. Eventually, I moved from the North Side to the eastern suburbs. We had a beautiful apartment on Bondi Beach. Selling that place is one of my biggest regrets in life. We sold it for a song, and, of course, now the real estate there is worth so much.

LODGING There is a charming little hotel on Bondi Beach called Ravesi's. It's been there for as long as I can remember. It started out as a two-star hotel and then they piled a lot of money into it. I'm not sure if they have their third or fourth star now. You overlook Bondi Beach there. That is just worth its weight in gold to me, because those are all my memories: just looking at that beach and walking on it and eating fish and chips and swimming. My favorite thing to do when I was living there was to get up every morning around 6 or 6:30 and run on the beach. Even better was the walk from Bondi to Bronte, which is about two or three beaches away. Bronte is approximately

forty-five minutes from the center of town and completely clean. The color of the water is extraordinary. The temperature of the water, depending on the time of year, is pretty great. I would say the walk from Bondi to Bronte, back and forth, takes forty-five minutes. It's got a lot of rocks and cliffs and beautiful beaches. It's just a priceless experience. For me, it's a nostalgic experience.

LUNCH/DINNER There are a number of great cafés on Bronte Beach. They are literally stacked up next to each other. They have great vegetable or chicken pies, great smoothies. And the coffee in Sydney is arguably the best coffee I have ever had in the world. Better than Italian, Parisian, or from any major city. I don't know, they just have it right. It's good, strong, bitter, and how it's supposed to taste. There's a famous restaurant in Watson's Bay called Doyle's on the Beach. You should take people who've never been to Australia before. It's very touristy, but it's a great spot. Watson's Bay is just so picturesque.

Kim Pin Tan/istockphoto.com

COFFEE On Bondi Beach, I go to Gusto. You sit on stools on the street and have your coffee and juice. You can grab a sandwich, too. There's another place called Bondi Aqua Bar, on the north end of Bondi that does great scrambled eggs. It's a very tiny place, a hole in the wall. It's

Those are all my memories: just looking at Bondi Beach and walking on it and eating fish and chips and swimming. My favorite thing to do when I was living there was to get up every morning around 6 or 6:30 and run on the beach.

sort of controlled chaos in there. The food is great, always fresh, but much of the allure is the ambience and spirit of fun.

SHOPPING There are great shops in Paddington along Oxford Street, but my favorite shops are on Williams Street. You've got Belinda, which is full of young designers, some of them local, some imported. It's expensive, but it has fantastic vintage stuff and some of the best finds I've ever come across. Then there's Collette Dinnigan, one of Australia's most famous designers. She sells all over America. She has shops in London and Paris. She's one of our biggest exports. Her dresses are very feminine but very modern and classic at the same time. She's a friend of mine and I have worn her things on several occasions and to several functions. There's also a fantastic shop called Orson and Blake that sells great clothes, but mainly what I like about it is the furniture. Then there's Queen Street, which has great antiques stores and galleries and things. Great shops and cafés, too.

LUNCH Right on Bondi Beach is a place called Bondi Surf Seafoods, on Campbell Parade, where I've been going since about 1990. You can get your greasy-style fish and chips or you can get it freshly grilled, without the batter. They sell extraordinary seafood as well, if you want to cook it yourself. But the fish and chips you just take away in a box and sit with there on the beach at sunset. It's beautiful. Hugo's, on Bondi Beach, was always my favorite. It's a small place and they do great seafood, great cocktails, fantastic daiquiris with fresh fruits, and a great balmain bug [a slipper lobster],

which is one of Australia's delicacies, somewhere between a crab and calamari. It's beautiful and fresh. I get a little upset with them now, because they always call the paparazzi. You can't go in there without it being in the paper the next day.

MASSAGE You can get a fantastic massage at the Ginseng Bath House. They soak you in all this great stuff and scrub you down. Then you get into these hot pools of special mineral water. I also go to this great woman named Eva Karpaty in Double Bay who gives incredible facials. You go in and she says, "Oh, we've got a skin emergency on our hands." She just gets down to it and does a thorough cleansing.

DINNER Icebergs, which is also on Bondi Beach, is more on the Italian side. It's quite rich, actually. Again, these are beachfront restaurants and, again, the experience is about more than just the food. It's what you're looking at and where you are. There are a number of great places in the city, too, especially on the wharf near the W Hotel. The one I go to is called Otto, which is also Italian. They make great risotto and do a great bellini. Then there's a landmark called Harry's Cafe de Wheels. He has always sold meat pies. I don't know if it exists anywhere else in the world. I'm not a meat lover, but it's a huge thing in Australia, so you go for the meat pie. It's sort of like a sausage roll. When I was a kid, the first thing we would do after school is grab a meat pie. You could probably get them then for twenty-five cents. Harry's used to be a rather low-rent place, but over the years it's become a landmark. Now they write about it in books and everything.

Some of my favorite restaurants are in east Sydney. All I keep telling you about is Italian restaurants, but they're all great, like Bill & Toni's and another one called No Names. I remember going there as a kid. There are only a few things to choose from, but it's really, really cheap and full of atmosphere. I might be biased, but I rate Australia as having some of the best food in the world. Yeah, other than Italy, I'd say it is probably the best food I've ever had in the world. Because everything is fresher and the tastes are much stronger and purer.

THEATER Doing theater in Sydney is on my list of things to do. I'm just trying to find the right time. I have kind of a fear about it, a bit of stage fright. The theater community in Sydney does really well. You have the Sydney Theatre Company, which is probably the biggest company, with fantastic directors and actors. Cate Blanchett had a play there. All of the great Australian actors have done at least one play out of STC, except me. There are also the Stables and Belvoir Street Theatres. There are a lot of little theater companies that manage to stay alive.

NIGHTLIFE My nightlife days are kind of long ago. There's a bar called Soho Bar in King's Cross that I'd go to. And I had my eighteenth birthday in a small club called the Freezer [now closed]. In those days I had aspirations to become a dancer, so I did a dance routine there that I had rehearsed. I actually performed at my eighteenth birthday. I don't know what I was thinking. Somebody should have stopped me. It was one of those classic dances to Janet Jackson, where I was the girl and

I was being fought over by two men. I did the routine. The music stopped and the lights went down and on I went. In front of about one hundred people! I mean, what a lunatic.

Sunday

EXCURSION Well, there's Palm Beach, which is beautiful. Sort of the equivalent of driving from the center of Los Angeles to Malibu. You've got the peninsula and the most beautiful beaches, both surf and calm beaches. A choice of waves or no waves, basically. There are also the Blue Mountains. I have a lot of memories of the two-hour drive from Sydney to mountain territory and its wonderful eucalyptus trees. We had a little cottage up there for a while, and we'd go there on the weekends. We would make fires and go for walks. It's really a different side of Australia, from the beaches to the cold, crisp mountains. There are waterfalls and some incredible wildlife as well, a lot of different animals.

Naomi Watt's Sydney Essentials

LODGING
Ravesi's, $$$, 011-61-2-9365-4422
Campbell Parade & Hall Street

DINING
Bill & Toni Italian Restaurant, Italian, $$,
011-61-2-9360-4702, 74 Stanley Street, East Sydney

Bondi Aqua Bar, breakfast/lunch, $, 011-61-2-9130-6070
266 Campbell Parade, Bondi Beach

Bondi Surf Seafoods, seafood, $$, 011-61-2-9130-4554
128 Campbell Parade, Bondi Beach

Doyle's on the Beach, seafood, $$$, 011-61-2-9337-2007
11 Marine Parade, Watson's Bay

Gusto, coffee shop, $, 011-61-2-9130-4565
16 Hall Street, Bondi Beach

Harry's Cafe de Wheels, Australian, $, 011-61-2-9211-2506, Cowper Wharf Roadway, Woolloomooloo

Hugo's, seafood, $$$, 011-61-2-9300-0900
70 Campbell Parade, Bondi Beach

Icebergs Dining Room and Bar, Italian, $$$$,
011-61-2-9365-9000, 1 Notts Avenue, Bondi Beach

No Names, Italian, $$, 011-61-2-9360-4711
2 Chapel Street, East Sydney

Otto Ristorante Italiano, Italian, $$$, 011-61-2-9368-7488, Area 8, Cowper Wharf Roadway, Woolloomooloo

SIGHTS

Blue Mountains Visitor Information, 011-61-2-4739-6266, http://www.bluemts.com.au/tourist/Default.asp

Sydney Opera House, 011-61-2-92-50-7111
Bennelong Point

SHOPPING

Belinda, young designers/vintage, 011-61-2-9380-8728
8 Transvaal Avenue, Paddington

Collette Dinnigan, designer fashions,
011-61-2-9361-0110, 33 William Street, Paddington

Orson and Blake, furniture, clothing, gifts,
011-61-2-9326-1155, 83-85 Queen Street, Woollahra

NIGHTLIFE

Soho Bar & Lounge, 011-61-2-9358-6511
171 Victoria Street, Potts Point

THEATER

Belvoir Street Theatre, 011-61-2-9699-3444
25 Belvoir Street, Surry Hills

Stables Theatre, 011-61-2-9361-3817
10 Nimrod Street, Kings Cross

Sydney Theatre Company, 011-61-2-9250-1777
Pier 6/7 Hickson Road, Walsh Bay

HEALTH/BEAUTY

Eva Karpaty, facials, 011-61-2-9363-2395
Double Bay

Ginseng Bath House, massage, 011-61-2-9356-6680
111 Darlinghurst Road, Kings Cross

Kiefer Sutherland

Toronto

Kiefer Sutherland had a kidney stone. We were scheduled to meet for lunch at L.A.'s venerable Chaya Brasserie, but as I drove toward Chaya, I got "the call." "He doubled over just before an appearance before the Hollywood Foreign Press Association," an assistant told me. Just when I was about to call it a day, my cell phone rang again. The kidney stone was gone and Sutherland had rallied. "He wants to do it," said the assistant.

"To stop a weapon that has no cure, you need a man who knows no limits," proclaimed the ad copy for *24,* Sutherland's hit Fox TV series, which plays out in real time, each episode tracking an impossibly frantic hour in the lives of government agents. Like Jack Bauer, the steely-nerved Fed who he portrays, Sutherland "knows no limits" when it comes to his acting career.

The son of actor Donald Sutherland, Kiefer has been on the fast track to fame since he first appeared as a knife-wielding punk in the film *Stand by Me.* In the years following, he spent time competing on the rodeo circuit in Montana, where he once owned a ranch. One of his film roles was as a WWII POW in *To End All Wars*, so he's not the type of guy to be laid low by a microscopic piece of calcium in the lower extremities. When Sutherland finally showed at Chaya, he fired up a Camel. "I've broken every bone in my body," he said of his time in the rodeo. "But I've never experienced pain like this"—referring to the morning's bronc-busting ride with the kidney stone.

Then he moved on to a story about a train, set in his hometown of Toronto, where he returned to launch his acting career after a college stint in Ottawa.

Friday

HIS ARRIVAL Actors like Timothy Hutton and Sean Penn had really broken down a lot of doors for younger actors, and I wanted to take advantage of that. I remember getting on a train to Toronto one night, and when I got there, I had maybe forty-six dollars or something frightening like that. The train station in Toronto is massive—it's like Grand Central Station. That morning, it was glorious and it was empty. I remember walking out of the station, seeing the pigeons take off, and thinking, *this is the first day of the rest of my life.* I remember feeling like Rocky. You know, when he's at the top of the stairs.

LODGING I have a house in Toronto, but I'll still go stay a night or two at the **Windsor Arms** for nostalgic reasons. It's right in the center of town, and I've stayed there forever. It's a really old, kind of funky hotel that has a minimalist feel. I remember how minimalist and sexy Mickey Rourke's apartment was in *9 1/2 Weeks,* and this hotel is very similar to that.

DINNER The Windsor Arms has a restaurant called the **Courtyard Café** that does literally the best mushroom soup you'll ever, ever, ever have. It would be like taking a regular mushroom soup and then sending it through a puree. It's got such a phenomenal taste and it's not too heavy.

Saturday

BREAKFAST Breakfast is not a huge meal of mine. Although there is a fantastic diner called **Flo's** in Yorkville. It looks like the diner in the movie *Diner.*

SKIING There's one area where I trained as a kid. It's like a four-hundred-foot hill called **Uplands,** which is just outside the city limits. A nice ski area is **Blue Mountain,** in Collingwood, which is about two hours away. It's got a nice elevation.

SHOPPING There's fantastic clothes shopping in Toronto. Throughout the Yorkville area there are fantastic boutiques, and **Holt Renfrew** is a fantastic store right there on Bloor Street. It's like Saks or Barneys, just a really nice, big

department store. The **Roots** store is there, too. They started off as a shoe company and made a very eco-friendly all-purpose shoe. They became famous for that, and then winter jackets and hats, and now it's a full clothing line, like the Gap. Toronto's **St. Lawrence Market** [St. Lawrence] will make you excited about cooking; the produce is so extraordinary and it changes every day. I remember the first couple of times I went there to do the groceries, it made me want to learn how to cook.

SIGHTS The **CN Tower** [downtown] is the largest freestanding structure in the world. Any time we have someone coming to visit, it's a mandatory stop. There's a restaurant at the top and a lookout deck. What's surprising is that the lookout deck is see-through. So as you step out, you're looking straight down. It usually has a much more profound effect than most people think as they're riding up the elevator.

LUNCH There are two fast-food chains that you can't find outside of Canada. One of them is **Mr. Sub,** which I think makes the best sub sandwiches I've ever had. The other is **Harvey's,** which is a hamburger stand. They do a thing there that you don't really do here in the States: French fries and gravy. They put the fries in the container, fill it halfway up with gravy, and it turns into the most delectable mush you've ever had. So generally, that's my morning meal. Which is probably why I had a kidney stone.

HISTORY A fantastic place to see is **Casa Loma,** which is a castle in the middle of the city with a very sad story. It was built by Sir Henry Pellatt, who was the richest man in Toronto. He lost all his money and ended up living with his chauffeur. But the castle stayed, and the city took it over and it's now operated by the Kiwanis Club. The architecture is extraordinary and is as opulent as it gets for a private residence.

WALK Toronto is one of the nicest cities for just walking around. But if you don't want to walk, the subway's not complicated. It runs east-west, north-south, that's it. If I were up at the Windsor Arms, I would take the subway down to Eaton Centre, and take a walk down Queen Street. There are two other areas I really love in Toronto. One is called the **Annex,** which is equivalent to New York's Greenwich Village. Musicians, painters, and writers all hang out there, and there are tons of restaurants and bars. The other area is the **Danforth.** It's predominantly a Greek neighborhood and has some of the most amazing Greek restaurants and bars and dance halls. Two of my favorite Greek restaurants there are **Christina's** and **Myth.**

EXERCISE L.A. is a city built around driving, but Toronto is built around taking the subway

Bistro 990

and public transportation and walking, very much like New York. I run. Unfortunately, a lot of it is done in a gym on a treadmill, but if I'm in Toronto, I'll absolutely try to run. Unlike L.A., it's possible to get away from the streets and actually not feel like you're running into traffic the entire time. **High Park** is the big park in Toronto. It's a very English park, with wild geese, ponds. A kind of less traditional park is **Taylor Creek Park,** which features a series of jogging trails. It's in an area called Don Valley, which is a very nice area of the city.

DINNER There's a fantastic restaurant in Yorkville called **Prego.** It's indoor/outdoor, and so in the summer months, or even the fall, it's stunningly beautiful during the day. It gets quite busy, so if you're a people watcher, it's a great place to go and just hang out. And it has fabulous food. **Sotto Sotto** [Yorkville] is another fantastic Italian restaurant. My mother and I go to **Bistro 990** [midtown]. It's her favorite restaurant. I went to Bistro 990 with the director of *24*—he's also from Toronto—and we took one of the writers. It reminded the writer of one of those fantastic underground German restaurants—real arches, kind of low ceilings, very intimate. And they have a fantastic bar downstairs.

I went to Bistro 990 with the director of 24—he's also from Toronto—and we took one of the writers. It reminded the writer of one of those fantastic underground German restaurants—real arches, kind of low ceilings, very intimate. And they have a fantastic bar downstairs.

THEATER I did stage work mainly in Toronto, and the [now defunct] Bayview Playhouse was the last long run I had before I started working in film. There are so many fantastic theaters in Toronto. The fact that there are as many theaters as there are in Canada and that they survive is a fantastic achievement. The last place I worked was the **Royal Alexandra** [downtown]. When I was young, the Alex was a place I had dreamed about.

NIGHTLIFE The Four Seasons Hotel is still where most of the people coming for the Toronto Film Festival stay. I made a joke once that there are so many films being made in Toronto at any given moment that **Avenue,** the Four Seasons bar, was probably Hollywood's hottest spot. I run into more people in that bar on any given night than I do out here in L.A. There's fantastic live music on Queen Street West, which I find increasingly difficult to find in any city. But Queen Street West has always had live bands, everything from reggae to rock to jazz. There's a fantastic restaurant there, too, that I've gone to for almost twenty years called **Peter Pan.** It looks like one of those old New York Italian restaurants. There are also phenomenal rock-and-roll bars. My brother and I couldn't wait to come of age to go to a bar called **El Mocambo.** The Rolling Stones played there one night on a whim. My brother saw the Police play there on their first tour of North America. There's an area called **Ontario Place,** where you can go and see concerts. They have a beautiful open amphitheater. I think I kissed my first girl at Ontario Place.

LATE-NIGHT SNACK People gather in Chinatown at the end of the night for some chow mein and tea. Chinese actor Chow Yun-Fat was actually quoted as saying that Toronto has the best Chinese food he's ever tasted outside of China. Chinatown in Toronto is huge and has an incredible variety where you can actually experience the difference between Szechwan and Hunan and Cantonese. If you're still awake after all that, check out **Club Lucky** [entertainment district] for late-night drinks, and **Montana,** a great lounge on John Street.

Sunday

SPORTS The **Toronto Blue Jays** are a huge attraction and the city has a good basketball team now, too. And the **Canadian Football League** is very exciting. But I don't think anything comes close to **Toronto Maple Leafs** hockey at the **Air Canada Centre.** That's where the Leafs and the basketball team, the **Raptors,** play. It's very safe to go to a hockey game in Toronto. I mean, it's not like going to an English football match in Chelsea, but the fan enthusiasm is incredibly exciting.

GOING UNDERGROUND Toronto's winters aren't as severe as those of Montreal or Winnipeg, but you do get a biting wind off the lake. But there's the **Eaton Centre** [downtown], with its underground shopping, where you can get a lot of stuff done without having to surface. The Yorkville area, all the way from the Hudson Bay Center to Holt Renfrew, is underground as well.

Kiefer Sutherland's Toronto Essentials

LODGING

Windsor Arms Hotel, $$$$, (416) 971-9666
18 St. Thomas Street, downtown

DINING

Bistro 990, continental, $$$$, (416) 921-9990
990 Bay Street, midtown

Christina's on the Danforth, Greek, $$$, (416) 463-4418
492 Danforth Avenue, Greektown

Courtyard Café, continental, $$$, (416) 971-9666
18 St. Thomas Street, Windsor Arms Hotel

Flo's Diner, diner, $, (416) 961-4333
10 Bellair Street, Yorkville

Harvey's, hamburgers, $, www.harveys.ca
multiple locations throughout Toronto

Mr. Sub, sandwiches, $, www.mrsub.ca
multiple locations throughout Toronto

Myth, Mediterranean, $$$, (416) 461-8383
417 Danforth Avenue, Greektown

Peter Pan Bistro, fusion, $$$, (416) 593-0917
373 Queen Street West, Queen West

Prego Della Piazza, Italian, $$$, (416) 920-9900
150 Bloor Street, Yorkville

Sotto Sotto, Italian, $$$, (416) 962-0011
116 Avenue Road, Yorkville

SIGHTS

Blue Mountain Ski Resort, (705) 445-0231
Collingwood

Casa Loma, castle, (416) 923-1171, 1 Austin Terrace

The CN Tower, world's tallest building, (416) 868-6937
301 Front Street West, downtown

High Park, www.toronto.ca/parks

Metro Toronto International Caravan, multicultural
festival, www.caravan-org.com

Taylor Creek Park, jogging, www.toronto.ca/parks
Don Valley

Toronto Blue Jays, baseball, toronto.bluejays.mlb.com
Rogers Centre, corner of Front and John Streets

Toronto Maple Leafs, hockey,
www.torontomapleleafs.com, Air Canada Centre

Toronto Raptors, basketball, www.nba.com/raptors
Air Canada Centre

SHOPPING

Eaton Centre, underground shopping area, (416) 598-8560
525 Bay Street, downtown

Holt Renfrew, department store, (416) 922-2333
50 Bloor Street West, downtown

Roots, clothing and accessories, (416) 323-3289
100 Bloor Street West, downtown

St. Lawrence Market Complex, farmer's market,
(416) 392-7219, 92 Front Street East, St. Lawrence

NIGHTLIFE

Avenue at the Four Seasons, bar, (416) 964-0411
21 Avenue Road, downtown

Club Lucky Kit Kat Too, nightclub, (416) 977-8890
117 John Street, entertainment district

El Mocambo, live music, (416) 777-1777
464 Spadina Avenue, Queen West

Montana, bar, (416) 595-5949
145 John Street, entertainment district

Ontario Place, live music, (416) 314-9989
955 Lakeshore Boulevard, waterfront, operates seasonally

Royal Alexandra, theater, (416) 872-1212
260 King Street West, downtown

Index of Celebrities

About the Author

A VETERAN MAGAZINE WRITER, MARK SEAL BEGAN WRITING the *Celebrated Weekend* feature in *American Way*, the magazine of American Airlines, in 1990, interviewing more than 300 celebrities about their favorite cities. He has served as a collaborator on numerous nonfiction books and is a contributing editor of *Vanity Fair*. He lives in Aspen, Colorado, and Dallas, Texas.